Enhancing Transatlantic Solidarity in Collective Defence

EMERALD STUDIES IN FINANCE, INSURANCE, AND RISK MANAGEMENT

Series Editor: Simon Grima

Books in this series collect quantitative and qualitative studies in areas relating to finance, insurance, and risk management. Subjects of interest may include banking, accounting, auditing, compliance, sustainability, behaviour, management, and business economics.

In the disruption of political upheaval, new technologies, climate change, and new regulations, it is more important than ever to understand risk in the financial industry. Providing high-quality academic research, this book series provides a platform for authors to explore, analyse, and discuss current and new financial models and theories, and engage with innovative research on an international scale.

Previously Published:

Uncertainty and Challenges in Contemporary Economic Behaviour
Ercan Özen and Simon Grima

New Challenges for Future Sustainability and Wellbeing
Ercan Özen, Simon Grima and Rebecca Dalli Gonzi

Insurance and Risk Management for Disruptions in Social, Economic and Environmental Systems: Decision and Control Allocations within New Domains of Risk
Simon Grima, Ercan Özen and Rebecca Emily Dalli Gonzi

Public Sector Leadership in Assessing and Addressing Risk
Peter C. Young, Simon Grima, and Rebecca Dalli Gonzi

Big Data Analytics in the Insurance Market
Kiran Sood, Balamurugan Balusamy, Simon Grima, and Pierpaolo Marano

Big Data: A Game Changer for Insurance Industry
Kiran Sood, Rajesh Kumar Dhanaraj, Balamurugan Balusamy, Simon Grima and R. Uma Maheshwari

The Adoption and Effect of Artificial Intelligence on Human Resources Management, Part A
Pallavi Tyagi, Naveen Chilamkurti, Simon Grima, Kiran Sood, and Balamurugan Balusamy

The Adoption and Effect of Artificial Intelligence on Human Resources Management, Part B
Pallavi Tyagi, Naveen Chilamkurti, Simon Grima, Kiran Sood, and Balamurugan Balusamy

Contemporary Studies of Risks in Emerging Technology, Part A
Simon Grima, Kiran Sood, and Ercan Özen

Contemporary Studies of Risks in Emerging Technology, Part B
Simon Grima, Kiran Sood, and Ercan Özen

The Framework for Resilient Industry: A Holistic Approach for Developing Economies
Narinder Kumar, Kiran Sood, Ercan Özen, and Simon Grima

VUCA and Other Analytics in Business Resilience, Part A
Deepmala Singh, Kiran Sood, Sandeep Kautish, and Simon Grima

VUCA and Other Analytics in Business Resilience, Part B
Deepmala Singh, Kiran Sood, Sandeep Kautish, and Simon Grima

Finance Analytics in Business: Perspectives on Enhancing Efficiency and Accuracy
Sanjay Taneja, Pawan Kumar, Kiran Sood, Ercan Özen, and Simon Grima

Enterprise Risk Management in Today's World: Enterprise-Wide Risk Management and Strategy, Part A
Author: Jean-Paul Louisot; Editor: Simon Grima

Enterprise Risk Management in Today's World: A Current and Futuristic View of the Complexity, Resilience, Responsibility and Tools in ERM, Part B
Author: Jean-Paul Louisot; Editor: Simon Grima

Green Management: A New Paradigm in the World of Business
Swati Gupta, Sanjay Taneja, Ercan Özen, Kiran Sood and Simon Grima

Business Challenges and Opportunities in the Era of Industry 5.0
Simon Grima, Salih Serkan Kaleli, Mehmet Baygin, and Engin Boztepe

Financial Landscape Transformation: Technological Disruptions
Manjit Kour, Sanjay Taneja, Ercan Özen, Kiran Sood, and Simon Grima

Sustainable Development and Green Innovation: Managing Risk Through Interdisciplinary Approaches and Policy Strategies
Adalat Muradov, Fariz Ahmadov, Nargiz Hajiyeva, Kiran Sood, and Simon Grima

Enhancing Transatlantic Solidarity in Collective Defence: Navigating Increased Defence Expenditures, Cyber Security, and Emerging Risks

EDITED BY

ANDRZEJ SOBOŃ

War Studies University in Warsaw, Poland

VLAD DUMITRACHE

National Defence University "Carol I", Romania

ELEFTHERIOS THALASSINOS

University of Piraeus, Greece

AND

SIMON GRIMA

University of Malta, Malta

emerald PUBLISHING

United Kingdom – North America – Japan – India – Malaysia – China

Emerald Publishing Limited
Emerald Publishing, Floor 5, Northspring, 21-23 Wellington Street, Leeds LS1 4DL.

First edition 2026

British Library Cataloguing in Publication Data
A catalog record for this book is available from the British Library

ISBN: 978-1-80686-260-3 (Print)
ISBN: 978-1-80686-259-7 (Online)
ISBN: 978-1-80686-261-0 (Epub)

Printed and bound by CPI Group (UK) Ltd, Croydon, CR0 4YY

Contents

About the Editors

Andrzej Soboń, PhD, is Colonel of Polish Armed Forces, Professor of War Studies University in Warsaw, and Founder of the Consortium of Uniformed Universities in Poland (2014). After earning the doctoral degree in the field of Security Studies in 2012, in 2017–2019, he had been the Vice Dean for student affairs, next Vice Dean for didactic affair. Since January 2020 is Dean of National Security Faculty, he is author of publications in the field of pro-defence, international cooperation. Latest publications in Emerald: Use of torture in areas of Ukraine occupied by the Russian Federation, *European Research Studies Journal*, Volume XXVII, Issue 1, pp. 50–64, 2024, https://doi.org/10.35808/ersj/3348. The impact of legal nihilism on the Russian Federation security, *European Research Studies Journal*, Volume XXVI, Issue 4, pp. 354–372, 2023, https://doi.org/10.35808/ersj/3289. ORCID: https://orcid.org/0000-0003-2540-2252.

Vlad Dumitrache is an Associated Professor at the Regional Department of Defence Resources Management Studies, a NATO Center for Training and Education, part of the National Defence University, located in Brasov, Romania. He has published over 50 papers on Defence, National Security, and Economic Studies, while also publishing over 10 books and chapters in books under international publishing houses including Cambridge Scholars Publishing. His fields of interest are Defence Economics, Financial Management, and Public Expenditures. His field of expertise and teaching domains are related to Defence Management Systems, particularly Planning, Programming, Budgeting, and System Evaluation; implemented in the DoD; and developed in all NATO member countries. ORCID: https://orcid.org/0000-0003-1215-3867.

Eleftherios Thalassinos holds a PhD in Quantitative Methods and International Economics (UIC, Chicago, 1983), an MBA in International Business (De-Paul U Chicago, 1979), and a BA in Economics (U of Athens, 1976). He also holds three DHC Degrees in Business and Economics from Danube's University of Galati 2013, University of Craiova 2015, and Rostov University of Economics 2018. He is Editor-in-Chief in three journals, Editor, Guest Editor, and Member of Editorial Board in few journals. He has an extensive record of lecturing in several universities around the globe (Europe, America, Asia) and hundreds of publications in journals, conference proceedings, collective volumes, and scientific series.

Professor Simon Grima is Dean of the Faculty of Economics, Management, and Accountancy and Head of the Department of Insurance and Risk Management. He is also a Professor at the University of Latvia and a visiting Professor at Haxhi Zeka University in Kosovo. He has served as President of the Malta Association of Risk Management and the Malta Association of Compliance Officers and has resumed this presidency in 2023. He chairs the Scientific Education Committee of the Federation of European Risk Managers and the Strategic Risk Leaders Association. With his research and vast experience spanning 35 years across financial services, academia, and public entities, he serves as an Editor and Reviewer for academic journals and book series. He is also an independent Director for financial services firms and sits on risk, compliance, investment, procurement, and audit committees while undertaking roles as compliance officer, internal auditor, and risk manager.

About the Contributors

Dorel Badea is Professor, with over 17 years of experience in military higher education. The areas of research are related to topics such as organisational resource management, critical infrastructure protection, and organisational resilience. He holds a PhD awarded in 2011 by the Technical University of Cluj-Napoca, in the field of Industrial Engineering. He has also professional experience, for more than 8 years, in educational management, as Director of the management department, Vice Dean for education, Vice Rector for research, and Strategic Adviser for education for a mission of EU in Africa. He participated in Erasmus teaching mobilities in Portugal, Czech Republic, Bulgaria, and Poland.

Robert Boroch holds a PhD in Security Studies and a PhD in Humanities. With Anna Korzeniowska-Bihun (PhD), he researches the concepts of anthropological defence and anthropological aggression in the context of hybrid warfare strategy. He specialises in military anthropology. His research area is Eastern and Central Europe. ORCID: https://orcid.org/0000-0002-2016-5449.

Gastone Breccia is PhD in History, thesis on the Byzantine Civilization under Norman rule in Southern Italy (1994, Scuola Superiore di Studi Storici, Università di San Marino). After a short period teaching Italian literature in high schools, since 1996, he is researcher and aggregate professor of Byzantine Civilzation, first at the Università della Basilicata (Potenza, Italy) and then (2001–present) at the Università di Pavia. He is a member of the scientific board of SISM (Società Italiana di Storia Militare). Since the academic year 2022/2023, he teaches History of Warfare at the Italian Military Academy in Modena. ORCID: https://orcid.org/0000-0002-4867-2805.

Eugeniusz Cieślak is the Director of the Higher Command Studies Course and the Senior Leaders' Course at the Baltic Defence College in Tartu, Estonia. His expertise combines military assignments with academic experience. He holds doctoral and post-doctoral degrees in military science. He has been recently involved in national and European research projects related to the development of comprehensive defence and air and missile defence systems. His research interests include military defence policies and strategies and air defence. ORCID: https://orcid.org/0000-0002-6476-3643.

Maria Constantinescu is Associate Professor at the Regional Department of Defence Resources Management Studies of the National Defence University

Carol I and an Associate Expert at the Euro-Atlantic Centre for Resilience. She completed doctoral studies in Economics – International Relations at the Academy of Economic Studies, Bucharest, and is a graduate of the Naval Postgraduate School in Monterey, USA. Her area of expertise is defence economics, defence planning, irregular warfare, and resilience. She has authored numerous books and research papers in her field of expertise, with focus on resilience and defence planning and defence resources management.

Nikolaos Deniozos is Senior Officer of the Hellenic Coast Guard (ret.), a graduate of the Naval Cadet School – School of Hellenic Coast Guard's Ensigns Cadets, graduate of the Department of Economics of AUEB (Athens University of Economics and Business), holder of a Master's and a PhD in Regional Development/Economic Geography from the Institute of Regional Development of Panteion University of Social and Political Sciences and from the University of the Aegean, respectively. He also holds a Master's in Quantitative Methods in Decision Making from the Postgraduate Department of Statistics of the Athens University of Economics and Business. He is a graduate from the School of National Defence of Greece (Degree in Strategic and Defence Studies) and from George Marshall European Center for Security Studies (Germany). He also teaches Economic Analysis, International Political Economy, and International Political Economy of Energy at LEDRA COLLEGE – CY.

Leszek Elak is Colonel of Polish Armed Forces and Professor and Vice-Rector for Didactic Affairs at WSU. His scientific interests include security issues focused on state defence. His efforts focus on defence capabilities, operations outside the country's borders, cooperation of the Polish Armed Forces with elements of the non-military system, Border Guard, military threats, hybrid conflict, security environments, defence, and security issues in the context of NATO and EU membership. He is also the author and co-author of about 120 domestic and foreign publications. His latest publication is Stany Zjednoczone jako hegemon XXI wieku, https://doi.org/10.34752/2023-c284. ORCID: https://orcid.org/0000-0002-5255-9768.

Bachuki Gakharia holds a master's degree in jurisprudence and is currently pursuing a PhD at the International Black Sea University in the American Studies Programme, focusing on the necessity of a Total Defence Strategy for Georgia to enhance security and ensure continued U.S. assistance. A graduate of Baltic Defence College and Ranger School (Fort Benning, USA), he served as a reconnaissance platoon commander during the 2008 Russia–Georgia war and later as a reconnaissance company commander. He was deployed twice to Afghanistan, first as an Infantry Company Commander (23rd Infantry Battalion) under ISAF and later as a Quick Reaction Force Commander in Mazar-i-Sharif. His research focuses on operational-level resilience and defence planning.

Piotr Gawliczek, PhD, dr h.c. multi, NATO DEEP eAcademy Director, University of Warmia and Mazury in Olsztyn. His research and educational activities are focused on Advanced Distributed Learning (ADL), information and communications technologies (ICT), mobile learning and AI/VR/AR/MR solutions within the education and training ecosystem. He supports the ADL efforts of the partner countries within the Defence Enhancement Education Programmes (DEEP). He has written numerous publications on e-learning questions, the Bologna Process, asymmetric threats, and leadership. He has implemented e-learning/ADL system solutions in many military and civilian educational entities based on the LMS ILIAS and the BigBlueButton platforms: Doctor Honoris Causa of the National Defence University of Ukraine in Kyiv (2020), Honorary Professor of the National Defence University of Ukraine in Kyiv (2023), and Professor Honoris Causa of the Korolov Zhytomyr Military Institute – ZMI (2023). ORCID: https://orcid.org/0000-0002-0462-1168.

Marta Gębska is an Associate Professor in Security Studies and PhD in Economics. She is Vice Dean on Academic Affairs at National Security Faculty and Head of postgraduate studies in International Military Relations. She is Research and Teaching Fellow at War Studies University. Previously, she is Head of the Department of International Security and Diplomacy. Her research interests include international aspects of economic policy and economic security. She is Intern at the World Bank and Fellow at the Universities of Manchester, London, and Rome. She is author of three books, including *The Economic Dimension of Security of the Three Seas Initiative States* and *Theory and Practice (2022)*. She is Academic Editor of 12 monographs, author of over 86 scientific articles and book chapters, and co-author and editor of 2 textbooks on international security. She is Project Manager of the Ministry of Defence Research Grant programme on 'The geopolitical, military and economic security dimensions of the Three Seas region. Contemporaneity and Prospects', 2018–2022. ORCID: https://orcid.org/0000-0002-2254-9366.

Jarosław Gryz is a researcher and teaching staff at the Department of National Security of the War Studies University and deals with issues of national and international security. He is Vice-Rector for Student Affairs at WSU. He is author of publications in security policy and strategy of states and organisations and management of entity security. His latest publication is Local water partnership: universal model of water resources management, https://doi.org/10.3920/9789004699069. ORCID: https://orcid.org/0000-0001-6671-2391.

Elisabeta-Emilia Halmaghi has a PhD in Management since 2021 and is currently a Lecturer in the Management Department of the Faculty of Military Management of the 'Nicolae Bălcescu' Land Forces Academy in Sibiu. Her areas of interest and research are management, sustainable development, organisational culture, and organisational theory.

Roman Janjulia holds a Master of Arts in Strategic Security Studies from the National Defence University, College of International Security Affairs (CISA, Washington, DC). He is a Project Management Professional (PMP) certified specialist and holds a CIPD Level 5 Associate Diploma in Organizational Learning and Development. A graduate of Ranger School (Fort Benning, USA), he served as a reconnaissance company commander during the 2008 Russia–Georgia war and later as Commander of 23rd Light Infantry Battalion. He was deployed twice to Afghanistan Helmand Province, first as a Battalion Commander under the Regional Command (SW), NATO lead ISAF (International Security Assistance Force) mission, and later as the Deputy Georgian Senior National Representative under the RSM (Resolute Support Mission) mission in Kabul. His research focuses on national security policy and strategy, including resilience, defence planning, and international security cooperation. ORCID: https://orcid.org/0009-0000-6444-3423.

Alexandru Lucinescu is a Senior Researcher at the Institute for Political Studies of Defence and Military History in Bucharest, Romania. He holds a PhD in Philosophy from the University of Bucharest and a PhD in Intelligence and National Security from Carol I National Defence University. His areas of expertise encompass European security and defence, civil-military relations, human security, and ethics of international relations. He has extensive experience in teaching and management positions at higher education institutions as well as in international academic cooperation. His research activity is reflected in five books, with the latest being Role of the United Nations in Providing Human Security by Exercising Responsibility to Protect (2024), and over 50 articles and studies. ORCID: https://orcid.org/0000-0001-9125-9605.

Ivan Okromtchedlishvili is an Associate Professor at Sulkhan-Saba Orbeliani University in Tbilisi, Georgia, specialising in Security and Defence Studies and Public Administration. With extensive experience in both academic and military settings, he has taught courses on Security and Defence Policy, Defence Management, and Public Sector Budgeting and Financial Management at leading universities. His research focuses on Security and Defence Policy, Defence Management, and Performance-Based Budgeting, with a particular emphasis on their practical application in national security contexts. He has published widely on these topics, contributing significantly to the advancement of military education, research, and public administration in Georgia.

Brîndușa Maria Popa, PhD, is a Lecturer at the Regional Department of Defence Resources Management Studies (DRESMARA) Brașov, which is part of the National Defence University 'Carol I', Bucharest, Romania. Along her years of teaching, she has a PhD in Military Sciences and her field of interest and competence is organisational and strategic communication and organisational culture and behaviour. She has developed course support materials and applications for her academic activity and has written numerous articles and chapters in books on communication, organisational effectiveness, and organisational culture. She is part of the Scientific Committees of several Conferences and reviews and she is an organiser for the Defence Resources Management in the 21st-century international conference. ORCID: https://orcid.org/0000-0002-3215-8000.

Diana Elena Ranf is Associate Professor at the Land Forces Academy 'Nicolae Balcescu' in Sibiu with a PhD in Management. In almost 20 years of experience in higher education, her areas of interest and research were general management, economics, project management, sustainability management, organisational culture. His teaching and research activity is coupled with administrative activity; since 2020, he has been the Director of the Management Department of the Military Management Faculty of the Academy.

Sandis Šrāders is a Researcher and Lecturer on Russian military and strategic studies at the Baltic Defence College in Tartu, Estonia. He served as the Secretary General of the Latvian Transatlantic Organisation (LATO) from 2007 until 2014. He was a Coordinator for research projects of the German Marshall Fund of the United States in the Baltic States between 2013 and 2015. He was responsible for the report addressing the EU's Eastern Partnership during Latvian Presidency at the EU Council in 2015. His academic interests include Russia foreign and security studies, US foreign policy, and role of small states in international affairs and the global political economy. ORCID: https://orcid.org/0000-0003-1082-7178.

Theodoros V. Stamatopoulos was born in Athens, Greece. He studied economics at the Athens School of Economics in Greece, and the University of Aix-Marseille in France, while at the University of Piraeus, Greece, he received his PhD in international economics. He has taught many economic courses, applied statistics, and econometrics at the Hellenic Mediterranean University in Heraklion-Crete, Greece, and the University of Piraeus (1990–2014). He has published two books for international economics and business statistics in Greek, while published papers in distinguished academic journals where he is also invited as an anonymous reviewer. He has worked in the private sector in financial services companies as CFO (1996–2004), while he has also served in academic administration positions (2009–2016). He writes articles in electronic newspapers or websites, intervening in political, social, and economic news. Since 2020–2021 academic year, he serves as Professor of Economics at the Accounting and Finance Department, of the School of Administrative, Economics and Social Science, of the University of West Attica, Athens, Greece. ORCID: https://orcid.org/0000-0002-9710-0870.

Vitalii Suprun is a PhD candidate in Political Science at the Vasyl Stefanyk Precarpathian National University and an expert in the EU Science Diplomacy Working Group at the European Commission. He is a graduate of the Faculty of Political Science and International Studies of the University of Warsaw and the Institute of Law of the Vasyl Stefanyk Precarpathian National University, where he received an MA in International Relations majoring in Security and Strategic Studies and an LL.M. majoring in Criminal Law. He was affiliated with the Polish Academy of Sciences, the University of Warsaw, and the University of Edinburgh. ORCID: https://orcid.org/0000-0002-6531-6765.

George Spencer Terry is a Lecturer in Strategic Studies at the Baltic Defence College. His research interests encompass the socio-political logics of actorship and legitimacy, with a focus on the Baltic Sea region, Russian domestic and foreign policy, and political ideologies. Some of his recent publications include 'Martial necropolitics: The position of the combatant in the Russo-Ukrainian war' in New Perspectives (2024) and 'Rearticulating the Italian right's perception of Russia: legitimacy and rupture in the post-invasion landscape' in European Politics and Society (2023). ORCID: https://orcid.org/0000-0002-1310-4138.

Jerzy Tomasik graduated of the Military Technical Academy (1990) and doctoral studies at the National Defence Academy (doctoral dissertation – 'Ukraine in the European Security Architecture' – 2015). He has many years of experience in service in the military diplomatic corps and the Ministry of National Defence. He deals with the issues of security policy and the construction and development of the Armed Forces of Ukraine. He advised the high-level Polish representative in the DRAB (Defence Reform Advisory Board) – the Advisory Board for the Reform of the Defence of Ukraine – an advisory body of the Ukrainian authorities reporting directly to the Ministry of Defence and the General Staff of the Armed Forces of Ukraine, which provides the authorities with constant strategic advice on institutional reforms of the Armed Forces and helps in their implementation. ORCID: https://orcid.org/0000-0001-7875-4994.

Paul Tudorache is a Field Artillery Officer in the Romanian Land Forces, currently working as a Professor at 'Nicolae Bălcescu' Land Forces Academy of Sibiu. He completed doctoral and habilitation studies in Military Sciences at 'Carol I' National Defence University where he is also a PhD coordinator. His areas of expertise cover multidomain operations, especially decision-making in full spectrum operations. He has authored valuable books and scientific papers in the field of Military Science, most of which focus on research directions and strategies for innovating and revolutionising military capabilities.

Ilona Urych is Professor of the War Studies University, Habilitated Doctor in security sciences, and Vice-Dean for Student Affairs National Security Faculty War Studies University. Her scientific interests include military education, education for security, societal security, health security, leadership, security psychology, and interdisciplinarity of security studies. Her most recent publications are What to do with free time? The prospect of strengthening societal security in the opinion of Polish theologians (2023), Youth and security. Theoretical and empirical aspects of defence education in Poland (2022), The Need for Leadership in Team Work. Prolegomenon, w: Person, Nation, State. Interdisciplinary Research in Security Studies (2021). ORCID: https://orcid.org/0000-0003-4868-9460.

Viljar Veebel is a Researcher and Lecturer at the Baltic Defence College in Tartu, Estonia. His expertise combines academic and fieldwork as consultant in the EU institutions, member states, and partner states. He has worked as an Academic

Advisor of the Estonian government in the European Future Convention, and as a Researcher for OSCE, SIDA, the European Council on Foreign Relations, Estonian Foreign Policy Institute and Eurasia Group. In recent years, he has been researching trends of Russian military capabilities and necessary counter-developments of the EU. Simultaneously, he has been involved in the UK and the US governments' financed defence projects in the Baltic States and Ukraine. ORCID: https://orcid.org/0000-0002-9122-0134.

Tadeusz Zieliński, PhD, is Associate Professor at War Studies University and Vice-Rector for Scientific Affairs at WSU. He is a Lecturer in the field of air power, unmanned aircraft systems, and global threats security. His scientific area emphasis is defence and security, in particular the EU Common Security and Defence Policy and the theory and practice of the use of military aviation and unmanned (autonomous) air systems in conflicts and crisis response operations. He is also engaged into projects related to broadminded security and military sciences. His latest publications are Challenges for Employing Drones in the Urban Transport Systems, https://doi.org/10.37105/sd.179; Zagrożenia i przeciwdziałanie bezzałogowym statkom powietrznym w ochronie portów lotniczych, https://doi.org/10.5604/01.3001.0016.1915. ORCID: https://orcid.org/0000-0003-0605-7684.

Foreword

The unfolding conflict in Ukraine represents a watershed moment in the global security paradigm. As the international community grapples with the implications of this war, a renewed emphasis on collective defence, military readiness, and economic resilience has emerged. This volume brings together leading scholars and practitioners to dissect these developments, offering critical insights into the future of European and transatlantic security.

As tensions continue escalating, NATO's response has been decisive and adaptive. The alliance has expanded its military presence on its eastern flank, reinforced deterrence measures, and enhanced defence cooperation among member states. The strategic realignment of NATO is explored in detail, providing a thorough assessment of its impact on the security architecture of Europe. The economic ramifications of the war extend far beyond Ukraine's borders, forcing European countries to navigate complex defence expenditures, shifting procurement policies and the challenges of maintaining industrial capacity. The war has also accelerated discussions on European strategic autonomy as member states seek to balance their commitments to NATO with the need for independent defence capabilities. These themes are meticulously analysed, illuminating the intricate relationship between economic policies and military strategies.

Beyond material resources, the human factor remains a critical component of national security. The ability to recruit, train, and retain skilled military personnel has become a pressing issue for many NATO members, particularly those on the alliance's eastern flank. A nuanced examination of workforce dynamics in the defence sector addresses how biases, recruitment incentives, and economic conditions shape military readiness.

Another dimension of security that has come to the forefront is maritime stability. The geopolitical crisis in the Middle East and the conflicts affecting the Red Sea region have significant implications for global trade and strategic navigation. The security of maritime routes, disruptions in trade corridors, and the broader economic consequences of these crises are integral to understanding the full scope of contemporary security concerns.

The war in Ukraine has demonstrated the enduring importance of alliances and the necessity of adapting to new security threats. As policymakers and military leaders confront the realities of modern warfare, the analyses presented in this book offer valuable guidance on strategic decision-making, economic resilience, and collective defence. By bridging historical perspectives with contemporary challenges, this volume is a crucial resource for anyone seeking to understand the evolving dynamics of European and transatlantic security.

The authors and editors of this book have produced a comprehensive and thought-provoking study that will undoubtedly contribute to the ongoing discourse on international security. As we look to the future, the lessons gleaned from this conflict will shape the policies and strategies of nations for years to come. We hope this work will serve as a foundation for continued dialogue and informed policymaking in pursuing global stability and peace.

NATO's Strategic Realignment

In response to Russia's invasion of Ukraine, NATO has undertaken significant measures to bolster its eastern defences and reaffirm its commitment to collective security. The alliance has increased its military presence along its eastern flank, deploying additional troops and establishing new battlegroups in member states bordering Russia. This enhanced posture aims to deter further aggression and reassure member nations of NATO's unwavering support.

The 2024 NATO summit in Washington, D.C., marked a pivotal moment in the alliance's evolution. During the summit, member states agreed to a comprehensive strategic plan emphasising rapid deployment capabilities, integrated air and missile defence systems, and advanced cyber defence initiatives. Establishing the NATO Security Assistance and Training for Ukraine (NSATU) command further exemplifies the alliance's commitment to supporting Ukraine's defence efforts and long-term military development.

Moreover, NATO has intensified its collaboration with non-member partners, particularly in the Indo-Pacific region. Recognising the interconnectedness of global security, the alliance has sought to strengthen ties with countries such as Japan, South Korea, Australia, and New Zealand. This approach aims to address emerging threats and ensure a cohesive response to challenges posed by nations like China and North Korea.

Economic Ramifications for Europe

The war in Ukraine has precipitated significant economic challenges across Europe. The disruption of trade routes, particularly in the Black Sea region, has led to supply chain bottlenecks and increased transportation costs. Additionally, Europe's reliance on Russian energy exports has necessitated a rapid diversification of energy sources, prompting investments in renewable energy and alternative suppliers.

In response to the heightened security environment, European countries have substantially increased their defence budgets. In 2024, NATO's European members and Canada collectively boosted defence spending by 20%, reflecting a concerted effort to enhance military capabilities and readiness.

This surge in defence expenditures has implications for national budgets, potentially affecting social programmes and other public services.

The conflict has also accelerated discussions on European strategic autonomy. While NATO remains the cornerstone of European defence, there is a growing emphasis on developing independent defence capabilities. Initiatives such as the European Defence Fund and Permanent Structured Cooperation (PESCO) aim to foster collaboration among EU member states in defence research, development, and procurement.

Human Factors in Military Readiness

Beyond material assets, a military force's effectiveness hinges on its personnel. NATO member states, particularly those on the eastern flank, face challenges in recruiting, training, and retaining skilled military personnel. Demographic trends, economic conditions, and societal attitudes towards military service influence the available talent pool.

Countries have implemented various strategies to address these challenges, including offering competitive compensation packages, educational opportunities, and career development programmes. Efforts to promote diversity and inclusion within the armed forces aim to broaden the recruitment base and enhance unit cohesion.

The war in Ukraine has underscored the importance of adaptable and resilient personnel. Ukrainian forces have demonstrated remarkable ingenuity and determination, often leveraging asymmetric tactics to counter a technologically superior adversary. This experience highlights the value of investing in training programmes emphasising critical thinking, adaptability, and leadership at all levels.

Global Security Concerns

The conflict's repercussions extend beyond Europe, influencing global security dynamics. The war has strained international arms control agreements, with Russia suspending its participation in treaties such as New START. This development raises concerns about a potential arms race and the erosion of established non-proliferation frameworks.

The involvement of external actors, including Iran and North Korea, has further complicated the security environment. Reports indicate that these countries have supplied military equipment and ammunition to Russia, thereby deepening their engagement in the conflict.

Maritime security has also emerged as a critical concern. The Black Sea, a vital corridor for energy and grain exports, has become a focal point of military activity. Ensuring the security of maritime routes is essential for global trade and economic stability.

The war in Ukraine represents a watershed moment in the global security paradigm. It has prompted a revaluation of defence strategies, economic policies, and international alliances. As the international community grapples with these challenges, a renewed emphasis on collective defence, military readiness, and financial resilience has emerged. The lessons learned from this conflict will undoubtedly shape the policies and strategies of nations for years to come, underscoring the importance of adaptability, unity, and foresight in navigating an increasingly complex security landscape.

Prof Simon Grima

Preface

This volume's collection of chapters encapsulates a comprehensive analysis of contemporary geopolitical challenges, with a primary focus on Europe's evolving security landscape. The Russian Federation's unprovoked aggression against Ukraine in 2022 has significantly altered the strategic considerations of NATO, the European Union, and their allies. This volume examines these transformations through various lenses, from collective defence and military expenditures to economic resilience and human resource mobilisation in the defence sector.

The authors contributing to this work are esteemed scholars and practitioners, each bringing a unique perspective to the discourse. Their analyses span the historical evolution of NATO's strategic posture, the impact of the Ukrainian conflict on European defence policies, and the imperative for stronger transatlantic solidarity. The insights provided here are not merely theoretical but have practical implications for policymakers, military strategists, and security analysts seeking to understand the trajectory of European security.

The importance of collective defence, as enshrined in NATO's founding principles, has been reaffirmed in the wake of Russia's renewed aggression. The alliance's response has demonstrated resilience and adaptability, with increased defence spending, strategic realignments, and an emphasis on interoperability among member states. At the same time, this conflict has underscored the vulnerabilities within European defence systems, prompting discussions on long-term investments in military capabilities, human resource development, and economic preparedness.

One of the crucial themes explored in this volume is the impact of defence policies on national economies. The war in Ukraine has forced European countries to reassess their defence budgets and industrial capacities, leading to a surge in military procurement and strategic investments. However, sustaining such spending levels over time presents economic challenges, further complicated by political shifts and public sentiment.

Another key area of focus is the role of human resources in modern defence strategies. The shift towards professionalised, technologically advanced armed forces has led to recruitment and retention challenges across NATO's eastern flank. This volume explores how cognitive biases, economic incentives, and social perceptions shape military recruitment and workforce management in the defence sector.

Furthermore, the analysis delves into economic defence strategies, emphasising the role of transatlantic cooperation in securing supply chains, fortifying financial resilience, and countering cyber threats. The necessity of a robust economic foundation for sustaining military efforts cannot be overstated, as seen in Ukraine's resilience despite prolonged conflict. NATO's changing preparedness and strategic orientation are examined in response to Russia's assertive stance, drawing lessons from the Baltic States. The Ukraine conflict has profoundly impacted European defence spending, procurement policies, and strategic coordination among EU member states, necessitating deeper cooperation and adaptability.

Beyond the battlefield, the conflict's implications extend into economic and maritime security concerns. Defence resource management has come under increased scrutiny as nations strive to maintain sustainable military operations and ensure operational readiness. Managing personnel recruitment and retention in the military has emerged as a critical challenge, with economic factors influencing decision-making and shaping the composition of modern armed forces. The issue of maritime security has also gained prominence, with geopolitical shifts in the Middle East and the Red Sea posing risks to global trade routes and economic stability.

These interconnected themes illustrate the broader narrative of contemporary security concerns. The war in Ukraine has catalysed significant strategic shifts in direct military engagements and the economic, human resource, and geopolitical spheres. The resilience of democratic nations, their ability to adapt to evolving threats, and their capacity to forge strategic partnerships are key factors that will determine the future security landscape.

This book serves as a testament to the resilience of allied nations in the face of aggression. It highlights the strategic adaptations required to maintain stability in an increasingly volatile world. The authors hope their analyses will contribute to a deeper understanding of the complexities of modern warfare, collective security, and economic defence strategies, fostering informed decision-making among policymakers and stakeholders in the international security community.

Prof Simon Grima

Chapter 1

Ukraine's Integration into NATO: Historical Processes, Strategic Dynamics, Scenarios and Policy Implications

Andrzej Soboń[a], Piotr Gawliczek[b] and Jerzy Tomasik[c]

[a] *War Studies University, Poland*
[b] *University of Warmia and Mazury, Poland*
[c] *NATO DEEP eAcademy, Poland*

Abstract

The aim of the chapter is to present the processes of transformation of Ukraine's mutual relations with the North Atlantic Treaty Organisation. The main goal of the chapter is to analyse the security policy and strategy of independent Ukraine, which led to the annexation of Crimea and the armed conflict in the Donbas region, and in the aftermath, a full-scale war started on 24 February 2022. Various possible scenarios were considered in the context of Ukraine's membership in NATO. The chapter also presents issues related to building the basis for cooperation, the dynamics of changes taking place in the way of implementing the strategic foreign policy, including balancing between decisions not to apply for full membership and obtaining the status of a partner of NATO. Work on the question: Did the Ukrainian authorities correctly define the main goals of Ukrainian security policy and strategy?

Keywords: Ukraine; NATO; process; bilateral relations; integration; full membership

JEL Codes: K10; F52; F20

Enhancing Transatlantic Solidarity in Collective Defence: Navigating Increased Defence Expenditures, Cyber Security, and Emerging Risks, 1–21

doi:10.1108/978-1-80686-259-720261001

Introduction

Referring to the issue of independent Ukraine, one cannot omit a critical moment in the history of its predecessor, the Ukrainian Soviet Socialist Republic (Ukrainian SSR), which existed for almost 70 years (1922–1991) and was the second largest state entity in terms of population and political and economic importance, which was part of the Union of Soviet Socialist Republics (SU–USSR). This event was the all-Ukrainian referendum on the declaration of Ukraine's independence on 1 December 1991 (Verkhovna Rada, 1991). Ukrainian citizens voted to maintain Ukraine's independence: 31,891,742 (84.18%) eligible voters participated, of whom 28,804,071 (90.32%) voted '*For*'. This resulted in, among other things, an excuse for the political leaders of the three main union republics of the USSR to state in a specially signed declaration that the USSR no longer exists (*without Ukraine, the empire could not survive*) (Bendyk, 2024) and, at the same time, establishing a new legal and political order – the Commonwealth of Independent States.

Ukraine has begun the process of creating its own independent entity in the international arena. However, throughout its existence, it was perceived by Moscow (the authorities in the Kremlin) as the cradle of Russian statehood and a strategic partner in areas including arms, space and aviation industries, etc., with which Russia shares common roots, culture and religion. Ukraine's location on the map of Europe, combined with its social, economic and military potential, created conditions for either mutually beneficial cooperation or conflict on many issues and at many levels – regardless of whether we mean Russian–Ukrainian cooperation or Ukraine's cooperation with member states of NATO and the EU (Bezhitashvili & Gerdes Scott, 2022). The referendum also showed that the society of Ukraine, its citizens, want to exist and function on the political map of Europe and the world as an independent entity, independent of anyone.

Ukraine's position, its geostrategic location at the junction of the East and the West, can be summed up in the words of President Carter's security advisor, Zbigniew Brzeziński, who believed that the importance of Ukraine '*does not result from power or ambition, but rather from its important geographical location and the effects of its potential instability*'. *for the behavior of geostrategic players. […] Without Ukraine, Russia ceases to be a Eurasian empire […], however, if Moscow regains power over Ukraine, with its 52 million citizens, enormous natural resources and access to the Black Sea, it will automatically regain the ability to become a powerful empire connecting Europe and Asia* (Brzezinski, 1998).

A new independent state taking into account its geostrategic location and key position in the regional and European security system, and as shown by the events of recent years (initiated in November 2013 with social unrest, the removal of the pro-Russian authorities, the occupation of part of the Donetsk and Luhansk voivodeships, the annexation of Crimea and the open attack of armed forces of Russia in February 2022) also worldwide. Experts dealing with security policy have emphasised for many years that the stability of Europe and the world largely depends on the stability and successful implementation of an independent domestic and foreign policy (Desai et al., 2016). This was highlighted, among others, in the words of former NATO Secretary General J. Solana, who announced during the summit in Washington that the Pact would support the independence and sovereignty of Ukraine. This was also reflected in NATO's Washington strategic concept, which stated: *Ukraine occupies a very special place in the Euro-Atlantic space and is an important and extremely valuable partner in the sphere of stability and shared democratic values*. When Ukraine started writing its own *history of independence*, it found itself in a very specific situation:

1. There was the *Homo Sovieticus* factor (Encyklopedia PWN, n.d.), as well as the Russian-speaking part of Ukrainian society and the Russian national minority living on its territory. Even attempts by the Ukrainian elites (political and cultural) to build a new state identity based on European standards and ideals were not able to quickly lead to a change in the social consciousness of that part of society that remained mentally in the social system of the former USSR and, therefore, in Russia's sphere of influence. Moreover, already at that time, on the emerging political scene in Ukraine, there were also political elites (parties) whose interests suited this state of affairs and tried to take advantage of it. This was also used by Russia, whose politicians tried to divide the society of independent Ukraine into those living in the East and parts of the South (according to them, more sympathetic to Russia) and in the West (strongly representing their pro-Ukrainian and pro-Western attitude).
2. Another extremely important factor was the strong trade, economic and social links with Russia in virtually every industry, with particular emphasis on the huge potential of the military–industrial complex located on the territory of Ukraine. The arms industry located in Ukraine was one of the largest in Europe and one of the largest in the world – it constituted approximately 1/3 of the defence industry of the former USSR and approximately 20% of its scientific and research potential. At the time of the declaration of independence, there were approximately 1,840 enterprises producing for the needs of the Armed Forces in Ukraine – they employed approximately 2.7 million. This was a very important element of influence on politics, politicians and society in Ukraine. Ukraine was also burdened by oligarchic industrial and financial empires, which were afraid of possible integration with the West, as it could result in breaking economic ties with Russia (Ptashchenko et al., 2022). An interesting fact was that the sons of Russian officers and generals served in the Armed Forces of Ukraine and Ukrainian sons in the Armed Forces of the Russian Federation.
3. The authorities of independent Ukraine, having on their territory approximately 15% of the nuclear weapons resources of the former USSR (at the time of independence, the third largest potential in the world), tried to *play this card*. After getting rid of tactical warheads based on a bilateral agreement with Russia, Prime Minister and later President of Ukraine Leonid Kuchma decided to preserve the existing resources of strategic missiles SS-19 *Stiletto* and SS-24 *Scalpel*. The Ukrainian Armed Forces formally took control of the units armed with these missiles, and the soldiers of the units using

them took an oath of allegiance to Ukraine. Ukraine's Ministry of Foreign Affairs informed ambassadors accredited in Kiev that Ukraine *has the right to retain full control over all components* of nuclear weapons on its territory. Washington feared that this situation could be used by terrorists and hostile states to obtain nuclear weapons and the technology for their production in Ukraine. Moscow, playing with the Americans, preferred not to have a heavily armed neighbour on its borders and to maintain its status as the only nuclear power in the region. Russia and the United States began to put political pressure on Ukraine and offer economic aid. After long negotiations, the Ukrainian side sought guarantees and compensation for the transferred arsenal – an agreement was reached, which culminated in the signing of the so called *Budapest Memorandum* (UN, 1994).

4. Ukrainian strategic dilemmas in the area of foreign and security policy. During the period of state-building, Ukraine had three options for shaping its policy:

- remain a neutral and non-bloc country – the so called Dmytro Pavlychko's doctrine;
- choosing a pro-Western orientation, consequently seeking integration with Euro-Atlantic structures and potential membership in NATO and the EU;
- return to the sphere of Russian influence – the option most expected by Russia.

As a result, during his duties as prime minister and two terms as president, Leonid Kuchma, the country constantly balanced between European countries, the United States and the Russian Federation. According to the assumptions of the authorities of independent Ukraine, the multi-vector policy preferred closer cooperation with the West without harming Ukrainian–Russian relations. Participation in Western (NATO) and Eastern political and military structures (all forms of institutionalised military cooperation within the CIS) was not taken into account. Ukraine is balanced between East and West, cooperating with the Russian Federation and NATO, without declaring its readiness to side with either side (Kuzio, 1998).

Changes started to take place in 2002, along with an interview by Yevhen Marchuk, Secretary of the National Security and Defence Council, who stated that Ukraine must adopt a strategy for relations with the North Atlantic Alliance. This was the beginning of legislative work, which resulted in the adoption by the Ukrainian parliament of the document *On Ukraine's strategy in relations with NATO*. The consequence was the president's declaration of willingness to join the Pact and a decree approving the decision of the National Security and Defence Council of Ukraine on the strategic goal of Ukraine's security policy, which is NATO membership. Subsequent actions of the executive and legislative authorities led to the preparation of the law *On the Foundations of Ukraine's National Security* and the adoption of a new version of Ukraine's military doctrine, which included the provision that the ultimate goal of the Euro-Atlantic integration policy is membership in the North Atlantic Alliance. These were preparatory activities for the participation of Ukrainian representatives at the upcoming NATO summit in Istanbul (28–29 June 2004). However, during the meeting of the NATO–Ukraine commission, this country did not receive an invitation to membership – the heads of NATO governments repeated the principle of the *open door* policy and emphasised the strategic nature of NATO–Ukraine relations. They called on Ukraine to implement political, economic, military and defence reforms. The response from Ukraine came almost immediately – President Leonid Kuchma once again approved the new text of Ukraine's military doctrine, which deleted the point regarding integration with NATO, leaving only a general statement about the policy of Euro-Atlantic integration (Meleshchenko, 2021).

The next president of Ukraine, Viktor Yushchenko, at the meeting of the Ukraine–NATO Commission during the NATO summit in Brussels (22 February 2005) again declared a return to full integration with the Alliance. The provision on the strategic goal of Ukrainian policy – membership in NATO – was restored in the military doctrine. In the subsequent Security Strategy, the first in the history of independent Ukraine (*Ukraine in a Changing World* of 12 February 2007), the Euro-Atlantic choice in Ukraine's security policy was confirmed. Possession of such a document, however, did not mean that it would be used in the activities of the authorities. The provisions focused primarily on achieving short-term political and economic goals, neglecting the strategic development needs of society and the state. As a result, the threat to national security has increased, and Ukraine's ability to defend its national interests has weakened (Skachko, 2020).

However, this was not the last turn in the security policy of independent Ukraine. Another change occurred in 2010 when the next government introduced the 'Act on the Principles of Internal and Foreign Policy' (3 June 2010), which included a provision prohibiting Ukraine's membership in military alliances. The document was created in connection with Ukrainian–Russian agreements on the expansion of the Black Sea Fleet base in Crimea (extending its basing until 2042, while it should have left Crimea in 2017) and reducing the price of gas supplied from Russia. They resulted in serious consequences: Russian influence in Ukraine was strengthened and consolidated, and Kyiv's sovereignty in security policy was limited. However, the Ukrainian authorities (President Viktor Yanukovych) believed that they had reached a favourable agreement due to the reduction in gas prices (an important element in the short term for stabilising the state budget and the metallurgical and chemical sectors recovering from the crisis, but at the same time, a very short-sighted action with regard to the issue of Ukraine's sovereignty) (Ilin & Nihmatova, 2023).

President Viktor Yanukovych, by building his position in Ukraine, resulted in the weakening of the Ukrainian state in relation to Russia. This simple conclusion can be drawn from the 4 years of his presidency. Turning a blind eye to the activities of Russian agents, disarming their own counterintelligence and army, unfavourable agreements with the Russian side, supporting their own *Familia* – a kind of political and business group based on the family connections of the Ukrainian president and his political and economic allies (Pogorzelski, 2013). Decisions made by V. Yanukovych, including the resignation from signing the Association Agreement between Ukraine and the EU at the Eastern Partnership, summit in Vilnius, on the grounds that this agreement, which also provides for the creation of a free trade zone with the EU, is not sufficiently favourable for Ukraine and may have a negative impact on economic relations with Russia and the Eurasian Customs Union. According to observers of the Ukrainian political scene (Popowski, 2014), this sudden turn was dictated not so much by the fear of opening the Ukrainian economy to the West, but rather by Russia's awareness that the association agreement would take Ukraine out of Russia's sphere of influence for good. Blocking Ukraine's association agreement was only a short-term goal of Russian policy. Russia's long-term goal was to permanently bind Ukraine through integration with the structures of the Eurasian Customs Union. The authorities in the Kremlin had and still have their own, quite clear vision of the political system and the geopolitical and economic status of Ukraine. Russia does not accept Ukrainians' desire to create a modern legal order in Ukraine based on proven European solutions; however, it expects that Ukraine will remain a post-Soviet state and, as such, will participate in the process of economic, political and perhaps military integration controlled by Russia (Fernández et al., 2023).

The effect is very well known. Removal as a result of the so called *Revolution of Dignity*, the authorities represented by V. Yanukovych and the government in which the Party of Regions, his political base, played the main role. The next consequences of the power crisis in Ukraine, exploited by Russia, were the occupation and subsequent annexation of Crimea, followed by Russian support for separatists in the eastern part of Ukraine, and the annexation of two self-proclaimed republics to Russia. This resulted in a breakdown of the existing security policy and the need to re-evaluate the methods used to ensure security not only in Ukraine but also in its neighbouring countries, as well as Western European countries and, to a large extent, even in the Euro-Atlantic zone (Maass, 2019).

The events at the turn of 2013 and 2014 led to strategic changes in Ukrainian foreign and security policy. Ukrainian citizens presented their own civilisational and identity choice for Ukraine, not those of the political elites in power.

Conditions of Ukraine's Cooperation with NATO

It can be said that the first attempts at their Euro-Atlantic aspirations were already included by Ukrainian political elites in the act *On the Proclamation of the Independence of Ukraine*, developed during the period of the Ukrainian Soviet Socialist Republic, which defined the direction of activities of the future, independent Ukrainian state: *Ukraine's direct participation in the pan-European process and European structures* (Aleksiievets & Aleksiievets, 2020; Vidnianskyi, 2011).

The history of establishing relations between Ukraine and NATO began in the fall of 1991, and already in January 1992. The representative of Ukraine took part in the meeting of the High-Level Working Group of the North Atlantic Cooperation Council (NACC). On 22–23 February 1992, the first official visit of NATO Secretary General Manfred Wörner to Kyiv took place, which marked the beginning of an active dialogue between Ukraine and the Alliance. On 8 July

1992, the first president of independent Ukraine, Leonid Kravchuk, visited the NATO Headquarters. Mutual positions were being established, and subsequent political and military visits were held: of the Supreme Commander of the NATO Arms, General John Shalikashvili, in Kiev (1992) and of the Minister of Foreign Affairs of Ukraine, A. Zlenko, in Brussels (1993). Also in September 1992, the ceremonial opening of the Embassy of Ukraine in Brussels took place, which has since become the main point of contact between Ukraine and the North Atlantic Alliance (Kuzio, 1998).

The next stage in the development and deepening of relations was Ukraine's accession (10 March 1992) to the NACC. However, in 1997, Ukraine became one of the founding countries and participants of its legal successor, the Euro-Atlantic Partnership Council (EAPC). In the meantime, in May 1992, Ukraine obtained the status of an associate member in the NATO Parliamentary Assembly, where it was represented by a permanent delegation of the Verkhovna Rada of Ukraine (parliament). Ukraine's activation of activities at the initial stage of cooperation with the Alliance was aimed at quickly establishing and deepening relations, which was positively received by both sides. Political and legal principles of cooperation were established, as well as programmatic tasks of state policy regarding cooperation with NATO in individual military and civilian spheres, and principles were also developed, the essence of which was the recognition of the integrity and inviolability of territorial borders and support for the democratic path of development of an independent Ukraine as well as the status of a non-nuclear state (Meleshchenko, 2021).

Taking into account the twists and turns of Ukrainian foreign and security policy described in the previous part of the article, it should be stated that Ukraine–NATO relations have developed depending on the political interests of politicians currently in power in Ukraine. However, chronologically, they can be divided into several time intervals (Aleksiievets & Aleksiievets, 2020):

1. (1991–1997) – preparatory and initial, which was characterised primarily by the expansion of the normative and legal base of bilateral cooperation, the creation of appropriate institutional structures, the implementation of visits at various levels, conducting consultations and determining the theoretical and conceptual basis, programme tasks of the Euro-Atlantic foreign policy factor and security of independent Ukraine.
2. (1998–2000) – continuation of political dialogue, searching for new forms and ways of cooperation between Ukraine and NATO within the framework of the EAPC and the action plan proposed by the Alliance for 1998–2000, which was adopted for more effective partnership, planned activities in external relations developed as a result of various trainings, seminars, conferences, working meetings, expert meetings, etc., in specific areas and directions;
3. (2001–2004) – with variable intensity of political contacts, pragmatic filling with specific content within the Charter on a special partnership between Ukraine and the Alliance, with increasing dynamics until mid-2004, when the decision was made to change the priorities regarding membership in the Pact (after the Istanbul summit);

4. (2004–2009) – Ukraine–NATO relations after the so called *Orange Revolution and the presidency of Viktor Yushchenko took on a new dimension, became more active, cooperation was strengthened*, and the process of Ukraine's integration with the Alliance was accelerated. This concerned the significant activation of Ukraine's individual participation in the 'Partnership for Peace' programme primarily and work in the NACC and then the EAPC. Moreover, during the meeting of the Ukraine–NATO commission (Vilnius, 21 April 2005), he initiated an intensified process of political dialogue on the issue of Ukraine's acquisition of full membership in the Alliance;
5. (2010–2019) – weakening of the political dialogue between Ukraine and the Alliance during the presidency of Viktor Yanukovych and its revival after his election in 2014. For the President of Ukraine, Petro Poroshenko, as a result of socio-political changes after the end of the so called '*Revolution of Dignity – Euromaidan*'. The priorities of Ukraine's national interests in the sphere of foreign and security policy also changed. The strategic goals were creating and deepening Ukraine–NATO relations, strengthening cooperation in the defence sphere and starting the process of adapting the state's defence structures to NATO standards, implementing projects supporting Ukraine in counteracting aggression and hybrid war from Russia.

Referring to the presented historical stages (due to the temporal division of the history of cooperation between independent Ukraine and the Alliance), it is worth emphasising the importance of the years 1994–1997. On 8 February 1994, Ukraine signed the framework document *Partnership for Peace*, and in May of the same year, at the NATO Headquarters in Brussels, Ukrainian representatives presented a document containing details of participation in the programme, with declarations of readiness to cooperate in specific military and civilian spheres and defining a number of priority directions. Consultations in the *16+1* format were also initiated (that was the number of member states of the Alliance at that time). During this period, Ukraine was included in the initiated *Planning and Review Process* (PARP) to provide it with the opportunity to prepare its armed forces for joint operations with NATO members, as well as to participate in the exchange of information on defence and budget planning issues. In 1995, the tasks of the first individual partnership programme between Kiev and Brussels, planned for 1996–1998, were also defined. As a result, it was possible to formalise a special partnership between Ukraine and the Alliance. Ukraine participated in peacekeeping operations and crisis resolution under NATO leadership (Meleshchenko, 2021).

A practical example of Ukraine's use of the opportunities offered by cooperation with NATO was the consultation mechanism provided for in paragraph 8 of the framework document of the *Partnership for Peace* programme. According to its content, NATO will consult with each active participant of the programme if it feels a direct threat to its territorial integrity, political independence, or security and will submit an appropriate request to Brussels. The existence of such a mechanism should have influenced countries that intended to make territorial claims against Ukraine. Ukraine once used the mechanism included in the programme, and in 1996, it obtained political support for its territorial integrity from the NACC, after the State Duma of the Russian Federation protested against the Ukrainian status of the city of Sevastopol. Cooperation under the *Partnership for Peace* programme assumed a number of goals:

- creating conditions for Ukraine's entry into the pan-European security system;
- ensuring democratic control over the armed forces;
- promoting openness in state defence planning and shaping the military budget;
- maintaining capabilities and readiness within the limits set by the Constitution;
- using the experience of NATO member states and partner countries in reforming and building modern Armed Forces.

A fundamental event in the development of relations between Ukraine and NATO was the signing in Madrid on 9 July 1997, by the President of Ukraine, L. Kuchma, and the leaders of all member states of the Alliance, of the *Charter on a special partnership between Ukraine and NATO*. It was signed with the aim of developing *special and effective* partnerships which, as stated in the Charter, *will contribute to greater stability and the promotion of common democratic values in Central and Eastern Europe*.

The principles of special partnership relations, the mechanisms for their implementation, as well as the areas of cooperation between Kyiv and Brussels are specified in the document, which refers directly to the military sphere of Ukraine. The consultative mechanism of the Ukraine–NATO Commission was one of the main achievements of the Charter, as well as the entire cooperation between Ukraine and NATO. He provided Ukraine with a theoretical opportunity to consult with NATO immediately in the event of an exacerbation of an external threat, at any time when Ukraine feels such a danger. The Charter stated that the Ukraine–NATO Commission, which was to meet at the level of the North Atlantic Council at least twice a year, would ensure mutual control over the implementation of the provisions of the document. It should be emphasised again that Ukraine has become the first country in Central and Eastern Europe to have a similar mechanism of consultation and cooperation with the Alliance. Time has confirmed that the Commission has proven to be an effective body. Regular meetings within the Ukraine–NATO Commission of the Ministers of Defence and Foreign Affairs of Ukraine and NATO countries allowed maintaining a high level of dialogue between the parties and contributed to the modernisation of the mechanism of Ukraine's relations with NATO, as well as the rapid resolution of problems that had arisen in the relations of both sides.

The Ukrainian authorities also adopted and approved several national legal acts supplementing bilateral agreements with NATO. At the end of 1998, the President of Ukraine, by his decree, approved the government's programme of activities in the field of cooperation between Ukraine and NATO. Only countries directly invited to join the Alliance had similar plans for cooperation with NATO, which in turn demonstrated the special nature of Ukraine's relations with NATO in the period after signing the Charter. The first state cooperation programme set itself the goal of achieving the main tasks specified in the Charter by the end of 2000 – it had a relatively simple structure consisting of 16 chapters. The next state cooperation programme of Ukraine with NATO for 2001–2004 was approved by the Decree of the President of Ukraine of 27 January 2001. The second programme had a much larger scope and content – it consisted of 7 large sections, which were in turn divided into 18 subunits and 14 smaller structural units. It also included provisions from the previous programme that were not implemented. Moreover, this programme had an annexe – a list of central executive bodies and institutions of Ukraine that are responsible for deepening cooperation with NATO.

Ukraine's cooperation with NATO was summarized in October 2002, during a parliamentary hearing. After its completion, it was concluded that Ukraine's Euro-Atlantic integration is an important factor in strengthening its national security, aimed at supporting the development of democratic institutions, civil society, protection of human rights and freedoms, which corresponds to the vital interests of Ukraine. The need to support Ukraine's course towards Euro-Atlantic integration, the ultimate goal of which is to obtain full membership in NATO and to consolidate the appropriate provision in legislation was also pointed out. The President of Ukraine was recommended to strengthen control over the timely and full implementation of acts of Ukrainian legislation in matters of mutual relations and cooperation between Ukraine and NATO.

As NATO approached the borders of independent Ukraine, its importance for the Alliance also increased. This value has and still has a geopolitical dimension primarily. Without Ukraine, it is impossible to complete Europe's political project. Therefore, the second wave will be followed by the third and fourth, and of course, the last wave of NATO expansion, which will end its expansion to the geographical borders of Europe. In this context, the new Action Plan for Ukraine's membership in NATO adopted in Prague was of fundamental importance. He clearly defined Ukraine's strategic directions and priorities to achieve the goal of full integration with the Euro-Atlantic security structures.

The Action Plan contained five chapters, covering political and economic issues, security and defence, military, information protection and security, legal issues and implementation mechanisms. Striving to achieve the strategic goal of full integration with the Euro-Atlantic security structures, Ukraine has undertaken to adapt its national legislation to the rules and procedures adopted in the Euro-Atlantic space, including the implementation of the principles of strengthening the market economy, protecting economic freedoms, ensuring stability and prosperity through economic freedom, social justice and a responsible attitude towards the environment.

The dynamics of activities aimed at adapting the Ukrainian state to the requirements of becoming a full member of the Alliance were stopped by the decision taken at the NATO summit in Bucharest in 2008, during which, due to the opposition of Russia, France, Germany and Great Britain, no *Membership Action Plan* (MAP) was offered to Ukraine and Georgia. However, NATO countries agreed to the future membership of both countries in the organisation. At the end of the meeting of the NATO–Russia Council, Russian President V. V. Putin added his proverbial '*five worst*' *words, giving a speech regarding, among others, the* situation in Eastern Europe, in which he recalled the issue of Russian interests. Media reports showed that Vladimir Putin allegedly said that *Ukraine is a very complicated country* that is plagued by various problems, including ethnic ones.

> Ukraine in its current form was created in Soviet times from the territories it received from Poland – after World War II, from Czechoslovakia, from Romania – and currently not all problems have been solved, such as those on the border with Romania in the Black Sea region. Ukraine received a huge territory from Russia in the east and south (…). If we introduce Ukraine to NATO problems and other problems, it may put this country on the brink of existence. There are complicated internal political problems there (Henzel, 2014).

This showed what policy Russia intended to pursue towards Ukraine.

This led to changes in Ukraine's strategic documents relating to foreign and security policy. The first was the Act *On the Principles of Internal and Foreign Policy* of 1 July 2010, which explicitly stated that Ukraine, as a European non-aligned (non-bloc) country, pursues an open foreign policy and seeks cooperation with all interested partners, avoiding dependence on individual countries, groups of states or international structures. The next step was the adoption of new editions of the National Security Strategy and the Military Doctrine of Ukraine.

The strategic goals and main tasks of national security policy include creating conditions for Ukraine's integration into one European political, economic and legal space, including through the development of sectoral cooperation with the European Union, expanding Ukraine's participation in programmes implemented under the European Union initiative *Eastern Partnership*, further development of mutually beneficial partnership with the European Free Trade Association and the member states of the European Free Trade Association, creation of general conditions for full membership of Ukraine in the European Union as one of the guarantees of its national security. Against this background, the provision regarding the formation of a new model of strategic partnership relations between Ukraine and the Russian Federation, based on the balance of national interests, expanding the dialogue on counteracting new security challenges and threats and finding a common approach to the formation of a new system of pan-European collective security looked very strange. NATO membership had not been the goal of Ukraine's foreign and security policy until then (Fiott, 2023). Only provisions were left stating the continuation of a constructive partnership with the North Atlantic Treaty Organisation and other military-political blocs on all issues of common interest. It was understood as one of the directions of Ukraine's security policy and was aimed at cooperation in overcoming traditional and new challenges and threats, as well as achieving leading standards of development and defence capabilities by the Ukrainian state.

The basis for implementing a constructive partnership became the Annual National Plans, which were adopted by the Ukrainian government with a considerable delay. Each such programme consisted of five chapters: political and economic, defence and military, raw materials, security and legal issues. The central executive authorities, their subordinate state structures, as well as non-governmental organisations were involved in the implementation. Despite the lack of consensus among member states, NATO tried to maintain an appropriate level of cooperation with Ukraine. Five joint working groups worked under the auspices of the Ukraine–NATO Commission:

1. On military reform (separate expert consultations were held within this working group on the reform of Ukraine's security and intelligence sector and cooperation in the field of cybersecurity).
2. For defence and technical cooperation.
3. For economic security.
4. For planning for civil emergencies.
5. For science and the environment.

Ukraine has remained the only partner country participating in all major ongoing NATO- and EU-led peacekeeping missions and various types of exercises – '*Ocean Shield*' (2013/2014), *EU NAVFOR ATALANTA*, '*Active Endeavour*', KFOR, Iraq, ISAF, '*Steadfast Jazz-2013*', NRF (*NATO Response Force*) NATO (2014). The issues of Ukraine's cooperation with the North Atlantic Alliance have definitely acquired a new dimension and scope after the *Revolution of Dignity – Euromaidan* at the turn of 2013/2014. The change of power that followed these events also led to a complete reorientation of Ukraine's security and foreign policy.

The catalyst for these actions was the aggression of the Russian Federation against Ukraine, the annexation of the Autonomous Republic of Crimea (Crimean peninsula), the conduct of *hybrid war* and military actions in the eastern regions of Ukraine. Constant military, political, economic and information pressure from Russia forced the Ukrainian authorities to look for new, more effective guarantees of maintaining independence, sovereignty, security and territorial unity. Practically since the beginning of 2014, Ukraine's consultations and cooperation with NATO have covered a very wide spectrum of various areas of the state's functioning. These include operations aimed at supporting peace, reforming security and defence structures, direct military cooperation and cooperation in the field of military equipment, planning in the event of emergency situations in the civilian environment, science and the environment and public diplomacy. Cooperation has become more active in the areas of increasing Ukraine's ability to guarantee its own security. The new president of Ukraine, P. Poroshenko, assessed that NATO is the only functional collective security organisation in the world (Skachko, 2020).

The words were also followed by actions. In December 2014, a new law was introduced into legal circulation, which cancelled Ukraine's non-bloc status and included provisions on its intentions to integrate with the Euro-Atlantic security structures. At the same time, President Poroshenko announced that he was in favour of holding an all-Ukrainian referendum (Kermacz, 2017) on NATO membership.

In order to increase public support for the state's policy on Euro-Atlantic integration and the level of citizens' trust in NATO as a key institution for strengthening international security, the President of Ukraine, on 21 February 2017, approved the '*Concept of improving society's information policy in the area of cooperation between Ukraine and NATO for 2017-2020*' (European Truth, 2017).

Overview of Ukraine–NATO Cooperation Programmes and Initiatives

Also, from NATO's side, since 2014, a number of active actions have been initiated to support Ukraine. NATO–Ukraine cooperation has been intensified in key areas. And since Russia's full-scale invasion of Ukraine began in February 2022, NATO and allies have provided unprecedented levels of support to Ukraine. Practical cooperation between NATO and Ukraine has been ongoing since the 1990s and significantly strengthened after 2014 was mutually beneficial and covered a wide range of activities – from building Ukraine's capabilities and interoperability with NATO forces, through promoting reforms in the Ukrainian defence and related security sector, to supporting non-military activities such as joint research and public diplomacy (Sydoruk et al., 2023).

Since the NATO Summit in Warsaw in July 2016, NATO's practical support for Ukraine has been set out in the Comprehensive Assistance Package (CAP) for Ukraine. During the 2022 Madrid summit, allies strengthened CAP to provide even greater support to Ukraine. At the 2023 Vilnius summit, it was agreed to further develop CAP and transform it into a multi-year Assistance Programme that will help rebuild the Ukrainian security and defence sector and transform Ukraine towards full interoperability with NATO. NATO cooperation with Ukraine took place at many levels and in many areas. In addition, cooperation was organised through several subgroups of the NATO–Ukraine Commission, including:

- the NATO–Ukraine Joint Working Group on Defence Reform (JWGDR);
- the Joint Working Group on Defence Technical Cooperation (JWGDTC) (NATO, 2024).

The last, most important accent in Ukraine–NATO relations was granting Ukraine the status of a country with extended possibilities of cooperation with the Alliance (12 June 2020) and the Alliance summit in Vilnius and in particular the decisions reached during it. It was agreed during the summit that the current forum for bilateral cooperation, the Ukraine–NATO Commission (1997–2023), will cease to exist and the Ukraine–NATO Council will be established. During its first meeting at the level of foreign ministers, the allies confirmed their long-term support for Ukraine and agreed on recommendations regarding the reform of Ukraine's security system. The Alliance will continue to support Kyiv on its path to NATO membership (Rublovskis, 2023). At the same time, Ukraine's full membership in NATO is impossible in war conditions. This was met with a negative comment from the head of Ukrainian diplomacy, Dmytro Kuleba, who stated that *establishing the Ukraine-NATO Council during the NATO summit in Vilnius without taking a decisive step towards our membership is like giving a tank without a gun*. Then, during a bilateral meeting with German Foreign Minister Annalena

Baerbock, he added: *Ukraine needs NATO as a member state of the Alliance, and not simply (as) a privileged partner* (Tkacz, 2023). It should also be recalled that three important decisions were made during the summit in Vilnius (Bohdaniok & Melnyk, 2023):

1. Ukraine's path to NATO membership was shortened from a two-stage to a one-stage process by removing the requirement to have a MAP.
2. NATO–Ukraine Council was created, which is an important body where Ukraine and all NATO members gather at the same table with the same rights and the same obligations, and decisions can be made together. This brings Ukraine closer to NATO through the creation of a decision-making body.
3. It was agreed to implement a comprehensive programme ensuring full interoperability between Ukrainian and NATO forces.

Scenarios and Implications

Referring to the words of the Secretary General of NATO, who stated that full-fledged membership of Ukraine in conditions of war is impossible, we decided to refer to possible scenarios for its ending. In this context, the prospects and consequences of Ukraine's membership for the Alliance will also be presented. Referring to the above, six possible scenarios for ending the Russian–Ukrainian war were considered.

Scenario first – Russia winning – the worst option for Ukraine, NATO, the EU and a number of other countries that support Ukraine. Unfortunately, this does not mean that, apart from Russia, there will not be countries for which this scenario may also be the best. The implementation of this scenario may lead to:

- a triumph for Putin, who may want to '*follow suit*';
- another large wave of emigration that will flow to NATO and EU countries;
- creating a power in Ukraine that is completely dependent on the Kremlin;
- creation of a Ukrainian government '*in exile*' in one of the NATO or EU countries;
- problems with members of the Armed Forces (people, equipment, etc.) and other formations of the defence forces of Ukraine who will remain in Ukraine or move to the territory of countries bordering Ukraine;
- starting repression against Ukrainian citizens and establishing a resistance movement in Ukraine (structures and formations that will strive to free Ukraine from Russian occupation);
- intensification of the activities of special services in Ukraine and the countries bordering it;
- problems for various national minorities living in Ukraine;
- further sanctions against Russia, which, however, will probably not receive such support from all countries (e.g. BRICS);
- isolating Russia in the international arena, which may lead to even greater unpredictability of its actions.

If this scenario occurs, Ukraine's membership in NATO and EU structures becomes impossible or postponed to a very distant, unknown time horizon.

Scenario second – victory for Ukraine (recovery of all occupied territories) – a variant desired by the authorities, the Ukrainian society, NATO and the EU. In such a case, Ukraine may very quickly become a full member of both NATO and the EU. However, even in this case, we will be faced with a number of problems that will need to be solved (both in Ukraine–Russian relations, as well as in NATO–Russia or EU–Russia relations):

- victory may be achieved thanks to successes on the battlefield or through an internal coup in Russia, which could lead to a change of power, although not necessarily to the immediate end of the war;
- there remains the issue of solving the problem of the Russian political, military and economic elites who supported Putin's regime (new Nuremberg?) and the Russian society itself, which will remain with the trauma of the lost war;
- there is a possibility of the disintegration of the Russian Federation as a federal state as a result of 'bottom-up initiatives' of any of the 85 federal entities that constitute it;
- the process of creating a new security architecture will begin – both European and global (China will certainly try to take advantage of Russia's defeat);
- there will still be a need to rebuild Ukraine's statehood as a unified socio-political entity and to face all the negative aspects of its current functioning as a state (corruption, oligarchic structures, building democratic mechanisms to control the activities of state structures, etc.) – this process will involve both EU and NATO structures;

Scenario third – freezing the conflict (e.g. in Transnistria) – a variant to some extent desired by the Kremlin in the event of creating a corridor connecting Russia with Crimea and retaining current territorial gains. In such a case, Ukraine's possible membership in NATO and the EU will require many efforts on the part of politicians, diplomats and military personnel, whose task will be to prepare their own societies, various international structures (UN, OSCE, etc.) and also the armed forces for possible variants of the development of the situation (peace talks, unfreezing the conflict, status quo). In this case, you should expect:

- Russian activities in the international arena (special and information operations), the aim of which will be to convince the international community of the fact that Ukraine does not meet the requirements of a country candidate for NATO and the EU;
- the need for the international community to engage in negotiation efforts, with particular emphasis on NATO, EU and UN structures;
- continuous smaller or larger armed skirmishes on the lines of separation of forces;
- 'earthquakes' in the structures of the political and military authorities of Ukraine, which led to this state of affairs.

In this case, we can also talk about the possibility of postponing Ukraine's membership in the Alliance, although this may also bring negative consequences in the form of a change in social mood in Ukraine (this will certainly be used by Russian propaganda).

Scenario fourth – the Russia–Ukraine peace agreement – a scenario that allows for the end of the war, but under conditions that are currently difficult to predict. Every peace agreement is a compromise. It does end military operations, but each side of the conflict must make some concessions. Given the current Russian authorities, such a compromise would be very difficult to achieve on terms acceptable to Ukraine. This may result in:

- relieving the international, Ukrainian and Russian communities from having to bear the costs of the war;
- the need to prepare Ukrainian society for this variant of the situation;
- wider participation of NATO and EU structures in the negotiation process (the format of possible peace talks is difficult to predict);
- the possibility of social unrest both in Russia and Ukraine – part of the societies that are dissatisfied with the effects of the armed conflict achieved by the political and military leadership of the countries.

In this case, of course, there is the possibility of Ukraine's membership in NATO and the EU, which will bring tangible benefits in the reconstruction of the country after the war. However, it cannot be ruled out that if the 'rotten compromise' is reached, the public attitude towards NATO and the EU on the part of the Ukrainian society will change, and it will not support the participation of its country in structures that have not brought a positive effect (e.g. only victory counts) in war with Russia.

Scenario fifth – Russia achieves its goals and manages, for example, to divide the territory of Ukraine into two parts along the Dnieper line – something like the division of the German state after World War II, known from the past – the Federal Republic of Germany and the German Democratic Republic – is created. The western part falls under the control of NATO and EU countries, while the eastern part and Crimea come under the control of the Russian Federation. As history shows, the process of reunification may take decades, but it is not impossible. The Western part receives help in the form of, for example, a new Marshall Plan and, over time, may become a member of the EU and possibly NATO. Another example showing that such coexistence is possible is the case of Cyprus – the southern part belongs to the EU, the northern part remains under the influence of Turkey. In such a case, we could expect similar problems that occurred in the relations of the two German states during the decades of their existence as separate structures on the world map. I mean both benefits (end of the war) and negative consequences (division of societies, political and economic problems, risk of conflict situations, the issue of the capitals of new *states*, the nationality of Kiev, etc.). Admission of the western part to NATO and the EU is possible in such a case, but at the expense of high costs of necessary investments related to post-war reconstruction and all state structures, with particular attention to the armed forces and other forces responsible for the safety and protection of the population.

Scenario sixth – considered purely theoretically due to the low possibility of its occurrence. *Russia and Ukraine reach a peace agreement and move to cooperation as in the past.* Ukraine is placed in Russia's sphere of influence in exchange for ending the war and access to natural resources (oil, gas, etc.) and markets for its own industry. This is an unacceptable option for Ukrainian society and the community of Western countries (NATO and the EU). It creates a problem for the authorities of countries supporting Ukraine in the war with Russia due to the fact that they were unable to achieve a positive effect, that is defeating Russian imperialism, which will continue to pose a threat to the international community. Of course, in this case, there are no prospects for Ukraine's membership in NATO and the EU.

Conclusions

To sum up, we would like to quote the opinion of Mr Maciej Popowski, a Polish diplomat who, since 1993, represented Poland in many EU structures. In his opinion:

> The events in Kiev's Independence Square, followed by the annexation of Crimea and the start of hybrid warfare in eastern Ukraine, increased the sense of threat in the countries of Central and Eastern Europe. However, the effects of the Ukrainian crisis reach further. First, Russia's forced confrontation with the West has breathed new life into the transatlantic community. This is very clearly visible in the example of the final declaration from the NATO summit in Newport, confirming the Alliance's return to its roots, i.e. common defence. Secondly, both Europe and the United States had to critically evaluate the current formula of cooperation with Russia. Thirdly, there has been a qualitative change in the perception of threats in Europe, which should have a significant impact on the implementation of allied obligations in NATO by European countries and on the further development of the Common Security and Defence Policy. Under the influence of the events in Ukraine, Europeans and Americans have realised that the transatlantic structures, encompassing a community of law and recognising common values in the field of democracy, human rights, as well as economic and political freedom, are at greater risk than previously assumed. Russian aggression against Ukraine has contributed to the rapprochement of NATO and the EU. The two organisations have not cooperated as closely as they do today in the wake of the Ukrainian crisis over the last 15 years. 'This can be considered an unintended consequence of President Putin's policy'. (Popowski, 2014)

Referring to these words, we would like to emphasise that the EU and NATO, responsible for ensuring security, prosperity and development for the citizens of the countries associated with them, are currently the only organisations capable of opposing the imperialist ambitions of the ruler sitting in the Kremlin (Ratti, 2023). Despite a number of differences and internal conflicts among member states, they are able to develop a consensus and achieve the assumed strategic goals of security, economic and social policy in today's extremely variable and unpredictable security environment (Orenstein, 2023). Membership in such structures should ennoble and give the countries seeking it an incentive to make even greater efforts to build state and social structures that recognise common values in the field of democracy, human and civil rights, economic, social and religious freedom and equality before the law. Simply put, the implementation of the basic values common to the EU and NATO: human dignity, freedom, democracy, equality, rule of law and human rights (Official Journal of the European Union, 2012).

Ukraine has been trying to become a member of the European community for many years. This is what the founding fathers of its independence fought for, which was achieved in 1991. Ukrainian society has many times confirmed its aspirations to be a member of the democratic part of Europe and the world. It is enough to mention here two important events in the history of independent Ukraine: the Orange Revolution of 2004 and 'Revolution of Dignity – Euromaidan' from the turn of 2013/2014. Following the aspirations of society, which, in 1991, in the independence referendum, confirmed the desire to build an independent, democratic, law-abiding state, the political elites at the helm of power did not always keep up. For them, it was enough to regain independence and try to build statehood according to their own ideas. Very often, their particular interests determined the current directions of security and foreign policy, leading to Ukraine balancing between the East and the West or remaining a state that was not an element of any collective international structures. The policy of indeterminacy or multiple vectors in the case of Ukraine's geopolitical location could only end in one thing – being constantly under the influence of the imperial aspirations of its great neighbour, Russia, which, under the rule of the current ruler of the Kremlin, is trying to rebuild its importance in the international arena using methods known from the distant political and historical past. What counts is strength, not dialogue and cooperation on equal terms of peaceful coexistence of states and nations. Only the real danger and threat from the neighbour changed the approach of the Ukrainian authorities dramatically (Demenko, 2023). You can say at this point, better late than never, but we have no right to forget about the costs, especially human ones, that it entailed. Considering the transformation of Ukraine's relations with NATO, it can be said that they were largely determined by the emergence of new security challenges and the need for an adequate response. An attempt to implement the idea of joining Western structures without any confrontation with Russia turned out to be impossible. This has led to a situation that is currently being faced not only by Ukrainians but also by the entire international community, including citizens of the Russian Federation, for whom participation in the war is not the main goal of their lives.

Ukraine's cooperation with the North Atlantic Alliance was established and developed over more than three decades. Many observers consider these relations to be the most effective and mutually beneficial of all Ukraine's relations with all other international organisations in the world. Therefore, obtaining full membership in NATO should become an indisputable goal of the security and foreign policy of all Ukrainian authorities, regardless of their political provenance. Currently, the main obstacle is Russia's full-scale military aggression, which has led to the annexation of part of the territory of an independent state in order to achieve particular interests by the authorities of that state.

Considering the above, the transformation of Ukraine–NATO relations was presented in the perspective of scenarios for the possible end of the armed conflict. However, this does not change the fact that Ukraine's membership in NATO and the EU would bring tangible benefits for the Alliance, the EU and Ukraine itself. Thanks to this, Ukrainian society could confidently say that after more than 30 years of wandering, it has finally found itself at home, in a democratic, law-abiding country that respects human and civil rights. This would seal the collapse of the evil empire that was the USSR and stand in the way of further development of Russia's imperial ambitions.

References

Aleksiievets, L., & Aleksiievets, M. (2020). The transformation of Ukraine – NATO relationships in 1991–2019: A historical aspect. *Ukrainian Historical Journal*, 126–142. https://doi.org/10.15407/uhj2020.01.126

Bendyk, E. (2024). *Lenin: wódz o wielu twarzach. Jego widmo ciągle krąży nad światem.* Lenin: The Many-Faced Leader. His Spectre Still Haunts the World. https://www.polityka.pl/tygodnikpolityka/historia/2243989,1,lenin-wodz-o-wielu-twarzach-jego-widmo-ciagle-krazy-nad-swiatem.read

Bezhitashvili, T., & Gerdes Scott, J. (2022). NATO-Russia clash over the Pro-Western Post-Soviet Republics. *Journal in Humanities, 11*(1). https://doi.org/10.31578/hum.v11i1.478

Bohdaniok, O., & Melnyk, C. (2023, November 27). *Stołtenberh: pownoprawne członstwo Ukrajiny w NATO w umowach wijny nemożływe* [Stoltenberg: full membership of Ukraine in NATO is impossible in the conditions of war]. https://suspilne.media/626365-stoltenberg-v-umovah-vijni-povnopravne-clenstvo-ukraini-v-nato-nemozlive/

Brzezinski, Z. (1998). *Wielka szachownica: główne cele polityki amerykańskiej* [The Grand Chessboard. American primacy and its geostrategic imperatives]. Świat Książki.

Demenko, O. (2023). The evolution of NATO policy in the conditions of the russian-Ukrainian war. *Diplomatic Ukraine, XXIV*. https://doi.org/10.37837/2707-7683-2023-5

Desai, R., Freeman, A., & Kagarlitsky, B. (2016). The conflict in Ukraine and contemporary imperialism. *International Critical Thought, 6*(4). https://doi.org/10.1080/21598282.2016.1242338

Encyklopedia PWN. (n.d.). *Homo sovieticus*. Retrieved June 3, 2024, from https://encyklopedia.pwn.pl/haslo/homo-sovieticus%3B3912513.html

European Truth. (2017, February 22). *Poroszenko zatwerdyw koncepciju informuwannia szczodo spiwpraci z NATO* [Poroshenko approved the concept of informing about cooperation with NATO]. https://www.eurointegration.com.ua/news/2017/02/22/7062028/

Fernández, Ó., Vandendriessche, M., Saz-Carranza, A., Agell, N., & Franco, J. (2023). The impact of Russia's 2022 invasion of Ukraine on public perceptions of EU security and defence integration: A big data analysis. *Journal of European Integration, 45*(3). https://doi.org/10.1080/07036337.2023.2183392

Fiott, D. (2023). In every crisis an opportunity? European Union integration in defence and the War on Ukraine. *Journal of European Integration, 45*(3). https://doi.org/10.1080/07036337.2023.2183395

Henzel, P. (2014, October 22). *Wracają kontrowersje wokół szczytu NATO w Bukareszcie. "Nowa linia podziału" w Europie* [Controversy returns over NATO summit in Bucharest. "New dividing line" in Europe]. https://wiadomosci.onet.pl/tylko-w-onecie/wracaja-kontrowersje-wokol-szczytu-nato-w-bukareszcie-nowa-linia-podzialu-w-europie/20pyss

Ilin, I., & Nihmatova, O. (2023). Exploring Russia's postponed war against Ukraine: A corpus-based analysis of strategic studies institutes' publications from 1991 to 2014. *Central European Journal of International and Security Studies, 17*(4). https://doi.org/10.51870/wujq2611

Kermacz, R. (2017, February 6). *Referendum szczodo członstwa w NATO: stratehiczna perspektywa czy instrument taktycznoji politycznoji hry?* [Referendum on NATO membership: A strategic perspective or a tool of tactical political game?]. https://novynarnia.com/2017/02/06/referendum-shhodo-chlenstva-v-nato-strategichna-perspektiva-chi-instrument-taktichnoyi-politichnoyi-gri/

Kuzio, T. (1998). Ukraine and NATO: The evolving strategic partnership. *Journal of Strategic Studies, 21*(2). https://doi.org/10.1080/01402399808437715

Maass, A. S. (2019). From Vilnius to the Kerch Strait: Wide-ranging security risks of the Ukraine crisis. *European Politics and Society, 20*(5). https://doi.org/10.1080/23745118.2019.1570667

Meleshchenko, T. (2021). Brothers in arms: Features of the Ukraine – NATO partnership in the 1990s. *Studia Warminskie, 58*. https://doi.org/10.31648/sw.7016

NATO. (2024, July 19). *Relations with Ukraine*. https://www.nato.int/cps/en/natohq/topics_37750.htm?selectedLocale=en#hybrid-warfare

Official Journal of the European Union. (2012). Consolidated version of the Treaty on European Union. *Official Journal of the European Union*. https://www.europarl.europa.eu/ftu/pdf/en/FTU_4.1.2.pdf

Orenstein, M. A. (2023). The European Union's transformation after Russia's attack on Ukraine. *Journal of European Integration, 45*(3). https://doi.org/10.1080/07036337.2023.2183393

Pogorzelski, P. (2013). *Barszcz ukraiński* [Ukrainian borscht]. Księgarnia informatyczna Helion.

Popowski, M. (2014). Transatlantyckie struktury bezpieczeństwa w obliczu kryzysu ukraińskiego. In *Bezpieczeństwo Narodowe* (32nd ed., Vol. *IV*, pp. 97–106). BBN. Bezpieczeństwo Biuro Bezpieczeństwa Narodowego. https://www.bbn.gov.pl › dok › BBN_32_calosc

Ptashchenko, O., Panasenko, H., Liapa, M., Sokhatskyi, O., Mudra, Y., & Pylypenko, N. (2022). Institutional instruments of Ukraine's Euro-Atlantic integration. *Economic Affairs (New Delhi), 67*(3). https://doi.org/10.46852/0424-2513.3.2022.26

Rada, V. (1991). *Widbuwsia Wseukrajinśkyj referendum szczodo prohołoszennia nezałeżnosti Ukrajiny* [An All-Ukrainian referendum on the declaration of Ukraine's independence was held]. http://www.nbuv.gov.ua/node/4475

Ratti, L. (2023). NATO and the CSDP after the Ukraine war: The end of European strategic autonomy? *Canadian Journal of European and Russian Studies, 16*(2). https://doi.org/10.22215/cjers.v16i2.4150

Rublovskis, R. (2023). Impact of Ukraine war on NATO development. NATO Vision 2030. *Doctrina. Studia Społeczno-Polityczne*, *20*(20). https://doi.org/10.34739/doc.2023.20.04

Skachko, L. (2020). Ukraine–NATO: State and prospects of cooperation development. *Visnyk of the Lviv University. Series International Relations*, *48*. https://doi.org/10.30970/vir.2020.48.0.11052

Sydoruk, T., Pavliuk, V., & Shuliak, A. (2023). Russia's war against Ukraine and the transformation of the Euro-Atlantic security architecture. *Politics in Central Europe*, *19*(2). https://doi.org/10.2478/pce-2023-0014

Tkacz, M. (2023, June 14). *Rada Ukraina-NATO bez kroku ku członkostwu to jak czołg bez działa* [The Ukraine-NATO Council without a step towards membership is like a tank without a gun]. https://www.gazetaprawna.pl/wiadomosci/swiat/artykuly/8733865,rada-ukraina-nato-bez-kroku-ku-czlonkostwu-to-jak-czolg-bez-dziala.html

UN. (1994). *Memorandum on security assurances in connection with Ukraine's accession to the treaty on the Non-Proliferation of Nuclear Weapons*. https://treaties.un.org/Pages/showDetails.aspx?objid=0800000280401fbb

Vidnianskyi, S. (2011). Nezalezhna Ukraina: dvadtsiat rokiv mizh Yevropoiu ta Yevraziieiu [Independent Ukraine: Twenty years between Europe and Eurasia]. *Ukraina – Yevropa – Svit: Mizhnarodnyi Zbirnyk Naukovykh Prats*, *6*(7), 24–38.

Chapter 2

Euro-Atlantic Integration of Ukraine: Experiences, Prospects, and Challenges

Ilona Urych[a], *Vitalii Suprun*[b], *Gastone Breccia*[c] *and Robert Boroch*[d]

[a] *War Studies University, Poland*
[b] *Vasyl Stefanyk Precarpathian National University, Ukraine*
[c] *University of Pavia, Italy*
[d] *University of Warsaw, Poland*

Abstract

In this chapter, we discuss the process of preparing Ukraine for integration with the North Atlantic Treaty Organization (hereafter NATO) and the need for additional change on both sides. Three research questions are posed in the chapter: (1) What legal and social efforts is Ukraine taking to standardise its integration? (2) What measures has NATO taken to prepare Ukraine for membership in the Alliance? (3) How does the Russian Federation influence the disruption of integration processes? Given these research questions, the chapter is divided into three components. The first presents Ukraine's legal and social preparations for integration into NATO. The second discusses integration-oriented moves made by NATO. Finally, the third part discusses the factors interrupting the integration process enforced by the Russian Federation in the form of anthropological aggression imposed in the Ukrainian socio-cultural environment. The conclusion contains recommendations for further Ukrainian–NATO integration, which indicate potential policy changes that NATO member states may need to make considering the Ukrainian occasion.

Keywords: Ukrainian–NATO integration; NATO criteria; standardisation; anthropological aggression of the Russian Federation; hybrid activities; Ukrainian at war

JEL Codes: K10; F52; F20

Enhancing Transatlantic Solidarity in Collective Defence: Navigating Increased Defence Expenditures, Cyber Security, and Emerging Risks, 23–35

doi:10.1108/978-1-80686-259-720261002

Introduction

The military strike initiated by the Russian Federation traces its roots back to the annexation of Crimea and the subsequent occupation of parts of eastern Ukraine in 2014. However, the escalation reached a critical point on 24 February 2022, when the Russian Federation launched a full-scale invasion of Ukraine, blatantly violating international law and disregarding established agreements. The military forces of the Russian Federation are consistently destroying not only military targets but also facilities that are significant to Ukrainian cultural development and a sense of being a part of a Western civilisation. An analysis of the politicians' statements and those of experts reveals a significant conclusion that the Ukrainian nation is standing up for its freedom and protecting Western civilisation values, which oppose, in fact, the Russian Federation's imperial ambitions. Needless to say, the Ukrainian nation is standing for fundamental rights – human rights – which include freedom, justice, and peace. As a consequence, Ukraine's aspiration for Euro-Atlantic integration comes as no surprise, driven by its steadfast commitment to implementing reform measures conducive to alignment with NATO standards.

This chapter analyses the process of preparing Ukraine for integration with NATO and the need for additional change on both sides. Three research questions need to be answered to conduct thorough research on this topic: (1) What legal and social efforts is Ukraine taking to standardise its integration? (2) What measures has NATO taken to prepare Ukraine for membership in the Alliance? (3) How does the Russian Federation influence the disruption of integration processes? The study considered various perspectives, including constructivism (Wendt, 1999), Chicago School empirical sociology (Bulmer, 1986), and engaged ethnography (Kirsch, 2018). The study used mixed research methods, including document analysis, visual analysis, and social network analysis techniques derived from critical discourse analysis. Through this interdisciplinary lens, we aim to shed light on the multifaceted dynamics underpinning Ukraine's integration with NATO and the complex interplay of geopolitical forces shaping its trajectory. Ultimately, the quest for a robust, resilient, and independent Ukraine emerges as indispensable for fostering stability within the Euro-Atlantic region.

Legal Actions of Ukraine Towards Euro-Atlantic Integration

The dynamics of relations between Ukraine and NATO have changed quite intensively depending on the Ukrainian internal political turbulence and the West's relations with Russia (Blyzniuk, 2023, p. 138). NATO's interest in Ukraine became evident in the early 1990s, when Ukraine became the first post-Soviet state to participate in the Partnership for Peace programme (Fasola & Wood, 2021, p. 45). In the late 1990s and early 2000s, Ukraine and NATO established a legal framework for cooperation, grounded in the Charter on a Distinctive Partnership between Ukraine and NATO and the Declaration to Complement the Charter on a Distinctive Partnership (Aleksiievets & Aleksiievets, 2020, pp. 131–137). During this period, the involved parties were moving towards deepening the partnership, culminating on 21 April 2005, when the NATO–Ukraine Commission in Vilnius launched an intensified political dialogue on membership and related reforms, which was reflected in a document entitled 'Enhancing NATO-Ukraine Cooperation: Short-Term Actions' (Blyzniuk, 2023, p. 138).

The impetus for Ukraine's Euro-Atlantic integration gained momentum after Russia's aggression on Ukrainian territory in 2014, which led to a change in the strategic thinking of the Ukrainian leadership (Maksak, 2020, p. 63). During this critical juncture, Ukraine renounced its ineffective non-aligned status and incorporated into the Law of Ukraine 'On the Principles of Domestic and Foreign Policy' a novel tenet, emphasising 'deepening cooperation with [NATO] in order to achieve the criteria necessary for membership in this organization' (Zakon Ukrainy, 2010; Zakon Ukrainy, 2014). This was also facilitated by the fact that, after the Russian aggression, NATO was the only international organisation that firmly supported the sovereignty and territorial integrity of Ukraine within its internationally recognised borders (Todorov, 2023, p. 12).

In subsequent years, pivotal legislative actions reinforced Ukraine's Euro-Atlantic course. In 2017, the Law 'On Amendments to Certain Laws of Ukraine on the Foreign Policy Course of Ukraine' confirmed that the ultimate goal of Ukraine's Euro-Atlantic integration is to join NATO (Zakon Ukrainy, 2017). The new Law 'On the National Security of Ukraine' of 2018 also confirmed that joining NATO is one of the most important interests of national security (Zakon Ukrainy, 2018). Fundamental legal changes regarding the foreign policy vector were made in 2019 to the Constitution of Ukraine, which confirmed the irreversibility of Ukraine's Euro-Atlantic course (Konstytutsiia Ukrainy, 1996; Zakon Ukrainy, 2019).

Consequently, the main legislative acts that regulate the Euro-Atlantic integration of Ukraine are the Constitution, the Law 'On the Principles of Domestic and Foreign Policy', and the Law 'On the National Security of Ukraine'.

In alignment with clearly articulated Euro-Atlantic aspirations, Ukraine took a decisive step in January 2020 by submitting an application to NATO for participation in the Enhanced Opportunities Partner programme, which provides for the achievement of sectoral (operational) interoperability with the Alliance, and joined it on 12 June 2020 (Todorov, 2022, pp. 131–132). Therefore, further strategic documents consider Euro-Atlantic integration within the framework of such a deepened partnership.

The lower legal level is strategies, and at the moment, the main strategic documents of Ukraine are National Security Strategy 2020, Military Security Strategy 2021, Foreign Policy Strategy 2021, and Strategic Defense Bulletin 2021.[1] In all strategic documents of Ukraine, partnership with NATO and the process of

---

[1]In addition to these main documents, references to Euro-Atlantic integration and deepening cooperation with NATO are covered in several sector-specific strategic documents, such as the Integrated Border Management Strategy 2019, the Information Security Strategy 2021, the Cyber Security Strategy 2021, the Energy Security Strategy 2021, the Economic Security Strategy 2021, the Strategy for the Development of the Defense-Industrial Complex 2021, the Strategy for Communication of National Euro-Atlantic Integration Policy 2021, and the Strategy for Ensuring State Security 2022.

Euro-Atlantic integration occupy a paramount position (Foreign Policy Council. Ukrainian Prism. Friedrich Ebert Foundation, 2020, p. 90).

The National Security Strategy of 14 September 2020 identified Russia as an aggressor, underscoring the imperative for a partnership with NATO (Singh, 2023, p. 86). The strategy defines the main steps for strengthening the special partnership with NATO and acquiring full membership in the Alliance, which include:

> achieving sufficient interoperability of the Armed Forces of Ukraine and other components of the security and defense sector with the relevant structures of the Alliance states in the shortest possible time; significantly intensifying the reforms that must be implemented in order to achieve compliance with NATO membership criteria within the framework of the implementation of annual national programs (ANP) under the auspices of the Ukraine-NATO Commission; and receiving an invitation and joining the NATO Membership Action Plan (MAP). (Stratehiia natsionalnoi bezpeky Ukrainy, 2020)

The Military Security Strategy of 25 March 2021 was created with the aim of preparing for the comprehensive defence of the state and promoting the integration of Ukraine into the Euro-Atlantic security space and the acquisition of NATO membership (Stratehiia voiennoi bezpeky Ukrainy, 2021). The acceleration of defence reform based on Euro-Atlantic principles and standards should facilitate integration into the Alliance, thereby ensuring the appropriate level of military security of Ukraine (Stratehiia voiennoi bezpeky Ukrainy, 2021). This reform encompassed several key aspects, including building defence forces compatible with NATO countries, capable of contributing to Alliance operations; developing the system of military education and professionalisation; developing the system of logistic support for the Armed Forces; and implementing NATO military standards (administrative, operational, and technical) (Stratehiia voiennoi bezpeky Ukrainy, 2021).

The first Foreign Policy Strategy in the history of Ukraine was adopted on 26 August 2021, which also confirmed the strategic course of the state towards full membership in NATO (Todorov, 2022, pp. 137–138). The strategy itself defines NATO as the main contributor to security in the Euro-Atlantic area (Stratehiia zovnishnopolitychnoi diialnosti Ukrainy, 2021). According to the strategy, the primary goals on the Euro-Atlantic track were:

> achieving compliance with the criteria for NATO membership through the purposeful and systematic implementation of a wide range of domestic reforms within the framework of the implementation of ANP under the auspices of the NATO-Ukraine Commission; effective use of all opportunities for the development of cooperation with the Alliance, provided to Ukraine in connection

> with obtaining the status of an Enhanced Opportunities Partner; [pursuing] the Alliance's decision to invite Ukraine to the MAP. (Stratehiia zovnishnopolitychnoi diialnosti Ukrainy, 2021)

The lowest tier in the hierarchy of strategic documents is the Strategic Defense Bulletin, which is developed based on the results of a defence review by the Ministry of Defense. The Strategic Defense Bulletin dated 17 September 2021 acknowledged that defence reform in accordance with NATO standards and participation in joint operations contributes to the achievement of the Alliance membership criteria and further integration into the Euro-Atlantic security structures (Stratehichnyi oboronnyi biuleten Ukrainy, 2021). It outlines five strategic goals for developing the defence forces, in particular: objective leadership of the defence forces in line with the principles and standards of NATO; effective planning and resource management following Euro-Atlantic principles; necessary capabilities of the defence forces; unified logistics and medical support systems; as well as the professionalisation of the defence forces and the establishment of the necessary military reserve (Stratehichnyi oboronnyi biuleten Ukrainy, 2021).

Separately, it is worth mentioning that in September 2022, Ukraine submitted an application to join NATO, which can be considered a political step since it has no legal significance (Suprun, 2022, p. 33). The process of joining NATO necessitates an invitation from the Alliance, which can be initiated only by consensus among allies in accordance with Article 10 of the Washington Treaty (Todorov, 2023, p. 15). The application itself signals Ukraine's intent to join the Alliance without the MAP, following the precedent set by Finland and Sweden, which is quite logical in view of the fact that since 2009 Ukraine has been implementing ANP, which is similar to the MAP in structure and content (Todorov, 2023, pp. 15–16).

Conclusively, the policy of Euro-Atlantic integration is deeply rooted in the constitutional foundations and legislative and conceptual frameworks. Ukraine is an excellent example of reformist success, as it has made persistent efforts to harmonise national planning and legislation with Euro-Atlantic standards. Against the backdrop of contemporary circumstances, Ukraine views integration into NATO as a vital national interest that will bring incomparable potential strategic advantages.

NATO Actions

Since 1994, NATO and Ukraine have shared a longstanding partnership aimed at bolstering operational interoperability and enhancing Ukraine's resilience against various threats. To improve operational interoperability, NATO and Ukraine have conducted joint exercises on Ukrainian territory since 1995. The Yavoriv training centre in the Lviv region, the largest in Europe, became a symbol of such a strategic partnership (Trembetska, 2013, p. 113). NATO recognised it as a national educational institution of the Partnership for Peace in 1999 (North Atlantic Treaty Organization, 2006). It conducts educational and training activities, including courses, seminars, and workshops for military and civilian audiences (North Atlantic Treaty Organization, 2006). Over the years, NATO's engagement with Ukraine has evolved through practical measures and collaborative initiatives, fostering a robust partnership that extends across multiple domains. This evolution prompts a pertinent question: what has NATO done on a practical level to increase the resilience of Ukraine?

NATO began active, practical activities in Ukraine in 1997, which consisted of signing a Memorandum of Understanding on the establishment of the NATO Information and Documentation Centre in Ukraine (Memorandum, 1997). This is the first information office created by NATO in a partner country dedicated to public diplomacy and strategic communications.

Immediately after creating the NATO Information and Documentation Centre, the parties signed a Memorandum of Understanding on the appointment of NATO Liaison Officers in Ukraine. This framework facilitated the operationalisation of the NATO Liaison Office, entrusted with pivotal responsibilities, including fostering relationships with Ukrainian ministries and governmental entities, delivering consultations to Ukrainian authorities on matters concerning the Ukraine–NATO partnership, relevant reforms, and fortifying the political and practical discourse between NATO and Ukraine (North Atlantic Treaty Organization, 2024).

In 2016, the NATO Representation in Ukraine was established to oversee the two existing offices, which became the largest NATO diplomatic office in a non-member country (Uhoda, 2015). It is an essential tool for strengthening NATO's role in supporting democratic transformations in Ukraine.

In July of the same year, during the NATO Warsaw Summit, a significant milestone was achieved with the approval of the Comprehensive Assistance Package (CAP). This initiative aimed to consolidate and fortify NATO's support for Ukraine, enhancing its resilience against a spectrum of traditional and hybrid threats while bolstering its security apparatus and facilitating the implementation of pivotal reforms aligned with Euro-Atlantic standards (North Atlantic Treaty Organization, 2024).

The CAP encompassed a comprehensive array of over 40 targeted support measures spanning across 13 key areas (North Atlantic Treaty Organization, 2016). Operational assistance was stratified into three principal categories: advisory support, trust funds, and capacity-building programmes.

Advisory support, spanning areas such as parliamentary affairs, security policy formulation, defence restructuring, security sector reform, gender mainstreaming in peace and security efforts, logistics and standardisation, professional development for non-commissioned officers, special operations forces enhancement, improvised explosive device countermeasures, and military medical advancements, is facilitated through a cadre of expert consultants seconded from NATO member states (North Atlantic Treaty Organization, 2024).

Trust funds are voluntary projects implemented at the national level and funded under NATO's Partnership for Peace programme, focusing on demilitarisation, security and defence transformation, and capacity building. Presently, seven targeted trust funds are operational, encompassing initiatives such as the

NSPA – Ukraine EOD & Counter IED, Destruction of Small Arms and Light Weapons, Medical Rehabilitation, Command, Control, Communications and Computers, Cyber Defense, Logistics and Standardization, and Military Career Transition (North Atlantic Treaty Organization, 2022).

In addition to these mechanisms, NATO's collaboration with Ukraine extends to various programmes and initiatives, including the NATO–Ukraine Platform on Countering Hybrid Warfare, the Air Situation Data Exchange Programme, the Partnership for Peace Planning and Review Process, the Operational Capability Concept Evaluation and Feedback Programme, the Building Integrity Programme, the NATO–Ukraine Professional Development Programme, the Defence Education Enhancement Programme, the NATO Resettlement Programme, the Psychological Rehabilitation, and the Science for Peace and Security Programme (North Atlantic Treaty Organization, 2018; North Atlantic Treaty Organization, 2024).

After the NATO Madrid Summit in 2022, the parties increased CAP funding to 640 million euros to provide non-lethal military assistance to Ukraine (North Atlantic Treaty Organization, 2024). For comparison, in 2021, this amount was 2–3 million euros (Niehus, 2023), which shows the growth of the Alliance's priorities on the Eastern Flank. During the Vilnius summit in 2023, NATO members agreed to continue the development of the CAP in the form of a multi-year assistance programme for Ukraine based on stable and pre-forecasted funding (North Atlantic Treaty Organization, 2024).

In the face of increased Russian aggression, NATO remains steadfast in its desire to strengthen support for Ukraine. On 3 April 2024, at a meeting of foreign ministers of NATO countries, the parties agreed to start long-term planning for Ukraine, in connection with which NATO Secretary General Jens Stoltenberg proposed to create a five-year fund for Ukraine in the amount of 100 billion euros (Gray & Irish, 2024). This ambitious project is poised for potential approval at the forthcoming Washington summit scheduled for July 2024. Such a step towards more active assistance to Ukraine aims to protect the structure from a reduction in US support, particularly amidst the impending presidential elections. According to the plan, NATO will take over some coordination work from the Ramstein Format, thereby giving the Alliance a more direct role in coordinating the supply of arms, ammunition, and equipment to Ukraine, which previously took place on a bilateral basis between NATO members (Gray & Irish, 2024). In addition, the proposal includes the creation of a NATO Mission for Ukraine. If such a decision is supported, it will lead to a change in the paradigm of the Alliance, which for a long time was limited to the supply of non-lethal aid to avoid exacerbating tensions with Russia.

While NATO's practical assistance is commendable, it must be accompanied by robust political–diplomatic actions to effectively deter aggression. The strategic documents of NATO emphasise that 'a strong independent Ukraine is vital for the stability of the Euro-Atlantic region' (NATO's 2022 Strategic Concept, 2022). Consequently, if the ultimate goal of the Alliance is to ensure the security of the Euro-Atlantic community, the acceptance of Ukraine into NATO is inevitable, since leaving Ukraine out of the Alliance in the grey zone will only lead to further instability in the region and the strengthening of Moscow's revisionist policy, which will soon lead to a direct confrontation with the Alliance.

Operational Area 6: Culture: Hybrid Warfare

According to Boroch and Korzeniowska-Bihun, Operational Area 6

> refers to military or military-like operations conducted in a social environment. These operations may include hybrid strikes, such as the crisis on the Polish-Belarusian border in 2021, or hybrid operations, such as separatist activities in Ukraine organised by the Russian Federation aimed at annexing Ukrainian lands. (Boroch & Korzeniowska-Bihun, 2023)

The activities in Operational Area 6 may indicate preparation for armed conflict. However, a hybrid warfare strategy aims to create an unstable social environment that can affect the development of state actors. Therefore, hybrid strikes or operations are not necessarily a sign of military conflict preparation.

Hybrid warfare can be easily transferred into the opponent's territory, forcing the authority to take action that consumes state social defensive resources. However, military anthropologists must acquire 'anthropological knowledge' to plan a hybrid attack or operation (Boroch & Korzeniowska-Bihun, 2023). The use of anthropological methods of cognition in such activities is called anthropological espionage (Boroch, 2021; Korzeniowska-Bihun, 2021).

It is necessary to recall that in 1999, Russian anthropologists announced the sociocultural environment in anthropological terms as a subject of military and non-military operations (Boroch, 2021). Traditional areas of non-military operations, such as political pressure, economic blackmail, and armed force threats, are effective against small state actors. All this was in the Ukrainian scenario, starting in the 1990s. Russia's hybrid war against Ukraine included economic, energy, political, diplomatic, informational, religious, and cultural methods. Since 2014, Russia has extended the list of pressure means added terrorist operational methods and cyberattacks (Suprun, 2023, p. 382).

Planning successful hybrid operations or attacks in Operational Area 6 against Ukraine requires solid socio-cultural knowledge that involves cooperating with random teams responsible for fieldwork planning, data gathering, field data analysis, operational planning, execution, and evaluation. Such complex activities cannot go unnoticed.

Operational Area 6, as Boroch and Korzeniowska-Bihun argue, is a natural environment for 7th-generation war: strategies of cultural warfare, psychological warfare, propaganda, information warfare, social warfare, etc., with progressive kinetic asymmetric actions.

Questions should be asked: (1) What support could NATO offer Ukraine in preparations for a hybrid war confrontation in the future? (2) What means of deterrence does NATO have in the case of hybrid operations and attacks? Answering these questions may take an effort, as Operational Area 6 has not been the subject of research and scenario planning by NATO analysts. However, analytical attempts underestimated the scale and degree of Russian anthropological infiltration in post-Soviet countries and the growing number of Russian supporters in Western communities. Needless to say, there are no scenarios or procedures regarding deterrence to stop hybrid operations or attacks against NATO members.

However, the Ukraine experience is a valuable lesson in understanding the Russian Federation's hybrid warfare strategy. In 2020, Vinnytsia Regional Universal Scientific Library gathered a large number of studies carried out by Ukrainian scholars on the Russian hybrid warfare strategy titled 'Hybrid War against Ukraine' (Vinnytska oblasna universalna naukova biblioteka, 2023).

In that collection, there is a chapter by Oleg Barna, in the chapter 'Ukraine's Information Space as a Factor of Social Consolidation in the Conditions of Hybrid Warfare' (Barna, 2019), the author brings attention to Russia's use of social stratification as a factor in disintegrating the nation – that well-crafted polarisation strategy brings to light religious, economic, and political differences to put pressure on society's capabilities to communicate, as a consequence that leads to the destruction of social leadership.

Another interesting study is a chapter written by Anhelika Dilai titled 'The War for Ukraine: From Information Operations to Direct Invasion' (Dilai, 2019). In this paper, Russian infiltration is treated as anthropological espionage. Such actions are carried out directly on Ukrainian soil using military anthropologists who recruit locals for collaboration. Such actions support spreading pro-Russian narration among Ukrainian countrymen.

The most comprehensive study in that collection is 'Russia's "hybrid" war is a challenge and a threat to Europe' (Tsentr Razumkova, 2016).[2]

---

[2]In that study took a part such experts as Maksym Rozumnyi, Head of the Centre for Russian Federation Studies at the National Institute for Strategic Studies; Anatolii Oktysiuk, Member of the Board of the International Centre for Policy Studies; Vadym Triukhan, Chairman of the Board NGO 'European Movement of Ukraine'; Kostiantyn Kononenko, Deputy Director of the National Institute for Strategic Studies; Dmytro Zolotukhin, Director of the Institute of Post-Information Society, Advisor to the Minister of Information Policy of Ukraine; Vitalii Martyniuk, an expert at the Ukrainian Independent Centre for Political Studies; Hryhorii Perepelytsia, Professor at the Department of International Relations and Foreign Policy, Institute of International Relations, National University of Kyiv, Institute Director of Foreign Policy; Volodymyr Ohryzko, Head of the Centre for Russian Studies, former Minister of Foreign Affairs of Ukraine; Leonid Poliakov, Chairman of the Expert Council of the Centre for Army Studies, Conversion and Disarmament Studies; Oleksandr Khara, expert at the Maidan of Foreign Affairs; Yevhen Mahda, executive director of the of the Centre for Public Affairs; Volodymyr Fesenko, Chairman of the Board Centre for Applied Political Studies 'Penta'; Oleksii Semenii, Director of the Institute for Global Transformation; Volodymyr Kopchak, deputy director of the Centre for Army Studies, Conversion and Disarmament Studies.

Intellectuals from numerous areas of science and practice examined the Russian hybrid warfare strategy from 2012 to 2016, which was applied in the Ukrainian scenario in Operational Area 6. A few experts pointed out that hybrid operations targeted Ukrainian values linked to national identity, language, history, traditions, etc.

In that case, simple propaganda techniques, such as bandwagon, transfer, repetition, and emotional appeal, were used. As Boroch argues, that was the first stage of operation (Boroch, 2021, pp. 68–69). The second stage targeted state institutions by questioning the credibility of the local and national authorities. As a result, the false authority image spread the message that Ukraine is a collapsed state. The consequences were the emergence of a pro-Russian lobbying social class. The third stage was to launch pro-Russian activists to organise social disturbances that allowed the building in Russia the narration of persecuted Russian-speaking citizens of Ukraine by Nazis. The fourth stage was the struggle for historical memory supported by social movements – the commemoration of Red Army veterans on 22 June called the 'Day of Remembrance and Sorrow' – and counted cultural groups such as the 'Night Wolves' motorbike club. That stage is the point of no return.

In 2014, after capturing Ukrainian Crimea, the 'Artek' major ideological brainwash factory became operational. A process of ideological and cultural erasing of Ukrainian identity is underway. As a further strategy of brainwashing, organisational 'Young Army' structures were brought to Ukrainian soil, recruiting Ukrainian juveniles aged 8–18, probably by force.

The Russian hybrid warfare strategy demonstrates the enormous scale of social operations. Thus, the questions asked above stay valid, but in a different order: first, what means of deterrence does NATO have in case of Russian hybrid operations and attacks; second, what support could NATO offer Ukraine in preparations for a hybrid war confrontation in the future?

Profound contemplation and decisive action concerning Operational Area 6 are imperative, demanding both meticulous analysis and pragmatic measures to confront the evolving tactics of hybrid warfare employed by Russia.

Conclusions

This paper discusses the process of preparing Ukraine for integration with NATO and the need for additional change on both sides. In essence, Russia is dead against Ukrainian integration with NATO. Thus, Russia does not hesitate to use all means of influence to stop this process. Hybrid warfare through violent conflict is an example of Russian toxic leverage, which is the constant creation and escalation of conflicts. Therefore, military and non-military objectives are targeted, especially those critical for the survival of Ukrainian values.

There is no doubt that the Russian Federation's strategy is to cause sociocultural stratification to create a crisis in areas of trust in state institutions, national values, and Ukrainian identity. The primary outcome of that is the emergence of an unstable social environment. The Russian Federation is effectively carrying out such operations not only in Ukraine but also against NATO members. Meanwhile, NATO is not prepared for hybrid warfare strategies such as cognitive impacts on societies or anthropological aggression. Needless to say, NATO uses soft defensive measures that are not effective.

However, NATO's engagement with Ukraine exemplifies a synergistic partnership founded on shared values and strategic objectives. Through practical measures and collaborative initiatives, NATO has demonstrated its commitment to upholding peace, security, and stability in the Euro-Atlantic region while strengthening Ukraine's resilience against contemporary security challenges.

NATO's efforts have contributed significantly to enhancing Ukraine's national security but have proved to be insufficient. This void can be attributed to a need for better synergy between the practical and political-diplomatic actions of the Alliance. Increasing practical assistance without a footpath to NATO membership leaves Ukraine powerless against a stronger aggressor. NATO must provide firm security guarantees for Ukraine, such as Article 5 of the North Atlantic Treaty, to suspend aggression and prevent future escalations effectively. Only a unified approach that brings together practical support and political solidarity will enable NATO to play a decisive role in the region.

Ukrainians' experience proved that building social resilience by building the credibility of state institutions is a powerful means against hybrid warfare. However, Ukraine's path to NATO seems extended. Given the key position of the United States in NATO, it can be argued that the American authorities are not spending enough effort to ensure international order in its superpower status. Observation of the international theatre allows us to conclude that the European members of NATO should become more active, since the political situation in the United States before the 2024 presidential elections limits stable support for Ukraine. There is a risk that if the United States does not abandon its democratic populism, it may lose its superpower status, and with it, NATO's role in the international arena will diminish, creating a security vacuum. This could result in a power shift from the West to the East, setting the stage for a global conflict among powers seeking to reshape the existing world order, with the unfortunate consequence of a belated awakening for the United States and its allies.

References

Aleksiievets, L., & Aleksiievets, M. (2020). Transformatsiia vidnosyn Ukrainy ta NATO v 1991–2019 rr. istorychnyi aspect. *Ukrainskyi istorychnyi zhurnal*, *1*, 126–142. https://doi.org/10.15407/uhj2020.01.126

Barna, O. (2019). Informatsiinyi prostir Ukrainy yak chynnyk suspilnoi konsolidatsii v umovakh hibrydnoi viiny. *Derzhava i pravo*, *86*, 365–376. http://nbuv.gov.ua/UJRN/dip_2019_86_35

Blyzniuk, M. (2023). Ukraine's attempts to join the West. In R. Zięba (Ed.). *Politics and security of Central and Eastern Europe: Contemporary challenges* (pp. 137–158). Springer Nature. https://doi.org/10.1007/978-3-031-16419-4_7

Boroch, R. (2021). Military anthropology – Specialisation frame. *Wiedza Obronna*, *274*(1), 63–73.

Boroch, R., & Korzeniowska-Bihun, A. (2023). City in conflict – Military anthropology perspective 2023. *Wiedza Obronna*, *285*(4), 1–3.

Bulmer, M. (1986). *The Chicago school of sociology: Institutionalization, diversity, and the rise of sociological research*. University of Chicago Press. https://press.uchicago.edu/ucp/books/book/chicago/C/bo5961517.html

Dilai, A. (2019). Viina za Ukrainu: Vid informatsiinykh operatsii do priamoho vtorhnennia. *Visnyk Lvivskoho universytetu. Seriia: Zhurnalistyka*, *45*, 13–20. http://nbuv.gov.ua/UJRN/VLNU_Jur_2019_45_4

Fasola, N., & Wood, A. J. (2021). Reforming Ukraine's security sector. In *Survival April–May 2021: Facing Russia*, Routledge. https://doi.org/10.1080/00396338.2021.1905990

Foreign Policy Council. Ukrainian Prism. Friedrich Ebert Foundation. (2020). *Ukrainska pryzma: Zovnishnia polityka 2019*. Analitychne doslidzhennia, Vistka, Kyiv. https://library.fes.de/pdf-files/bueros/ukraine/16141.pdf

Gray, A., & Irish, J. (2024). *NATO to plan long-term Ukraine aid, mulls 100-billion euro fund, Reuters, 3 April*. https://www.reuters.com/world/europe/nato-ministers-mull-100-billion-euro-military-fund-ukraine-2024-04-02/

Kirsch, S. (2018). *Engaged anthropology: Politics beyond the text*. University of California Press. https://www.ucpress.edu/book/9780520297951/engaged-anthropology

Konstytutsiia Ukrainy. (1996). *254к/96-ВР*. https://zakon.rada.gov.ua/laws/show/254%D0%BA/96-%D0%B2%D1%80

Korzeniowska-Bihun, A. (2021). Cultural projects as a tool of anthropological defense. Ukraine example. *Wiedza Obronna*, *274*(1), 35–47.

Maksak, H. (2020). The security perception and security policy of Ukraine, 1991–2018. *Defense & Security Analysis*, *37*(1), 53–65.

Memorandum pro vzaiemorozuminnia mizh Uriadom Ukrainy ta NATO shchodo zasnuvannia Tsentru informatsii ta dokumentatsii NATO v Ukraini. (1997). https://zakon.rada.gov.ua/laws/show/950_019/ed19970507#

NATO's 2022 Strategic Concept. (2022). https://www.nato.int/nato_static_fl2014/assets/pdf/2022/6/pdf/290622-strategic-concept.pdf

Niehus, G. (2023, August 30). Op-Ed: How NATO is helping Ukraine. *Internationale Politik Quarterly*. https://ip-quarterly.com/en/op-ed-how-nato-helping-ukraine

North Atlantic Treaty Organization. (2006). *NATO military liaison officer in Kyiv*. https://www.nato.int/structur/nmlo/nmlo_kyiv.htm

North Atlantic Treaty Organization. (2016). *Comprehensive assistance package for Ukraine*. https://www.nato.int/nato_static_fl2014/assets/pdf/pdf_2016_09/20160920_160920-compreh-ass-package-ukraine-en.pdf

North Atlantic Treaty Organization. (2018). *NATO's support to Ukraine*. https://www.nato.int/nato_static_fl2014/assets/pdf/pdf_2018_11/20181106_1811-factsheet-nato-ukraine-sup.pdf

North Atlantic Treaty Organization. (2022). *NATO-Ukraine trust funds*. https://www.nato.int/cps/en/natohq/topics_153288.htm?selectedLocale=en

North Atlantic Treaty Organization. (2024). *Relations with Ukraine*. https://www.nato.int/cps/en/natohq/topics_37750.htm

Singh, D. (2023). *The tripartite realist war: Analysing Russia's invasion of Ukraine*. Springer Nature Switzerland. https://doi.org/10.1007/978-3-031-34163-2

Stratehiia natsionalnoi bezpeky Ukrainy. (2020). *392*. https://zakon.rada.gov.ua/laws/show/392/2020

Stratehiia voiennoi bezpeky Ukrainy. (2021). *121*. https://zakon.rada.gov.ua/laws/show/121/2021

Stratehiia zovnishnopolitychnoi diialnosti Ukrainy. (2021). *448*. https://zakon.rada.gov.ua/laws/show/448/2021

Stratehichnyi oboronnyi biuleten Ukrainy. (2021). *473*. https://www.president.gov.ua/documents/4732021-40121

Suprun, V. (2022). Mizhnarodni harantii bezpeky dlia Ukrainy: Vid Budapeshtskoho memorandumu do Kyivskoho bezpekovoho dohovoru. In V. Makar, O. Shorodok, B. Kudelko, A. Eksman, & V. Rudka (Eds.), *Aktualni problemy zovnishnoi polityky Ukrainy* (pp. 32–34). Yuriy Fedkovych Chernivtsi National University. http://www.interrel.chnu.edu.ua/index.php?page=ua/08sciencessa

Suprun, V. (2023). Trójkąt zagrożeń bezpieczeństwa zewnętrznego Ukrainy w okresie prezydentury Wołodymyra Zełenskiego: Aspekty militarno-polityczne. In L. Elak, T. Zieliński, Z. Ciekanowski, & S. Żurawski (Eds.), *Odporność społeczeństwa, państwa na zagrożenia hybrydowe* (pp. 379–398). Publishing House of the Management Academy of Applied Sciences in Warsaw.

Todorov, I. (2022). *Yevroatlantychna intehratsiia Ukrainy. Istoriia ta suchasnist*. TOV RIK-U. Uzhhorod. http://eurodev.uzhnu.edu.ua/images/files/2023_T.pdf

Todorov, I. (2023). Ukraina–NATO: Suchasnyi stan vidnosyn i perspektywy. *Mizhnarodnyi naukovyi visnyk*, *1–2*(27–28), 10–20. http://visnyk-international.uzhnu.edu.ua/issue/view/17082

Trembetska, Y. (2013). Osoblyvosti orhanizatsii mizhnarodnoho spivrobitnytstva u systemi pidhotovky maibutnikh ofitseriv Zbroinykh Syl Ukrainy. *Visnyk Lvivskoho universytetu. Seriia: Pedahohichna*, *29*, 110–119. http://publications.lnu.edu.ua/bulletins/index.php/pedagogics/article/view/4840

Tsentr Razumkova. (2016). *"Hibrydna" viina Rosii – vyklyk i zahroza dlia Yevropy, Kyiv*. https://razumkov.org.ua/images/Material_Conference/2016_12_14/GIBRID-WAR-FINAL-1-1.pdf

Uhoda mizh Uriadom Ukrainy ta NATO pro status Predstavnytstva NATO v Ukraini. (2015). https://zakon.rada.gov.ua/laws/show/950_033#

Vinnytska oblasna universalna naukova biblioteka. (2020). *Hibrydna viina proty Ukrainy: istoriia, instrumenty, tekhnolohii*. Retrieved January 10, 2024, from https://library.vn.ua/news-and-events/novini/gibridna-vijna-proti-ukraiini

Wendt, A. (1999). *Social theory of international politics*. Cambridge University Press. https://doi.org/10.1017/CBO9780511612183

Zakon Ukrainy. (2010). *Pro zasady vnutrishnoi i zovnishnoi polityky*. № 2411-VI. https://zakon.rada.gov.ua/laws/show/2411-17

Zakon Ukrainy. (2014). *Pro vnesennia zmin do deiakykh zakoniv Ukrainy shchodo vidmovy Ukrainy vid zdiisnennia polityky pozablokovosti*. x№ 35-VIII. https://zakon.rada.gov.ua/laws/show/35-19/ed20141223

Zakon Ukrainy. (2017).*Pro vnesennia zmin do deiakykh zakoniv Ukrainy shchodo zovnishnopolitychnoho kursu Ukrainy*. № 2091-VIII. https://zakon.rada.gov.ua/laws/show/2091-19/ed20170608

Zakon Ukrainy. (2018).*Pro natsionalnu bezpeku Ukrainy*. № 2469-VIII. https://zakon.rada.gov.ua/laws/show/2469-19

Zakon Ukrainy. (2019). *Pro vnesennia zmin do Konstytutsii Ukrainy (shchodo stratehichnoho kursu derzhavy na nabuttia povnopravnoho chlenstva Ukrainy v Yevropeiskomu Soiuzi ta v Orhanizatsii Pivnichnoatlantychnoho dohovoru)*. № 2680-VIII. https://zakon.rada.gov.ua/laws/show/2680-19

Chapter 3

Evolution of Baltic and Polish Defence Budgets Amidst Russian Aggression

Eugeniusz Cieślak[a], Sandis Šrāders[b], George Spencer Terry[a] and Viljar Veebel[a]

[a]*Baltic Defence College, Tartu, Estonia*
[b]*National Defence Academy of Latvia, Riga, Latvia*

Abstract

The article aims at preliminary assessment of defence budgets of the Baltic States (Estonia, Latvia and Lithuania) and Poland, as NATO member states bordering the Russian Federation, in wake of Russian aggression against Ukraine in 2022. The topic is timely and relevant to recent dynamics of geopolitical situation in Central and Eastern Europe. Financial decisions made and the budgets adopted will shape defence of abovementioned states for coming decade and will impact regional military balance of power. The research attempts a comparative analysis of defence budgets in terms of their overall size, percentage of GDP and main components. Official governmental documents and statistics are used as primary sources for analysis. The research suggest that despite substantial increase in defence budgets of the Baltic States and Poland after 2022, this may not be sufficient to meet all the requirements tied to development and sustainment of required military capabilities. Additional taxation and foreign debt as sources for military modernisation cast some doubt on ability of respective states to sustain increased defence budgets over long term. The results of research may be used to inform ongoing political discourse and enrich

Enhancing Transatlantic Solidarity in Collective Defence: Navigating Increased Defence Expenditures, Cyber Security, and Emerging Risks, 37–61

Published under exclusive licence by Emerald Publishing Limited
doi:10.1108/978-1-80686-259-720261003

expert debate on strengthening deterrence and defence of the NATO Eastern Flank amidst Russian aggression against Ukraine.

Keywords: Estonia; Latvia; Lithuania; Poland; defence budget; 2022; war in Ukraine; Russian aggression

JEL Codes: F52; F20

1. Introduction

The Baltic states (Estonia, Latvia and Lithuania) and Poland, as NATO member states bordering the Russian Federation and having undergone political and economic transformations post-Cold War, exhibit significant responsiveness in their defence budgets to the Russian threat. Initial changes in defence budgets occurred following the Russian annexation of Crimea in 2014. However, it was Russia's full-scale invasion of Ukraine in 2022 that marked a pivotal shift in the defence strategies of the Baltic States and Poland. The substantial increase in defence budgets since 2022 has led to intensified arms procurement and the development of armed forces. The urgency and existential nature of these needs have necessitated the search for additional financing for the technical modernisation and expansion of their respective armed forces. In the forthcoming years, increased weapons purchases and organisational changes within the armed forces will result in a continual rise in operations and maintenance costs.

Ultimately, defence budgets will need to be augmented at the expense of other governmental expenditures or through the identification of new revenue sources. This chapter will comparatively analyse the evolution of the defence budgets of the Baltic States and Poland from 2014 to 2022, as well as from 2022 onwards, to assess the feasibility of the adopted budgetary decisions and their impact on technical modernisation and force development. It will also provide insights into the planned fiscal decisions related to defence in the Baltic States and Poland, arguing that two strategies – investment in the arms industry and the implementation of new taxation schemes – have emerged. However, the economic and political viability of covering these substantial cost increases largely depends on heightened threat perceptions, both within the studied countries and globally.

2. 2014–2022

2.1. Estonia

Russia's aggression against Ukraine has brought the war directly into Estonia's backyard in many ways. The country has been one of the most vocal advocates for the fight against Russia's aggressive ambitions in both the European Union and the NATO alliance since 2007, after Estonia itself came under hybrid attack in 2007. The annexation of Crimea by the Russian Federation in 2014 has urged

Estonia to both enormously increase its military capabilities and seek additional security guarantees from its allies. Over the past decade, turbulence in the global security environment has also been reflected in the dynamics of threat assessments of those residing in Estonia. Russia's ongoing military actions in Ukraine have also significantly increased the share of those people in Estonia who consider either a large-scale military attack against Estonia or a limited military attack against some strategic object in Estonia either very or reasonably likely in the coming years. Since 2014, this share has more than tripled, currently situated around 40% (Public Opinion on National Defence, 2024, p. 21).

Estonia's defence strategy against potential military attacks has undergone many changes since 2014. Still, the core principles – having a robust initial self-defence capability and being a member of the NATO alliance – have remained unchanged. National strategy documents developed during that period addressed this challenge specifically. The development plan for 2013–2022 primarily focused on improving the rapid response capabilities of the Estonian Defence Forces (National Defence Development Plan 2013–2022, 2012a, 2012b). This concerned the establishment of two infantry brigades instead of an initially planned five, strengthening anti-tank defence, development of armoured manoeuvre capabilities, the establishment of the military intelligence unit and several supportive and coordinative structures, the formation of territorial defence districts, etc. (National Defence Development Plan 2013–2022, 2012a, 2012b; National Defence Development Plan 2017–2026, 2016a, 2016b). These developments could be viewed as a direct response to Russia's actions in Ukraine in 2014 (Hurt, 2014).

The national defence development plan for 2017–2026 continued the path set earlier and prioritised military readiness and improvement of response capabilities of national defence forces. The first infantry brigade was reorganised into a mechanised infantry brigade and the second into a combat-capable motorised light infantry brigade (Development of Combat Capability, 2023). The number of people employed in rapid reaction structures gradually increased. However, the document also highlighted an imbalance between a wide range of security threats and the country's limited financial resources (National Defence Development Plan 2017–2026, 2016a, 2016b).

Regarding the defence budget over the past decade, neither Estonian politicians nor the public have questioned the necessity of spending money on national defence. Regardless of the political parties included in the government, they all have supported maintaining national defence expenditures above 2% of the GDP. The commitment to keep the defence budget at 2% of the GDP was formulated in the agreement between the political parties that formed the Estonian government in 2012, that is before Russia annexed Crimea, and has remained valid since then. In practice, real investment into national defence capabilities, together with additional resources spent to host allied forces and investments made in the framework of the defence investment programme, have exceeded 2% since 2015. The size of the defence budget has more than doubled in 10 years, from €340 million in 2012 to €771 million in 2022 (Defence Expenditures, 2023), being in absolute numbers within the same range as in Latvia and half of the size of the defence budget in Lithuania.

2.2. Latvia

Between 2012 and 2023, Latvia developed three national security concepts, prioritising national armed forces to address military threats. Yearly reports highlight accomplishments and challenges, providing a framework for managing security risks and aligning budgetary priorities with threat levels. The 2012–2016 concept, approved by Parliament, emphasised the Baltic Nordic region and the United States as key partners and reiterated Latvia's NATO obligation to meet the 2% defence spending target by 2020. However, the 2008–2009 financial crisis reduced defence spending to 1% in 2014. Despite a low probability of direct military attack, the concept stressed developing land forces and preparing for hybrid warfare, cyber threats, and terrorism. It also emphasised host nation support for NATO deployment and integrating security structures into international frameworks. This laid the foundation for national defence plans, which shifted priorities after Crimea's annexation in 2014.

Before 2014, Latvia's defence strategy aligned with global challenges, focusing on NATO missions and EU anti-piracy operations. Efforts centred on air force capabilities and host nation support, justified by frequent Russian airspace incursions. The 2012 milestone report identified four major projects: communication systems, naval patrol ships, a national cartography system, and international defence agreements. It emphasised sustaining military personnel, reducing administrative burdens, and gradually increasing the defence budget to meet NATO's 2% target and address emerging threats. In 2014, Latvia's defence budget accounted for 0.94% of GDP. Only 7.6% of the defence budget at that time was spent on equipment (Eng.LSM.lv, 2024).

The 2016–2020 national security concept identified Russia's military aggression in Ukraine, the revision of international borders, and the undermining of the liberal democratic world order as the primary threats to the EU, NATO, and Latvia (Valsts Aizsardzības Koncepcija, 2016; Valsts Aizsardzības Koncepcija, 2017; Valsts Aizsardzības Koncepcija, 2018; Valsts Aizsardzības Koncepcija, 2019; Valsts Aizsardzības Koncepcija, 2020). The document highlighted Russia's shift from rhetorical threats to military aggression, portraying NATO and the EU as major security threats. Russia's alignment with autocratic regimes like Assad's Syria further exacerbated these concerns. Domestically, Russia's 2015 National Security Strategy consolidated the external threat narrative with domestic social and political interests. Modernising Russian rapid reaction forces, improved military mobility, and developing air and special forces near the Baltic region were major security challenges for Latvia, the Baltic States, and the transatlantic security community. The vivid surge of Russia as the primary security threat for Latvia caused the shift in political priorities and the allocation of financial resources for defence.

Before 2012, Latvia's defence focus was on counterterrorism and international peacekeeping missions. However, after 2014, Latvia's security assessment shifted to prioritising the threat an increasingly aggressive Russia posed. The 2016–2020 concept emphasised the defence of NATO's Eastern flank and placed Russia as the primary security concern, with terrorist groups like Daesh being secondary.

Latvia's strategy focused on deterring Russia, enhancing domestic defence structures, establishing the NATO STRATCOM Center of Excellence and developing a domestic military industry to ensure crucial wartime supplies. Although conscription was debated, it was not reinstated during this period, despite pressures and deteriorating security in the Baltic region (Kond, 2022). Russia's aggression against Ukraine in 2014 triggered a substantial hike in Latvia's defence budget. By 2018, the budget increased almost threefold from €223 million to €590 million. Consequently, the defence budget reached 2.02% of GDP in 2018 as compared to only 0.94% of GDP in 2014 (Andžāns, 2023). The decisions on establishment of NATO's forward presence made at the Summit in Warsaw in 2016 paved the way for deployment of a multinational battalion-size battlegroup in Latvia following year. Preparations for hosting allied troops increased the share of infrastructure spending in Latvian defence budget to 12.83% of the defence budget in 2016 and 15.02% in 2017, twice as much as in previous years (The Secretary General's Annual Report 2023, 2023, p. 165).

The 2020–2023 concept reflected a deteriorating security environment in Europe and the United States, focusing on the impact of the fourth industrial revolution and global competition on military and civilian sectors. The concept highlighted vulnerabilities exposed by the COVID-19 pandemic and noted that diplomacy alone was insufficient to address the growing challenges posed by Russia, which remained a direct military threat. Russia's novel methods, including election meddling, military posturing, and ideological confrontations with the West, were seen as escalating risks. The concept advocated for decentralised, high-firepower defence units, addressing gaps in naval, long-range, and air defence capabilities, typically supplemented by transatlantic allies. In addition to military objectives, the concept emphasised societal resilience and cooperation across sectors to ensure the continuity of critical infrastructure during crises. Latvia's defence spending was planned to increase to 2.27% of GDP by 2023, but concerns remained about the adequacy of military capabilities to meet rising challenges. The solid defence posture was considered essential not only for the military security of Latvia but also as the basis for healthy investment and economic climate in the region.

The security landscape in the Baltic Sea Region drastically changed after Russia annexed Crimea in 2014. By 2015, the continuous application of Russian military power in its neighbourhood reaffirmed the need for Latvia to enhance its air defence and surveillance systems (State Defence Concept, 2020–2023). Increased public interest and the need to expand military structures led to improvements in training, reorganisation of national guard units, and the mechanisation of Latvia's infantry brigade, significantly boosting the readiness and firepower of its National Armed Forces in response to threats along NATO's Eastern borders (Report 2015). After 2014, the acceleration of existing modernisation plans took place. The mechanised brigade was armed with 170 armoured fighting vehicles and 59 self-propelled howitzers, which were used but modernised (Pallin et al., 2024). In August 2021, Latvia procured 200 armoured personnel carriers, which will be delivered by 2029. Extensive infrastructure projects initiated then served NATO's enhanced Forward Presence and increased Latvia's Host Nation

Support capabilities. Infrastructure investment in Latvia exceeded, except 2018, 10% of the defence budgets from 2016 to 2020 (The Secretary General's Annual Report 2023, 2023).

2.3. Lithuania

In the decade following Lithuania's accession to NATO, the defence budget was influenced by two primary considerations. Firstly, there was a sense of stability due to the collective defence commitments within the Alliance. Secondly, as a NATO member, the Lithuanian Armed Forces primarily engaged in supporting expeditionary international missions, such as the International Security Assistance Force in Afghanistan and the NATO Kosovo Force. Consequently, financial allocations were made within a political climate shaped by these two planning assumptions. Despite intermittent periods of Russian aggression, such as the 2008 Russo-Georgian war, the Lithuanian defence budget fluctuated around 1% of GDP (Defence Data Portal, 2023). On the eve of the annexation of Crimea in 2014, Lithuanian defence spending accounted for only 0.88% of GDP (Defence Data Portal, 2023).

During this period, Vilnius' threat assessment mainly reflected perceptions of Russia's 'desire to control or influence Lithuanian decision-making and policy-implementation processes' through different ways of pressure, 'purposeful and calculated actions... that threaten Lithuanian energy, economic, social, and information security' and erode trust in public institutions (The State Security Department of the Republic of Lithuania Annual Threat Assessment 2013, 2013). However, such activities were not considered an existential threat to continued survival of the Lithuanian state, so military spending before the 2014 annexation of Crimea took this threat landscape as a planning assumption (Balčytienė & Lauk, 2005). However, after the annexation of Crimea and the ensuing war in eastern Ukraine, certain policy adjustments were made due to the shifted threat landscape and the realisation that Russian aggression might not only persist below the threshold of open conflict.

The one crucial policy adjustment was the reinstatement of conscription in 2015. At that point, up to 4,000 Lithuanian citizens were conscripted annually for 9 months, with conscript soldiers receiving monthly allowances and a cumulative payment of up to €3,600 based on performance (Conscripts, 2022). Additionally, employers of conscripted soldiers receive a 6-month subsidy after their service. In practice, the reinstatement of conscription institutionalised the constitutional 'right to oppose anyone who encroaches on the independence, territorial integrity, or constitutional order' as outlined in Article 3 (Seimas, 2003). However, such a practice also meant additional lines of spending for new personnel and infrastructure for training and lodging.

Another significant factor in defence spending considerations was the establishment of enhanced Forward Presence as a result of the 2016 NATO Warsaw Summit. An additional consideration is that Lithuania had just joined the euro area in 2015, which meant that new budgets, unlike previous ones, had to adhere to the EU Stability and Growth Pact. This includes the submission of any draft budgets to the European Commission to guarantee financial solvency (Draft Budgetary Plans 2016, 2015). All defence budgetary considerations, including the necessary efforts to strengthen host nation support capabilities to effectively accommodate the presence of allied troops, had to pass such a stress test. As a result, the subsequent budgets had to be designed to support both the deployment and sustainment of Allied multinational battalion-sized battle groups while also aligning with EU-mandated fiscal responsibility.

Another factor influencing the incrementally increasing defence budget during this period was the infamous statement by US President Trump, calling on NATO allies to spend their fair share on defence (Joint Press Conference by NATO Secretary General Jens Stoltenberg and the President of the United States, Donald Trump, 2017). This highlighted some of the US domestic discontent regarding the perceived free riding on US defence guarantees through Article 5 and the peace dividend. Although Lithuania had already committed to reaching the 2% GDP threshold by 2020, it was still considered among these perceived free-riders in 2017, spending only 1.7% of GDP on defence (Defence Data Portal, 2023). Vilnius views collective defence to be 'of the critical importance for deterrence and defence', so any risk to 'the continued and long-term deployment of [US] military capabilities' would constitute a potential existential threat to the Lithuanian state (Strategic Provisions, 2023). Therefore, reaching the 2% threshold became important not only in terms of defence spending but also in politically signalling investment into the Alliance.

This interconnected shift back to conscription, paired with the establishment of NATO eFP, and anxieties over potential frictions within NATO due to US displeasure with allied defence spending, was met with increased spending across the board. From 2014 to 2022, Lithuania significantly increased its defence spending, rising from €322 million (0.9% of the GDP) to €1.649 billion (2.5% of the GDP) (Defence Expenditure of NATO Countries 2014–2023, 2024). This period saw annual expenditures grow steadily, with notable increases in 2015 (€425 million), 2016 (€575 million), and 2022 (€1.649 billion). The allocation of the defence budget varied, with spending on equipment peaking at 37.57% in 2019, personnel costs fluctuating from 57.53% in 2014 to 33.43% in 2023, and infrastructure spending reaching 33.21% in 2022. Other expenses, including operations, maintenance, and R&D, ranged from 26.24% in 2014 to 30.11% in 2022.

2.4. Poland

Before 2014, Poland, similar to the strategic assessments of NATO and the European Union, assessed the risk of an armed conflict in the Euro-Atlantic area as negligible. After the suspension of conscription in 2009, the focus was on developing the operational capabilities of the reduced armed forces, declaring a balance between preparations for expeditionary operations and collective defence. Poland's involvement in operations in Iraq and Afghanistan required significant resources, which is why the technical modernisation of the armed forces was to be spread over many years, and new weapon systems were to be acquired in relatively small quantities. Russian aggression against Ukraine and the annexation of Crimea in 2014 resulted in a re-evaluation of the plans for the development of the armed forces and the initiation of the acquisition of anti-access area denial systems, which could strengthen military deterrence. The change of government in 2015 and the strategic defence review conducted in 2016–2017 led to a redefinition of the military strategy. The priority was to defend territorial integrity and the readiness of the armed forces to defend Poland (Ministerstwo Obrony Narodowej, 2017). Despite the rhetoric, technical modernisation slowed, new weapons systems were acquired in homoeopathic quantities. The exception was initiating the first phase of the Patriot programme in 2018, purchasing two of the eight planned batteries of this set, and signing a contract to purchase F-35 fighters in January 2020 (Cieślak, 2022).

The rules for defining Poland's defence budget specify, since 2001, the requirement to spend 1.95% of the Gross Domestic Product from the previous year on national defence (Kancelaria Sejmu, 2022). The internal structure of the budget is flexible, and depending on needs, investments may be balanced with ongoing operations. From 2014 to 2022, Poland's defence budget systematically increased while maintaining expenditure on equipment above 20% of the total budget. Analysing the proportions of spending on equipment, infrastructure, personnel and other activities in 2014–2022, a relatively constant level of proportions between the above budget elements can be noticed. The increased equipment expenditure in 2015 resulted from the settlement of deferred payments for multi-role combat aircraft purchased in 2006–2008. Similarly, spending on infrastructure remained at several percent in the analysed period and did not differ significantly from that in other NATO countries (Gręzicki & Płaczek, 2019). Similarly, spending levels on personnel have been relatively stable. To sum up, the changes in Poland's defence budget in 2014–2022, despite the nominal increase, needed to reflect the rhetoric regarding the increase in armed forces and their generational modernisation (Ministerstwo Obrony Narodowej, 2017). To a large extent, this was due to the need for more decisions and contracts in the analysed period regarding basic categories of weapon systems that required generational replacement. This mainly concerned tanks, infantry fighting vehicles, artillery and rocket systems, short-range air defence systems, attack and multi-role helicopters, and submarines. Funds from the Technical Modernization Fund supplemented the defence budget before 2022 obtained from the sale of materials and real estate previously transferred to the Military Property Agency by the Ministries and investments by the Military Housing Agency. The funds obtained this way constituted a marginal part of the budget until 2022. After 2014, it was not decided to finance any technical modernisation programmes from funds outside the national defence budget.

3. Beyond 2022

3.1. Estonia

In Estonia, the most recent national defence development plan for 2022–2031 was adopted in December 2021. Still, because of the outbreak of Russia's aggression against Ukraine, the military chapter of the document was revised in June 2023.

Several significant steps to increase the country's preparedness for the crisis were taken in early 2022, before the war broke out, or in spring 2022. In January 2022, around €340 million was allocated to buy ammunition and build ammunition storage. In March 2022, another allocation of money was agreed to in the amount of €15.44 million for 2022 and €476.77 million for 2023–2025 to deploy short-range air defence systems, upgrade anti-tank capabilities, improve indirect fire capabilities, build infrastructure to allies, and conduct other activities (Defence Budget, 2024a). The national defence development plan for 2022–2031 and its amendment directly reflect the changes in the global security environment and the NATO defence plans agreed upon at the Madrid summit in June 2022. The most significant organisational change was establishing the Estonian division based on the two Estonian infantry brigades, intelligence and support units of the Estonian defence forces, and the NATO allied brigade in Estonia (Government, 2022). Since the division is transferred to the NATO chain of command, it is expected to enhance the military defence planning process for Estonia and the Baltic countries and contribute to the rapid and well-coordinated deployment of local military capabilities and the NATO allies (Palm, 2022).

In 2023, the updated national security concept was approved, and a target was set that Estonian defence expenditures should be at least 3% of the GDP plus the host nation support costs (The National Security Concept Presented by the Prime Minister Is Approved in the Riigikogu, 2023). As a follow-up, the coalition agreement between the political parties that formed the government in 2023 after the national parliamentary elections stated that the defence spending would be increased to 3% of the GDP for the next four years (Government: Coalition Agreement 2023–2027, 2023). This principle is also reflected in the state budget strategy for 2024–2027, which states that defence expenditures for 2024 are expected to be about 3.21% of the GDP (i.e. around €1.33 billion in 2024 as assessed in the budget strategy document) (State Budget Strategy 2024–2027, 2023, p. 148). Since the budget strategy was based on the somewhat optimistic economic forecast of the Estonian Ministry of Finance in autumn 2023, it was expected that defence spending in absolute numbers would increase over 2024–2027 gradually, but in contrast, expenditures as shares of GDP will decrease but remain above 3% of the GDP in the next four years.

The significant increase in defence costs as a share of the GDP is directly linked to Russia's aggression in Ukraine. Estonia needs to replace the military capabilities the country has delivered to Ukraine since 2022, prepare itself for a potential conflict with Russia in the future, and, finally, increase the defence spending due to the intensified cooperation towards the NATO alliance, for example the formation of the Estonian Division. On the other hand, the idea that defence costs should be higher than 2% is nothing new in Estonia. Since 2017, Estonian politicians have constantly called to increase defence expenditures. To reflect the overall sentiment in Estonian society at that time, it has occasionally been proposed in the media statements of various local politicians that 2% of the GDP should 'not be a ceiling, but a minimum level' in Estonia. In times of economic boom (as was the financial situation in 2017), this view was broadly supported and almost self-evident in Estonia because everybody wanted to be better protected against

Russia. At that time, I deemed necessary to increase defence spending constantly above 2% of the GDP in Estonia to be able to maintain the defence forces as they were planned to develop at that time. Such financing did not account for a possible increase of the defence forces. The need for at least a decade of long-term planning and financing was also voiced due to time needed to develop military capabilities (Sõdur, 2018).

Based on the national budget strategy assessment in 2023, the total defence expenditures for 2024–2027 were meant to be about €5.6 billion. However, since the Ministry of Finance revised its forecast downwards in spring 2024, the defence expenditures, in absolute terms, will be smaller by about €60 million annually than assessed a year ago. In 2023–2026, about half of the budget (54%) will be spent on various procurements, 20% on personnel costs, 12% on operating expenditures, 6% on intelligence, 5% on logistics investments, and 3% on benefits for conscripts and reservists (Ministry of Defence, 2023). In Estonia, €185 million is meant for procurements for 2024, and primarily anti-tank, short-range anti-aircraft, artillery ammunition and small-calibre ammunition will be procured (Defence Budget, 2024b).

The Estonian economy faces turbulent times because of multiple crises worldwide over the past years. This has also left its mark on how much the country should spend on defence. In April 2024, the Estonian Chief of Defence, Gen. Martin Herem, expressed that the defence expenditures should temporarily increase to 5% of the GDP in 2025 and 2026 because Estonia needs to buy additional ammunition to deter Russia. However, this time, support for this idea was not as overwhelmingly positive among politicians as it had been earlier. Some of them strongly supported the idea (Kaljulaid, 2024a, 2024b), but others did not so much. For example, the Estonian Minister of Defence, Hanno Pevkur stated already in January 2024 that it is impossible to increase defence spending to around 4.5% of the GDP and a 'reasonable limit must be drawn somewhere' because other areas like health care, social security, and education also need financing (Ehand, 2024).

Changes to the coalition government in Estonia in July 2024 may help in sorting out some of the immediate concerns related to the defence budget. One of those may be allocation of additional resources for munition stocks, mainly long-range rockets and 155 mm artillery shells. The gap between current levels of munitions for Estonian Defence Forces and those needed to thwart potential Russian military aggression was estimated at €1.6 billion over the coming five years by the former CHOD and the MOD Secretary General. Investment in loitering munitions and unmanned technologies is considered a way to decrease costs while keeping up the deterrent potential (Klementi, 2024). The new Estonian government is vocal about increasing the defence budget levels in the coming years. The Minister of Defence stated on 1 September 2024 that the fulfilment of the new NATO force capability goals presented to Estonia in July 2024 would require the defence budget to be increased to up to 5% GDP. The initial Estonian long-term development plans until 2044 suggest that additional €250–300 million annually would be needed to achieve NATO force capability goals (Kiisler, 2024). To achieve and sustain the level of defence budget that is one and a half times higher than the current defence spending will require additional money.

The current government coalition in Estonia agreed to introduce the defence tax package as a part of coalition agreement announced on 19 July 2024. Both VAT and income tax will be raised to 24%. VAT will increase from July 2025, and income tax from the beginning of 2026. Additionally, from the beginning of 2026, a 2% tax on corporate profits will be introduced. These taxes would be temporary until the end of 2028 at which point the new government (after elections in 2027) decides whether they need to be prolonged (New Government to Raise VAT and Income Tax to 24%, 2024).

In the short term, the main challenges for Estonia are related to practical questions of how to prepare itself in a relatively short time frame against Russia's possible attack soon. In this respect, questions like where to get money to buy ammunition and weapons, where to buy them in the nearest future, and how to get the lowest price in procurements are highly relevant today. As regards the defence budget, the current situation in Estonia looks somewhat awkward. While focusing so much on the development of self-defence capabilities, Estonia has, to some extent, gone to extremes and convinced itself that only Estonians must protect the country in a wider conflict between Russia and NATO. This approach is reflected in the former discussion on how high the national defence expenditures should be and practical preparations for the conflict.

On the one hand, there is a need to find more money to finance national defence in Estonia, as pointed out in 2018. However, it is very challenging for Estonia to find more resources under current economic circumstances.

Some Estonian politicians have recently recommended taking a loan, raising taxes, or cutting expenditures in other areas to cover the increase in defence spending (Kaljulaid, 2024a, 2024b). This decision is closely related to recent attempts to reduce the budget deficit in Estonia, which is currently higher than permitted by the rules of the EU, that is based on the assessment of the IMF, the budget deficit is about 3.5% in Estonia in 2024 (Eesti Pank, 2024). More precisely, both Estonian governments from 2023 and 2024 have focused on reducing the budget deficit as much as possible by increasing tax rates, introducing new taxes, and cutting costs. The decisions to raise the tax rates or to introduce new taxes (like the car tax) in times of economic recession have faced heavy criticism recently in society. In July 2024, the newly formed government of Estonia agreed that a temporary broad national defence tax would be introduced until end-2028 by combining increases in several tax rates (ERR, 2024a, 2024b, 2024c). Somewhat surprisingly, the overall feedback to the government's plan to introduce a defence tax was more positive (about 30% of the respondents of the respective public survey supported it) compared to other options like the introduction of the car tax or increase in the VAT tax (Stamberg, 2024). In this respect, the defence tax might be the most acceptable option for Estonian taxpayers. It could bring temporary financial relief, assuming that the revenues will be directed to national defence only as expected by the taxpayers; however, it could also demotivate people in Estonia to pay taxes, and this further jeopardised the budget deficit and harm the financing of other areas like health care and so on. On the other hand, whatever the share of the GDP spent on national defence will be in the coming years in Estonia, the reality is that the sums are tiny in absolute terms. At the same time, the main idea behind the wide range of procurements and the strategic narrative in 2024 seems to be that Estonia deters Russia by showing that it can destroy Russian military forces already on Russian territory, which is not credible.

3.2. Latvia

The state defence concepts from 2012 to 2023 laid the groundwork for Latvia's latest 2023–2027 defence strategy. While building on past successes and addressing identified threats, the new concept focuses on Russia as the foremost military challenge (Valsts Aizsardzības Koncepcija, 2023). This strategy highlights Russia's attempts to revert NATO to its 1997 borders and its ideological warfare against Ukraine and the West. Russia's consistent framing of the United States as the main adversary and Ukraine as an obstacle to its broader goals has shaped its aggressive posture (Šrāders, 2021). The 2023–2027 defence concept goes beyond identifying challenges, offering specific scenarios, such as a potential Russian military campaign against Latvia, including nuclear blackmail and the use of Belarus as a staging ground. Russia's ability to mobilise large numbers of troops poses a serious threat. The concept concludes that Russia, learning from its ongoing war in Ukraine, will continue to strengthen its military capabilities while the support from the West to Ukraine has thus far been far from necessary and consistent (Megerian et al., 2024).

To counter these threats, Latvia emphasises broad societal involvement and the State Defence Service, initiated in 2023, as key responses to Russia's revisionist aggression. The strategy calls for mobilising national resources and ensuring resilience in crises or attacks, prioritising an active military reserve, national guard training, and widespread military education. The concept also stresses the need for societal resilience through cooperation between educational institutions, churches, civil society, the private sector, local municipalities, and public institutions. Latvia aims to draw on Ukraine's experience in defending against Russian aggression as well as support of Ukraine until the complete liberation from the Russian occupation.

The concept envisions a profound increase from around 20,000 to a 61,000-strong military force, with 31,000 active personnel and 30,000 in reserve, as the backbone of Latvia's defence (Valsts Aizsardzības Koncepcija, 2023). An increase in the peacetime strength of the armed forces to 31,000 active and 30,000 reserve troops is planned by 2028. It will require conscription of 4,000 soldiers annually. From 2028, women will be eligible for conscription to alleviate demographic shortages. However, additional investments may be needed for that (Latvia's Defense Minister Wants to Conscript Women by 2028, 2024). Estimated costs for conscription may amount to approximately €120 million annually (Hurt et al., 2023).

Financially, Latvia planned to increase defence spending from 2.4% of GDP in 2024 to 3% by 2027, reflecting the growing importance of security considering existing and emerging threats (Valsts Aizsardzības Koncepcija, 2023). The year 2022 already marked a significant shift when Russia launched a full-scale invasion of Ukraine, prompting Latvia to accelerate defence projects. The defence budget 2023 also exceeded initial planning figures, and actual spending was 3.15%

of GDP on defence in 2023 (Lazdiņa, 2024). The budget for 2024 key initiatives included enhancing air defence systems, including anti-drone measures, and improving naval defence to protect territorial waters, ports, and coastal areas. An additional €200 million will be apportioned yearly in the defence budget between 2023 and 2027 to strengthen air defence capabilities, including purchasing the IRIS-T short-range air defence system (Defence Budget, 2024c). In cooperation with the United States, Latvia procured anti-ship missile systems and launched a long-range artillery project with HIMARS.

Additionally, the year 2023 saw the launch of the State Defence Service, allowing eligible individuals to join the armed forces voluntarily or through mandatory service. Learning from Ukraine's defence strategies, Latvia prioritised replenishing artillery reserves and developing UAV systems to bolster combat capabilities (Lazdiņa, 2024). Establishing a new military base, Sēlija further underscores Latvia's commitment to strengthening its defence infrastructure (Reihenbaha, 2023). Over the next five years, the Latvian defence budget will spend around €303 million to reinforce the eastern border under the Eastern Border Fortification and Counter-mobility Plan, part of the Baltic Defence Line initiative (Baltic Defence Line: Latvia Approves EUR 300 Million Investment Plan, 2024). One major lesson for Latvia and its allies is the critical need for a robust domestic military industry. Ensuring the availability of essential military supplies has become a top priority, especially considering the logistical challenges faced by Ukraine's supporters in Europe and North America. Latvia has focused on developing its domestic military industry, launching the state-owned State Defence Corporation (in Latvian, *Valsts aizsardzības korporācija*) to ensure a reliable supply chain for military needs (Aizsardzības ministrijas gada pārskati, 2023).

Latvia will continue to support Ukraine via the operation of a Latvian-led drone coalition, supplies of ammunition, provision of materiel, and training of Ukrainian soldiers. The 12-year development plan allocates 0.25% of GDP to support Ukraine annually. In 2024, it will be approximately €112 million, and this burden will most likely impact the Latvian defence budget for the coming decade (Lazdiņa, 2024).

The capacity of Latvia's social, economic, and political fabric to sustain high levels of defence spending in the long term depends heavily on the geopolitical environment and the security situation in and around Europe. The defence concepts and annual reports demonstrate a strong correlation between deteriorating security conditions and the increased prioritisation of military spending in Latvian domestic politics. The coming decade will see Latvian armed forces introduce new major weapon systems, reintroduce conscription, and expand its personnel and infrastructure. Despite the ongoing commitment to keep the defence budget over 3% of the GDP, one may wonder whether this level of defence spending will satisfy growing costs (Pallin et al., 2024).

3.3. Lithuania

Lithuania has significantly increased its defence spending compared to Estonia and Latvia in both relative and absolute terms, nearly doubling its budget to around 2 billion euros between 2022 and 2024. This increase includes a rise of €352.8 million (almost 22%) in 2023, with an additional €97.6 million allocated in Q1 2023 to maintain a 2.52% GDP level (The Government Allocated Almost EUR 300 Million to Finance Military Infrastructure and Military Mobility Projects Still This Year, 2023). The MoND used a total of €2.001.7 million in 2023, including unused appropriations from 2022. Almost half of the 2024 defence budget was dedicated to modernisation projects, with €128.3 million allocated for military infrastructure, sourced from the Law on Temporary Solidarity Contribution and state-borrowed funds. Lithuania plans to have a division reach full combat readiness by 2030, including HIMARS capabilities with eight launchers. If the National Defence Plan 2024–2030 is fulfilled as envisioned, Lithuania would have the largest NATO presence in the Baltic states (Chmielewski & Tarociński, 2024).

In the year 2024 alone, Lithuania plans to enhance its combat power, protection, manoeuvre, air defence, intelligence, and logistics through various ongoing arms and equipment projects as part of the National Defence Plan 2024–2030. Key projects include combat drones, mine countermeasures, search and rescue vessels, radars for patrol vessels, and counter-unmanned aerial systems. Major ongoing projects include HIMARS, Medium Range Air Defence Systems, JLTV armoured all-terrain vehicles, 155 mm howitzers, Medium Range Mobile Radars, artillery radars, multi-purpose helicopters, and electronic warfare equipment (Budget Statement, 2024). Additionally, individual weapons and CBRN protective gear will be supplied to troops, and MSHORAD mobile air defence systems procurement has begun from Saab Dynamics (Andrašiūtė, 2024). Over 45% of the 2024 defence budget is allocated to modernisation. The Iron Wolf brigade is set to receive German Boxer APCs (locally called *Vilkas*),[1] and there are plans to purchase 54 Leopard 2 tanks (Lithuania's State Defence Council Agrees to Buy German Leopard Tanks – Adviser 2024), as well as 28 CAESARS for the Žemaitija brigade.

On 5 December 2023, the Seimas approved the Law on the Approval of Financial Indicators for 2024, with MoND appropriations amounting to €2.0917 billion. This includes €134.8 million from the Law on Temporary Solidarity Contribution and €31.4 million from the European Peace Facility (2023–2027). An additional €58.1 million is allocated for 2024, with €48.5 million for international assistance to Ukraine, €7.9 million for the National Cyber Security Development Programme, €1.5 million for UAV capability development in the Lithuanian Riflemen's Union, and €0.2 million for other MoND needs (Budget Statement, 2024).

[1]There were significant delays in fulfilling a 2015 order for Samson MKII turrets for the Boxer APCs from the arms manufacturer Rafael, which was originally scheduled for completion by 2021. This delay resulted in a minor diplomatic incident between Israel and Lithuania, although the issue was resolved by the summer of 2022 (Yaron & Tibon, 2023). Nonetheless, this acts as an illustrative case of how apportionment and budgetary planning does not necessarily translate into defence planning fulfilment, especially in terms of combat readiness.

The total MoND appropriations for 2024, including unused appropriations from 2023, amount to €2,292.0 million. In the near future, Lithuania envisions joining Estonia in reaching a 3% defence spending threshold by 2025. Upgrades to Rukla and the expansion of Rūdininkai by 2026 are also planned in order to enhance HN capacities for hosting allied forces, which is paired with the development of new bases at Pajūris, Šiauliai, and Rokantiškės.

Despite these ambitious plans, which would be continued and refined until 2030, some significant challenges still remain in meeting these stated goals. First, reforms in basic military training, reducing the period to six months, are hostage to deliberations related to the parliamentary elections in late 2024, showing the political contingency of even staffing reservists, let alone raising funds for such a level of expansion. The second and more pressing of these issues comes in the form of the sustainability of such levels of military expenditure over 3% of the gross domestic product, which necessarily entails decreased apportionment to social spending or increased taxation – or both.

The Defence Fund, approved by the Lithuanian Ministry of Finance in 2024, is one such strategy for ensuring the sustainability of this level of spending, at least until 2030. The concept behind the project, as explained by Lithuanian Minister of Finance Gintarė Skaistė, consists of four pillars: 'the extension of the solidarity contribution, corporate income tax decisions, excise duty decisions, and the concept of the security contribution' (Seimas Approves the Defence Fund Package, 2024). The Defence Fund package would ensure around €1.128 billion between 2025 and 2027, around a fifth of envisioned spending on defence during each of the upcoming financial years. Through such an approach, funding for increased defence expenditure would not impact budgetary lines for social spending as heavily, as this budgetary apportionment would come through new lines of taxation.

Nonetheless, the risk with the Defence Fund approach is that it, similar to the reforms hostage to political deliberations after the parliamentary elections, is only contingent on a coalition government with priorities similar to that of the current one led by *TS–LKD*, *LS*, and *LP*. As budget laws are finalised annually in November and December, the sustainability of finances for defence planning would be audited yearly. As tax increases have been shown to weakly impact support for incumbent governments (Kone & Winters, 1993), which would affect voting preferences and turnout for a right to centre-right party more than left-leaning ones (Jaime-Castillo & Sáez-Lozano, 2016). While the *TS-LKD*-led coalition may have been able to break out of a predicted budgetary status quo due to the Russian full-scale invasion of Ukraine shifting threat perceptions significantly (Blais et al., 2010), such levels of increased taxation are only tenable insofar as they represent democratic preferences (Mutascu, 2011). The challenge until 2030, therefore, is maintaining democratic preferences towards increased defence spending as the threat perception of an immediate Russian invasion might dwindle, and if this perceived threat of military aggression recedes in an international structural condition, the political opposition could capitalise on dissatisfaction with the sustainment of higher tax rates for the express purposes of defence spending – higher tax rates, as envisioned by the Prime Minister, that are intended to impact all citizens equally.

3.4. Poland

The outbreak of the war in Ukraine made Poland realise that the previously adopted plans for the development of the armed forces must be implemented much faster than planned. Military assistance to Ukraine consisted of transferring weapons systems and ammunition from the armed forces. This resulted in the need to urgently replace the tanks, artillery, and rocket systems transferred to Ukraine in the Polish Armed Forces and to acquire short-range anti-aircraft systems. The quick availability of weapon systems was one of the essential purchase criteria. In 2022, a contract was signed for the supply of 250 M1A2 SEPv3 Abrams tanks, and in January 2023, for another batch of 116 M1A1 tanks of the older version with delivery by the end of 2024. In 2023, a contract was signed for six Patriot medium-range anti-aircraft systems batteries and an executive contract for 23 short-range CAMM-ER anti-aircraft systems batteries (Cieślak, 2024). Since Poland's defence budget in 2022 was insufficient for equipment expenditure, actions were taken to increase it. The Homeland Defence Act passed in March 2022 increased required defence spending to 3% of the Gross Domestic Product (Kancelaria Sejmu, 2024). The above change will increase the defence budget by 50% in the coming years. However, the creation of the Armed Forces Support Fund, which can take out loans and issue bonds to obtain funds for the technical modernisation of the armed forces, was of crucial importance. Consequently, defence spending could exceed 3% of GDP. More importantly, the Armed Forces Support Fund increases the availability of funds for technical modernisation. This means a sharp increase in equipment spending, allowing for purchasing large quantities of weapon systems relatively quickly (Gębska, 2023). According to NATO estimates, total defence expenditure devoted to equipment rose to 53.57% from a level between 20% and 30% seen in the preceding decade. In 2023, this fund spent (on a cash basis) PLN 24.2 billion. The fund's debt amounted to PLN 47 billion at the end of 2023. It was expected that by 2027, the fund would provide a total of over PLN 300 billion, becoming an increasingly important source of financing for the development of the capabilities of the Polish Armed Forces. The fund is supplied with loans granted by countries supplying weapons subsequently purchased by Poland (e.g. the Republic of Korea, the United States, the United Kingdom, and Sweden) and by issuing bonds through BGK. The volume of loans necessary to implement the framework agreements with Korea is estimated at USD 20 billion and exceeds the limit on loans granted by Korea to one country. It was feared that this might limit the possibility of introducing all the planned equipment into service and limit purchases to those for which implementing contracts had been signed. Changes to Korean law in 2024 have resolved this problem. The Ministry of Finance estimated that the costs of loans taken out by the Armed Forces Support Fund are higher than the funds from the budget, which may negatively affect the debt servicing costs. With this approach, the fund may not be approved to obtain new funds (loans). Consequently, there will be a need for some of the financial resources necessary to implement the technical modernisation programmes of the armed forces. The above problem is the subject of an expert debate in which arguments of an economic nature are opposed to reasons related to the imperative of ensuring state security. Work on Poland's defence budget for 2025 indicates continued upward trends in the overall budget size resulting from allocating 3% of GDP for national defence and additional financing from the Armed Forces Support Fund for up to PLN 70 billion. If the above solution is maintained, Poland's expenditure on equipment and infrastructure may be at PLN 226.3 up to PLN 234.1 billion (Dmitruk, 2023). The government's political declarations indicate the desire to increase the defence budget to 5% of GDP starting in 2025 (Rabij, 2024). The increased defence spending in Poland is expected to last until 2027 or 2028 and decrease slightly.

Political discourse in Poland emphasises that negative changes in the security environment will persist for at least the next decade. During this time, it will be necessary to continue the technical modernisation of the armed forces and increase their numbers. Experts indicate that acquiring weapon systems is only part of life cycle costs. Operating and maintenance costs and midlife upgrades over the life cycle may constitute up to two-thirds of overall spending. As the information related to the contracts remains classified, it only allows for an educated guess based on historical cases. It suggests that overall costs for procurement and operating new weapon systems over approximately three decades may be up to three times higher than those for procurement. Without reliable and relatively precise data on this subject, it is difficult to judge the needs in terms of the size and components of Poland's defence budget over the next decade. The Minister of Defence claimed in August 2024 that up to approximately PLN 140 billion will be needed in addition to foreseen spending by 2035 to finance pre planned purchases of the new weapon systems. The infrastructure will need approximately additional PLN 46 billion by that time. Those figures resulted, according to the audit, from underestimation by the previous government (Bankier.pl, 2024a). The Armed Forces Support Fund is to repay loans taken out from 2028, which will generate specific financial needs for the state and the defence budget. The level of financing of national defence in Poland will probably have to remain above the statutory level of 3% of GDP after 2028. This will result, among other things, from the operating and maintenance costs of the weapon systems currently being purchased and the increased number of armed forces. There is no consensus among financial market experts on the potential costs associated with maintaining the state's ability to provide increased financing for national defence. According to some experts representing Leviatan Confederation (the association of Polish employers), ING Bank and PKO BP Bank, in the longer term, there is a risk of increasing the state's debt above 60% of GDP and the need to cut budget expenditures in other areas of the state's activities (Bankier.pl, 2024b). Using funds from the Armed Forces Support Fund would allow some of the expenditures to be moved outside the state budget. The costs of obtaining these funds could turn out to be higher than in the case of increasing the budget for national defence by introducing additional fiscal burdens. Therefore, Poland has accordingly sought to exempt increased defence expenditure from the Excessive Deficit Procedure and avoid triggering an EU fiscal response (Palowski, 2021). Some experts believe that increasing spending on purchasing new weapon systems may be an economic opportunity. They estimate that around 26% of orders will be placed in the Polish arms industry, generating new jobs and increasing tax revenues for the budget (CreditAgricole, 2024). The inclusion of Polish companies in the supply chain of global arms corporations may increase the competitiveness of the Polish arms industry in the long term. Such an optimistic scenario is not widely accepted. Sceptics believe that, at least initially, most of the arms purchases abroad will concern finished products, which puts the possibility of the Polish defence industry being involved in deliveries into question. With that, some new taxes to support the future budgets for national defence are deemed quite possible.

4. Conclusions

The threat from Russia was perceived by the Baltic States and Poland long before the Russian aggression against Ukraine in February 2022. Russia's support for separatists in eastern Ukraine and the annexation of Crimea in 2014 resulted in increased defence budgets for these countries, optimisation of plans for the development of armed forces, and technical modernisation of their armed forces taking into account the needs of defending territorial integrity. However, these plans were to be spread over years and implemented within the framework of the availability of funds in the budget. Russian armed aggression against Ukraine in February 2022 caused major changes in the approach of countries bordering Russia to financing defence. The perception of the threat has changed. The most likely hybrid threats have given way to a scenario of a full-scale armed invasion and occupation, which could be realised within a few years of Russia ending the war against Ukraine. It is expected that such a threat will be present for at least the next decade. The experience of the Ukrainian conflict has exposed existing gaps in operational capabilities and the need to quickly eliminate them. Further challenges are related to the implementation of the new generation of NATO defence plans requiring an increased number of high-readiness forces and increased capacity for operational capabilities critical to collective defence. Finally, it is necessary to continue military support for Ukraine, enabling long-term, multiyear resistance to Russian aggression. The defence budgets of the Baltic States and Poland will remain above 3% of GDP in the coming years. Based on the current plans for the development of the armed forces of the above countries, it can be stated that expenditure on weapon systems and equipment will constitute the largest part of their defence budgets. In the case of Lithuania and Latvia, an important category will be expenditure on infrastructure enabling the deployment and sustained presence of allied troops there. Due to the urgency of the needs, the main part of the purchases of new weapons will take place in the next five years, and later deliveries will concern weapon systems that are not available in the shorter term. The coming years will also generate additional costs due to the increase in the number of troops, to include raising the number of conscripts or introduction of conscription. In the longer term, we should expect a constant increase in the costs of maintaining new operational capabilities, training, and the increased number of armed forces.

The perception of the threat from Russia will be a fundamental factor motivating the Baltic States and Poland to increase their defence spending. As long as Russia is perceived as having the ability to continue armed aggression against more countries, there will be a political and social consensus for increased defence spending. A hypothetical collapse and weakening of Russia may have a demotivating effect on Western countries, including the Baltic States and Poland, discouraging them from further increases in defence budgets. Russia's success in the war with Ukraine will in turn lead to the perception of a 'lack of time' and will create pressure on the speed of development of the capabilities necessary for defence.

The period from 2022–2024 has shown that defence budgets at the level of 3% of GDP are insufficient to fully develop the operational capabilities required to defend against Russian military aggression. Poland's budget decisions and political discourse in Estonia suggest that potential requirements for the defence budgets may reach up to 5% of GDP to develop and maintain required military capabilities. Such defence spending will result in additional tax burdens and a real decline in the standard of living of citizens, which will negatively affect public support for greater defence spending. Taking out debt to purchase new weapon systems, as is the case in Poland, allows for the rapid development of operational capabilities but generates high costs in subsequent years related to debt servicing. In the event of a worse economic situation in the future, high costs of servicing foreign debt may have serious consequences for expenditures in all areas of the state budget. In light of the declarations of the governments of the Baltic States and Poland, maintaining increased defence budgets is to take place over the next few years, during the period of purchases of the basic part of new weapon systems. In subsequent years, defence budgets are to stabilise at a slightly lower level. However, it seems that a slight reduction in the size of defence budgets in subsequent years may not be clearly felt by the societies of these countries or their economies.

In the long term, it may be beneficial for individual countries to develop their defence industries. Placing arms orders in their own industry will generate additional jobs and revenues for the budget. Cooperation with large international companies will increase the chances of arms exports, generating additional funds that can be spent on defence. The potential benefits of developing the defence industry will not appear immediately, but rather over the course of several or even a dozen years. To sum up, the significant increase in defence budgets by the Baltic States and Poland is directly motivated by the perception of an existential threat from Russia. The programmes for the development of armed forces and technical modernisation initiated after 2022 indicate that in the event of a deterioration in the geostrategic situation, actions are possible to increase the defence budgets of these countries even above the currently observed levels. In the long term, even if the threat from Russia decreases, it should be expected that the defence budgets of the Baltic States and Poland will be maintained at the currently observed levels.

This will result from the need to maintain and operate generationally modernised and numerically increased armed forces.

In broad terms, two strategies have emerged in the Baltic states and Poland to sustain increased defence spending. Poland and Latvia are focusing on expanding their industrial base through investments in arms manufacturing and the development of a nascent drone industry. This approach aims to mitigate some of the negative impacts of increased defence spending by fostering domestic arms industries. The critical question is whether these countries can achieve economies of scale to compete globally, making their products competitive for export beyond domestic military consumption. Without this, long-term subsidies would become a significant budgetary burden. Poland's existing industrial base could make this strategy somewhat viable, provided market conditions are favourable.

In contrast, Estonia and Lithuania have adopted a more nuanced political approach, framing new taxation schemes as essential for defence. This strategy supports current spending targets of around 2% of GDP but would be insufficient to meet short-term peaks of 3%–5% of GDP projected for 2025–2026.

To ensure sustainability for the forecasted defence spending levels, these strategies require that threat perceptions in the Baltic Sea region and globally remain at current levels or increase, particularly if the Russo-Ukrainian war deteriorates or escalates significantly. The profitability of manufacturing and exporting materiel, arms, and drones depends on the presence of willing buyers, which in turn grows the tax base. For rhetorically based, morally charged taxation policies to remain politically viable, Russia must be perceived as an imminent existential threat rather than merely willing but incapable adversary.

If the Russo-Ukrainian war were to become frozen in the coming years, neither of these conditions for the two sustainment strategies would be met. Historical precedent following the annexation of Crimea illustrates this dynamic: threat perceptions surge in the immediate aftermath of aggression, prompting plans to deter further aggression, but these perceptions tend to wane over time, leading to the incomplete realisation of initially grand plans, whether for defence or other purposes.

References

Aizsardzības ministrijas gada pārskati. (2023). *Aizsardzības ministrija.*

Andrašiūtė, S. (2024, July 8). *Ministry of National Defence Acquires MSHORAD Air Defence System.* LR Krašto Apsaugos Ministerija (blog). https://kam.lt/en/ministry-of-national-defence-acquires-mshorad-air-defence-system/

Andžāns, M. (2023, May 31). *Latvia's military industry marks its first decade.* Foreign Policy Research Institute. Retrieved September 3, 2024, from https://www.fpri.org/article/2023/05/latvias-military-industry-marks-its-first-decade/

Balčytienė, A., & Lauk, E. (2005). Media transformations: The post-transition lessons in Lithuania and Estonia. *Informacijos Mokslai, 33*, 96–109.

Baltic Defence Line: Latvia Approves EUR 300 Million Investment Plan. (2024, March 9). *Defence Industry Europe.* Retrieved September 3, 2024, from https://defence-industry.eu/baltic-defence-line-latvia-approves-eur-300-million-investment-plan/

Bankier.pl. (2024a). *MON kupuje Apache i Patrioty. Ponownie zwraca uwagę na niedofinansowanie* [MoD buys Apache and Patriot. Again draws attention to underfunding], Bankier.

Bankier.pl. (2024b, August 28). *Eksperci i politycy już analizują kształt zaproponowanej ustawy budżetowej*, Bankier. Retrieved September 4, 2024, from https://www.bankier.pl/wiadomosc/Eksperci-i-politycy-juz-analizuja-ksztalt-zaproponowanej-ustawy-budzetowej-8803537.html

Blais, A., Kim, J., & Foucault, M. (2010). Public spending, public deficits and government coalitions. *Political Studies*, *58*(5), 829–846. https://doi.org/10.1111/j.1467-9248.2010.00842.x

Budget Statement. (2024, July 5). *LR Krašto Apsaugos Ministerija*. https://kam.lt/en/facts-and-trends/budget-statement/

Chmielewski, & Tarociński, J. (2024, May 10). *On the warpath: The development and modernisation of the Baltic states' armed forces*. OSW Centre for Eastern Studies. Retrieved August 30, 2024, from https://www.osw.waw.pl/en/publikacje/osw-commentary/2024-05-10/warpath-development-and-modernisation-baltic-states-armed

Cieślak, E. (2022). Responding to evolving military threat. Development of polish armed forces after 2014. *Challenges to National Defence in Contemporary Geopolitical Situation*, 264–274. https://doi.org/10.47459/cndcgs.2022.34

Cieślak, E. (2024). Siły Zbrojne Rzeczypospolitej Polskiej w NATO. Refleksje z perspektywy ćwierćwiecza [Armed forces of the Republic of Poland in NATO. Reflections from a perspective of a quarter of century]. *National Security*, *44*(1), 57–90. https://doi.org/10.59800/bn/187300

Coalition Agreement 2023–2027. (2023). *Eesti Vabariigi Valitsus*. Retrieved September 3, 2024, from https://www.valitsus.ee/en/coalition-agreement-2023-2027

Conscripts. (2022). *Karys.Lt*. Retrieved September 2, 2024, from https://www.karys.lt/en/military-service/conscript-service/conscripts/400

CreditAgricole. (2024). *Czy wydatki na zbrojenia przyspieszą wzrost gospodarczy w Polsce?* [Will armament spendings accelerate economic growth in Poland?]. Makro Mapa. Tygodnik Ekonomiczny.

Defence Budget. (2024a). *Kaitseministeerium*. Retrieved September 3, 2024, from https://kaitseministeerium.ee/en/objectives-activities/defence-budget

Defence Budget. (2024b). Kaitseministeerium. Retrieved September 3, 2024, from https://kaitseministeerium.ee/en/objectives-activities/defence-budget

Defence Budget. (2024c). *Aizsardzības ministrija*.

Defence Data Portal. (2023, November 30). *Default*. Retrieved September 2, 2024, from https://eda.europa.eu/publications-and-data/defence-data

Defence Expenditure of NATO Countries (2014–2023). (2024, February 7). *NATO*. https://www.nato.int/nato_static_fl2014/assets/pdf/2024/3/pdf/240314-def-exp-2023-en.pdf

Defence Expenditures. (2023). *Estonian national defence development*. Retrieved September 3, 2024, from https://riigikaitseareng.ee/en/defence-expenditures/

Development of Combat Capability. (2023). *Estonian national defence development*. Retrieved September 3, 2024, from https://riigikaitseareng.ee/en/development-of-combat-capability/

Dmitruk, T. (2023). *Finansowanie modernizacji technicznej Wojska Polskiego w latach 2023-2026* [Financing the technical modernization of the Polish Armed Forces in 2023-2026].

Draft Budgetary Plans 2016. (2015). *European commission*. Retrieved September 2, 2024, from https://economy-finance.ec.europa.eu/economic-and-fiscal-governance/stability-and-growth-pact/annual-draft-budgetary-plans-dbps-euro-area-countries/draft-budgetary-plans-2016_en

Eesti Pank. (2024). *Republic of Estonia: Staff concluding statement of the 2024 Article IV mission.* https://www.eestipank.ee/en/press/republic-estonia-staff-concluding-statement-2024-article-iv-mission-15042024

Ehand, E. (2024, January 1). *Minister: EDF thinks defense spending should be 4.5% GDP – But there is a limit.* ERR. Retrieved September 3, 2024, from https://news.err.ee/1609209245/minister-edf-thinks-defense-spending-should-be-4-5-gdp-but-there-is-a-limit

Eng.LSM.lv. (2024, July 4). *Latvia currently in NATO's top four on defense spending.* LSM+. Retrieved September 3, 2024, from https://eng.lsm.lv/article/society/defense/04.07.2024-latvia-currently-in-natos-top-four-on-defense-spending.a560311/

ERR. (2024a, April 22). *EDF chief: Estonia's defense spending could rise to 5% of GDP in coming years.* Estonian Public Broadcast (ERR). https://news.err.ee/1609321011/edf-chief-estonia-s-defense-spending-could-rise-to-5-of-gdp-in-coming-years

ERR. (2024b, January 1). *Minister: EDF thinks defense spending should be 4.5% GDP – But there is a limit.* Estonian Public Broadcast (ERR). https://news.err.ee/1609209245/minister-edf-thinks-defense-spending-should-be-4-5-gdp-but-there-is-a-limit

ERR. (2024c, July 3). *Defense tax likely to come from multiple sources.* Estonian Public Broadcast (ERR). https://news.err.ee/1609387892/defense-tax-likely-to-come-from-multiple-sources

Estonian National Defence Development: Defence Expenditures. (2023). https://riigikaitseareng.ee/en/defence-expenditures/

Gębska, M. (2023). Finansowanie celów militarnych w Polsce – wybrane aspekty teoretyczne w kontekście ustawy o obronie ojczyzny oraz praktyka [Financing military objectives in Poland – selected theoretical aspects in the context of the Homeland Defense Act and practice]. *Problemy Techniki Uzbrojenia, 167*(5). https://doi.org/10.5604/01/3001.0054.3021

Government. (2022, December 8). *Government passes decision to establish defence division.* https://valitsus.ee/en/news/government-passes-decision-establish-defence-division

Government: Coalition Agreement 2023–2027. (2023). https://valitsus.ee/en/coalition-agreement-2023-2027

Government Passes Decision to Establish Defence Division. (2022). *Eesti Vabariigi Valitsus.* Retrieved September 3, 2024, from https://valitsus.ee/en/news/government-passes-decision-establish-defence-division

Government: The National Security Concept Presented by the Prime Minister Is Approved in the Riigikogu. (2023, February 22). https://www.valitsus.ee/en/news/national-security-concept-presented-prime-minister-approved-riigikogu

Gręzicki, M., & Płaczek, J. (2019). Statystyczna korelacja wydatków obronnych i PKB w Polsce w Latach 2010-2019 [Statistical correlation of defense expenditure and GDP in Poland in the years 2010-2019]. *Gospodarka Materiałowa i Logistyka, LXXI*(5). https://doi.org/10.33226/1231-2037.2019.5.43

Hanso, H. (2017, December 1). *Kaks protsenti ei saa olla kaitsekulutuste lagi, vaid pigem alguspunkt (available in Estonian only).* Postimees. https://www.postimees.ee/4330667/hanso-kaks-protsenti-ei-saa-olla-kaitsekulutuste-lagi-vaid-pigem-alguspunkt

Hurt, M. (2014, May). *Krimmi sündmuste õppetunnid: kas Eesti riigikaitsemudel vastab täielikult meie vajadustele?* (available in Estonian only). Diplomaatia, No. 129. https://diplomaatia.ee/krimmi-sundmuste-oppetunnid-kas-eesti-riigikaitsemudel-vastab-taielikult-meie-vajadustele/

Hurt, M., Vargulis, M., & Zdanavičius, L. (2023). *Baltic defence development: Adding value to the defence of the Baltic Sea region.* ICDS, Tallinn.

Jaime-Castillo, A. M., & Sáez-Lozano, J. L. (2016). Preferences for tax schemes in OECD countries, self-interest and ideology. *International Political Science Review, 37*(1), 81–98. https://doi.org/10.1177/0192512114539716

Joint Press Conference by NATO Secretary General Jens Stoltenberg and the President of the United States, Donald Trump. (2017). *NATO*. Retrieved September 2, 2024, from http://www.nato.int/cps/en/natohq/opinions_143135.htm

Kaljulaid, R. (2024a, January 18). *Eesti kaitsekulutused peavad olema vahemikus 4–5% SKTst!* (available in Estonian only). Eesti Päevaleht. https://epl.delfi.ee/artikkel/120263333/raimond-kaljulaid-eesti-kaitsekulutused-peavad-olema-vahemikus-4-5-protsenti-sktst

Kaljulaid, R. (2024b, January 18). *Raimond Kaljulaid: Eesti kaitsekulutused peavad olema vahemikus 4-5 protsenti SKTst!* Eesti Päevaleht. Retrieved September 3, 2024, from https://epl.delfi.ee/artikkel/120263333/raimond-kaljulaid-eesti-kaitsekulutused-peavad-olema-vahemikus-4-5-protsenti-sktst

Kancelaria Sejmu. (2022). *Ustawa z dnia 25 maja 2001 r. o przebudowie i modernizacji technicznej oraz finansowaniu Sił Zbrojnych Rzeczypospolitej Polskiej* [Act of 25 May 2001 on the reconstruction and technical modernization and financing of the Armed Forces of the Republic of Poland].

Kancelaria Sejmu. (2024). *Ustawa z dnia 11 marca 2022 r. o obronie Ojczyzny* [Act of March 11, 2022 on the defence of the homeland].

Kiisler, I. (2024, September 2). *Minister: New NATO plan may hike Estonia's defense spending to 5 percent*. ERR. Retrieved September 3, 2024, from https://news.err.ee/1609441616/minister-new-nato-plan-may-hike-estonia-s-defense-spending-to-5-percent

Klementi, J. (2024, June 18). *Agency: Delivery of EDF's long-range munitions could happen in 2027–2028*. ERR. Retrieved September 3, 2024, from https://news.err.ee/1609374212/agency-delivery-of-edf-s-long-range-munitions-could-happen-in-2027-2028

Kone, S. L., & Winters, R. F. (1993). Taxes and voting: Electoral retribution in the American states. *The Journal of Politics*, *55*(1), 22–40. https://doi.org/10.2307/2132226

Latvia's Defense Minister Wants to Conscript Women by 2028. (2024). *Politico*.

Lazdiņa, A. (2024, July 24). *Latvian 12-year military development plan updated*. LSM+. Retrieved September 3, 2024, from https://eng.lsm.lv/article/society/defense/24.07.2024-latvian-12-year-military-development-plan-updated.a562501/

Lithuania's state defence council agrees to buy German Leopard tanks – adviser. (2024). *LRT.lt*. Retrieved August 30, 2024, from https://www.lrt.lt/en/news-in-english/19/2177909/lithuania-s-state-defence-council-agrees-to-buy-german-leopard-tanks-adviser

Megerian, C., Corbet, S., & Miller, Z. (2024, June 7). *Biden apologizes to Zelenskyy for monthslong congressional holdup to weapons that let Russia advance*. AP. Retrieved September 3, 2024, from https://apnews.com/article/russia-ukraine-war-biden-zelenskyy-a77546e23fa571eb7f6509d4e14b89b3

Ministerstwo Obrony Narodowej. (2017). Koncepcja Obronna Rzeczypospolitej Polskiej [The defence concept of the Republic of Poland]. Warszawa, Poland.

Ministry of Defence. (2023). *Riigikaitse arengukava 2022-2031 sõjalise kaitse osa uuendamine* (available in Estonian only). https://www.kaitseministeerium.ee/sites/default/files/rkak_2031_uuendamine_09062023.pdf

Ministry of Defence: Defence Budget. (2024). https://kaitseministeerium.ee/en/objectives-activities/defence-budget

Ministry of Finance. (2023). *State budget strategy 2024–2027*. https://www.fin.ee/sites/default/files/documents/2024-02/State%20Budget%20Strategy%202024-2027.docx

Mutascu, M. (2011). Taxation and democracy. *Journal of Economic Policy Reform*, *14*(4), 343–348. https://doi.org/10.1080/17487870.2011.635037

National Defence Development Plan 2013–2022. (2012a). *Defence forces*. https://www.kaitseministeerium.ee/riigikaitse2022/riigikaitse-arengukava/index-en.html

National Defence Development Plan 2013–2022. (2012b). *Republic of Estonia defence forces*. Retrieved September 3, 2024, from https://www.kaitseministeerium.ee/riigikaitse2022/riigikaitse-arengukava/index-en.html

National Defence Development Plan 2017–2026. (2016a). *Ministry of Defence/Defence Forces*. https://kaitseministeerium.ee/riigikaitse2026/arengukava/eng/

National Defence Development Plan 2017–2026. (2016b). *Republic of Estonia Ministry of Defence; Republic of Estonia Defence Forces*. Retrieved September 3, 2024, from https://kaitseministeerium.ee/riigikaitse2026/arengukava/eng/

National Defence Development Plan 2031. (2021). *Ministry of defence*. https://kaitseministeerium.ee/en/national-defence-development-plan-2031

New Government to Raise VAT and Income Tax to 24%. (2024, July 19). *ERR*. Retrieved September 3, 2024, from https://news.err.ee/1609401448/new-government-to-raise-vat-and-income-tax-to-24

Pallin, K., Ottosson, B., Aronsson, A., Engqvist, M., Engström, A., Gustafsson, J., Gunnarson, C., Häggblom, R., Jonsson, M., Svedin, A. L., & Thorburn, E. (2024). *Western Military Capability in Northern Europe 2023*. Part 1: National Capabilities. *Totalförsvarets forskningsinstitut*, Stockholm, Sweden.

Palm, V.-V. (2022, November 24). *Diviisi loomine aitab koordineerida koostööd liitlastega* (available in Estonian only). Estonian Public Broadcast (ERR). Retrieved September 3, 2024, from https://www.err.ee/1608798727/diviisi-loomine-aitab-koordineerida-koostood-liitlastega

Palowski, J. (2021, September 22). *Poland boosts 2021 defence budget by more than 1.5 billion*. Defence24.Com. Retrieved December 9, 2021, from https://www.defence24.com/poland-boosts-2021-defence-budget-by-more-than-15-billion

Public Opinion on National Defence. (2024). *Eesti Uuringukeskus OÜ, Tallinn*, pp. 1–80.

Rabij, M. (2024). *Pięć procent PKB na wojsko? Tego nie unikniemy* [Five percent of GDP for the military? We can't avoid it]. Tygodnik Powszechny.

Reihenbaha, D. (2023, November 29). *Reģistrēts valsts uzņēmums SIA 'Valsts aizsardzības korporācija'*. Aizsardzības ministrija.

Republic of Estonia: Staff Concluding Statement of the 2024 Article IV Mission. (2024, April 15). *Eesti Pank*. Retrieved September 3, 2024, from https://www.eestipank.ee/en/press/republic-estonia-staff-concluding-statement-2024-article-iv-mission-15042024

Riigikaitse arengukava 2022–2031 sõjalise kaitse osa uuendamine. (2023). Kaitseministeerium.

Seimas. (2003). *Constitution of the Republic of Lithuania*. Retrieved January 30, 2024, from https://e-seimas.lrs.lt/portal/legalActPrint/lt?jfwid=rivwzvpvg&documentId=TAIS.211295&category=TAD

Seimas Approves the Defence Fund Package. (2024). *Ministry of finance of the Republic of Lithuania*. Retrieved August 29, 2024, from https://finmin.lrv.lt/en/news/seimas-approves-the-defence-fund-package/

Sõdur. (2018, September 17). *Kaitsekulutused suurenevad või kaitsevägi kahaneb* (available in Estonian only). No 4/2018, pp. 18–23. https://issuu.com/sodur/docs/0418sodur

Šrāders, S. (2021). *Small Baltic states and the Euro-Atlantic security community*. Palgrave Macmillan, Tartu.

Stamberg, T. (2024, May 31). *Võrreldes käibemaksu tõusu ja automaksuga leiab elanike seas enam toetust riigikaitsemaks*. Turu-Uuringute AS. Retrieved September 3, 2024, from https://turu-uuringute.eu/vorreldes-kaibemaksu-tousu-ja-automaksuga-leiab-elanike-seas-enam-toetust-riigikaitsemaks/

Strategic Provisions. (2023). *LR Krašto Apsaugos Ministerija*. Retrieved January 12, 2024, from https://kam.lt/en/strategic-provisions/

The Government Allocated Almost EUR 300 Million to Finance Military Infrastructure and Military Mobility Projects Still This Year. (2023, July 28). *Ministry of finance of the Republic of Lithuania*. Retrieved September 4, 2024, from https://finmin.lrv.lt/en/news/the-government-allocated-almost-eur-300-million-to-finance-military-infrastructure-and-military-mobility-projects-still-this-year/

The National Security Concept Presented by the Prime Minister Is Approved in the Riigikogu. (2023, February 22). *Eesti Vabariigi Valitsus*. Retrieved September 3, 2024, from https://www.valitsus.ee/en/news/national-security-concept-presented-prime-minister-approved-riigikogu

The Secretary General's Annual Report 2023. (2023). *NATO*.

The State Security Department of the Republic of Lithuania Annual Threat Assessment 2013. (2013). *Valstybės Saugumo Departamentas*. https://www.vsd.lt/senoji/Files/Documents/635448351234307500.pdf

Turu-uuringute, A. S. (2024, May 31). *Võrreldes käibemaksu tõusu ja automaksuga leiab elanike seas enam toetust riigikaitsemaks* (available in Estonian only). https://turu-uuringute.eu/vorreldes-kaibemaksu-tousu-ja-automaksuga-leiab-elanike-seas-enam-toetust-riigikaitsemaks/

Valsts Aizsardzības Koncepcija. (2016). *Aizsardzības ministrija*.

Valsts Aizsardzības Koncepcija. (2017). *Aizsardzības ministrija*.

Valsts Aizsardzības Koncepcija. (2018). *Aizsardzības ministrija*.

Valsts Aizsardzības Koncepcija. (2019). *Aizsardzības ministrija*.

Valsts Aizsardzības Koncepcija. (2020). *Aizsardzības ministrija*.

Valsts Aizsardzības Koncepcija. (2023). *Aizsardzības ministrija*.

Yaron, O., & Tibon, A. (2023, April 22). Major Israeli arms deal created diplomatic crisis with Lithuania. *Haaretz*. Retrieved August 30, 2024, from https://www.haaretz.com/israel-news/security-aviation/2023-04-22/ty-article/.premium/israel-lithuania-rafael-major-arms-deal-created-diplomatic-crisis/00000187-98e6-d6e9-a997-9eef46a80000

Chapter 4

War-Weariness and National Defence Spending in the Context of the Russian Federation's Aggression Against Ukraine: The Case of Romania and Poland

Alexandru Lucinescu[a] *and Marta Gębska*[b]

[a]*Institute for Political Studies of Defence and Military History in Bucharest, Romania*
[b]*War Studies University, Poland*

Abstract

War-weariness gained currency in connection to support provided to Ukraine for resisting the Russian aggression. The use of the concept is split from the theoretical background of the war-weariness theory and this chapter frames the issue of succouring Ukraine by introducing a version of this theory that is tailored to the security environment shaped by the war in Ukraine and which is applied to Romania and Poland. Against the background of the prospect of a possible aggression by Russian Federation against NATO European members, it is highly alarming the decline in willingness to adequately finance national defence that the tailored war-weariness theory anticipates for states already under the strain of supporting Ukraine. For applying the developed version of war-weariness theory, a combination of qualitative and quantitative methods has been integrated within a case study approach where the decrease of public and political support for meeting the NATO guideline on national defence expenditures is made dependent on the decrease of the same type of support for assisting Ukraine. The tailored war-weariness theory fails to operate for both

Enhancing Transatlantic Solidarity in Collective Defence: Navigating Increased Defence Expenditures, Cyber Security, and Emerging Risks, 63–85

doi:10.1108/978-1-80686-259-720261004

Romania and Poland with the effect that consistent assistance to Ukraine does not necessarily undermine the will to effectively resist a potential Russian aggression. Considering the current European security environment through the lens of the tailored war-weariness theory contributes to assessing vulnerabilities of NATO.

Keywords: War-weariness; aggression against Ukraine; assistance to Ukraine; defence spending; NATO; Romania; Poland

JEL Codes: F52; F20

Introduction

War-weariness, more frequently referred to as war fatigue, figured in analysis of the war in Ukraine months after its outbreak (Koshiw, 2022; Talant, 2022), but this topic has attracted increasing attention in 2023, especially in its second half (Bond, 2023; Cohen & Gentile, 2023; Dennison & Zerka, 2023; Doncel, 2023; Hasselbach, 2023; Jankowicz & Southern, 2023; Joyner, 2023; Sandbu, 2023), and continues to do so (Khromeychuk, 2024; Koenig & Schütte, 2024, pp. 49, 52). This term is used to designate the decrease of the willingness among countries supporting Ukraine to continue the provision of assistance it needs to fight against the Russian aggression. War fatigue with respect to Ukraine also gained currency among politicians on both sides of the Atlantic who usually denied its existence by pointing out that political will to support Ukraine was not weakening (Cook & Lee, 2023; Higgins, 2024; Pamuk & Gray, 2023).

This phenomenon brings to attention the well-known war-weariness theory according to which states affected by war-weariness are, for a long period of time, unwilling to fight a war. This anticipated behaviour is highly worrisome in the context of a possible aggression against European members of NATO initiated by the Russian Federation not too long after the end of the war in Ukraine, a scenario that is frequently mentioned by European politicians and high-ranking military officials (Camut, 2024; Cole, 2024; Haynes, 2024; Kirby, 2024; Milne & Dunai, 2024; Reuters, 2024). It could be argued that, in line with the mentioned theory, war-weariness hampers not only the ability of affected states to defend themselves against the Russian Federation but also their capacity to deter a Russian aggression, given that a state lacking a strong will to fight a would-be aggressor is more likely to be attacked by it (Stapleton, 2015, p. 37).

Authors discussing war-weariness generated by the support provided to Ukraine do not refer to war-weariness theory so that they do not consider the implications of this phenomenon for the capacity of states supporting Ukraine to defend or deter a potential Russian aggression against them. Therefore, war-weariness is discussed with a focus on the present situation and on the ongoing war in Ukraine and it is used only to describe the exhaustion resulting from a sustained effort to support Ukraine. War-weariness as discussed in connection with the war in Ukraine turns out to be distinct from war-weariness theory, but this disconnection is not unusual as experts operate with it in various other contexts (German Marshall Fund of the United States & Bertelsmann Foundation, 2021; Rudolf, 2011).

However, given the significant implications of the war-weariness theory for the current security situation in Europe, it is important to consider the possibility for the Ukraine-related war-weariness to be analysed through the lens of this theory. The exploration of such a theoretical framing of it is pursued in the next section.

Ukraine-related War-weariness Through the Lens of War-weariness Theory: The Interplay Between Supporting Ukraine and Financing National Defence

War-weariness theory is a well-established one whose origins go back to Oswald Spengler and his famous interwar book *The Decline of the West*, and which received authoritative formulations in the mid-20th century by Arnold J. Toynbee and Lewis Fry Richardson (Garnham, 1986, p. 280). According to this theory, a state which fought a war, particularly a lasting and highly demanding one, will evince a long-time reluctance to engage in a new war (Garnham, 1986, pp. 279–280; Pickering, 2002, p. 315).

The viability of this theory began to be disputed in the 1970s (Levy & Morgan, 1986; Stapleton, 2015, p. 37) but, despite controversies it generated, the theory continued to enjoy currency among both journalists and experts writing on foreign policy of the United States who wrote about the so-called Korea, Vietnam, Iraq, or Afghanistan syndromes (Minakov, 2021; Stapleton, 2015, pp. 36, 37).

Circumscribing Ukraine-related war-weariness to war-weariness theory requires the war in Ukraine to generate a war-weariness phenomenon like the one from the war-weariness theory. This means that states supporting Ukraine develop a long-lasting inhibition to participate in a future war following the significant costs entailed by their participation in the war in Ukraine. It is clear that authors discussing the assistance to Ukraine do not use the term of war-weariness in the sense it is employed in the war-weariness theory firstly because Ukraine's supporters do not fight in the war and, secondly, because there is no reference to the unwillingness of these states to be a party to a future war.

The use of war-weariness theory in connection with states significantly assisting Ukraine implies changes to its original formulation leading to a version of it that could be conveniently called tailored war-weariness theory: a state experiencing war-weariness caused by lasting substantial material and financial support to another state that fights a war will develop a long-time inhibition to become itself a warring party in potential future wars.

Applied to European supporters of Ukraine and the dangerous evolutions in the security situation of Europe that it could trigger, the tailored war-weariness theory would predict that European states experiencing distressing consequences resulting from their commitment to Ukraine would develop a long-term inhibition to resist a Russian aggression against them. The presence of such an inhibition at the level of these states could be said to be well captured in the support among their population and decision-makers for meeting the NATO guideline of spending 2% of GDP on defence; given that prior to the 2023 Vilnius Summit, the 2% of GDP was the threshold and that after this summit, the 2% of GDP became only a minimum threshold, and the NATO guideline will be broadly referred to as the 2% of GDP spent on defence.

The position on the issue of the percentage of GDP spent for defence is indicative for the determination to oppose an would-be Russian aggression because of two main reasons. Firstly, resisting to such an aggression is largely dependent upon possessing significant military capabilities which, in turn, requires substantial financial resources. Secondly, both the 2014 and 2023 NATO Defence Investment Pledge have been agreed upon in direct connection with the aggression of the Russian Federation against Ukraine.

The following section builds the framework for the tailored war-weariness theory to be applied to Romania and Poland, the largest states on NATO's Eastern Flank that share a border with Ukraine and which are considered among its strongest supporters.

Groundwork for Applying War-weariness Theory as Tailored to the European Security Landscape Shaped by the War in Ukraine

An analysis of how Ukraine-related war-weariness among public opinion and politicians is identified by experts mentioned in the first section of the chapter is helpful for applying the tailored war-weariness theory. With respect to public opinion, the presence of this phenomenon at national level is registered by means of results of opinion polls about supporting Ukraine in fields like economic, financial, political, military, and humanitarian and also by means of sanctions against the Russian Federation. A constant decrease of even a few percentage points (p.p.) (minimum 4 p.p.) in public support, regardless of whether it takes place within a favourable majority or minority, is treated as war-weariness.

Within the framework of this chapter, which operates with the specific meaning of war-weariness corresponding to the war-weariness theory, the level of public opinion support for assisting Ukraine does not account for the presence or the absence of war-weariness among the public, but only for the existence or the lack of a factor that war-weariness depends on. The public support in Romania and Poland for the assistance provided to Ukraine will be analysed by means of public pools covering the period 2022–2023. The decline in support would be recognised as a phenomenon with implications for tailored war-weariness theory if it registers a downward trend of at least 4 p.p. when measured as an overall attitude covering all forms of assistance and as an attitude towards its following constituents: humanitarian support, financial/economic support, imposition of economic sanctions against the Russian Federation, financing of military equipment.

As for the Ukraine-related war-weariness manifested at political level, various experts mentioned in the first section refer to public messages delivered by high-ranking decision makers (Koshiw, 2022). War-weariness within legislative bodies is not treated by the reviewed experts as being dependent on a minimum number of their members making public statements in favour of assistance for Ukraine or voting for legislation counter to it, but the formation of majorities opposing support for Ukraine is mentioned as a clear sign of war-weariness (Bond, 2023; Jankowicz & Southern, 2023; Koenig & Schütte, 2024, p. 49).

In this chapter, the decrease of political support for assisting Ukraine does not represent war-weariness but, similar to the case when there is a reduction of the support by public opinion for this assistance, only a factor on which war-weariness depends. The level of political support for the assistance provided to Ukraine will be assessed on the basis of public declarations by presidents and prime ministers of Romania and Poland that have been made in the period 2022–2023. It is assumed that a decrease of support means that an initial strong support for assisting Ukraine against the Russian aggression is replaced with wavering support for it or even blatant opposition towards it. The decrease of support among members of legislative bodies from the two countries will be established by means of a constant decrease in the number of those ones voting in the period 2022–2023 in favour of assisting Ukraine; the value of minimum 4 p.p. will be considered a threshold for the existence of a reduction relevant for tailored war-weariness theory.

Returning to the support for meeting the 2% of GDP NATO guideline for defence spending, it could be maintained that, in connection with war-weariness, its decrease among public opinion from the two countries, measured by means of opinion polls, is relevant when, for the 2022–2023 period, it was a constant one and had a minimum value of 4 p.p.. A drop in political support for this NATO guideline means that, between 2022 and 2023, high-ranking decision-makers (presidents and prime ministers) from the two countries initially expressed strong public support for complying with the NATO defence spending guideline, but afterwards their publicly stated support for it started to fade away or was replaced by direct opposition to it. In the case of members of legislative bodies from the mentioned countries, a decrease of their support for the NATO guideline in the period 2022–2023 will be reflected in the decrease of the number of those ones voting against the state budget law for 2023 and for 2024 when it allocates to defence the financial resources required for meeting those guidelines.

It is assumed that the political support for designing the defence budget by taking into account the NATO 2% of GDP guideline implies support for the actual spending of these budgetary allocations, even if it is possible for the defence budget not to be fully spent (NATO, 2024).

It could be summed up that the tailored war-weariness theory, as applied to Romania and Poland in the context of the security situation generated by the war in Ukraine, is likely to be valid if (1) the public opinion support for providing assistance to Ukraine, considered in its entirety and from the viewpoint of four of its constituents (humanitarian support, financial/economic support, imposition of economic sanctions against the Russian Federation, financing of military equipment), has constantly dropped in the period 2022–2023, and this decrease was accompanied during this time by a constant decrease of its support for meeting the 2% of GDP defence expenditures NATO guidelines; (2) the constant decrease of political support for assisting Ukraine was accompanied by a constant decrease of political support for meeting the NATO defence spendings guideline. In case there is a mismatch between (1) and (2), priority will be given to (1) on grounds that public opinion views are more basic and will finally prevail upon the viewpoints of politicians.

Linking Support for Ukraine with Defence Spendings: Applying to Romania and Poland a Tailored War-weariness Theory

Romania

From April–May 2022 to October–November 2023, the support among Romanian public opinion for the assistance provided to Ukraine constantly declined, in the case of its components under consideration here the range of decline varying from a maximum of 16 p.p. to a minimum of 9 p.p., while, with respect to assistance taken as a whole, the decrease registered a 9 p.p. value. The approval for humanitarian support registered a 12 p.p. drop: 82% (April–May 2022) (European Commission, 2022), 71% (January–February 2023) (European Commission, 2023a), 70% (May–June 2023) (European Commission, 2023b), and 70% (October–November 2023) (European Commission, 2023c). The backing for the provision of financial support decreased by 13 p.p.: 69% (June–July 2022) (German Marshall Fund of the United States & Bertelsmann Foundation, 2022), 59% (January 2023–February 2023) (European Commission, 2023a), 58% (May–June 2023) (European Commission, 2023b), 56% (October–November 2023) (European Commission, 2023c). The imposition of economic sanctions against the Russian Federation generated a 9 p.p. decrease of support: 72% (April–May 2022) (European Commission, 2022), 72% (June–July 2022) (German Marshall Fund of the United States & Bertelsmann Foundation, 2022), 67% (January 2023–February 2023) (European Commission, 2023a), 65% (May–June 2023) (European Commission, 2023b), 63% (October–November 2023) (European Commission, 2023c). As for the financing for military equipment, the backing dropped by 16 p.p.: 65% (April–May 2022) (European Commission, 2022), 55% (January 2023–February 2023) (European Commission, 2023a), 55% (May–June 2023) (European Commission, 2023b), 49% (October–November 2023) (European Commission, 2023c). Considering the assistance for Ukraine as a whole, there was a 9 p.p. decrease of public opinion support for continuing to provide it at national level, the variation ranging from 66% in November–December 2022 (NATO, 2022b) to 57% in April–May 2023 (NATO, 2023a).

It follows that, at the level of Romanian public opinion, the decrease of support for assisting Ukraine met the threshold of 4 p.p. and the condition of continuity in case of both the assistance as a whole and each of its components. Equally, with respect to assistance taken as a whole and to three out of four constituents of assistance, the downward tendency manifested within the limits of a clear majority favourable to providing assistance to Ukraine.

Turning towards the political side of support for Ukraine, it is to be mentioned that during his visit to Kyiv from June 2022, the President of Romania recalled the strong support that Romania provided to Ukraine since the start of the aggression against it and emphasised that it would continue to act in this way on a broad spectrum of areas (President of Romania, 2022). Addressing the heads of the diplomatic missions accredited in Romania, Iohannis declared in January 2023 that the assistance given to Ukraine by Romania would continue to be both multidimensional and comprehensive and would be provided for as long as it takes (President of Romania, 2023a). In the margins of the second summit of European Political Community, which took place on 1 June 2023 in the Republic of Moldova, the presidents of Romania and of Ukraine signed a joint declaration which stated that Romania was committed to multidimensional support to Ukraine for as long as it would be needed and that the assistance already provided by Romania encompassed military aspects (President of Romania, 2023b). In the context of the official visit to Romania by Volodymyr Zelenskyy from October 2023, the joint statement he signed together with his Romanian counterpart, Klaus Iohannis, mentioned that bilateral relationships would develop within the framework of a strategic partnership and that Romania was determined to provide Ukraine with the practical assistance until victory over the Russian Federation (President of Romania, 2023d).

Immediately after the initiation of aggression against Ukraine, the Romanian Prime Minister Nicolae Ciucă declared that the Government was willing to provide a comprehensive support to Ukraine. When Ciucă visited Kyiv on April 2022, he made clear that Romania plainly proved its solidarity with Ukraine and intended to offer it a broad support (Government of Romania, 2022b). When, in June 2023, a new government was formed with Marcel Ciolacu as prime minister, the solid, constant, and multidimensional assistance for Ukraine was made part of the government programme (Government of Romania, 2023a, p. 146). In line with this approach Ciolacu and his counterpart, Denys Shmyhal, organised in Kyiv in October 2023 the first ever joint meeting of the governments of the two countries, an event which provided the opportunity for the two prime ministers to sign a joint statement mentioning that Romania would continue to assist Ukraine as long as required (Government of Ukraine, 2023).

A few days after the beginning of the Russian aggression, the Romanian Parliament adopted in a joint session held on 28 February 2022 a declaration on the situation from Ukraine in which was expressed complete solidarity with Ukraine and the support for providing it with humanitarian assistance, for imposing sanctions against the Russian Federation, and also for the Euro-Atlantic integration of Ukraine (Chamber of Deputies, 2022a). The declaration was adopted with 339 votes in favour from 346 attending members (Chamber of Deputies, 2022b) which means that 72.4% from all members of the Parliament supported the document. One year later, the Romanian Parliament marked the start of the war in Ukraine by adopting a special declaration which expressed solidarity with Ukraine, firm support for the fight of Ukraine against the Russian aggression, approval of imposition of sanctions against Russia, and alignment with the policy towards Ukraine pursued by Romania's allies and partners (Chamber of Deputies, 2023a). The declaration was adopted with 285 votes in favour from 294 members present at the meeting (Chamber of Deputies, 2023b) with the effect that 60.9% of the total members of the Parliament endorsed the document.

Summing up, at the level of the President and the Prime Minister of Romania, there was no decrease of the support for assisting Ukraine which constantly remained a strong one. This support was also significant among members of the Romanian Parliament, albeit it fluctuated therein with the number of supporters decreasing at the beginning of 2023, as compared with the same period of 2022. Under such a reading, between 2022 and 2023, there was a 11.5 p.p. decrease of support on the part of parliamentarians, which met the condition of being relevant for the tailored war-weariness theory.

Considering now the support for meeting the 2% NATO guideline, the second element with relevance for the tailored war-weariness theory alongside the support for assisting Ukraine, it is first necessary to analyse the budget that Romania allocated to defence in 2022 and 2023.

The raise of defence budget to 2% of GDP took effect in 2017 (President of Romania, 2015) and, in response to the 2022 Russian aggression against Ukraine, Romania decided to increase its defence budget up to 2.5% of GDP beginning with 2023 (Supreme Council of National Defence, 2022a; Supreme Council of National Defence, 2022b). It is to be mentioned that both the President and the Prime Minister of Romania, who at that moment was Nicolae Ciucă, are members of the Supreme Council of National Defence, a body whose decisions are adopted by consensus (Supreme Council of National Defence, 2002, art. 3). Ahead of the NATO Vilnius Summit from 2023, President Iohannis reaffirmed the importance of Romania allocating 2.5% of its GDP to defence (President of Romania, 2023c). Also, after taking office from Nicolae Ciucă, Marcel Ciolacu clearly expressed his support for the allocation of 2.5% of GDP to defence (Government of Romania, 2023b).

At the level of the Parliament, the State Budget Law for 2023 which allocated for defence 2.5% of GDP was adopted with 251 votes from 369 attendants (Chamber of Deputies, 2022d) which represented 53.6% of the total number of the members of Parliament (Chamber of Deputies, 2022c; Chamber of Deputies, 2022e); it is to be mentioned that, for the adoption of a state budget law, only the affirmative vote of the majority of the present members of the Parliament is required (Chamber of Deputies, 1992, art. 51). Consequently, it could be rightly said that the increase of the defence budget enjoyed a wider supported than 53.6% among the members of the Parliament. When the State Budget Law for 2024, which included the 2.5% from GDP being directed towards the defence budget (Chamber of Deputies, 2023c), was subjected to a vote in Parliament, it secured 294 votes for from 378 attendees, a value that constituted 62.8% from the total number of the members of the Parliament (Chamber of Deputies, 2023d).

With respect to the public opinion, from April 2022 to December 2023, the support for increasing the defence budget which in the case of Romania meant support for the defence budget receiving a 2.5% share of GDP, inconstantly fluctuated: 53% (April–May 2022) (NATO, 2022a), 40% (November–December 2022) (NATO, 2022b), 42% (April–May 2023) (NATO, 2023a), 44% (November–December 2023) (NATO, 2023b). There was a drop from a majority support to an ascending minority support with both the highest (13 p.p.) and the lowest (9 p.p.) difference meeting the 4 p.p. threshold but not the constancy condition. Therefore, one could refer to a decrease of support when compares the figures from Spring 2022 with those from the end of 2022 and throughout 2023, but he could equally observe a trend of increasing support with an overall 4 p.p. value when the comparison operates between December 2022 and December 2023. When we consider for the same period the position of the public opinion on the issue of maintaining the current level of defence spending, which for Romania meant already 2% of GDP, the situation looks different because there was only a minority support for this view and within it there was a constant upwards trend that was slightly reverted (but below the 4 p.p. threshold) at the end of 2023: 33% (April–May 2022) (NATO, 2022a), 36% (November–December 2022) (NATO, 2022b), 37% (April–May 2023) (NATO, 2023a), 34% (November–December 2023) (NATO, 2023b). Given that people supporting the increase of the defence budget above 2% of GDP were obviously not opposed to the 2% of GDP guideline, it follows that the public support for meeting this guideline evolved as follows in the period under consideration: 86% (53% + 33% for April–May 2022), 76% (40% + 36% for November–December 2022), 79% (42% + 37% for April–May 2023), 78% (44% + 34% for November–December 2023). The summed-up values indicate that there was a consistent majority in favour of meeting the 2% of GDP guideline and that within it there has been a downward variation well beyond the 4 p.p. threshold but not a constant tendency of decrease.

Summing up, at the level of the President and the Prime Minister of Romania, there was no decrease of the support for allocating 2% of GDP or for increasing this value at 2.5% of GDP, the commitment of the officeholders being constantly a strong one. The support for meeting the NATO guideline was also significant among members of the Romanian Parliament whose support for the State Budget Law that allocated 2.5% of GDP to defence increased with 9.17 p.p. between 2022 and 2023 and formed each year a majority. It follows that, politically, the compliance with NATO guideline enjoyed a broad support. With respect to the public opinion, there was a significant decrease of support for meeting that guideline (10 p.p. from Spring to Winter 2022) but did not take the form of a constant trend entirely falling under the scope of the 4 p.p. threshold.

Considering now the first condition for the validity of the tailored war-weariness theory, it is to be observed that in 2022 and 2023 the decrease of public opinion support for assisting Ukraine decreased with more than 4 p.p. and represented a continuous tendency which, however, did not affect the existence of a favourable majority. Considering all components of the assistance to be provided to Ukraine, the decrease of public support reached 9 p.p., while in case of its components taken individually, the drop of support on the part of public opinion was 12.5 p.p., on average: 16 p.p. for financing of military equipment, 13 p.p. for financial support, 12 p.p. for humanitarian support, 9 p.p. for the imposition of economic sanctions against the Russian Federation. The public support for meeting the NATO 2% of GDP guideline equally registered a decrease which exceeded the 4 p.p. threshold but did not follow a continuous trend and there was always a substantial favourable majority. The maximum percentage of decrease was 10 p.p., a value which comes close to the drop registered at the level of both the support for all areas of assistance for Ukraine (9 p.p.) and the average support for individual components of this assistance (12.5 p.p). However, the constant tendency of decrease that manifested within the area of support for assisting Ukraine was not present at the level of support for meeting the NATO 2% of GDP guideline. It could be thus concluded that the first condition of validity is only partly fulfilled: there was a decrease of more than 4 p.p. of the public support for assisting Ukraine and for complying with the NATO 2% of GDP guideline but this decrease was a constant one only in case of support on the part of public opinion for the assistance to be provided to Ukraine.

With respect to the second condition for the validity of the tailored war-weariness theory, the political support for assisting Ukraine was constantly very high on the part of the President and the Prime Minister of Romania and registered a constant decrease of 11.5 p.p. at the level of the members of the Parliament where it continued to enjoy majority support. The support expressed by the President and the Prime Minister of Romania for meeting the NATO 2% from GDP guideline was also a constantly very high one and the support among the members of the Parliament for this guideline marked an increase with 9.2 p.p.. Consequently, one could conclude that the second condition failed to be met.

The overall conclusion is that, in case of Romania, the validity of the tailored war-weariness theory cannot be confirmed so that Romania could be rightly said not to be affected by the war-weariness phenomenon as described in this version of the war-weariness theory.

Poland

Surveys conducted by the European Commission[1] in the period 19 April–11 May 2022, that is very soon after Russia's attack on Ukraine, show that the level of satisfaction with Poland's response towards the invaded Ukraine was 75%, compared to a level of 59% on average in the EU. At the same time, the Polish public's support for humanitarian aid provided to those affected by the war was 95%, while no support was declared by 4% of respondents. Support for the reception in the EU of people fleeing war among the Polish population was 94%, disapproval of such action was declared by 5% of respondents. Acceptance of

[1] All surveys based on face-to-face questionnaire interviews.

financing the supply of military equipment to Ukraine was 93% in Poland, and disapproval was 6%.[2] It is worth noting that at the same time on average in the European Union support for the above-mentioned indicators was lower by 2, 3, and as much as 23 percentage points, respectively. In turn, support for imposing economic sanctions on the Russian government, companies, and individuals was 94%. The same survey found that Poles were most concerned about the expansion of the war to Poland, with 38% of respondents, the spread of the war to other countries, with 24%, and nuclear war, with 29% of respondents. These indicators justify the high level of Poles' support for the fighting Ukraine (European Commission, 2022).[3]

Another survey conducted by the European Commission between 12 January 2023 and 30 January 2023 shows that the level of satisfaction with Poland's support for the Ukraine was 72%, compared to a level of 59% on average in the EU. At the same time, Polish public support for humanitarian aid provided to those affected by the war decreased to 91% in the period (a decrease of 4 percentage points – p.p.), while no support was declared by 8% of respondents (an increase of 4 p.p.). At the same time, acceptance of financial support for Ukraine was declared by 86% of respondents, lack of support was reported by 13% of respondents, while support for making purchases and providing military equipment to Ukraine amounted to 89%, lack of support for this type of support amounted to 9%, respectively, which means a 4 p.p. deterioration in attitudes towards Ukraine. In contrast, support for imposing economic sanctions on the Russian government, companies, and individuals was 90%, down 4 p.p. (European Commission, 2023a).

It is interesting to note that in the next survey conducted from 31 May to 19 June 2023, the level of satisfaction with Poland's response towards the invaded Ukraine increased to 74%, compared to a level of 54% on average in the EU. This represents an increase in approval of Poland's actions by 2 p.p. and a decrease in approval on average in the EU to 1 p.p. Meanwhile, Polish public support for humanitarian support provided to those affected by the war stood at 89%, another decline, this time by 2 p.p. (31 May 2023–19 June 2023). At the same time, the Polish public's support for making purchases and providing military equipment to Ukraine amounted to 86%, disapproval of such support amounted to 12%, respectively, indicating a 4 p.p. deterioration in attitudes towards Ukraine. According to a further part of the survey, 86% of respondents voted in favour of Polish financial support for Ukraine, disapproval was declared by 12% of respondents, which means that the sentiment remained at the current level. In turn, support for making purchases and providing military equipment to Ukraine in the case of Poland was 86%, disapproval of such support was 12%, which means a decrease in support for both indicators for Poland by 3 p.p.

[2]The survey did not include information on support for financial support for Ukraine.
[3]The Special Eurobarometer 526 Key Challenges of our Times – The EU released by the European Commission in 2022 (European Commission, 2022) did not include a question about the financial or economic support for Ukraine.

In contrast, support for imposing economic sanctions on the Russian government, companies, and individuals was 89%, another 1 p.p. decrease (European Commission, 2023b).

The last survey presented, conducted between 23 October and 12 November 2023, shows that the level of satisfaction with Poland's response towards the invaded Ukraine decreased to 70%, compared to the level of 54% on average in the EU. This means that acceptance of Poland's actions fell by 4 p.p. and acceptance remained at its current level on average in the EU, compared to the previous survey. At that time, Polish public support for humanitarian aid provided to those affected by the war was 93%, an increase of 4 p.p. from the previous period. At the same time, acceptance of financial support for Ukraine was declared by 84% of respondents, while disapproval was reported by 14% of respondents, indicating a 2 p.p. deterioration in sentiment towards Ukraine in both cases. Simultaneously, the support of the Polish public for making purchases and providing military equipment to Ukraine was 85%, and the disapproval of such support was 12%, which means a deterioration of the first indicator by 1 p.p. In turn, support for imposing economic sanctions on the Russian government, companies, and individuals amounted to 89%, which is the same level as before (European Commission, 2023c).

Summarising the above data, it should be said that from April–May 2022 to October–November 2023 the support among Polish public opinion for the assistance provided to Ukraine fluctuated. For some indicators, there was a steady decline in support, while in other cases, support decreased and then increased. The range of decline varied from a maximum of 8% to a minimum of 2%, while, with respect to assistance taken as a whole, the decrease registered a 5% value. Support for providing humanitarian aid in the April–May 2022–May–June 2023 period fell by 5 p.p., but the level of support still remained very high, far exceeding majority support. This indicates a lack of realisation of the requirement for war-weariness, especially since support for such aid increased by 4 p.p. in the October–November 2023 period. On the other hand, there was a slow decline in support for the indicator of sanctions imposed on Russia, reaching a decline of 5%, but by the end of the period under review the downward trend had stopped, support for sanctions was still around 90%, that is the level of a clear majority. We cannot speak of the war-weariness in the case of financial support for Ukraine, as the decline in support amounted to only 2 p.p. during the period under study. Support for financing military equipment for Ukraine decreased much more, as the decline in support was continuous, with a final decline of as much as 8 p.p.

In summary, none of the four indicators analysed exceeded the tipping point leading to minority support for providing political and public support to Ukraine. Also, the indicator of overall support, although it decreased by 5%, did not reach the tipping point, so the condition for the fulfilment of the war-weariness theory was not met.

The support for Ukraine by the Polish President and ruling prime ministers since Russia's attack on Ukraine has been constant, unwavering and undeniable, as they mention at every opportunity. This support includes political, social, economic, and military issues. Poland has become an extremely important logistics and coordination centre for the delivery of humanitarian and military aid. It is noteworthy that from 24 February 2022 to 25 October 2023, more than 16.66 million people from Ukraine crossed the Polish border. From Poland to Ukraine during this period, 14.84 million people crossed the border. Refugees submitted 1,639,725 applications for various forms of temporary protection to the relevant institutions in Poland (Zyzik et al., 2023). With such a significant influx of Ukrainians in the first days after the Russian attack, it should be noted that no refugee camps were established in Poland, and those arriving in Poland were welcomed by civilians in private apartments, hotels, guesthouses, or by Ukrainian families previously residing in Poland.

Due to the undeniable support for Ukraine and awareness of threats from the Russian Federation, in recent years, there was no doubt that increasing military spending was necessary. A steady upward trend in the defence expenditure as a share of GDP and annual real change indicator has been observed since 2020. The requirement of spending 2% of GDP on military purposes indicated by NATO was achieved in Poland already in 2015 (2.23% of GDP), that is in the first budget year after the Russian Federation occupied the eastern part of Ukraine and Crimea. Only in 2017 and 2019 did the value of military expenditures not exceed 2% of GDP and amounted to 1.89% and 1.99% of GDP, respectively. In 2020–2022, expenditures were stable and ranged between 2.22% of GDP and 2.23% of GDP. According to NATO estimates for 2023 and 2024, defence expenditures as a share of GDP amounted 3.26% and 4.12%, which means a strong increase in expenditures. According to the results of the same study, in 2020–2024, there was an increase in the number of military personnel from 116.2 thousand to 216.1 thousand people, which reflects, on the one hand, the perception of strong threats to security and the determination of successive governments to prepare for a possible escalation of threats and the desire to deter a potential enemy (NATO, 2024).

With respect to the public opinion, from April 2022 to December 2023, the support for increasing the defence budget, inconstantly fluctuated: 59% (April–May 2022) (NATO, 2022a), 38% (November–December 2022) (NATO, 2022b), 41% (April–May 2023) (NATO, 2023b), 40% (November–December 2023). There was a drop from a majority support to an ascending minority support with both the highest (21%) and the lowest (18%) difference meeting the 4% threshold but not the constancy condition. The drop in support from spring 2022 to autumn 2023 in the period under review turned out to be drastic. However, if we take into account the respondents' answers in favour of maintaining the defence budget at the current level, the situation looks different. The value of this indicator fluctuated, but it had an upward trend, from the level of 30% (April–May 2022) (NATO, 2022a), 42% (November–December 2022) (NATO, 2022b), 39% (April–May 2023) (NATO, 2023b), to 43% (November–December 2023). This means an overall increase in support for maintaining the defence budget at its current level by 13 p.p., which means a significant increase in support for maintaining the high expenditures already incurred. In turn, adding up both indicators above (increasing and maintaining the defence budget), these values amounted to 89% (59% + 30% for April–May 2022),

80% (38% + 42% for November–December 2022), 80% (41% + 39% for April–May 2023), and 83% (40% + 43% for November–December 2023). This means that Polish public opinion clearly supported NATO's basic requirement of 2% of GDP, and some respondents were in favour of increasing spending. Moreover, within indicators, there have been a downward variation well beyond the 4% threshold but not a constant tendency of decrease.

The need to increase spending was repeatedly mentioned in speeches by both President Andrzej Duda and the ministers in charge of the national defence ministry. The basic issue, therefore, was not whether spending would be increased, but to what extent and with what economic tools. Work on a new law dedicated to national defence and its financing has been going on since 2021. Their result is the Law on Homeland Defence, which comprehensively normalises and describes broadly defined defence issues and new solutions and regulations for financing the armed forces. The law was adopted on 11 March 2022 and came into force on 23 April 2022, shortly after the start of Russian aggression against Ukraine. The draft law envisaged raising defence spending to 2.5% of GDP starting in 2026, but in the course of legislative work, the provisions in this regard were amended and a requirement to spend at least 3% of GDP was introduced starting in 2023. It is interesting to note that 450 deputies voted in favour of the law (a document of more than 800 pages), no one voted against it, and five abstained. The bill was thus the result of a consensus, rarely seen in the Polish parliament (Polska Zbrojna, 2024).

Under the law, new and sometimes controversial ways of financing the armed forces were introduced, with the overriding goal of increasing military spending and increasing the size of the armed forces. The law provided for the creation of an off-budget Armed Forces Support Fund (FWSZ), which replaced the former Armed Forces Modernization Fund (FMSZ) [4](Ciślak, 2022; Ciślak, 2023; Dz.U.2022.0.2305, 2022, Dziennik Urzędowy Ministra Obrony Narodowej, 2022). It is administered by the Polish development bank – Bank Gospodarstwa Krajowego (BGK). A direct reference to the financing of the army is found in Article 40 of the Law on Homeland Defence. In accordance with it, the financing of the defence needs of the Republic of Poland shall be allocated annually for expenditures from the state budget in an amount not lower than: 2.2% of the GDP – in 2022 and at least 3% of the GDP – in 2023 and subsequent years. The share of property expenditures in the expenditures of the mentioned 2.2% shall be at least 20%. The Minister of Defence, when planning expenditures on technical modernisation of the Armed Forces, is to take into account the Polish industrial defence potential and expenditures on scientific research and development

[4]The FMSZ operated pursuant to Article 11 of the Act of 25 May 2001 on the reconstruction and technical modernisation and financing of the Polish Armed Forces. Interestingly, on the day of the liquidation of the FMSZ (23 April 2022), its budget amounted to PLN 10.001 billion, consisting of cash in the amount of PLN 5.042 billion and receivables from unsettled advances in the amount of PLN 4.959 billion. The funds were transferred to the account of the FWSZ, the successor of the FMSZ.

work in the field of national defence. The aforementioned principles of financing are to be taken into account in draft budget bills, or in draft budget provisional laws. Additional financing of armaments expenditures is made possible by a provision stating that the Minister responsible for public finance, at the concurring requests of the Minister of Defence and the competent administrator of the budgetary part, may transfer expenditures scheduled in the 'national defence' section between parts of the state budget, and that the Minister responsible for public finance, at the request of the Minister of Defence, may transfer expenditures scheduled in the 'national defence' part of the state budget between divisions of the state budget expenditure classification.

In addition to the 'traditional regulations' related to revenues to the state budget earmarked for defence purposes, a provision was introduced that is controversial from the point of view of economic security, stating that if it is not possible to recover the State Treasury's claims arising under the guarantee, the Council of Ministers, at the request of the minister responsible for public finance, may cancel the claim in whole or in part. In turn, BGK is exempted from the obligation to establish collateral for the guarantee. The financial conditions covering the economic parameters of loans or credits require the prior approval of the minister responsible for the budget. In addition, BGK may, with the approval of the minister responsible for public finance, make other financial commitments for the Fund to obtain repayable funds. The State Treasury guarantee is granted up to 100% of the liability arising from the guarantee of an entity other than the State Treasury 100% of the interest on the disbursed liability under this guarantee and 100% of the costs directly related to this guarantee. On the other hand, it is advantageous that the BGK can enter into transactions to hedge foreign exchange risk and interest rate risk on the financial obligations incurred. The Polish authorities are acutely aware of the military threat coming from the Russian Federation, hence the justification for both increasing spending from the state budget and increasing the potential state debt.

A very interesting analysis was conducted by a researcher from Dziennik Zbrojny – a portal devoted to military topics. On 28 August 2024, the Council of Ministers adopted a draft budget law for 2025. It planned state budget revenues of PLN 632.6 billion, a state budget expenditure limit of PLN 921.6 billion and a state budget deficit of no more than PLN 289 billion (7.3% of GDP). For defence in 2025, a total of PLN 186.6 billion is planned to be spent from the state budget and the FWSZ, which is expected to account for *4.7%* of Poland's planned GDP in 2025 (at PLN 3,973.1 billion) and nearly 19% of total state budget and FWSZ spending. This means an increase in the defence spending plan compared to the 2024 plan by PLN 28.6 billion, or 18.1%. The total defence spending planned for 2025 in the amount of PLN 186.548 billion consists of expenditures from the state budget in the amount of PLN 124.302 billion (3.13% of GDP), of which PLN 14.021 billion is to be transferred to the FWSZ, as well as expenditures from the FWSZ in the amount of PLN 76.267 billion. It should additionally be pointed out that the total defence spending in 2025 is the sum of funds from the state budget and the FWSZ, minus the amount transferred from the state budget to the FWSZ (Dmitruk, 2024).

Planned expenditures on purchases of military equipment and armaments included in the 'Centralny Plan Rzeczowy – CPR'[5] are likely to be carried out to a greater extent with funds from the FWSZ and, to a lesser extent, with funds from the state budget. On the one hand, this decision has the effect of reducing the state budget deficit and the funds included in the FWSZ do not expire at the end of the year, which gives greater flexibility in their spending, but on the other hand, the budget funds are relatively certain, while receipts for the FWSZ have to be raised in large part only from repayable mechanisms (loans and bonds) (Dmitruk, 2024).

Expenses related to the technical modernisation of the Armed Forces in 2025 are also to be financed from off-budget funds of the FWSZ, managed by BGK. At this point, it should be recalled that under the FWSZ, accumulated funds are not forfeited at the end of the fiscal year, but are transferred for use in the following year. The funds of the FWSZ are also not included within the budget law. It is planned that at the beginning of 2025, the FWSZ will have saved funds in the amount of PLN 3.287 billion (Dmitruk, 2024).

All in all, defence spending in 2025 is planned at a record level of 4.7% of GDP. If this level of spending is realised, it could place Poland in fourth place in terms of defence spending among European NATO members, behind the UK, Germany, and France, and ahead of Italy or Spain and the Netherlands. This means that almost every fifth PLN from the state budget and the FWSZ (counting spending from these sources together) will be spent on national defence.

The above data confirm that with such high financing of the armed forces, it will be possible to maintain support for Ukraine and prepare Poland to defend itself in the event of an escalation of the conflict. It is important to emphasise that Poland supports Ukraine not only in the military sphere, but also economically and socially, and has been doing so for many years. Ukraine has been on the list of priority partners of Polish development cooperation since 2005. Cooperation at the level of both governments covers areas important for the success of Ukraine's transformation and implementation of the Association Agreement with the EU, including support for the reform process – decentralisation, education and vocational education, public finance and fight against corruption, as well as the development of national and regional systems of crisis management. Poland is also taking steps to for the formation of professional civil servants in Ukraine (Ministry of Foreign Affairs, no date).

To sum up the above considerations, it should be said that the war-weariness theory does not work in the case of Poland. Despite a partial decline in support for providing humanitarian aid, providing military aid, and imposing sanctions on Russia, the indicators overall did not exceed the critical point causing a minority support for providing aid to Ukraine. The tipping point was exceeded only in

---

[5]CPR – Central Material Plans are plans drawn up for the period covered by the development programming of the Armed Forces of the Republic of Poland and updated annually for: technical modernisation, purchase of material resources, construction investments, investments made under NATO Security Investment Program.

the case of the military aid funding indicator, but this is insufficient to meet the theory. Moreover, the Polish public clearly supported NATO's basic requirement of 2% of GDP, some respondents were even in favour of increased spending. Moreover, within indicators, there have been a downward variation well beyond the 4% threshold but not a constant tendency of decrease. Other indicators, despite the decrease, did not meet a constant tendency of decrease.

The survey of European Commission found that at the beginning of the Russian attack to Ukraine Poles were most concerned about the expansion of the war to Poland, with 38% of respondents, the spread of the war to other countries, with 24%, and nuclear war, with 29% of respondents. These indicators justify the high level of Poles' support for the fighting Ukraine next months (European Commission, 2022). The Polish historical experience of Germany and the USSR attacking Poland during World War II, the lack of sufficient support from Western countries at the time, the very clear awareness of the threat occurring today from the Russian Federation, and the possibility of the war spreading to further territories such as Moldova, Georgia, or even the Baltic states, which are part of NATO, means that in practice, in the case of Poland, there is no question of the war-weariness theory coming true. Despite shaky public support for increased military spending, in reality, the state authorities are deciding on a significant increase in spending, as evidenced by the draft budget law for 2025 and the military spending target of almost 4.7% of GDP. Thus, it can be concluded that the awareness of real threats, the responsibility of state authorities for the defence of the homeland, and its population are becoming stronger than the results of surveys and the resulting indicators of public support.

Conclusions

Highlighting the difference between war-weariness as an atheoretical concept and war-weariness as a phenomenon embedded in a theory made possible for an analysis in broader terms to be conducted with respect to the security implications that the assistance provided to Ukraine entails for NATO. The extended analytical framework, tailored to account for the new European security reality created by the Russian aggression, indicated that the willingness of Ukraine's supporters to defend themselves, measured by means of determination to meet the NATO guideline on defence spendings, weakens when their commitment to assist Ukraine diminishes.

However, the tailored war-weariness theory could not be proved viable in case of both Romania and Poland which means that the general applicability of this version of the theory is called into question. The flaws bear consequences for the viability of the original war-weariness theory by adding to various arguments against its confirmation another one that, unlike those already developed, is of an indirect nature.

The absence of the war-weariness at the level of two states that play a significant role in supporting Ukraine has relevant consequences within the context brought about by the possibility of a Russian aggression against NATO members. It shows that consistent assistance provided to Ukraine is not necessarily conducive to a dramatic downfall of public support for such an approach towards Ukraine which means, in turn, that arguing for reducing assistance to it out of fear for public opinion massive negative reactions is exaggerated. The lack of an automatic connection between reducing public and political backing for assisting Ukraine and the downward trend in public and political support for meeting the NATO defence-expenditure guideline proves as doubtful the contention that insistence on high levels of assistance for Ukraine is a contributing factor to undermining Alliance solidarity.

Elements of similarity between Romania and Poland with respect to both assistance provided to Ukraine and financial resources allocated to defence facilitate closer relations and convergence in bilateral and allied format with positive effects on NATO's deterrence and defence posture on the Eastern Flank and sends a firm message to the Russian Federation.

The fact that, in both Romania and Poland, there is a broad support on the part of high-level politicians and ordinary citizens for financing defence in line with NATO guideline brings a significant contribution to further consolidate transatlantic relations irrespective of who will be the next president of the United States.

References

Bond, I. (2023, November). *Ukraine fatigue Bad for Kyiv, bad for the West.* https://www.cer.eu/sites/default/files/pb_IB_ukraine_21.11.23.pdf

Camut, N. (2024, January 24). *British public should be ready to fight Putin, UK army chief says.* https://www.politico.eu/article/hold-uk-army-chief-calls-on-government-to-mobilize-the-nation-if-theres-a-war-with-russia/

Chamber of Deputies. (1992, March 4). *Regulation on the joint meetings of the chamber of deputies and of the senate.* https://www.cdep.ro/pls/dic/site.page?id=748&idl=2

Chamber of Deputies. (2022a, February 28). *Declarația Parlamentului României cu privire la situația din Ucraina* [Declaration of the Romanian Parliament on the situation in Ukraine]. https://www.cdep.ro/pls/legis/legis_pck.htp_act?ida=183224&frame=0

Chamber of Deputies. (2022b, February 28). *Sedinta comuna a Camerei Deputaților și Senatului din 28 februarie 2022* [Joint meeting of the Chamber of Deputies and the Senate of 28 February 2022]. https://www.cdep.ro/pls/steno/steno2015.stenograma?ids=8391&idm=2&idl=1 and https://www.cdep.ro/pls/steno/eVot2015.Nominal?idv=29542

Chamber of Deputies. (2022c, December 13). *Sedinta comuna a Camerei Deputaților și Senatului din 13 decembrie 2023, Prezentarea și dezbaterea Proiectului Legii bugetului de stat pe anul 2023* [Joint meeting of the Chamber of Deputies and the Senate of 13 December 2022, Presentation and debate of the Draft State Budget Law for 2023]. www.cdep.ro/pls/steno/steno.stenograma?ids=8478&idm=2&idl=1

Chamber of Deputies. (2022d, December 14). *Sedinta comuna a Camerei Deputaților și Senatului din 14 decembrie 2022* [Joint meeting of the Chamber of Deputies and the Senate of 14 December 2022]. https://www.cdep.ro/pls/steno/evot2015.Nominal?idv=31397

Chamber of Deputies. (2022e, December 14). *Sedinta comuna a Camerei Deputaților și Senatului din 14 decembrie 2023. Continuarea dezbaterilor și adoptarea Proiectului Legii bugetului de stat pe anul 2023* [Joint meeting of the Chamber of Deputies and the Senate of 14 December 2022. Continuation of debates and adoption of the Draft State Budget Law for 2023]. https://www.cdep.ro/pls/steno/steno.stenograma?ids=8484&idm=2&idl=1

Chamber of Deputies. (2022f, December 19). *Legea bugetului de stat pe anul 2023* [State Budget Law for 2023]. https://www.cdep.ro/pls/proiecte/docs/2022/pr756_22.pdf

Chamber of Deputies. (2023a, March 7). *Declarația Parlamentului României la împlinirea pe 24 februarie 2023 a unui an de la declanșarea războiului de agresiune al Federației Ruse împotriva Ucrainei* [Declaration of the Romanian Parliament on the 24 February 2023 at one year after the outbreak of the Russian Federation's war of aggression against Ukraine]. https://www.cdep.ro/pls/legis/legis_pck.htp_act?ida=192437&frame=0

Chamber of Deputies. (2023b, March 7). *Sedinta comuna a Camerei Deputaților și Senatului din 7 martie 2023* [Joint meeting of the Chamber of Deputies and the Senate of 7 March 2023]. https://www.cdep.ro/pls/steno/steno2015.stenograma?ids=8499&idm=5&idl=1 and https://www.cdep.ro/pls/steno/eVot2015.Nominal?idv=31562

Chamber of Deputies. (2023c, December 19). *Legea bugetului de stat pe anul 2024* [State Budget Law for 2024]. https://mfinante.gov.ro/static/10/Mfp/buget2024/legeabugetuluidestat2024.pdf

Chamber of Deputies. (2023d, December 20). *Sedinta comuna a Camerei Deputaților și Senatului din 20 decembrie 2023. Vot electronic* [Joint meeting of the Chamber of Deputies and the Senate of 20 December 2023. Electronic vote]. https://www.cdep.ro/pls/steno/evot2015.nominal?idv=33278&idl=1

Ciślak, J. (2022). *66 miliardów z nowego funduszu na modernizację Sił Zbrojnych*. https://defence24.pl/polityka-obronna/66-miliardow-z-nowego-funduszu-na-modernizacje-wojska-polskiego-w-dwa-lata

Ciślak, J. (2023). *Rośnie zadłużenie Funduszu Wsparcia Sił Zbrojnych*. https://defence24.pl/przemysl/rosnie-zadluzenie-funduszu-wsparcia-sil-zbrojnych

Cohen, R. S., & Gentile, G. (2023, January 3). *The myth of America's Ukraine fatigue*. https://www.rand.org/pubs/commentary/2023/01/the-myth-of-americas-ukraine-fatigue.html

Cole, B. (2024, February 20). *Germany issues ominous warning about attack on NATO country*. https://www.newsweek.com/germany-russia-nato-pistorius-1871150comments/2011

Cook, L., & Lee, M. (2023, November 29). *Ukraine insists it sees no sign of NATO war fatigue even as fighting and weapons supplies stall*. https://apnews.com/article/ukraine-kuleba-nato-eu-russia-security-f440bb7b708be96c4889aacb5c06bb40

C31_rdf_ks.pdf

Dennison, S., & Zerka P. (2023, December 18). *Europe's emerging war fatigue, how to shore up falling support for Ukraine*. https://www.foreignaffairs.com/eastern-europe-and-former-soviet-union/europes-emerging-war-fatigue

Dmitruk, T. (2024, August 24). *Blisko 4,7% PKB na obronność Polski w 2025 roku* [Nearly 4.7% of GDP for Poland's defense in 2025]. https://dziennikzbrojny.pl/aktualnosci/news,1,12061,aktualnosci-z-polski,blisko-47-pkb-na-obronnosc-polski-w-2025-roku

Doncel, L. (2023, November 26). *Ukraine fights against one of its worst enemies: Oblivion*. https://english.elpais.com/international/2023-11-26/ukraine-fights-against-one-of-its-worst-enemies-oblivion.html#

Dz.U.2022.0.2305. (2022). *Ustawa z dnia 11 marca 2022 r. o obronie Ojczyzny*. https://arslege.pl/likwidacja-funduszu-modernizacji-sil-zbrojnych/k1978/a138602/

Dziennik Urzędowy Ministra Obrony Narodowej. (2022, February 15). *Poz. 1*, https://www.dz.urz.mon.gov.pl/zasoby/dziennik/pozycje/tresc-aktow/pdf/2022/02/bpoz._16_dec._nr_14-sig.pdf

European Commission. (2022, June). *Special Eurobarometer 526 key challenges of our times – The EU in 2022* (field work April–May 2022). https://europa.eu/eurobarometer/surveys/detail/2694

European Commission. (2023a, April). *Standard Eurobarometer 98 – Winter 2022–2023* (field work January–February 2023). https://europa.eu/eurobarometer/surveys/detail/2872

European Commission. (2023b, July). *Standard Eurobarometer 99 – Spring 2023* (field work May–June 2023). https://europa.eu/eurobarometer/surveys/detail/3052

European Commission. (2023c, December). *Standard Eurobarometer 100 Autumn 2023* (field work October–November 2023). https://europa.eu/eurobarometer/surveys/detail/3053

Garnham, D. (1986). War-proneness, war-weariness, and regime type: 1816-1980. *Journal of Peace Research, 23*(3), 279–289. https://doi.org/10.1177/002234338602300306

German Marshall Fund of the United States & Bertelsmann Foundation. (2021). *Transatlantic Trends 2021*. Transatlantic opinion on global challenges, The German Marshall Fund of the United States and Bertelsmann Foundation. https://www.gmfus.org/sites/default/files/2021-08/TT2021_Web_Version.pdf

German Marshall Fund of the United States & Bertelsmann Foundation. (2022, September). *Transatlantic Trends 2022*. Public Opinion in Times of Geopolitical Turmoil (field work June–July 2022). https://www.gmfus.org/news/transatlantic-trends-2022

Government of Romania. (2022a, February 27). *Press statements by Prime Minister Nicolae-Ionel Ciucă at the beginning of the Cabinet meeting of February 27, 2022*. https://gov.ro/en/news/press-statements-by-prime-minister-nicolae-ionel-ciuca-at-the-beginning-of-the-cabinet-meeting-of-february-27-2022

Government of Romania. (2022b, April 27). *Statements by Prime Minister Nicolae-Ionel Ciucă after meeting his Ukrainian counterpart Denys Shmyhal in Kyiv*. https://gov.ro/en/news/statements-by-prime-minister-nicolae-ionel-ciuca-after-meeting-his-ukrainian-counterpart-denys-shmyhal-in-kyiv

Government of Romania. (2023a). *Program de Guvernare 2023-2024. Viziune pentru națiune. Partidul Social Democrat. Partidul Național Liberal* [Governance Programme 2023–2024. Vision for the Nation. Social Democratic Party. National Liberal Party]. https://gov.ro/fisiere/pagini_fisiere/23-06-16-12-32-52Programul_de_Guvernare_2023-2024.pdf

Government of Romania. (2023b, August 15). *Prime Minister Marcel Ciolacu attends the Romanian Navy Day celebrations*. https://gov.ro/en/media/video/prime-minister-marcel-ciolacu-attends-the-romanian-navy-day-celebrations

Government of Ukraine. (2023, October 18). *Joint statement of the Prime Ministers of Ukraine and Romania on the results of the first meeting of the Cabinet of Ministers of Ukraine and the Government of Romania*. https://www.kmu.gov.ua/en/news/spilna-zaiava-premier-ministriv-ukrainy-ta-rumunii-za-rezultatamy-pershoho-zasidannia-uriadiv-dvokh-krain

Hasselbach, C. (2023, December 12). *Rising Ukraine war fatigue endangering US, EU support*. https://www.dw.com/en/rising-ukraine-war-fatigue-endangering-us-eu-support/a-67154224

Haynes, B. (2024, July 23). *UK must be ready for war in three years, head of British Army warns*. https://news.sky.com/story/uk-must-be-ready-for-war-within-three-years-head-of-british-army-warns-13183844

Higgins, A. (2024, February 1). *For Orban, Ukraine is a Pawn in a longer game*. https://www.nytimes.com/2024/02/01/world/europe/orban-ukraine-funding-hungary.html

Iohannis, K. (2022, February 27). *Message on Twitter*. Retrieved March 09, 2024, from https://twitter.com/KlausIohannis/status/1497870278780768257

Jankowicz, N., & Southern, T. (2023, May 04). *The War-Weary West. How governments can keep their citizens committed to Ukraine's defense*. https://www.foreignaffairs.com/ukraine/russia-war-fatigue-weary-west

Joyner, E. (2023, November 27). *NATO, Ukraine swat away talk of war fatigue*. https://www.dw.com/en/nato-ukraine-swat-away-talk-of-war-fatigue/a-67588964

Khromeychuk, O. (2024, January 25). *'Ukraine fatigue': Why I'm fighting to stop the world forgetting us*. https://www.theguardian.com/world/2024/jan/25/ukraine-fatigue-why-im-fighting-to-stop-the-world-forgetting-us?ref=upstract.com

Kirby, P. (2024, January 11). *Swedish alarm after defence chiefs' war warning*. https://www.bbc.com/news/world-europe-67935464

Koenig, N., & Schütte, L. (2024). Shades of gray zone. In T. Bunde, S. Eisentraut, & L. Schütte (Eds.), *Lose-lose? Munich security report 2024, Munich: Munich security conference* (pp. 47–53). https://doi.org/10.47342/BMQK9457

Koshiw, I. (2022, November 06). *US says Zelenskiy risks allies' 'Ukraine fatigue' if he rejects Russia talks – Report*. https://www.theguardian.com/world/2022/nov/06/us-says-zelenskiy-risks-allies-ukraine-fatigue-if-he-rejects-russia-talks-report

Levy, J. S., & Morgan, C. T. (1986). The war-weariness hypothesis: An empirical test. *American Journal of Political Science*, *30*(1), 26–49.

Milne, R., & Dunai, M. (2024, February 09). *Russia could attack a NATO country within 3 to 5 years, Denmark warns*. https://www.ft.com/content/b3101099-9516-4b0b-92c6-179997d7e4cf

Minakov, M. (2021, September 27). *The Afghanistan syndrome and U.S.–Ukraine relations*. https://www.wilsoncenter.org/blog-post/afghanistan-syndrome-and-us-ukraine-relations

Ministry of Foreign Affairs. (no date). *Ukraina znajduje się na liście priorytetowych partnerów polskiej współpracy rozwojowej od 2005 roku. Polska pomoc dla tego kraju utrzymuje się niezmiennie na wysokim poziomie* [Ukraine has been on the list of priority partners for Polish development cooperation since 2005. Polish aid to the country has remained consistently high]. https://www.gov.pl/web/polskapomoc/ukraina3

NATO. (2022a, June). *NATO audience research: Pre-Summit polling results 2022* (field work April–May 2022). https://www.nato.int/nato_static_fl2014/assets/pdf/2022/6/pdf/220622-pre-summit-research-2022.pdf

NATO. (2022b, December). *NATO Annual tracking research 2022* (field work November 2022). https://www.nato.int/nato_static_fl2014/assets/pdf/2023/3/pdf/230320-annual_tracker_report.pdf

NATO. (2023a, July). *NATO audience research: Pre-Summit polling results 2023* (field-work April–May 2023). https://www.nato.int/nato_static_fl2014/assets/pdf/2023/7/pdf/2300707-pre-summit-research-2023.pdf

NATO. (2023b, December). *NATO Annual tracking research 2023* (field work November–December 2023). https://www.nato.int/nato_static_fl2014/assets/pdf/2024/3/pdf/240314-annual-tracking-2023-en.pdf

NATO. (2023c, December). *NATO Annual tracking research* 2023 (field work November–December 2023). https://www.nato.int/nato_static_fl2014/assets/pdf/2024/3/pdf/240314-annual-tracking-2023-en.pdf

NATO. (2024, June 17). *Defence Expenditure of NATO Countries* (2014–2024) (data at 12 June 2024). https://www.nato.int/nato_static_fl2014/assets/pdf/2024/6/pdf/240617-def-exp-2024-en.pdf

Pamuk, H., & Gray, A. (2023, November 29). *'No sense of fatigue' when it comes to support for Ukraine, Blinken says*. https://www.reuters.com/world/europe/no-sense-fatigue-when-it-comes-support-ukraine-blinken-says-2023-11-29/

PAP. (2024, February 11). *Trump grozi, że nie będzie chronił przed Rosją krajów NATO zalegających z płatnościami* [Trump threatens not to protect defaulting NATO countries from Russia]. https://www.pap.pl/aktualnosci/trump-grozi-ze-nie-bedzie-chronil-przed-rosja-krajow-nato-zalegajacych-z-platnosciami

Pickering, J. (2002). War-weariness and cumulative effects: Victors, vanquished, and subsequent interstate intervention. *Journal of Peace Research*, *39*(3), 313–337. https://doi.org/10.1177/0022343302039003004

Polska Zbrojna. (2024). *Posłowie za ustawą o obronie ojczyzny* [Deputies in favor of homeland bill]. https://www.polska-zbrojna.pl/home/articleshow/36738?t=Poslowie-za-ustawa-o-obronie-ojczyzny

President of Romania. (2015, January 13). *National political agreement on increasing defence funding*. https://www.presidency.ro/en/president/core-documents/national-political-agreement-on-increasing-defence-funding-13-january-2015

President of Romania. (2022, June 16). *Conferința de presă comună a Președintelui României, Klaus Iohannis, cu Președintele Ucrainei, Volodâmâr Zelenski, Președintele Republicii Franceze, Emmanuel Macron, Cancelarul Republicii Federale Germania, Olaf Scholz, și Președintele Consiliului de Miniștri al Republicii Italiene, Mario Draghi* [Joint Press Conference of the President of Romania, Klaus Iohannis, with the President of Ukraine, Volodymyr Zelenskyy, the President of the French Republic, Emmanuel Macron, the Chancellor of the Federal Republic of Germany, Olaf Scholz, and the President of the Council of Ministers of the Italian Republic, Mario Draghi]. https://www.presidency.ro/ro/media/declaratii-de-presa/conferinta-de-presa-comuna-a-presedintelui-romaniei-klaus-iohannis-cu-presedintele-ucrainei-volodamar-zelenski-presedintele-republicii-franceze-emmanuel-macron-cancelarul-republicii-federale-germania-olaf-scholz-si-presedintele-consiliului-de-ministri-al-republicii-italiene-mario-draghi

President of Romania. (2023a, January 17). *Speech held by the President of Romania, Mr. Klaus Iohannis, on the occasion of the annual meeting with the heads of the diplomatic missions accredited in Romania*. https://www.presidency.ro/en/media/speeches/speech-held-by-the-president-of-romania-mr-klaus-iohannis-on-the-occasion-of-the-annual-meeting-with-the-heads-of-the-diplomatic-missions-accredited-in-romania

President of Romania. (2023b, June 1). *Joint declaration of President of Ukraine Volodymyr Zelenskyy and President of Romania Klaus Werner Iohannis on the Euro-Atlantic integration of Ukraine*. https://www.president.gov.ua/en/news/spilna-deklaraciya-prezidenta-ukrayini-volodimira-zelenskogo-83317

President of Romania. (2023c, July 11). *Declarațiile de presă susținute de Președintele României, Klaus Iohannis, înaintea participării la Summitul NATO de la Vilnius* [Press statements by Romanian President Klaus Iohannis ahead of the NATO Summit in Vilnius]. https://www.presidency.ro/ro/media/declaratiile-de-presa-sustinute-de-presedintele-romaniei-klaus-iohannis-inaintea-participarii-la-summitul-nato-de-la-vilnius

President of Romania. (2023d, October 10). *Joint statement by the President of Romania Klaus Iohannis and the President of Ukraine Volodymyr Zelenskyy*. https://www.presidency.ro/en/media/press-releases/joint-statement-by-the-president-of-romania-klaus-iohannis-and-the-president-of-ukraine-volodymyr-zelenskyy

Reuters. (2024, April 18). *Russia may be ready to attack NATO in 5-8 years, German official says*. https://www.reuters.com/world/europe/russia-may-be-ready-attack-nato-5-8-years-german-official-says-2024-04-18/

Rudolf, P. (2011). *War-wearines and change in strategy in US policy on Afghanistan*. Research Report. SWP Comments, 31. https://www.swpberlin.org/publications/products/

Sandbu, M. (2023, December 17). *'Ukraine fatigue' is a problem of western leaders' own making*. Retrieved February 04, 2024, from https://www.ft.com/content/dcc28873-b462-4382-8bc7-08d7557deb4e

Stapleton, B. I. (2015). The Korea syndrome, an examination of war-weariness theory. *Journal of Cold War Studies*, *17*(3), 36–81. https://doi.org/10.1162/JCWS_a_00561

Supreme Council of National Defence. (2002, June 27). *Legea nr. 415 din 27 iunie 2002 privind organizarea şi funcţionarea Consiliului Suprem de Apărare a Ţării* [Law no. 415 of 27 June 2002 on the organization and functioning of the Supreme Council of National Defence]. https://csat.presidency.ro/ro/prima-pagina/legea-de-organizare

Supreme Council of National Defence. (2022a, March 01). *Declaraţia de presă susţinută de Preşedintele României, Klaus Iohannis, la finalul şedinţei Consiliului Suprem de Apărare a Ţării* [Press statement by the President of Romania, Klaus Iohannis, at the end of the meeting of the Supreme Council of National Defence]. https://csat.presidency.ro/ro/comuni/declaratia-de-presa-sustinuta-de-presedintele-romaniei-klaus-iohannis-la-finalul-sedintei-consiliului-suprem-de-aparare-a-tarii1646215121

Supreme Council of National Defence. (2022b, October 25). *Şedinţa Consiliului Suprem de Apărare a Ţării* [Meeting of the Supreme Council of National Defence]. https://csat.presidency.ro/ro/comuni/sedinta-consiliului-suprem-de-aparare-a-tarii1666774824

Talant, B. (2022, June 30). *War fatigue in the West*. https://www.lowyinstitute.org/the-interpreter/war-fatigue-west

Zyzik, R., Baszczak, Ł., Rozbicka, I., & Wielechowski, M. (2023). *Uchodźcy z Ukrainy na polskim rynku pracy: możliwości i przeszkody*. Polski Instytut Ekonomiczny.

Chapter 5

NATO's Collective Defence: Lessons from the Russia–Ukraine War

Leszek Elak, Jarosław Gryz and Tadeusz Zieliński

War Studies University, Poland

Abstract

The chapter considers the issues of collective defence of the North Atlantic Alliance in the context of the conclusions resulting from the second phase of the Russian–Ukrainian war, which took place in 2022–2024. The aim of the chapter is to analyse strategic, operational and tactical actions in terms of the identified solutions that the parties to the war have carried out and implemented against each other, with an indication of those that should potentially be adopted by NATO. In terms of strategic activities, the method of their implementation in 2022–2024 and their consequences have been indicated. They have been included in the operational dimension of operations on the ground and air theatre, and selectively at the tactical level in the ways of conducting combat. In a general way, there will be a reference to the accompanying cyber activities. The cognitive value of this chapter is an attempt at a comprehensive, holistic approach to political activities and their strategic consequences in the activities carried out during the Russian–Ukrainian war in 2022–2024. Causal relationships between successes or lack thereof on the battlefield, the prose of combat and diplomacy have been inscribed in the narrative of advantages or weaknesses of both warring parties, with reference to the experiences that should be shared by the collective defence of NATO and individual member states. From them, final conclusions for the North Atlantic Alliance were introduced.

Keywords: NATO; collective defence; Russia's war against Ukraine; military operations; political decision-making

JEL Codes: F52; F20

Enhancing Transatlantic Solidarity in Collective Defence: Navigating Increased Defence Expenditures, Cyber Security, and Emerging Risks, 87–114

doi:10.1108/978-1-80686-259-720261005

Introduction

Russia's war against Ukraine, initiated in its second phase on 24 February 2022, prompts us to take up the issues of conclusions for NATO, as an alliance, and the member states in the context of ensuring collective defence and preparing the armed forces for it in the political and military aspects, as well as strategic, long-term actions. The ultimate strategic goal of the Russian Federation is to take over the role of a leading state in international relations on the European continent, guaranteeing its continued influence. Russia coordinates these activities with China, which provides it with logistical support for its military operations and diplomatic support in international forums (Bossuyt & Kaczmarski, 2021). The idea of both countries is to completely change the forms of international security architecture and deprive the United States of its importance in it, with the participation of broadly defined Western countries, including South Korea and Japan (Sagild & Hsiung, 2024). Thus, Russia's war against Ukraine is one of the puzzles of the global puzzle, the pieces of which are located around the globe and correlate with each other, creating a narrative for Russian and Chinese international policy.

Russia's preparations for the second phase of the war against Ukraine and the confrontation with the West have been carried out since the end of the fighting in 2014 (Bartosiewicz et al., 2024). They were comprehensive in nature encompassing all forms of struggle, that is political, economic, informational, psychological, and other (Petrenko, 2024). Each of them was aimed at gaining an advantage in a situation in which NATO would act inadequately to the situation, weakening its condition as a political and military alliance (Tardy, 2020). This situation did not occur, because from the meeting of NATO heads of state and government in Newport in 2014 to Washington in 2024, the adaptation process that NATO has gone through over the past decade has become a response to Russian and Chinese efforts to revise the international order (Calmels, 2020).

In 2014, NATO responded to the challenges to international security and allied defence generated by the Russian Federation. It has taken important decisions and actions in this regard at meetings of heads of state and government (Wales 2014, Warsaw 2016, Brussels 2018, London 2019, Brussels 2021). As it turned out, however, all these provisions were not enough to stop Russia from escalating the war in Ukraine. In response to this situation, the heads of state and government adopted the NATO 2022 Strategic Concept in 2022. It contains a catalogue of actions in relation to the identified challenges and threats (Szenes, 2023). In addition, the following has become a response to the challenges related to ensuring international order and security:

- the enlargement of the alliance to include Finland and Sweden;
- support for Ukraine;
- recognition of Russia as a state seeking to undermine the European and global international order;
- recognition of China as a challenge to the transatlantic community (Washington Summit Declaration, 2024).

Not without significance for Russia's efforts to revise the existing international order was the withdrawal of the Russian Federation from treaties creating confidence-building measures in Europe since the late 1980s and early 1990s. Since Russia unilaterally suspended the application of the Treaty on Conventional Armed Forces in Europe (CFE Treaty) in 2007, and violated the terms of the Open Skies Treaty, there has been an erosion of confidence-building measures on the European continent (Engvall, 2020). The result was Russia's formal denunciation of the treaty in 2021, of the Treaty on Open Skies, and in 2023, the termination of the Treaty on Conventional Armed Forces in Europe (Rodkiewicz, 2023). At the same time, NATO countries maintained the provisions of the NATO–Russia Founding Act adopted in 1997 (m.in. restrictions on the construction of allied military infrastructure and the deployment of armed forces in the countries of the alliance's eastern flank) (Hanson, 1998). This created a favourable situation for Russia, in which it questioned the actions of the North Atlantic Alliance as inconsistent with the provisions of the founding act. As a result, in 2021, the Russian Ministry of Foreign Affairs announced a 'halt' (i.e. de facto liquidation) of the Permanent Mission of the Russian Federation to NATO Headquarters in Brussels (Rodkiewicz, 2020).

In the Russian approach, one of the key elements was military preparations for war, based on the experience gained from the first phase of the conflict in 2014, when it was possible to annex part of Ukraine with relatively little effort and resources (Snegovaya, 2015). In its second instalment, it was intended to repeat the situation in which Russian troops take control of Ukrainian territory through combined, synergistic actions of regular and irregular forces (Muradov, 2022). The intention was to repeat the situation that occurred during the occupation of Crimea (Pokorzyński, 2022). The adoption of a strategy to take control of Ukraine with forces intended not for war, but for short-term fighting, quickly brought results in the form of shortcomings in command and control, a breakdown of supplies in logistics chains, poor equipment and morale of soldiers, terrible communications, unsatisfactory actions of the Russian aerospace forces, air defence, and the use of cruise and ballistic missiles (Dalsjö et al., 2022).

Russia's predominance in actions against the West, as well as in waging war, was determined by its readiness to confront in the information sphere using information bubbles and echo chambers in troll farm activities (Greenberg, 2021), the use of 'useful idiots' and other forms of building influence in opinion-forming and leadership communities (Natorski, M. 2020). Russia's actions are consistent with the understanding of propaganda as a broadly understood communication encompassing all forms of narrative and media, which strongly favours a specific form of interest in global communication strategies in a connected network environment (Tolz & Hutchings, 2023).

In the case of Russia's war against Ukraine, two currents of Russian strategic culture have been identified that affect the form of its message. The first is a deep-seated sense of vulnerability, especially in relation to the 'West', which must be countered with strategic depth and buffer zones. The second is a special position, and the resulting prerogatives of a great power. Hence, central to the vision of a greater Russia is the right to have a sphere of influence in its Eurasian neighbourhood (Götz & Staun, 2022). Together, these two factors create an imperative for Russian elite thinking and Russian society. The manipulation of information in relations between Russia and the West and Russia in the Global South has become part of the information war aimed at disavowing Russian opponents and using lies in their own actions (Baumann, 2020).

The Course of Military Operations During the Russian–Ukrainian War in Years 2022–2023

Military operations during the Russia–Ukraine war were characterised by intense actions on various fronts and changing dynamics. The initial phase of the conflict, which began with Russia's invasion on 24 February 2022, included large-scale attacks on Ukraine from three main directions: the north (Belarus and Bryansk Oblast), the east (Donbas), and the south (Crimea). Russian ground forces, supported by artillery and aviation, attempted to quickly capture strategic cities such as Kyiv, Kharkiv, and Mariupol in order to neutralise the Ukrainian government and dismantle Ukraine's defence forces. The deployment of Russian troops to Belarus before the invasion of Ukraine on 24 February 2022, was of key strategic importance (Dalsjö et al., 2022).

Russian forces, despite numerous logistical and operational problems, tried to use their numerical superiority and superiority in heavy weapons such as tanks and artillery. Russian troops sought to quickly capture key cities to weaken the morale of Ukrainian defenders and force surrender. However, they have encountered strong resistance from the Ukrainian army, which has used flexible defences, guerrilla tactics, and support from the local population (Snegovaya, 2022). In addition, their rapid adaptation and support from the West allowed them to successfully repel further attacks (Baumann, 2023).

Ukrainian ground troops used a combination of manoeuver and permanent defence, focusing on holding key strategic points such as the cities of Kyiv, Kharkiv, and Mariupol. Using the advantage of knowledge of the terrain and the support of the local population, the Ukrainians organised ambushes, surprise attacks and precise strikes on Russian logistics columns. Effective cooperation with allies was also a key element, which provided access to modern anti-tank defence systems, such as Javelin or NLAW, which played a significant role in defence against Russian tanks (Gibadło, 2024).

The Russians ignored the basic principle of the art of war, which is to provide logistical support and operational support for advanced troops. The lack of adequate supplies, especially in fuel and ammunition, has significantly limited the ability of Russian forces to conduct long-term offensive operations. In addition, the Russian command did not adapt its plans to the actual situation on the battlefield, which led to chaos and losses (Engvall, 2023).

Prior to 22 February 2022, Russian forces were deployed along the border with Ukraine in several key groupings: in Belarus, Donbas, Crimea, and in the western regions of Russia. These groupings were prepared to quickly strike Ukrainian positions in several directions, which were intended to weaken Ukrainian defences by attacking from multiple sides at once. This deployment was crucial for the rapid seizure of Ukrainian territories, especially the capital, Kyiv (Dodds, 2023).

The operational plan of the Russian Federation assumed the rapid occupation of Kyiv through coordinated attacks from Belarus and the north-eastern regions of Ukraine. A key role was played by the airborne operation, aimed at seizing the airfields around Kyiv, which was to enable the rapid transport of additional forces and supplies. However, this plan failed, mainly due to strong Ukrainian defences and logistical problems that affected Russian troops (Snegovaya, 2022).

On the eve of its invasion of Ukraine in February 2022, Russia deployed its armed forces at key points to make the most of the element of surprise and numerical superiority. The main Russian forces were concentrated in the north, in the region of Belarus, which allowed for a quick march towards Kyiv. Additional groups were located in the east, in Donbas, and in the south, in Crimea. Military operations were carried out in accordance with the assumption of a massive attack in several directions at the same time. The Russian strategy was based on the rapid capture of key cities, which was supposed to destabilise Ukrainian defences. In practice, however, these operations met with strong resistance, resulting in a protracted conflict and the need for Russia to change its operational plans (Javelin & Hawn, 2022).

The military potential of the army of the Russian Federation before 22 February 2022 was impressive in terms of numbers and technology. The Russian armed forces consisted of about 900,000 active-duty soldiers and more than 2 million reservists. Russia had one of the largest armies in the world, equipped with modern weapons systems, including T-90 tanks, Su-35 fighter planes, S-400 air defence systems, and advanced artillery and rocket assets. The Russian armed forces were also supported by advanced logistics infrastructure and a well-developed command network. Despite this, despite its impressive potential, the Russian military also had significant weaknesses, such as a complicated command structure, morale problems, and dependence on outdated war doctrines (Giles, 2022).

Ukraine's military potential before 22 February 2022 was much smaller than Russia's, both in terms of numbers and technology. The Ukrainian army, numbering about 250,000 soldiers, was in the process of modernisation after decades of underfunding and neglect. Ukraine's main forces relied on older weapons systems, such as T-64 and T-72 tanks and MiG-29 and Su-27 aircraft. Despite these limitations, the Ukrainian army gained combat experience during the conflict in Donbas, which increased its operational capabilities. In addition, Ukraine began cooperation with Western allies, which allowed for partial modernisation of weapons and the development of defence strategies based on mobility and flexibility (Kofman, 2022).

Hostilities in Ukraine since February 2022 have been characterised by intense fighting on multiple fronts, with key battles for Kyiv, Kharkiv, Mariupol, and Sumy. Russian forces initially achieved significant territorial successes, but over time, thanks to Ukrainian counterattacks and the support of Western allies, Ukraine managed to regain some of the lost territory, especially in the northeastern and southern parts of the country (Watling & Reynolds, 2023).

The defence of Kyiv was one of the key moments of the conflict. Ukrainian forces have effectively exploited the urban area, organising ambushes and blocking key access roads to the capital. The support of the local population, well-planned fortifications, and the use of modern anti-tank systems played a key role in repelling the Russian attack on Kyiv (Mitrokhin, 2023).

The battles for Sumy, Kharkiv and Mariupol were among the most intense clashes of this period of the conflict. Sumy and Kharkiv became the scene of fierce fighting, where Ukrainian forces successfully repelled Russian attacks, often with the support of artillery and drones. Mariupol, on the other hand, was the site of a dramatic defence that, despite a prolonged siege, attracted international attention due to the scale of destruction and suffering of the civilian population. The Ukrainian counteroffensive in the Sumy area, carried out in the late summer of 2022, was a key moment that forced the Russians to retreat from many of the occupied areas (Kofman, 2022).

The war went through several distinct phases. The first phase was a rapid Russian advance, which, however, was stopped by Ukrainian defences. The second phase is Ukrainian counteroffensives, which led to the recapture of part of the territory. The third phase is the stabilisation of the front, where both sides have strengthened their positions, preparing for a long-term conflict (Reynolds, 2023).

Russia went on the counteroffensive in early 2024, after significantly strengthening its forces and improving logistics. Despite large losses, Russia has been gradually regaining lost territories, but its progress has been limited by the effective defence of Ukraine (Bowen, 2024).

Russia has used hypersonic weapons, including Kinzhal missiles, during the war in Ukraine mainly to carry out precision strikes on strategic targets, such as ammunition depots, critical infrastructure, and command centres. These missiles, due to their ability to reach extreme speeds (over Mach 5) and high manoeuvrability, were virtually impossible to intercept by Ukrainian missile defence systems. The use of these weapons was aimed not only at destroying key targets but also at demonstrating Russia's technological superiority and exerting psychological pressure on Ukraine and its allies (Bronk et al., 2024).

Ukraine's air defence has proven to be crucial in protecting the country from Russian aggression. Before the war, Ukraine relied mainly on older systems such as the S-300, which, however, were relatively effective against aircraft, cruise missiles and ballistic missiles. As the conflict continued, Ukraine received modern air defence systems from the West, such as IRIS-T from Germany and NASAMS from the United States. These systems have significantly increased Ukraine's ability to shoot down Russian missiles and drones, which has significantly reduced Russian air superiority and contributed to the protection of key cities and infrastructure (Foltynova, 2022).

The Russian–Ukrainian war is making intensive use of armoured and mechanised troops. Russia, which has one of the largest armoured fleets in the world, in the initial phase of the conflict tried to use its armoured troops to carry out quick, massive attacks aimed at breaking through Ukrainian defences and capturing key cities. However, Russian armoured troops have encountered serious difficulties, especially in urban areas and densely built-up areas. Ukrainian ground forces, equipped with modern anti-tank systems provided by the West, such as Javelin and NLAW missiles, successfully stopped Russian armoured columns. The Ukrainians used the tactic of driving Russian tanks into narrow streets or wooded areas where their forces were more vulnerable to ambush attacks (Fox, 2022).

The Russians, using battalion tactical groups, have tried and are currently trying to organise their operations in a way that allows them to quickly carry out offensives. However, the structure of these units turned out to be inadequate for the needs of a full-scale conflict, which resulted in problems with coordination of activities and logistics. Russian armoured troops were often isolated and forced to abandon equipment on the battlefield due to a lack of adequate logistical support (Marinko et al., 2023).

Artillery was one of the most important elements in Ukraine's defence strategy during the war with Russia. The Ukrainian Armed Forces, despite limited artillery resources, have effectively used modern technologies and precision artillery shells provided by the West. Ukrainian artillery was mainly used to destroy Russian positions, ammunition depots and supply lines, which significantly limited the offensive capabilities of the Russians. The Ukrainians used the tactic of mobile and flexible use of artillery, which allowed them to move quickly and avoid counterattacks. The Russians, despite their significant numerical superiority in artillery, often relied on indiscriminate shelling, which was not always precise, leading to large civilian casualties and ineffective destruction of military targets. This tactic, known as a 'war of attrition', involved intense and prolonged artillery fire, while Ukrainian artillery focused on precision strikes to eliminate key enemy assets and support defensive and counteroffensive operations.

Russia had a large number of artillery systems, which allowed it to conduct massive shelling on a large scale. Russian artillery units often adopted the tactic of 'fire fences', where large areas were systematically shelled in order to completely destroy the infrastructure and forces of the enemy in the area. This type of shelling was carried out by both barrel artillery and rocket systems, such as the BM-21 Grad or BM-30 Smerch. Ukrainian artillery, on the other hand, focuses on precision strikes aimed at eliminating key enemy assets and supporting defensive and counteroffensive operations. Russian troops used 20 to 60 thousand artillery shells per day, while Ukrainian troops used up to 5 thousand. Russian artillery tactics in the war in Ukraine are based on intense, indiscriminate shelling that aims to completely destroy Ukrainian positions and resources, which is implemented at the expense of precision and often leads to significant civilian casualties (DePetris, 2022).

The training of Ukraine's ground troops was the result of intensive training programmes conducted in cooperation with many NATO countries, including the United Kingdom, Canada, the United States, and other international partners. As part of Operation Interflex, which is the largest training programme conducted on British soil since World War II, more than 30,000 Ukrainian recruits have undergone training since 2022 (Shapps & Sunak, 2023). This programme includes training in basic combat skills such as weapon handling, battlefield first aid, patrol tactics, and urban operations. As a result, Ukrainian soldiers have gained the skills necessary to effectively conduct defensive and offensive operations at the front (Gressel, G. 2022). In addition, the Ukrainian ground forces are receiving training in the use of advanced military equipment provided by Western partners, such as Challenger 2 tanks and Patriot missile systems. These trainings increase the ability of Ukrainian forces to effectively use modern technologies in the fight against Russian aggression.

The combat training of the ground troops of the army of the Russian Federation is more diverse, depending on the unit and type of soldiers (Conenell et al., 2023). The Russian armed forces consist of a mixed cadre, including both professional soldiers and conscripts. Since 2009, Russia has implemented reforms to improve the quality of training, including an increase in the number of live ammunition exercises and the introduction of surprise exercises to check the combat readiness of units. In addition, Russia has invested in new training centres, such as the Mulino complex, aimed at raising training standards. However, despite these reforms, the Russian armed forces continue to face problems such as a lack of standardisation in training, an over-reliance on simulations instead of actual field exercises, and problems with logistics and coordination in combat operations. These shortcomings came to light during the invasion of Ukraine, where Russian units often failed to cope with the more flexible and well-trained Ukrainian forces (McKew, 2022). One of the greatest combat successes of the Ukrainian ground forces was the destruction of a Russian battalion in Bilohorivka, on the Donets River in the Luhansk region. In May 2022, the Ukrainian Armed Forces carried out a successful attack on a Russian column trying to cross the river. This event not only inflicted serious losses on the Russians but also demonstrated Ukraine's ability to deal significant blows to the enemy on the frontline. The greatest combat success of the ground forces of the Russian Federation was the battle for Mariupol, which ended in May 2022. After a three-month siege and brutal fighting, Russian forces captured the city, which was of strategic importance due to its location on a 'land bridge' between Crimea and Russia. Despite long-term resistance from Ukrainian defenders, especially in the area of the Azovstal plant, the Russians managed to take full control of the city, which was a propaganda and strategic victory (Weber, 2023).

The domain of cyber warfare should be indicated here. Cyberspace activities aimed at disrupting enemy communications and command play an essential role on the battlefield, which also played a vital role throughout the conflict. Russia has also carried out cyberattacks on Ukraine's critical infrastructure, but Ukraine, supported by international partners, has managed to successfully defend itself against these threats. In space, both sides used satellites to monitor the situation on the front and direct artillery fire, which emphasises the growing importance of this domain in modern armed conflicts (Gibadło, 2024). Russian air operations during the invasion of Ukraine have been the subject of detailed analysis and often extreme assessments from the beginning, both among military experts and internationally. Initial expectations for the Russian Aerospace Forces (VKS) were high, assuming that numerical and technological superiority over the Ukrainian Air Force would allow Russia to quickly gain air dominance, which could determine the outcome of the war. Russia had some of the most modern combat aircraft, such as the Su-35, MiG-31, and advanced long-range missile systems, including R-37M and Kh-101 missiles. In addition, Russian forces were supported by advanced air defence systems, such as the S-400, which were theoretically intended to prevent Ukraine from conducting effective air operations.

The first days and weeks of the invasion showed that Russia was unable to effectively neutralise Ukrainian air defence, which, despite limited resources, proved to be extremely effective and flexible. Ukrainian air defence systems, such as the S-300 and Buk, were not only well integrated but also skilfully used in combination with mobile units and MANPADS systems, which became the bane of Russian pilots. Despite numerous attempts, Russia was unable to destroy these systems enough to gain unimpeded air superiority. This meant that Russian aircraft had to operate at higher altitudes, which not only reduced their combat effectiveness but also increased the risk of being shot down by Ukrainian missiles (Henriksen & Bronk, 2024).

In the initial phases of the war, Russia carried out a number of massive missile and air strikes aimed at destroying key military and civilian infrastructure of Ukraine, including command centres, ammunition depots, and power grids. These attacks, based on the doctrine of 'non-contact warfare', were intended to cripple Ukrainian defences and allow Russian ground forces to quickly gain control of strategic areas, including the country's capital, Kyiv. However, Ukrainian defences, supported by Western intelligence and the supply of modern air defence systems, managed to successfully repel these attacks, which prevented Russia from implementing its original plans. A particularly dramatic example was the failure of the Russian landing operation on Hostomel airfield near Kyiv, which was supposed to open the way for the rapid capture of the capital, but ended in failure due to Ukrainian resistance (Ichaso, 2023).

The Russian Air Force has also encountered serious difficulties in coordinating air operations with ground operations. Unlike NATO forces, which have developed complex joint operations over the years, integrating air operations with land and sea operations, Russia has failed to fully integrate its air force with other branches of the military. The lack of an advanced command and control system and insufficient situational awareness on the battlefield were factors that significantly limited the capabilities of the Russian Military Forces to effectively support ground operations. For example, Russian aircraft often operated without sufficient intelligence support, leading to inefficient use of available resources and losses in people and equipment (Bronk, 2023).

One of the most serious mistakes made by Russia was its inability to effectively conduct the SEAD (Suppression of Enemy Air Defences) operation, which is a key element in gaining air superiority, destroying or neutralising enemy air defence systems. It seems that the Russian command underestimated the strength of the Ukrainian air defence and was not able to react quickly to the changing situation on the battlefield. As a result, Russian planes and helicopters were often shot down, and the VKS were unable to provide uninterrupted support for ground operations (Galamison & Petersen, 2023).

As time passed, Russia was forced to adapt its strategies, which was associated with some successes, but also with clear failures. Faced with problems with the coordination and effectiveness of traditional air operations, Russia has increasingly relied on long-range missile attacks and the use of drones to fill the gaps in traditional air operations. In particular, the Shahed-136 drones, provided by Iran, have become one of the main tools of Russian strategy, allowing it to carry out attacks on Ukrainian targets from a long distance at a relatively low cost (Zampronha & Albuquerque, 2024). These drones, despite being relatively cheap and slower compared to other systems, were difficult to intercept by Ukrainian air defence systems and posed a serious threat to Ukraine's energy and civilian infrastructure (Sankaran, 2024). However, despite these efforts, the effectiveness of Russian air attacks has been limited. The Ukrainian Armed Forces, with advanced air defence systems provided by the West, were able to shoot down most of the drones and missiles launched by Russia, minimising losses in people and infrastructure. Additionally, the Ukrainian army has effectively used its own drones to conduct attacks on Russian targets, including air bases and command centres, which have further weakened Russia's combat capabilities (Gunzinger, 2024).

At the end of 2022, Russia began to experience serious problems related to the depletion of resources, including precision-guided munitions and modern combat assets. In response to these problems, Russia began to produce Iranian Shahed drones on the spot, which was aimed at filling the shortage of weapons and increasing strike capabilities. The production of these drones, carried out under the name 'Geran', has enabled Russia to continue its offensive operations in the face of increasing losses. Nevertheless, even these actions were not able to compensate for the lack of air superiority, which ultimately contributed to the overall ineffectiveness of Russian offensive actions (Méheut, 2024). The Russian Air Force, despite having modern weapon systems, has not been able to effectively integrate them with other types of troops as part of complex joint operations. In particular, the lack of cooperation between the air force and the ground forces, as well as communication and command problems, were factors that significantly limited the ability of the WCS to conduct effective combat operations. In many cases, Russian aircraft operated on their own, without adequate support from ground forces, leading to losses and failures in the implementation of tasks (Jensen, 2024).

Russia has not been able to fully use its potential in terms of precision air strikes. Although the initial missile attacks were well coordinated and accurate, over time the effectiveness of these attacks began to decline, which was the result of both Ukrainian defence and logistical problems on the Russian side. Supply shortages, depleting ammunition stocks, and problems with maintaining and servicing equipment meant that the Russian Air Force gradually lost its effectiveness, which in turn had an impact on the course of the conflict (Wiswesser, 2023). Ultimately, Russia's failures in air operations have shown that technological superiority does not always translate into operational success, especially when effective strategy, coordination and the ability to respond quickly to a changing battlefield situation are lacking.

In turn, Ukraine's air defence strategy, implemented during the war with Russia, has become a key element of national defence and one of the pillars of resistance to Russian aggression. In the face of the enemy's numerical and technological superiority, Ukraine built a system that not only effectively countered air attacks but also limited the operational capabilities of the Russian Air Force.

The basis of Ukraine's air defence strategy was an integrated air defence system, which consisted of multi-layered anti-aircraft and anti-missile systems. Older Soviet-derived systems, such as the S-300, Buk and Strela, played a key role in this system and were supplemented by modern systems supplied by Western countries. The S-300 system, which is one of the most important components of Ukraine's air defence, provided the ability to intercept both aircraft and ballistic missiles at long distances, often exceeding 150 kilometres. Its role was crucial in defending against Russian cruise missiles, which posed one of the main threats to Ukraine's critical infrastructure and armed forces (Integrated Air and Missile Defence, 2024).

The second layer of Ukrainian air defence was the Buk mobile systems, which, like the S-300, date back to the Soviet era but were upgraded in the years leading up to the war. These systems were characterised by high mobility and the ability to quickly regroup, which made it significantly difficult for the Russians to target and destroy them. The Buk played a key role in defending against mid-range air attacks, which was especially important in areas where the main Ukrainian forces were concentrated (Stoll et al., 2024).

At the lowest level of the Ukrainian air defence system were short- and very short-range systems. These include portable air defence systems (MANPADS) such as the Igla, Stinger, and Piorun. They were particularly effective against low-flying targets, including Russian cruise missiles and drones, which Russia has often used to attack Ukrainian civilian and military targets. An example of their effectiveness can be the shooting down of numerous drones and cruise missiles during Russian attacks on Ukrainian energy infrastructure in 2022 and 2023.

An important element of Ukraine's air defence strategy was the supply of modern systems from the West. The Ukrainian army has received a variety of air defence systems from its allies, which have significantly increased its defence capabilities. These systems included m.in, NASAMS, Patriot, IRIS-T, and SAMP/T. Each of these systems brought unique capabilities to the Ukrainian air defence. NASAMS, a medium-range system, has been particularly effective in defending against missile and air attacks, providing Ukraine with the ability to protect vital facilities in urban areas and key transportation hubs. The Patriot system, famous for its high effectiveness against ballistic missiles, has played a key role in protecting Ukrainian airspace from the most advanced threats, including Russian Iskander missiles (Piotrowski, 2022).

The support of NATO and partners in the form of modern air defence systems has not only increased Ukraine's defence capabilities but also enabled it to respond flexibly to evolving threats. The Ukrainian armed forces, thanks to Western assistance, were able not only to effectively repel air attacks but also to adapt their strategies depending on the development of the situation on the front. Mobility and the ability to quickly redeploy air defence systems have become key factors that have allowed Ukraine to maintain effective air defences throughout the conflict.

One of the most important elements of Ukraine's air defence strategy was the anti-access/aera-denial (A2/AD) strategy. Instead of seeking full air dominance, which may have proved impossible in the face of Russia's numerical and technological superiority, Ukraine has focused on limiting the enemy's operational capabilities in specific areas. This strategy was aimed at preventing Russia from gaining air superiority that could decide the fate of the war. Instead of focusing on destroying Russian air forces in direct clashes, Ukraine's strategy has been to gradually reduce its effectiveness by reducing operational capabilities (Verville & Buchatskiy, 2023).

The basic tool for implementing the A2/AD strategy was the maintenance of mobile air defence units, which could be quickly relocated as needed. The Ukrainian Armed Forces have understood that stationary air defence systems are too easy a target for Russian cruise missiles and aviation, so they have focused on mobility. Systems such as the Buk or S-300 regularly changed their location, which made it significantly difficult for the Russians to recognise and destroy them. As a result, Ukraine has been able to effectively protect its key areas while minimising the risk of equipment losses (Bremer & Grieco, 2022).

The effectiveness of this strategy was manifested in a significant limitation of the operational freedom of the Russian Air Force. Russian aircraft, forced to operate at higher altitudes and from greater distances, lost combat effectiveness, which translated into less effectiveness of Russian attacks. Ukraine's air defence, combined with mobility and adaptability, has created a kind of protective 'umbrella' over the armed forces and critical infrastructure, effectively reducing the effectiveness of Russian air and missile attacks.

One of the most telling examples of the effectiveness of Ukraine's A2/AD strategy was Ukraine's shooting down of large numbers of Russian cruise missiles and drones. For example, in May 2023, Ukraine reported that it had shot down about 90% of Russian cruise missiles and drones, and 80% of air- and ground-launched ballistic missiles. This effectiveness was possible thanks to the skilful use of a multi-layered air defence system, which was regularly reinforced with the supply of modern systems from the West.

The lessons that NATO and Western countries can draw from the air operations conducted by Russia and Ukraine during the current conflict are multifaceted and crucial for future military operations. Analysing both the successes and failures of both sides in the fight for air superiority provides valuable lessons that can shape future military strategies, particularly in the context of the changing nature of modern armed conflicts.

The experience from Ukraine shows that air superiority is not an automatic result of having a more numerous and technologically advanced fleet of combat aircraft. Russia, despite its significant technological and numerical superiority, was not able to achieve full air dominance. The reason for this failure was not only Ukraine's effective air defence but also the lack of an appropriate strategy that could neutralise this defence. NATO must, therefore, understand that in future conflicts, even with technological superiority, flexibility and the ability to adapt quickly to dynamically changing battlefield conditions will be crucial. In addition, it is necessary to develop the capabilities to conduct effective SEAD operations, which are necessary to achieve and maintain air superiority. NATO, which for years has based its air operations on the ability to neutralise enemy air defences, must constantly improve these capabilities, taking into account modern air defence systems that can be used by potential adversaries (Goodwin, 2024).

The conflict in Ukraine has also highlighted the importance of integrated air defence, which has been able to effectively counter Russia's air and missile attacks. Ukraine's defence strategy, based on mobile and integrated air defence systems, created a highly contested airspace in which Russia was unable to act freely. For NATO, there is a clear lesson to be learned: future air operations will need to take into account the existence of advanced, multi-layered air defence systems that can effectively counter air attacks. This means that NATO must invest not only in the ability to conduct offensive operations but also in the development of its own air defence systems that will be able to protect allied forces against potential enemy attacks.

Another important conclusion from the analysis of air operations in Ukraine is the importance of mobility and flexibility in conducting operations. Russia, despite having technologically advanced aircraft and weapons systems, has often encountered problems related to the lack of operational flexibility. Ukraine's A2/AD strategy proved effective in large part due to the mobility of Ukrainian air defence systems, which were regularly deployed, making it difficult for the Russians to target and destroy them. For NATO, this means the need to further develop its ability to react and adapt quickly depending on the situation on the battlefield. NATO forces must be ready to operate in an environment where the adversary will use advanced and mobile air defence systems, which requires not only appropriate training but also investment in technologies that enable the rapid movement and concealment of weapon systems (Bowsher, 2023).

An equally important aspect that NATO should pay attention to is the role and importance of drones in modern air operations. Both Ukraine and Russia have intensively used unmanned aerial vehicles for a variety of purposes, from reconnaissance and guidance to carrying out precision strikes on enemy territory. The conflict in Ukraine has shown that drones have become an integral part of modern warfare, offering a cost-effective way to conduct combat operations without risking the lives of pilots. For NATO, the development and integration of advanced unmanned aerial vehicle systems should become a priority. Future armed conflicts will require NATO forces to be able to operate in airspace saturated with enemy drones, which means the need to invest in technologies capable of intercepting and neutralising UAVs, as well as developing their own advanced drone systems capable of performing complex combat tasks (Husain, 2024).

However, it is not only the development of technology that is crucial. It's equally important to understand how technology affects tactics and strategy. The conflict in Ukraine has shown that technology alone does not guarantee success if it is not properly integrated into operational tactics and strategy. Russia's failure to gain air superiority is partly due to a lack of proper coordination between the various branches of the armed forces. In contrast, NATO must continue to develop its combined operations capabilities that combine air, land and sea operations into a coherent, integrated operational plan. This requires not only advanced command and control systems but also close cooperation and coordination between different branches of the military and with allies.

For NATO, the need to invest in electronic warfare and cyber warfare capabilities is also an important lesson. The conflict in Ukraine has shown how important it is to neutralise the enemy's ability to use communication and control systems, as well as to conduct operations in cyberspace. NATO must be ready to conduct complex operations that combine traditional military operations with advanced electronic and cyber warfare. The ability to disrupt adversary systems, disable its means of communication and command, and protect its own systems from cyberattacks will become key elements of future armed conflicts (Patterson, 2024).

It is also worth highlighting the importance of international cooperation and interoperability. NATO, as a multi-member alliance, must ensure that all its forces can work together effectively on the battlefield. The conflict in Ukraine has highlighted the importance of ensuring that different air defence systems, armaments and technologies are compatible and can be used effectively in integrated allied operations. NATO must, therefore, continue to develop interoperability standards and promote industrial cooperation that will enable the development and deployment of systems that can interact in complex multinational operations.

Ultimately, one of the key lessons NATO must learn from the conflict in Ukraine is the need to develop the ability to conduct operations in a contested airspace environment. This conflict has shown that future wars can be fought in an airspace that is not dominated by any one side. NATO must be ready to operate in such an environment, which requires investment in technologies that enable temporary, local air superiority, which can be crucial to operational success. In this context, the development of advanced fighter jets, such as the F-35, which can operate in a high-threat environment, and advanced electronic and cyber warfare systems, is becoming a priority for the Alliance.

The second phase of Russia's war against Ukraine has provided NATO and Western countries with many valuable lessons in the conduct of air operations and the fight for air superiority. Key findings include the need to invest in SEAD capabilities, the development and integration of advanced air defence systems and drones, and the need to increase operational flexibility and the ability to operate in contested airspace. NATO must also continue to develop its capabilities for joint operations, electronic and cyber warfare, and interoperability within the alliance. These lessons are crucial to maintaining NATO's advantage in future armed conflicts, which will be conducted in an increasingly complex and technologically advanced environment.

NATO Support for Ukraine in the War Against Russia

The outbreak of the second phase of Russia's war against Ukraine on 24 February 2022 was preceded by actions taken by Ukraine after it began in 2014. Their political, informational, economic, and military nature was intended to prepare international public opinion to accept the Russian narrative of the 'Russian mir' as a permanent, historical element of cultural heritage in the former areas of the USSR (Mälksoo, 2022). At the same time, these actions were an important element of the 'cultural fog' directed against Ukraine, its subjectivity and statehood in its current, sovereign form. In parallel, those aimed at weakening the unity of Western countries within the so called Minsk format and the Normandy group were carried out (Helwig, 2019). Their role was to consolidate the belief that the leading countries of the European Union, Germany and France, together with the Russian Federation, are able to resolve the conflict (Siddi, 2018). Even without the participation of the United States. In addition, this political construct has made it possible to create a platform for economic cooperation with Russia with political support from the governments of these countries, giving them political, international legitimacy to act together for the benefit of Ukraine and the good of the entire European Union. The adoption of the above narrative in 2014–2022 gave Russia the ability to prepare militarily combined with economic benefits. In this strategic pause, it managed to maintain the gross domestic product and increase it significantly just before the start of operations (Melkadze, 2024).

In parallel with its political and economic activities, the Russian Federation has been conducting military operations since 2014. Their consequence was the occupation of Crimea and the war in Donbas. On the basis of the experience gained, selected segments of the armed forces and their armament were modernised. This process, due to the size of the Russian army, took the form of an evolutionary one and was related, m.in other things, to efficiency problems, as well as corruption. Expenditures oscillated from USD 84 billion in 2014, through sums of USD 66–65 billion in the years 2015–2021, to an expenditure of USD 86 billion in 2022, the year of the beginning of the second phase of the war (Macrotrends, 2024). At that time, new systems were incorporated into the existing armament. Since 2014, the Russian land, air and naval forces have become better trained and equipped. Therefore, the failure they suffered in their attempt to seize Kyiv between 24 February and April 2022 should be attributed to improper operational planning (the march of columns of troops exposed to constant losses in logistically difficult terrain with poor supplies) that did not take into account Ukraine's readiness to defend itself (Plokhy, 2024). This is a sign of disregard for the enemy, his potential, and above all, the lack of proper recognition by Russian intelligence (the attitude of the Ukrainians to the confrontation with Russia, the operational capabilities of the Ukrainian army). Underestimating the intentions and will of the United States and the role of Germany, its attitude towards Russia. This resulted in Ukrainian successes in the August–November 2022 period, when some of the territories occupied by Russia in the north-eastern and southern parts of the front were regained.

The year 2023 brought fundamental changes in the conduct of the war by both sides. In the initial period of 2022–2023, Russia and Ukraine operated in diverse formations. The Ukrainians are relatively small units, that is brigades, while the Russians are corps and armies. During this period of fighting, taking advantage of climatic conditions and the lack of proper coordination of activities at the corps level, the Ukrainian army achieved significant successes by liberating the northern areas of the country in September–October and the southern areas in September–November 2022. The turn of 2022 and 2023 did not change the overall state of the war, but it allowed the army of the Russian Federation to make preparations for both defence and further attack on Ukrainian troops. This period ended with the attempted Ukrainian counteroffensive against the fortified Russian positions of the so called Surovikin Line, a heavily fortified belt of fortifications built by Russian troops in the east and south of Ukraine in August 2023, with extensive, diverse, appropriately located minefields covered by barrage fire (Jones et al., 2024). The lack of success of the Ukrainian troops resulted in Russia going on the offensive, which, despite large losses in personnel and equipment, has been progressing steadily since March 2024.

Therefore, the will and nature of support by NATO countries and partner countries for Ukraine remains an open question. Since 2016, it has been provided with the Comprehensive Assistance Package (CAP), which was adopted during the meeting of heads of state and government in Warsaw (The CAP). In this way, the Alliance has helped Ukraine transform its security and defence sector, providing advice at the strategic level through the NATO representation in Ukraine, NATO headquarters, practical support for many programmes and initiatives dedicated to building Ukraine's military capabilities, defence capabilities in the broadest sense. The Ukraine CAP Trust Fund has become part of this aid package. It was launched in 2014 and was included in the aid package in 2021. It remained focused on providing resources to support capability development and sustainable capacity building in key areas.

In 2021, NATO consolidated and converted all pre-existing trust funds supporting Ukraine into a single CAP trust fund in Ukraine. The Trust Fund of Ukraine allows for fundraising to provide Ukraine with short-term non-lethal military assistance and long-term capacity-building support in areas such as: (1) Command, Control, Communications and Computers (C4) to help Ukraine reorganise and modernise its C4 structures and capabilities. (2) Medical rehabilitation, the purpose of which is to provide patients with long-term benefits, services, m.in. active and released Ukrainian soldiers, women and civilian personnel of the defence and security sector. (3) A professional development programme aimed at developing the skills of civilians working in defence and security institutions of Ukraine. Since February 2022, the fund has provided Ukraine with combat rations, fuel materials (including jet fuel), clothing (including winter clothing and military boots), medical supplies (m.in. first aid kits, pharmaceuticals and ambulances), shelters and generators, chemical, biological, radiological and nuclear (CBRN) detectors and safeguards, explosives removal (EOD) and demining equipment, anti-drone equipment and communication systems (including enhanced communications) (NATO, 2024).

In 2023, during a meeting of heads of state and government in Vilnius, the allies agreed to further develop the aid package, transforming it into a long-term aid programme for Ukraine, based on sustainable and predictable financing. Its objectives are multi-domain and include ensuring that Ukraine continues its transition towards full interoperability with NATO, including its transformation to NATO standards, training and doctrines as it develops its capabilities, as agreed in NATO's jointly developed initial interoperability requirements. In addition, reform Ukraine's defence procurement system to align it with NATO best practices and promote greater efficiency, accountability and transparency.

This is complemented by the creation of the NATO–Ukraine Joint Analysis, Training and Education Centre (JATEC) in Bydgoszcz, Poland, to identify and apply lessons learned from Russia's war against Ukraine and contribute to increased interoperability. New joint actions were also launched to support Ukraine's self-defence through the first NATO–Ukraine Innovation Roadmap. In addition, continue to support Ukraine's self-defence with essential non-lethal equipment and supplies through the CAP, including contributions from NATO partners. The activities also include the reconstruction of destroyed military infrastructure (including three training grounds), demining the territory of Ukraine and strengthening its own capabilities in this area. There is also an emphasis on the rehabilitation of wounded personnel of the armed forces and security forces and their return to service or civilian life, which includes many projects organised under the Human Centric Framework programme (NATO, 2024).

On 9–11 July 2024, at a meeting of heads of state and government in Washington, D.C., Allies agreed to establish NATO Security Assistance and Training for Ukraine. The aim is to coordinate the provision of military equipment and training to Ukraine by NATO member states and partner countries and to provide logistical support. The sustainable consolidation of security assistance to Ukraine, providing strengthened, predictable and coherent support in the long term (Graca, J., & Rudnik, F. 2024, July 17). In Washington, NATO pledged long-term security assistance to Ukraine. It includes support for it with USD 40 billion per year and includes the purchase of military equipment for Ukraine; in-kind support provided to Ukraine; costs related to the maintenance, logistics and transport of military equipment for Ukraine; military training costs for Ukraine; operational costs related to the provision of military support to Ukraine; investments and support for Ukraine's defence infrastructure and industry; all contributions to the NATO Trust Funds for Ukraine, including non-lethal assistance. Ukraine's needs in this area are demanding and should be met by the North Atlantic Alliance on a regular basis (Washington Summit Declaration, 2024). According to expert Leon Komornicki, the Ukrainian army needs about 1,200 155 artillery systems and 3.5 million 155 mm shells in order to hit the Russian army in 80 percent and move from defensive to offensive operations. The Ukrainian army should obtain about 400 HIMARS rocket artillery systems, ATACMS long-range missiles and 160 F16 or other multirole aircraft. Such a number would cause an anti-access barrier, cutting off Russians from their own resources from Russian territory. The Ukrainians also do not have a sufficient number of kamikaze drones, which they need about 1000 units per year (Gen, 2024).

A constant element of this war are Russian attacks on Ukrainian critical infrastructure as well as civilian targets. In response, Ukraine is attacking elements of Russia's critical infrastructure, primarily energy installations and those used to supply the Russian army. Logistics, both military and civilian, is a key factor in determining their capabilities for both sides. In the case of Ukraine, it plays a greater role because it determines the quality of life of society and the survival and defence of the armed forces on the battlefield. This includes proper supply management, an effective system, both civilian and military, including m.in, the reconstruction of material and personnel reserves, in which the Energy

Community of the European Union, including some NATO countries belonging to this community, has its share. It implements a total of six projects in this area: Ukraine support activities in milestones, Ukraine Energy Support Fund, Ukraine Support Task Force, Ukraine Whistleblower hotline, Ukraine Energy Market Observatory, Ukraine Legal Support Platform (Ukraine Support Activities, 2024). In the context of attacks on energy infrastructure from Ukraine, the Russian Federation has gained an advantage by using its own resources, as well as supplies from China and other countries, such as Iran or North Korea, which do not respect the sanctions imposed on it by the West. This assistance is used to successively renew attacks on military and civilian targets of Ukraine.

The effect of Russian attacks on critical infrastructure and civilian targets is the lowering of the morale of Ukrainian society, the violation of the will of its readiness to defend the country, reinforced by disinformation campaigns in the media. This is the result of the introduction of civil society standards in Ukraine only after 2014, after the Euro Maidan, which were not consistently implemented (Harasymiw, 2019). The effects of Russia's coordinated actions, both kinetic and propaganda, are, m.in, problems with mobilisation to the Ukrainian army, or the strengthening of corruption processes among Ukrainians. The strategic goal of Russia's actions is to deprive the current Ukrainian government of legitimacy, to destabilise the internal situation as a result of protests and social unrest, and above all to win as a result of internal disintegration, allowing pro-Russian groups to take power. In fact, turning Ukraine and its society back from the path of integration with the European Union, and thus squandering several decades of Ukrainian transformation initiated by the Orange Revolution, but which can only exist thanks to the institutions of this country (Samokhvalov & Strelkov, 2020). That is why it is so important to implement Western standards in Ukraine (Králiková, 2021).

Russia's Experience Against Ukraine for NATO

Between 2022 and 2024, the message in Russia's information war against Western countries was significantly weakened and then devalued just before the second phase of the conflict. Since November 2021, representatives of U.S. President Joe Biden's administration have extensively reported on the deployment of Russian troops along the borders with Ukraine in preparation for an invasion of the country. As part of the disinformation campaign and psychological warfare, Russia systematically denied this until its aggression on 24 February 2022. At the same time, actions were carried out by the United States against the Russian authorities and allies to stop the Russian strike. NATO has also been involved in them. As a result, conditions have been created in which Russia, after the start of the second phase of the war against Ukraine on 24 February 2022, failed to convince international opinion that it is not an aggressor despite its efforts to do so. The Russian message was devalued after the scale of the murders of civilians in Bucha, Irpin, and Hostomel and was discovered after the recapture of the areas around Kyiv as a result of the successful Ukrainian counteroffensive in April 2022. As a result of this situation, Russia's information warfare in the international message has been focused on:

- gaining influence on the course of political actions, cooperation between the West and Ukraine – resolving the conflict in favour of Russia in the 'hearts and minds' of the societies of the European Union countries and the North Atlantic Alliance.
- undermining the trust of Western societies in the government in information messages leading to a weakening of the will to support Ukraine politically, economically and militarily.
- disavowing the international position of Western countries in relation to the countries of the Global South in order to maintain their political neutrality, which would allow, for m.in, to circumvent the economic sanctions imposed on Russia.
- undermining the unity of the North Atlantic Alliance countries, their readiness to provide mutual military assistance, especially to the countries of the so called eastern flank.
- taking advantage of the differences in economic interests between the European Union countries and Ukraine in terms of opening transport and agricultural markets to Ukrainian companies.

In response to Russia's actions, the U.S. Congress in 2022–2024 undertook and implemented a number of measures to limit Russia's influence, continuing and strengthening earlier ones. Firstly, he has assisted Ukraine by providing it with financial support. Secondly, it strengthened international sanctions. Thirdly, it has implemented procedures for the confiscation of Russian property located abroad. Fourthly, it implemented responsibility for war crimes. Fifthly, it has strengthened the position of the United States and NATO in the field of collective defence on the European continent (Welt et al., 2024). The countries of the North Atlantic Alliance have joined these activities.

Along with disinformation activities, the Russian Federation has taken active measures with the use of migrants against NATO countries located on the borders of Belarus and Russia, launching an attack on alliance countries below the threshold of war (Fraszka, 2021). Since May 2021, groups of people from the Middle East, North Africa, and other regions have begun to emerge looking for opportunities to get to European Union countries, primarily those with a high level of social care and social benefits (Walsh, 2024). At the same time, the pressure of migrants has become the result of the ability to transport them to Belarus, preparations to cross the borders in places that are not allowed to do so, and the accompanying narrative about human rights violations by the countries bordering Belarus and Russia. By conducting synergistic activities in different geographical areas, that is in Europe, in Asia, Syria, in North and Central Africa, in the Balkans, the Russian Federation has gained the ability to exert influence by increasing or intensifying the phenomena determining the security and internal stability of NATO countries and geographical regions bordering it.

Since 2008, the North Atlantic Alliance has successively faced the assertive policy of the Russian Federation. Its intensification since 2014 has resulted in the adoption of many functional solutions. These were arrangements on the transformation of organisational structures, action plans, and the deployment of forces of the alliance countries in the countries of NATO's eastern flank (Connell, M., Lennox, B., & Schwartz, P. 2023). The essence of these solutions is to ensure the security and freedom of all members by political and military means based on the United Nations Charter and the Washington Treaty. The security of NATO countries on both sides of the Atlantic has been and has remained indivisible, based on solidarity, shared goals and responsibility. They ensure that the alliance continues to be a source of stability in an unstable world (Karásek, 2020).

When considering the scope of Russian activities in land, air, sea, space, and cyber areas, it is necessary to indicate strategic goals related to the subordination of Ukraine to Russia. Elements of force, political terror combined with military terror are expected to bring Russia results in the form of shifting its borders and subordinating selected geographical areas (Suslov, 2018). Following the compilation of diplomatic and military actions:

1. The takeover and incorporation of Ukrainian territories in the form of Kharkiv, Luhansk, Donetsk, Kherson, Mykolaiv and Odessa into the territory of Russia, and the creation of a federal union state with Russia from the remaining territories (Düben, 2023).
2. Reunification of Transnistria with Moldova and its incorporation as a union state into the Russian Federation (Pieper, 2018).
3. Pushing NATO out of Finland, Sweden, Denmark, Lithuania, Latvia, Estonia along with the subordination of areas belonging to these countries, including m.in Åland Islands, Gotland, Bornholm (Szumski, 2024).
4. Pushing NATO out of Norway and subordinating the country's area, that is Svalbard (Staalesen, 2024).
5. The expulsion of NATO from Polish, Slovakia, the Czech Republic, Hungary, Romania, and Bulgaria on the basis of recognizing Russia's rights to a special sphere of influence in Europe. (Beebe et al., 2024)

As a result, a change in the European security architecture with the elimination of NATO as a tool and a form of projection of American policy in Europe, a political weakening of the unity of the European Union (its decomposition) and giving form to a special relationship between this organisation and the Russian Federation. The consequence would be the restoration of Russia's international position as a leading subject of international relations and its special guarantee for participation in European affairs. In addition, a strengthened geopolitical position in relations with China on the basis of Russia's dominant relations with Western Europe – the European Union in political and economic terms, and the countries of the global south within the BRICS (in the extended geopolitical formula of this organisation).

The political goals listed above are pursued in the form of diplomatic and military actions. The successes of the Russian Federation include the fact that the countries of the global south and their societies remain neutral towards Russia's war against Ukraine (Foa et al., 2024). This allows it to participate in international trade bypassing the sanctions of the broadly defined West, with the participation of Japan and South Korea. In addition, the successive impact on the form of international relations based on the Russian imperative of their formula leading to a change in the architecture of international security both on the European continent and in the global formula with the participation of China, India, and other countries (Dodds et al., 2024).

The indicated actions of the Russian Federation, coordinated in its agreement with China, make it possible to determine their consequences for the North Atlantic Alliance.

Firstly, in the form of an intensifying political confrontation between NATO and Russia, culminating in a possible armed clash in one of the regions indicated above. The course and scale of this confrontation depends on many factors, the most important of which are the degree of political and social integration or disintegration of the North Atlantic Alliance countries subjected to Russian disinformation activities, using all means to undermine the political legitimacy of the ruling elites, as well as allied military actions (Frangeul-Alves et al., 2024). The aim of Russia's actions is to consolidate the uncertainty of Western societies and to permanently undermine their morale and social integrity in political and economic terms. The tools used for this are varied, from pointing out their impoverishment as a result of the European Union's policy (e.g. the Green New Deal), through population migrations and the consequences caused by it in the form of social unrest, to the delegitimisation of actions supporting collective conduct, policy, for example towards the countries of NATO's eastern flank or Ukraine.

Secondly, in the form of the degree of political and military integration or disintegration of the countries of the North Atlantic Alliance, with the participation of the United States as the leading entity generating the objectives of NATO's policy and strategy, guaranteeing support in every security domain (land, sea, air, space, cyber). The final form of the test of strength with the United States, the broadly defined West, with the participation of South Korea and Japan, may be the use of tactical nuclear weapons and their targeted use against one of the countries of NATO's eastern flank (the most advantageous due to their rank in the organisation would be Norway, Finland, Sweden, Poland, Romania). Taking into account the potential retaliation from the United States (e.g. against the Kaliningrad Oblast or, more likely, Belarus), the effect would still be calculated as intimidating Western societies, confirming the Russian Federation's determination to achieve its goals related to changing the European and global security architecture.

Thirdly, increased or decreased pressure on the borderland of NATO and European Union countries in the form of border incidents (migration of people to the territories of countries such as Norway, Finland, Estonia, Latvia, Lithuania, Poland, Mediterranean countries) aimed at deepening social and political unrest.

Fourthly, the deployment of weapons in the form of nuclear weapons, as well as other forms of nuclear weapons, near the borders of the countries of NATO's eastern flank in Russia (Kaliningrad Oblast) and Belarus as an element of escalation of armaments and intimidation.

Conclusion

With the Russian Federation continuing its war against Ukraine, political, economic and military issues on the European continent and in other parts of the world have become key for the countries of the North Atlantic Alliance. Among them, we can point out political ones concerning:

1. the political leadership of the United States in the broadly defined Western bloc with the participation of NATO and European Union countries, as well as Australia, New Zealand, Japan, South Korea, aiming, m.in other things, to maintain the current form of the international security architecture based on American alliances (Flockhart & Korosteleva, 2022). The political and military challenges and threats created by the Russian Federation, as well as the political, military and economic ones created by China, generate a formula for change (Arts, 2024). The result is to determine the direction of action of the broadly understood bloc of Western countries. It concerns a comprehensive approach inscribed in the formula of changes in the global economy 4.0 and 5.0 and the policy pursued not only on the European continent but also in Asia, Africa, and other parts of the globe.
2. Support for the policy based on forms of international cooperation, from the United Nations to regional organizations combining the approach of Western countries with those located in the global South. The point is to maintain and strengthen the existing international security architecture with the leadership role of the United States. The argument and, at the same time, the field of cooperation is the political economy shared by the countries of the broadly understood West, including South Korea and Japan.

In the geoeconomically terms, political and economic support for Ukraine with leading role of the United States, the European Union as well as from the International Monetary Fund, created its resilience. In geopolitically terms, Ukraine's military resilience was created by United States and NATO states. In the military dimension, providing assistance to Ukraine from NATO and the EU. In addition, the correlation of political, economic and military activities of American, European and non-European countries in the form of supplies of weapons, ammunition, logistical support for the armed forces of Ukraine. Actions in the intra-allied dimension, dictated by the experience of Russia's war against Ukraine, include, m.in:

- ensuring adequate financing of military spending, at least 2% of the country's GDP.
- creating mobilisation capabilities and strengthening the conditions for resilience in every domain of the Alliance's operations, that is social, economic (including food and energy).
- development of NATO's operational capabilities in the following domains: land, air, sea, space, cyber, along with interoperability in each of them at the level of the entire alliance and with the participation of individual member states.

- Continuously and actively countering Russian disinformation and propaganda in strengthening national security and defence, involving a variety of actors that should work together to ensure a given level of resilience (Christie & Berzina, 2022).

Taking into account the above, additional elements are those that are strictly military in nature and which will allow NATO to strengthen operational capabilities in various dimensions in a synergistic and holistic way, taking into account the form of the emerging conflict with Russia and, in the future, with China.

The formula of NATO's strategic activities towards the conduct of the Russian Federation, as an element of 'lessons learned', should take into account:Constant, flexible in terms of forms strategic communication addressed to the societies of the North Atlantic Alliance with the participation of expert centres of individual member states, taking into account their social and cultural specificity. The essence of the message should be to clearly indicate the common goals of NATO countries. In addition, the ways of their implementation in order to ensure the development of democratic societies, aware of responsibility for their fate and the fate of humanity.Development and strengthening of forms of political and military cooperation within the North Atlantic Alliance, as well as between NATO and the European Union with the participation of partner countries in each of the domains (land, sea, air, space, cyber), as well as in the economic dimension through the implementation of joint armament programs, their acquisition, and the development of capabilities in the formula of a flexible response to challenges and threats, regardless of their source. In addition, the adoption of the escalation of Russian military actions as the norm, in response to which the formula of sharing tactical nuclear weapons (Nuclear Scharing) should be extended to include the countries of NATO's eastern flank.A flexible formula of political and military action combined with economic pressure in response to the challenges and threats generated by the Russian Federation with the participation of the countries supporting it, regardless of their formula or geographical location.Continuous strengthening of defence readiness and capabilities in the field of effective response to military and political actions of Russia and its allies as a factor of military deterrence in every domain: cyber, land, air, space, sea.

Taking into account the interdependence of events, phenomena, processes, trends in different regions of the planet, sharing responsibility within NATO between European members and the United States is a requirement of the effectiveness of the alliance. The key factors are joint actions to strengthen the resil ience of societies, defence programmes, their implementation by all Member States along with the projection of development over time. The requirement not only of this moment is the correlation of political, economic and military actions. They will determine the security of NATO countries in the next decades of the 21st century, which is the result of the transformation of the security environment generated by countries such as the Russian Federation and China, but also the condition and importance of liberal democracy in the 21st century.

References

Arts, S. (2024, August 18). *Vulnerable, strategically critical, and underfunded*. https://www.gmfus.org/download/article/23509

Bartosiewicz, M., Chawryło, K., Domańska, M., Menkiszak, M., Rodkiewicz, W., Rudnik, F., Wilk, A., Wiśniewska, I., & Żochowski, P. (2024). *Rosja po dwóch latach pełnoskalowej wojny krucha stabilność i narastająca agresywność, Raport OSW, Warszawa*, pp. 22–24.

Baumann, M. (2020). 'Propaganda Fights' and 'Disinformation Campaigns': The discourse on information warfare in Russia-West relations. *Contemporary Politics*, *26*(3), 288–307.

Baumann, M. (2023). The impact of logistics on the Russian invasion of Ukraine. *Journal of Strategic Studies*, *46*(2), 245–267.

Beebe, G., Episkopos, M., & Lieven, A. (2024, August 18). *Right-sizing the Russian threat to Europe*. https://quincyinst.org/research/right-sizing-the-russian-threat-to-europe/#

Bronk, J. (2023). *Russian combat air strengths and limitations: Lessons from Ukraine*. Retrieved July 12, 2024, from https://www.cna.org/reports/2023/04/Russian-Combat-Air-Strengths-and-Limitations.pdf

Bronk, J., Reynold, N., & Watling, J. (2024, September 4). *The Russian air war and Ukrainian requirements for air defence*. https://rusi.org/explore-our-research/publications/special-resources/russian-air-war-and-ukrainian-requirements-air-defence

Bossuyt, F., & Kaczmarski, M. (2021). Russia and China between cooperation and competition at the regional and global level. *Eurasian Geography and Economics*, *62*(5–6), 539–556.

Bowen, A. S. (2024). Russian counteroffensives in Ukraine: A strategic assessment. *International Security Review*, *49*(1), 45–69.

Bowsher, H. (2023). *Air denial lessons from Ukraine*. Retrieved August 31, 2024, from https://www.usni.org/magazines/proceedings/2023/september/air-denial-lessons-ukraine

Bremer, M. K., & Grieco, K. A. (2022). *In denial about denial: Why Ukraine's air success should worry the West, war on the rocks*. Retrieved November 28, 2023, from https://warontherocks.com/2022/06/in-denial-about-denial-why-ukraines-air-success-should-worry-the-west/

Calmels, C. (2020). NATO's 360-degree approach to security: Alliance cohesion and adaptation after the Crimean crisis. *European Security*, *29*(4), 416–435.

Christie, E. H., & Berzina, K. (2022). *NATO and societal resilience: All hands on deck in an age of war*. Retrieved August 18, 2024, from https://www.gmfus.org/sites/default/files/2022-07/NATO%20and%20Societal%20Resilience%20All%20Hands%20on%20Deck%20in%20an%20Age%20of%20War.pdf

Connell, M., Lennox, B., & Schwartz, P. (2023). *Training in the Russian armed forces an assessment of recent reforms and their impact on Russian operations in Ukraine*. Retrieved September 4, 2024, from https://www.cna.org/reports/2023/09/training-in-the-russian-armed-forces

Dalsjö, R., Jonsson, M., & Norberg, J. (2022). A brutal examination: Russian military capability in light of the Ukraine war. *Survival*, *64*(3), 7–28.

DePetris, D. R. (2022). *The strengths and weaknesses of the Russian military*. Retrieved September 4, 2024, from https://nationalinterest.org/feature/strengths-and-weaknesses-russian-military-201983

Dodds, K., Taylor, Z., Akbari, A., Broto, V. C., Detterbeck, K., Inverardi-Ferri, C., & Woon, C. Y. (2023). The Russian invasion of Ukraine: Implications for politics, territory and governance. *Territory, Politics, Governance*, *11*(8), 1519–1536.

Düben, B. A. (2023). Revising history and 'Gathering the Russian Lands': Vladimir Putin and Ukrainian nationhood.*LSE Public Policy Review*, *3*(1), 1–12.

Engvall, J. (2020). Military confidence-building in crises: Lessons from Georgia and Ukraine. *Defence Studies*, *20*(3), 250–270.

Engvall, J. (2023). Military failures in Ukraine: A case study on Russia's operational art. *Defense and Security Analysis*, *39*(1), 85–102.

Flockhart, T., & Korosteleva, E. A. (2022). War in Ukraine: Putin and the multi-order world. *Contemporary Security Policy*, *43*(3), 466–481.

Foa, R. S., Mollat, M., Isha, H., Romero-Vidal, X., Evans, D., & Klassen, A. J. (2024). *A world divided Russia, China and the West, centre for the future of democracy* (pp. 2–28). University of Cambridge.

Foltynova, K. (2022). *Protecting the skies: How does Ukraine defend against Russian missiles?*https://www.rferl.org/a/ukraine-missile-defense-weapons-charts-russia/32192132.html

Fox, A. C. (2022). *Reflections on Russia's 2022 invasion of Ukraine: Combined arms warfare, the Battalion tactical group and wars in a fishbowl*. Retrieved September 4, 2024, from https://www.ausa.org/publications/reflections-russias-2022-invasion-ukraine-combined-arms-warfare-battalion-tactical

Frangeul-Alves, A., de Hoop Scheffer, A., Hsakou, A., & Weber, W. (2024, August 18). *Transatlantic trends Washington, DC Ankara Belgrade Berlin Brussels Bucharest Paris Warsaw takeaways from public opinion for NATO's path forward*. https://www.gmfus.org/sites/default/files/2024-07/Transatlantic%20Trends_Takeaways%20From%20Public%20Opinion%20for%20NATO%E2%80%99s%20Path%20Forward%20.pdf

Fraszka, B. (2021). *Sytuacja na granicy polsko-białoruskiej: przyczyny, aspekt geopolityczny, narracje*. Retrieved August 16, 2024, from https://warsawinstitute.org/pl/sytuacja-na-granicy-polsko-bialoruskiej-przyczyny-aspekt-geopolityczny-narracje/

Galamison, M. S., & Petersen, M. B. (2023). Failures of the Russian aerospace forces in Ukraine. *Air & Space Operations Review*, *2*(3), 4–19.

Gen. (2024, July 23). *Komornicki: armii rosyjskiej nie chodzi o zdobywanie terytorium*. https://www.onet.pl/biznes/biznesalert/gen-komornicki-armii-rosyjskiej-nie-chodzi-o-zdobywanie-terytorium/z6hvlvv,30bc1058?2376

Gibadło, L. (2024, April 9). *W obliczu kolejnej Zeitenwende. RFN wobec perspektywy zwycięstwa Trumpa*. https://www.osw.waw.pl/sites/default/files/komentarz_588.pdf

Giles, K. (2022). *Russia's military capabilities and limitations*. Chatham House. Retrieved July 23, 2024, from https://www.chathamhouse.org/2022/02/russias-military-capabilities-and-limitations

Goodwin, J. (2024, August 31). *Allied air command lessons from Ukraine – Joint air power competence centre*. https://www.japcc.org/articles/allied-air-command-lessons-from-ukraine/

Graca, J., & Rudnik, F. (2024, July 17). *Nowy pakiet wsparcia USA dla Ukrainy i groźba konfiskaty rosyjskich aktywów*. https://www.osw.waw.pl/pl/publikacje/analizy/2024-04-24/nowy-pakiet-wsparcia-usa-dla-ukrainy-i-grozba-konfiskaty-rosyjskich

Greenberg, A. (2021). *SANDWORM Nowa era cyberwojny i polowanie na najbardziej niebezpiecznych hakerów Kremla, Wydawnictwo PWN, Warszawa*.

Gressel, G. (2022). *Ukraine's military preparedness before the invasion*. Retrieved April 9, 2024, from https://ecfr.eu/article/ukraines-military-preparedness-before-the-invasion/

Götz, E., & Staun, J. (2022). Why Russia attacked Ukraine: Strategic culture and radicalized narratives. *Contemporary Security Policy*, *43*(3), 482–497.

Gunzinger, K. (2024, August 31). *The significance of air superiority: The Ukraine-Russia war, Mitchell Institute for Aerospace Studies*. https://mitchellaerospacepower.org/the-significance-of-air-superiority-the-ukraine-russia-war/

Hanson, M. (1998). Russia and NATO expansion: The uneasy basis of the founding act. *European Security*, *7*(2), 13–29.

Harasymiw, B. (2019). Civil society as an anti-corruption actor in post-Euromaidan Ukraine. *Canadian Slavonic Papers*, *61*(3), 288–320.

Helwig, N. (2019). Germany in European diplomacy: Minilateralism as a tool for leadership. *German Politics*, *29*(1), 25–41.

Henriksen, D., & Bronk, J. (2024). *The air war in Ukraine: The first year of conflict*. Taylor & Francis.

Husain, A. (2024, August 31). *Learning lessons: Air warfare in Ukraine*. https://medium.com/@amirhusain_tx/learning-lessons-air-warfare-in-ukraine-93cfb14aa1b8

Ichaso, R. (2023). *Russian air force's performance in Ukraine – Joint air power competence centre*. Retrieved August 31, 2024, from https://www.japcc.org/articles/russian-air-forces-performance-in-ukraine-air-operations-the-fall-of-a-myth/

Integrated Air and Missile Defence. (2024, August 31). https://rusi.org/explore-our-research/topics/null

Javelin, J., & Hawn, M. (2022). *The Russian Blitzkrieg: How the initial offensive unraveled, war on the rocks*. Retrieved September 4, 2024, from https://warontherocks.com/2022/05/the-russian-blitzkrieg-how-the-initial-offensive-unraveled/

Jensen, B. (2024, August 31). *Extending air defense East*. https://www.csis.org/analysis/extending-air-defense-east

Jensen B., & Hoffman, E. (2024, August 18). *Victory in Ukraine starts with addressing five strategic problems*. https://csis-website-prod.s3.amazonaws.com/s3fs-public/2024-05/240515_Jensen_Victory_Ukraine.pdf?VersionId=Z.f9IB3u0biHu6rgtv6.G77hzyprEKL

Jones, S. G., Palmer, A., & Bermudez Jr., J. S. (2024, July 17). *Ukraine's offensive operations: Shifting the offense-defense balance*. https://www.csis.org/analysis/ukraines-offensive-operations-shifting-offense-defense-balance

Karásek, T. (2020). Between Pastiche and sampling: NATO's strategic adaptation to Russian revisionism. *Europe-Asia Studies*, *72*(6), 996–1009.

Kofman, M. (2022). *The Ukrainian military's evolution and modernization*. Retrieved July 17, 2024, from https://www.cna.org/reports/2022/the-ukrainian-militarys-evolution-and-modernization

Králiková, M. (2021). Importing EU norms: The case of anti-corruption reform in Ukraine. *Journal of European Integration*, *44*(2), 245–260.

Macrotrends. (2024, June 19). https://www.macrotrends.net/global-metrics/countries/RUS/russia/military-spending-defense-budget

Mälksoo, M. (2022). The postcolonial moment in Russia's war against Ukraine. *Journal of Genocide Research*, *25*(3–4), 471–481.

Marinko, A., Sead, C., & Božović D. (2024, September 4). *Analysis of land army maintenance techniques in the war in Ukraine*. https://www.armyupress.army.mil/Journals/Military-Review/English-Edition-Archives/May-June-2023/Land-Army-Maintenance-Techniques/

McKew, M. (2022). *Ukraine's defiance: How the war unfolded*. Retrieved September 4, 2024, from https://www.politico.com/news/2022/03/03/ukraine-defiance-war-00013687

Méheut, C. (2024, March 5). Shift in Russian tactics intensifies air war in Ukraine. *The New York Times*. Retrieved August 31, 2024, from https://www.nytimes.com/2024/03/05/world/europe/ukraine-war-russia-planes.html

Melkadze, A. (2024, April 5). *Annual gross national income (GNI) volume in Russia from 2013 to 2022*. https://www.statista.com/statistics/1059680/gni-of-russia/

Mitrokhin, N. (2023). Defending Kyiv: Ukrainian strategies and tactics. *Slavic Review*, *82*(2), 333–354.

Muradov, I. (2022). The Russian hybrid warfare: The cases of Ukraine and Georgia. *Defence Studies*, *22*(2), 168–191.

NATO 2022 Strategic Concept Adopted by Heads of State and Government at the NATO Summit in Madrid 29 June 2022. (2024, June 19). https://www.nato.int/nato_static_fl2014/assets/pdf/2022/6/pdf/290622-strategic-concept.pdf

Natorski, M. (2020). United we stand in metaphors: EU authority and incomplete politicisation of the crisis in Ukraine. *Journal of European Integration*, *42*(5), 733–749.

Patterson, K. S. (2024, August 31). *Reevaluating modern warfare: Lessons from Ukraine's air defense strategies*. The Defense Post. https://www.thedefensepost.com/2024/07/05/ukraine-air-defense-strategies/

Petrenko, L. (2024, August 16). *Як Україна готувалася до вторгнення*. https://wszystko-conajwazniejsze.pl/lubko-petrenko-Як-Україна-готувалася-до-вторгнення

Pieper, M. (2018). *Russkiy Mir*: The geopolitics of Russian compatriots abroad. *Geopolitics*, *25*(3), 756–779.

Piotrowski, M. (2022). *Effectiveness of Ukraine's air defence, Polski Instytut Spraw Międzynarodowych*. Retrieved August 31, 2024, from https://pism.pl/publications/effectiveness-of-ukraines-air-defence

Pokorzyński, M. (2022). *Co oznaczają symbole na rosyjskich pojazdach? Ukraina rozszyfrowała znaki*. Retrieved August 13, 2024, from https://www.auto-swiat.pl/wiadomosci/aktualnosci/rosyjskie-pojazdy-wojskowe-maja-dziwne-symbole-ukraina-rozszyfrowala-te-znaki/cngdbn0

Plokhy, S. (2024). *Rosja-Ukraina. Największe starcie XXI wieku, Znak, Warszawa.*

Reynolds, N. (2023). Phases of the war in Ukraine: An analytical overview. *Journal of Military History*, *87*(3), 788–812.

Rodkiewicz, W. (2020). *Roska zamraża stosunki z NATO*. Retrieved August 13, 2024, from https://www.osw.waw.pl/pl/publikacje/analizy/2021-10-20/rosja-zamraza-stosunki-z-nato

Rodkiewicz, W. (2023). *Gest bezsilności. Rosja wypowiada Traktat CFE*. Retrieved August 13, 2024, from https://www.osw.waw.pl/pl/publikacje/analizy/2023-05-17/gest-bezsilnosci-rosja-wypowiada-traktat-cfe

Sagild, R. Å., & Hsiung, C. W. (2024). Chinese re-examinations of Russia? The strategic partnership in the wake of Russia's war against Ukraine. *Journal of Contemporary China*, 1–16.

Samokhvalov, V., & Strelkov, A. (2020). Cross-dimensional network of democracy promotion: Public administration reform in post-Euromaidan Ukraine. *Journal of European Integration*, *43*(7), 799–814.

Sankaran, J. (2024). The failures of Russian aerospace forces in the Russia–Ukraine war and the future of air power. *Journal of Strategic Studies*, 1–28.

Shapps, G., & Sunak, R. (2023). *30,000 Ukrainian recruits trained in largest UK military training effort since Second World War*. Retrieved September 4, 2024, from https://www.google.com/search?q=https%3A%2F%2Fwww.gov.uk%2Fgovernment%2Fnews%2F30000-ukrainian-recruits-trained-in-largest-uk-military-training-effort-since-second-world-war&sca_esv=c7a01837b1eb8e0f&hl=pl&sxsrf=ADLYWIJzWtOrNquoJFeoVr8I4T9M51_8WA%3A1725446171559&source=hp&ei=GzjYZo_3HoCWxc8Pp86kKQ&iflsig=AL9hbdgAAAAAZthGK-B7ZbTxzCcH1UZJSmrMi9HkIdOq&ved=0ahUKEwjP8Ibxi6mIAxUAS_EDHScnKQUQ4dUDCBk&uact=5&oq=https%3A%2F%2Fwww.gov.uk%2Fgovernment%2Fnews%2F30000-ukrainian-recruits-trained-in-largest-uk-military-training-effort-since-second-world-war&gs_lp=Egdnd3Mtd2l6IoEBaHR0cHM6Ly93d3cuZ292LnVrL2dvdmVybm1lbnQvbmV3cy8zMDAwMC11a3JhaW5pYW4tcmVjcnVpdHMtdHJhaW5lZC1pbi1sYXJnZXN0LXVrLW1pbGl0YXJ5LXRyYWluaW5nLWVmZm9ydC1zaW5jZS1zZWNvbmQtd29ybGQtd2FySABQAFgAcAB4AJABAJgBAKABAKoBALgBA8gBAPgBAvgBAZgCAKACAJgDAJIHAKAHAA&sclient=gws-wiz

Siddi, M. (2018). A contested Hegemon? Germany's leadership in EU relations with Russia. *German Politics*, *29*(1), 97–114.

Snegovaya, M. (2015). *Putin's information warfare in Ukraine Soviet origins of Russia's hybrid warfare* (pp. 9–21). Institute for the Study of War.

Snegovaya, M. (2022). *Putin thought Russia's military could capture Kyiv in 2 days, but it still hasn't in 20*. Retrieved September 4, 2024, from https://www.cnas.org/press/in-the-news/putin-thought-russias-military-could-capture-kyiv-in-2-days-but-it-still-hasnt-in-20

Staalesen, A. (2024). *Deputy Prime Minister sends warning to Oslo: Russian rights at Svalbard must not be challenged*. https://thebarentsobserver.com/en/2024/02/deputy-prime-minister-sends-warning-oslo-russian-rights-svalbard-must-not-be-challenged

Stoll, H., Hoehn, J., & Courtney, W. (2024, August 31). *Air defense shapes warfighting in Ukraine*. https://www.realcleardefense.com/articles/2024/02/22/air_defense_shapes_warfighting_in_ukraine_1013615.html

Suslov, M. (2018). "Russian World" concept: Post-soviet geopolitical ideology and the logic of "Spheres of Influence". *Geopolitics*, *23*(2), 330–353.

Szenes, Z. (2023). Reinforcing deterrence: Assessing NATO's 2022 strategic concept. *Defense & Security Analysis*, *39*(4), 539–560.

Szumski, Ch. (2024, August 16). *Russia's push to change Baltic Sea border sparks concern in the region*. https://www.euractiv.com/section/defence-and-security/news/russias-push-to-change-baltic-sea-border-sparks-concern-in-the-region/

Tardy, T. (2020). The risks of NATO's maladaptation. *European Security*, *30*(1), 24–42.

Tolz, V., & Hutchings, S. (2023). Truth with a Z: Disinformation, war in Ukraine, and Russia's contradictory discourse of imperial identity. *Post-Soviet Affairs*, *39*(5), 347–365.

Ukraine Support Activities. (2024, August 16). https://www.energy-community.org/Ukraine/overview.html

Walsh, N. P. (2024, June 20). *Belarus floods the European Union with migrants, taking a page out of Putin's playbook*. https://edition.cnn.com/2021/08/13/europe/belarus-lithuania-border-migrants-eu-cmd-intl/index.html

Watling, J., & Reynolds, N. (2023). The first year of war in Ukraine: Strategic and tactical shifts. *RUSI Journal*, *168*(4), 22–39.

Washington Summit Declaration issued by the NATO Heads of State and Government Participating in the Meeting of the North Atlantic Council in Washington, D.C. (2024, July 10).

Wiswesser, S. M. (2023). Potemkin on the Dnieper: The failure of Russian airpower in the Ukraine war. *Small Wars & Insurgencies*, *34*(7), 1205–1234.

Weber, P. (2023). *Ukraine's biggest victories and defeats in its war against Russia*. Retrieved September 4, 2024, from https://theweek.com/russo-ukrainian-war/1021250/ukraines-biggest-victories-and-defeats-in-its-war-against-russia

Welt, C., Belkin, P., Bowen, A. S., Nelson, R. M. (2024, August 16). *Russia's war on Ukraine: U.S. policy and the role of congress*. https://crsreports.congress.gov/product/pdf/IF/IF12277

Verville, F., & Buchatskiy, C. (2023). *Russia and Ukraine are locked into mutual air denial*. Retrieved August 16, 2024, from https://icds.ee/wpcontent/uploads/dlm_uploads/2023/10/ICDS_Brief_In_a_State_of_Denial_Verville_Buchatskiy_October_2023.pdf

Zampronha, D., & Albuquerque, A. (2024). Cheaper precision weapons: An exploratory study about the HESA Shahed 136. *Advances in Aerospace Science and Technology*, *9*(1), 40–59.

Chapter 6

Economic Defence and Readiness in Total Defence Systems: A Comparative Perspective

Ivan Okromtchedlishvili

Sulkhan-Saba Orbeliani University, Tbilisi, Georgia

Abstract

This chapter examines the concept of economic defence as a core pillar of total defence through a comparative analysis of national strategies adopted by Singapore, Israel, Sweden, and Switzerland. It explores how these countries integrate economic resilience, industrial policy, technological innovation, and public–private coordination into their national security frameworks. Building on international experiences, the chapter develops the concept of economic readiness by adapting Richard Betts' military readiness model to the economic domain. It introduces the key strategic questions of readiness for when, readiness for what, and readiness of what, and identifies the essential components of economic readiness, including financial stability, supply-chain resilience, infrastructure protection, human capital development, and innovation policy. The chapter provides a theoretical and comparative foundation for understanding economic defiance as a strategic capability within modern total defence systems.

Keywords: Economic defence; economic readiness; total defence; national security; resilience; innovation; public–private cooperation

JEL Codes: H56; D74; O38; O31; I25

Enhancing Transatlantic Solidarity in Collective Defence: Navigating Increased Defence Expenditures, Cyber Security, and Emerging Risks, 115–130

Published under exclusive licence by Emerald Publishing Limited
doi:10.1108/978-1-80686-259-720261006

Introduction

In an era marked by dynamic security landscapes, intricate economic interdependencies, and rapid technological advancements, the notion of total defence serves as a cornerstone in the national defence strategies of many nations. Within this framework, the concept of economic defence emerges as a pivotal pillar, emphasizing the critical role of economic resilience and preparedness in safeguarding national security.

This paper delves into the evolving paradigm of economic defence by examining international experiences and drawing insights from diverse national strategies, particularly those of Singapore, Israel, Sweden, and Switzerland. The comparative analysis of national security strategies provides valuable insights into the multifaceted nature of economic defence, highlighting the importance of comprehensive, adaptive approaches that integrate economic resilience with military preparedness, societal cohesion, and technological innovation. By synthesizing lessons learned from various national contexts, this study seeks to inform strategies for bolstering economic defence capabilities, strengthening resilience, and safeguarding shared interests in an increasingly complex and interconnected world.

By considering the case of Ukraine, the paper underscores the critical role of a strong economy, effective economic defence mechanisms, and international support in navigating crises. Proper organization of economic defence in peacetime significantly influences the sustainability of a country's economy and its ability to cope with crises or conflicts. Despite Ukraine's pre-existing economic challenges, exacerbated by the conflict, international support has played a vital role in stabilizing the economy and supporting recovery efforts. Key policies during wartime include fiscal discipline, monetary stability, financial sector resilience, governance reforms, and debt sustainability. While corruption and reconstruction pose ongoing challenges, optimism remains for Ukraine's post-conflict recovery, fueled by its resilience and continued international backing.

The chapter suggests a comprehensive definition of economic readiness, which refers to a nation's ability to swiftly mobilize economic resources to withstand crises, and discusses key questions that are critical to making the best decisions about economic readiness. Economic readiness involves assessing risks, contingency planning, ensuring financial stability, strengthening supply chains, diversifying industries, protecting infrastructure, maintaining reserves, developing human capital, fostering public–private cooperation, and promoting innovation and technology. Similar to military readiness, economic readiness requires accurate t iming, understanding potential crises, and preparing various economic sectors. Both concepts aim to ensure timely and effective responses to crises while upholding national security and economic stability.

Furthermore, amidst the backdrop of escalating defence expenditures and the omnipresent specter of cyber threats, the imperative for transatlantic solidarity in economic defence assumes unprecedented significance. As nations confront multifaceted security challenges that transcend traditional boundaries, the need for collaborative action among transatlantic partners becomes increasingly pronounced. The transatlantic alliance, rooted in shared values, interests, and commitments to collective defence, represents a cornerstone of global security architecture. By fostering collaboration and mutual assistance among allied nations, transatlantic partners can leverage resources efficiently, mitigate duplication of efforts, and enhance overall defence capabilities to address evolving security challenges effectively.

Moreover, as cyber threats continue to proliferate and pose significant risks to both national security and economic stability, cooperation in cybersecurity emerges as a critical component of collective economic defence. By sharing intelligence, best practices, and technological expertise, transatlantic partners can fortify their cyber defence capabilities, bolster resilience against emerging threats, and mitigate the disruptive impact of cyber incidents on economic activities.

In summary, this paper underscores the imperative for transatlantic solidarity in navigating the complexities of modern security challenges, emphasizing the importance of collective economic defence as a cornerstone of shared resilience and prosperity. By embracing a collaborative approach and drawing upon lessons learned from international experiences, transatlantic partners can forge a path toward enhanced security, stability, and prosperity in an ever-evolving global landscape.

Economic Defence: Overview of International Experience

In today's interconnected global economy, nations wield economic interdependencies and disparities as tools for influence, coercion, and dominance, even within alliances. This contemporary landscape is characterized by a spectrum of nuanced economic defence strategies, ranging from overt force actions such as lawfare and cyber-attacks to influential maneuvers like shaping standards and diplomatic initiatives, alongside efforts to bolster resilience and autonomy.

Within this context, a strategic economic defence approach emerges, encompassing several key pillars:

- Safeguarding economic interests through regulatory frameworks on foreign investments, robust counter-intelligence efforts, combating misinformation campaigns, and fostering political backing for exports.
- Ensuring access to vital resources through proactive measures, adaptive economic policies, and diplomatic or military interventions.
- Cultivating an enabling environment by reinforcing digital and technological sovereignty and advocating for equitable trade practices in international forums.
- Leveraging economic instruments for political security imperatives, which may involve actions such as countering proliferation, controlling technology transfers, imposing embargoes or sanctions, and utilizing economic leverage in diplomatic negotiations (IHEDN, 2023).

The proper organization of economic defence in peacetime largely determines the sustainability of the country's economy and its ability to survive in a crisis or conflict. This section of the paper delves into the experiences of selected nations like Singapore, Israel, Sweden, and Switzerland, shedding light on their approaches to navigating the complexities of economic defence in the modern era.

Singapore's Total Defence Model

Singapore's Total Defence model, established in 1984, has proven effective in addressing national security challenges, offering valuable policy insights for resource utilization and fostering a collective commitment to defence. Contrary to its name, the model didn't draw inspiration from Japan but was influenced by the defence and resilience strategies of smaller states like Sweden and Switzerland (Factsheet – About Total Defence, n.d.).

The Total Defence model in Singapore adopts a "whole-of-society" approach, involving government, business, and the public. Total Defence Day on February 15th annually commemorates Singapore's fall to the Japanese during World War II, underscoring citizens' collective responsibility for national defence. Initially focused on conventional military threats, the model evolved to encompass non-traditional security risks arising from within the nation.

The Total Defence model consists of several pillars: military defence, civil defence, economic defence, social defence, psychological defence, and digital defence. Initially, there were five, but a sixth was added in 2019 to address challenges from the digital revolution. There have been calls for a seventh pillar, "climate" defence, reflecting Singapore's vulnerability to climate change, especially rising sea levels. Each pillar is subordinate to the overarching goal of uniting all stakeholders for the defence of Singapore, given its small size, limited resources, and diverse population.

Public campaigns play a crucial role in inculcating Total Defence into the public psyche, targeting adults and instilling responsible societal values in children. The model has been invoked during various threats, including pandemics, economic turbulence, and environmental challenges, demonstrating its adaptability.

Singapore's Total Defence model can serve as a benchmark for other countries, particularly small ones, showcasing the importance of a comprehensive, multifaceted approach to national security. The success lies in its ability to address both traditional and nontraditional threats, unite diverse sectors, and instill a sense of collective responsibility among the population. This approach is particularly relevant in the face of emerging global challenges such as terrorism, natural disasters, pandemics, and disinformation campaigns.

The Economic Pillar of Total Defence Model

The Economic Pillar within Singapore's Total Defence model is a critical component that underscores the interdependence of economic strength and national security. The country recognizes the importance of a robust economy not only for prosperity but also for sustaining defence capabilities. Given its small size and lack of self-sufficiency, Singapore is deeply integrated into the global economy, making economic resilience crucial.

Economic defence refers to a comprehensive approach to organizing government, business, and industry to support the economy at all times, especially in times of war or the threat of war. While total defence encompasses a wide range of areas, including military, civil, social, and psychological aspects, economic defence specifically focuses on protecting a country's economic stability and security. The main goals of economic defence are to strengthen the competitiveness and attractiveness of the economy so that the country is special and relevant to the world; keeping the economy viable and sustainable, which will allow it to continue to function and quickly "recover" if the country faces a challenge (crisis or conflict) in the future (Factsheet – About Total Defence, n.d.).

The Economic Pillar addresses various aspects, including the need to stockpile essential supplies such as food, medication, and protective equipment to guard against international supply chain vulnerabilities. Furthermore, the scarcity of water resources, with Malaysia being the primary supplier, poses a significant challenge, making water security a fundamental component of economic and national security (Matthews & Bintang Timur, 2023).

Economic strength directly supports military capabilities, aligning with the belief that a strong economy is closely tied to military power and vice versa. The government adopts an interventionist approach to economic, industrial, and technological development, actively seeking dynamic comparative advantages. Over the years, Singapore has transitioned through different economic stages, emphasizing R&D, STEM activities, bio- and nano-technology, cyber, artificial intelligence, space, and digital systems in the current knowledge-intensive stage.

The government's proactive and interventionist stance in economic development is exemplified by the establishment of the Economic Development Board (EDB) in 1961. The EDB plays a crucial role in identifying and developing strategic industries, with a particular focus on defence and aerospace as strategically integrative sectors. This approach involves market interventions, government funding, business incentives, and the creation of industrial clusters, such as the advanced aerospace cluster at the Seletar Aerospace complex. The EDB's "visible hand" facilitates capability development by attracting major overseas players and local contractors to contribute to the dynamic aerospace cluster (Singapore Economic Development Board, 2020).

Singapore's push for technological advancement is influenced by the model of fellow small nation Israel, where "National Security through economic means" is seen as crucial for technological innovation and educational opportunities (Eisenkot & Siboni, 2019).

To further accelerate technological progress, Singapore established the Defence Science and Technology Agency (DSTA), which invests in deep technology companies through CapVista, its strategic investment arm. The DSTA serves as the central procurement agency for the Ministry of Defence, and the Singapore Armed Forces (DSTA, n.d.).

In summary, the Economic Pillar of Singapore's Total Defence model emphasizes the integral connection between economic strength, resilience, and national security. The proactive and interventionist approach of the government, as seen through the EDB and DSTA, contributes to Singapore's global competitiveness and readiness in advanced manufacturing and technology development.

National Security Through Economic Means: The Case of Israel

The economic component of national security is paramount in Israel's national security strategy, which is deeply rooted in the principles of Zeev Jabotinsky's "iron wall" concept and David Ben-Gurion's ideas on the interconnectedness of society, the economy, science, and technology. This strategy asserts that peace can only be achieved when Israel's adversaries realize the futility of violence and opt for dialogue instead. Central to this approach is the recognition that national security encompasses various dimensions beyond the purely military, including economic, social, political, and demographic factors (Segell, 2020).

Israel's economic security strategy focuses on leveraging economic development to strengthen society, education, and culture, thereby fostering social cohesion and solidarity. By positioning itself as an economic growth engine driven by technological innovation, Israel aims to contribute to global human development while building mutual interests and partnerships with international actors. Moreover, the development of economic infrastructures is tailored to meet national security needs, such as ensuring physical reinforcement, functional continuity, and energy sources to support the war effort (Segell, 2020).

Crucially, Israel's economy is structured to allocate resources for the development and maintenance of the security establishment, including military and civilian components. This includes investing in military research and development to maintain technological superiority and a competitive defence industry. By leveraging defence exports and research capabilities, Israel strengthens not only its security but also its political and economic ties globally.

In preparation for wartime, Israel emphasizes the uninterrupted function of critical economic infrastructure, diverting resources to support the military and ensuring the continuity of essential economic activities. This involves establishing systems to support businesses during wartime and facilitating reconstruction efforts afterward. Additionally, an inter-ministerial organizational system is vital to sustain necessary economic activities throughout periods of conflict (Eisenkot & Siboni, 2019).

Overall, Israel's economic defence strategy is integral to its broader national security framework, emphasizing the importance of economic development, innovation, and preparedness in safeguarding the country's interests and ensuring its long-term security and prosperity.

The Economic Component of Total Defence: Lessons from Sweden

Sweden's approach to national security, encapsulated within the framework of total defence, exemplifies a holistic strategy that encompasses military preparedness, civil resilience, and crucially, economic defence. With a rich historical context dating back to the post-war period, Sweden's total defence concept has evolved to adapt to changing geopolitical landscapes and industrial realities.

Total defence in Sweden is a multifaceted endeavor that involves the entire society, aiming to prepare the nation for potential conflict scenarios. This comprehensive approach is delineated into two main areas of activity: military defence and civil defence. The direction of Sweden's total defence strategy is determined by the Riksdag, with periodic updates to align with prevailing security challenges and national priorities. The recent Totalförsvaret 2021–2025 bill underscores the ongoing evolution of Sweden's defence posture in response to contemporary threats (Government Offices of Sweden, 2024).

The role of industry within Sweden's total defence framework has been pivotal throughout its history, encompassing past, present, and future trajectories. During the Cold War era, Sweden's economic defence strategy was characterized by collaboration between public and private entities to ensure self-sufficiency in critical areas such as food, energy, and essential goods. This collaboration, facilitated by agreements with crisis and war-important companies, formed the cornerstone of Sweden's economic resilience during times of crisis.

However, the post-Cold War era ushered in a period of transition marked by globalization, deregulation, and increased reliance on international markets. These shifts posed new challenges to Sweden's economic defence strategy, necessitating a reassessment of industry's role within the total defence framework. Rising foreign ownership in strategic sectors and the proliferation of international supply chains underscored the need for adaptive strategies to safeguard Sweden's security of supply.

In response to these challenges, Sweden has embarked on a journey to revitalize its total defence strategy, with a renewed emphasis on integrating industry into civil defence efforts. This entails fostering collaboration between state agencies and private enterprises to safeguard critical societal functions and maintain the supply of goods and services. Recent legislative initiatives and policy directives aim to redefine the role of industry within Sweden's total defence architecture, reflecting a forward-looking approach to national preparedness.

Looking ahead, Sweden faces several unresolved questions and challenges as it seeks to strengthen its total defence posture. These include the need for a national coordination mechanism for security of supply, resolution of legal obstacles, and enhanced collaboration with international partners, particularly with NATO members, given Sweden's accession to the alliance.[1] Furthermore, companies themselves must undertake important development work to ensure wartime readiness and protective security measures (KKRVA, 2023).

In conclusion, the economic component of total defence in Sweden serves as a critical pillar of national security, underpinning the nation's resilience and readiness in the face of evolving threats. By embracing innovation, collaboration, and adaptive strategies, Sweden is poised to reinforce its readiness and security in the

[1]Sweden became NATO's newest member on Thursday (7 March 2024), upon depositing its instrument of accession to the North Atlantic Treaty with the Government of the United States in Washington DC. With Sweden's accession, NATO now counts 32 countries among its members. https://www.nato.int/cps/en/natohq/news_223446.htm

years to come, ensuring the continued prosperity and well-being of its citizens in an increasingly complex geopolitical landscape.

The Economic Dimension of Swiss Total Defence

Security has been a central concern for Switzerland for nearly 700 years, rooted deeply in its history and political evolution. From its origins in the 13th century to the present day, Switzerland's approach to security has undergone significant transformations, shaped by both internal and external factors.

The early origins of Swiss security can be traced back to 1291 when various city-states and rural communities formed a confederation to protect themselves against external threats. Initially driven by the need for defence against lawlessness and outside interference, Switzerland experienced a phase of expansionism in the 14th and 15th centuries, positioning itself strategically in European politics. However, a decisive defeat in 1515 marked the end of this expansionist period, leading to the adoption of a policy of neutrality (FDFA, n.d.).

Switzerland's neutrality was not initially a deliberate strategic choice but rather a result of internal tensions and external pressures, including the reformation and conflicts between cities and rural states. However, over time, neutrality emerged as a cornerstone of Swiss security policy, providing stability and allowing Switzerland to navigate the turbulent waters of European conflicts while avoiding direct involvement.

The Napoleonic era highlighted the limitations of neutrality without credible defence capabilities, leading to a reevaluation of Swiss defence strategy. The Congress of Vienna in 1815[2] recognized Switzerland's neutrality, laying the foundation for its international recognition as a neutral state. The Swiss Constitution of 1848 emphasized the preservation of independence as a primary objective, with neutrality serving as a means to that end (Internet Archive, n.d.).

The 20th century brought new challenges, including the rise of nuclear weapons and the Cold War. In response, Switzerland developed the Concept of General Defence in 1973, acknowledging the interconnectedness of modern society and the need for a comprehensive defence strategy. This concept integrated military preparedness with civil defence, national supply, information, and psychological defence, reflecting Switzerland's commitment to peace in independence (Fedlex, n.d.).

The economic dimension of Swiss total defence is multifaceted, encompassing national supply, infrastructure development, and crisis management. Civil defence plays a crucial role in ensuring the survival of the population and maintaining essential services during crises. Switzerland's strong emphasis on

---

[2]Congress of Vienna, assembly in 1814–1815 that reorganized Europe after the Napoleonic Wars. It began in September 1814, five months after Napoleon I's first abdication and completed its "Final Act" in June 1815, shortly before the Waterloo campaign and the final defeat of Napoleon. The settlement was the most-comprehensive treaty that Europe had ever seen. https://www.britannica.com/event/Congress-of-Vienna

economic preparedness reflects its recognition of the interdependence between economic stability and national security.

To conclude, Switzerland's security policy has evolved over centuries, shaped by its historical experiences and geopolitical realities. The Swiss concept of total defence combines military readiness with economic preparedness, emphasizing the importance of neutrality, independence, and peace. As Switzerland continues to navigate an uncertain global landscape, its commitment to comprehensive security remains unwavering, serving as a model for other nations seeking to balance defence capabilities with economic resilience (Spillmann, 1987).

Comparative Analysis of National Security Strategies: Economic Defence Perspectives from Singapore, Israel, Sweden, and Switzerland

National security strategies encompass various dimensions beyond traditional military defence, including economic resilience, technological innovation, and societal cohesion. This section of the paper compares the approaches of Singapore, Israel, Sweden, and Switzerland to economic defence within their broader national security frameworks, highlighting key policy insights and implications for other countries, particularly small states.

Singapore's Total Defence model

Singapore's Total Defence model, established in 1984, emphasizes a "whole-of-society" approach to national security, drawing inspiration from smaller states like Sweden and Switzerland. The model comprises multiple pillars, including economic defence, aimed at uniting stakeholders for the defence of Singapore. Public campaigns and commemorations play a crucial role in instilling societal values and collective responsibility. The Economic Pillar underscores the interdependence of economic strength and national security, focusing on stockpiling essential supplies, water security, and technological innovation through interventionist government policies.

Implications

Singapore's Total Defence model serves as a benchmark for small countries, showcasing the importance of a comprehensive, multi-faceted approach to national security. The model's success lies in addressing both traditional and nontraditional threats, fostering societal resilience, and instilling collective responsibility among the population.

National security through economic means: The case of Israel

Israel's national security strategy prioritizes economic development and technological innovation as integral components of its defence posture. Rooted in the principles of Zeev Jabotinsky and David Ben-Gurion, Israel's strategy aims to build mutual interests and partnerships while maintaining technological superiority and a competitive defence industry. The economy is structured to allocate resources for military research and development, leveraging defence exports to strengthen political and economic ties globally.

Implications
Israel's approach highlights the importance of economic development in enhancing security and building international alliances. Small countries can emulate Israel's focus on technological innovation and defence industry collaboration to bolster their defence capabilities and global influence.

The economic component of total defence: Lessons from Sweden
Sweden's total defence concept integrates military preparedness with civil resilience and economic defence, reflecting its historical context and geopolitical realities. The role of industry is pivotal, with past collaboration between public and private entities ensuring self-sufficiency in critical areas. However, globalization and foreign ownership challenges necessitate adaptive strategies, prompting Sweden to revitalize its total defence posture through enhanced collaboration and legislative initiatives.

Implications
Sweden's experience underscores the importance of industry government collaboration and adaptability in economic defence. Small states can learn from Sweden's approach to ensure resilience in the face of evolving security challenges and global economic dynamics.

The economic dimension of Swiss total defence
Switzerland's security policy, rooted in neutrality and independence, combines military readiness with economic preparedness to ensure comprehensive defence. The Concept of General Defence integrates civil defence, national supply, and crisis management, emphasizing the interdependence between economic stability and national security. Switzerland's commitment to neutrality and peace serves as a model for other nations seeking to balance defence capabilities with economic resilience.

Implications
Switzerland's approach highlights the importance of neutrality, independence, and comprehensive security in safeguarding national interests. Small countries can draw lessons from Switzerland's emphasis on economic preparedness and neutrality to navigate uncertain global landscapes effectively.

Economic Readiness Concept

Military Readiness Concept by Richard Betts

In "Military Readiness: Concepts, Choices, Consequences," Richard Betts presents a comprehensive definition of military readiness. According to him, *a nation is considered militarily ready if the time needed to transform its potential military capabilities into the required actual capabilities does not surpass the period available between the decision to mobilize and the actual outbreak of hostilities.* This is achieved when the government *accurately estimates mobilization time before war, ensures sufficient potential capabilities, and maintains an optimal gap between actual and potential capabilities in peacetime or compensates for uncertainty by retaining surplus capabilities* (Betts, 1995).

According to Betts, a nation demonstrates its lack of military readiness when a *disparity between its current and potential capabilities leads to a gap between the supply of capability and the demand for it*. The crucial aspect here is the causal relationship. During peacetime, there typically exists a certain gap between the potential and actual military capabilities of a country, which is then addressed through mobilization efforts. If a sufficient portion of this gap is closed within a timely manner, the supply of military capability aligns with the demand. However, unreadiness arises when a nation enters a conflict with forces that are insufficient for the task at hand and unable to engage as swiftly or effectively as necessary. This inadequacy may stem not from a lack of potential capability, but rather from delays in making the decisions needed to convert potential military capability into readily available and operational forces.

Therefore, readiness depends on how time affects two key ratios: firstly, *the balance between the supply of combat capability and the demand for it*, and secondly, *the relationship between actual capability and potential capability*. The former ratio pertains to the requisites necessary for successful combat, focusing on the relative military strength required. The latter ratio pertains to conversion, representing the variance between forces ready for immediate deployment and those that can be mobilized after thorough preparation. It is essential to note that neither ratio in isolation can ascertain readiness.

A disparity between the available combat capability and the requirements does not inherently signify unreadiness. This is because certain countries may lack the capability to fulfill their demands regardless of the timing and intensity of their preparations. For instance, a nation like Poland facing a more powerful adversary like Germany in World War II would encounter this lack irrespective of how promptly and thoroughly it readied its forces. Therefore, a nation's primary objective is to ensure it possesses adequate potential military capability, either through internal resources or collaborative efforts with allies, to match its adversary. Without this underlying potential, readiness to utilize it becomes irrelevant. A government that fails to secure sufficient military potential, either through alliances or economic means, should not contemplate defending itself militarily and need not concern itself with military readiness, as war in this case will not "serve his interests better than surrender" (Betts, 1995, p. 29).

Betts formulates the three questions discussed below for policy and strategy, the right answers to which are critical to making optimal decisions about readiness.

Readiness for When?

The time available to convert potential capabilities into actual capabilities must be determined. There are not enough funds or national will to have all military units ready to launch at a moment's notice. By answering this question correctly, strategists and those working on institutional capabilities can determine what the peacetime gap between actual and potential military capabilities should be, which capabilities should be in reserve and which should be in active service. The answer to this question depends more on political considerations than on technical calculations.

Readiness for What?

This question focuses on what kind of conflict is expected, who will be the adversary, what tasks the military will have to perform, and according to what strategy. Understanding potential adversaries and scenarios is critical to determining how the military should assess the readiness of various units and combat equipment.

Readiness of What?

The processes of mobilization and preparation for the launch of each element of the joint forces have their own specifics. Air, naval, and land forces (as well as their constituent elements) require different timelines and different tasks to bring units to combat readiness. The readiness "of what" is tied to "for what" and "for when." With a consensus on what type of conflict the military should prepare for and in what time frame it can do so, the services and combined forces can determine what capabilities should be kept available in the short term.

To summarize, Richard Betts defines military readiness as the nation's ability to transform potential military capabilities into actual ones within the available timeframe between mobilization and the outbreak of hostilities. Betts emphasizes accurate estimates of mobilization time, ensuring sufficient potential military capabilities and maintaining an optimal gap between actual and potential capabilities. Additionally, he underscores the government's role in securing adequate potential capabilities, both internally and through alliances. Betts poses three pivotal questions for policy and strategy: *Readiness for When, Readiness for What*, and *Readiness of What*. These questions guide decisions on timing, understanding potential conflicts and adversaries, and the specifics of mobilization and preparation for joint forces.

Economic Readiness: Definition and Key Questions to be Answered

Economic readiness is a crucial aspect of economic defence and refers to the preparedness and ability of a country's economy to effectively respond to and withstand various challenges, crises, and threats. It encompasses a set of policies, strategies, and measures designed to enhance the resilience, adaptability, and stability of the economic system, ensuring its ability to function efficiently even in the face of disruptions or adverse events. The concept of economic readiness recognizes that economies are susceptible to a wide range of risks, including financial crises, natural disasters, pandemics, global economic downturns, cyber attacks, trade conflicts, and geopolitical tensions and wars. To mitigate the impact of such challenges and safeguard the national security and well-being of its citizens, a nation must proactively prepare its economy to handle these situations and recover as swiftly as possible.

When examining readiness within the economic domain of total defence, Betts' approach offers valuable insights. *A country will be considered ready for a crisis situation (or war) in terms of the economic component of total defence only if the time required for the conversion of various sectors of the economy, as well as for the mobilization of elements of the economic system and the material and technical base to ensure economic resilience, does not exceed the timeframe between the decision to initiate the above-mentioned activities and the outbreak of actual hostilities.* It should be noted that in this case the term "conversion" refers to the transfer of civilian sectors of the economy to military production. This refers to a situation where the necessities of war force a country to reduce its civilian industry and increase its military industry.

The proposed definition of economic readiness captures key aspects of economic preparedness for crisis situations, particularly in the context of war or conflict. It emphasizes the importance of timing in converting various sectors of economy and mobilizing economic resources to meet the demands of the crisis. This definition underscores the necessity for efficient coordination and timely action in deploying economic capabilities to support national defence efforts. Additionally, it highlights the critical role of decision-making in initiating necessary economic activities before the outbreak of hostilities to ensure readiness. Overall, this definition provides a clear framework for evaluating and achieving economic readiness in times of crisis or war.

A nation reveals its lack of economic readiness when the gap between its actual economic defence capability, including the level of reserve resources and potential capability that the nation is able to provide, results in a gap between the supply of resources and the demand for them. The crucial aspect here is the causal relationship. During times of stability, there typically exists a certain gap between a country's potential and actual levels of economic defence capabilities, including the levels of material resources for contingencies, which, in the event of a crisis, is addressed through various economic measures. If a sufficient portion of this gap is closed within a timely manner, the supply of resources aligns with the demand. However, economic unreadiness arises when a nation faces economic challenges that are beyond its ability to handle effectively, leading to disruptions in economic support of defence activities and instability. It should be noted that this inadequacy may stem not from a lack of potential economic capability, but rather from delays in making the decisions needed to convert it into readily available and operational resources.

Therefore, economic readiness is contingent on how time affects two key ratios: firstly, the relation between the supply of economic and material resources and the demand for them, and secondly, the relation between a country's potential and actual economic defence capabilities. The former ratio pertains to the requisites necessary for ensuring economic resilience and stability, focusing on the relative economic capacity required to provide effective resource support. The latter ratio pertains to conversion, representing the variance between currently functioning economic systems and resources that are ready for immediate deployment and those that can be mobilized after thorough preparation. It is essential to note that neither ratio in isolation can ascertain economic readiness.

A discrepancy between the supply of available economic and material resources and demand does not inherently signify economic unreadiness. This is because certain countries may lack the economic capacity to meet their requirements regardless of the timing and intensity of their economic preparations. For instance, a nation facing significant economic challenges or crises due to internal or external factors would encounter this lack irrespective of how promptly and thoroughly it readied its economic systems and resources. Therefore, a nation's primary objective is to ensure it possesses adequate potential economic defence capability, either through internal resources or collaborative efforts with allies, to address its economic challenges effectively.

To achieve economic readiness, the government needs to estimate as accurately as possible the time that will be available to prepare the economy from the onset of a likely crisis and the decision to mobilize to the outbreak of actual hostilities. It must also ensure the adequacy of economic resources and the proper functioning of relevant systems. During peacetime, it should determine and maintain the optimal level of material and technical supply, which can be augmented in a crisis, using both the country's own economic capabilities and support from partner nations. Additionally, the government must ensure that its potential economic defence capabilities, both domestically and in collaboration with allies, are sufficient to effectively address the challenges and threats facing the country.

When discussing economic readiness decisions, the questions proposed by Betts can be considered follows:

Readiness for When?

Determine as accurately as possible the time that will be available for the transformation of the potential economic defence capabilities into actual ones. That is, when the necessary measures in the part of the economic component of total defence should be started, in order to be able to respond to the crisis in a timely and adequate manner. By accurately addressing this question, strategists and individuals involved in institutional economic defence capabilities can ascertain the peacetime disparity between current and potential economic capacities, discerning which of them ought to be reserved and which should remain active in service.

Readiness for What?

This question focuses on what kind of crisis or conflict is coming and how it will affect the country's economy. Understanding potential crises, adversaries, and scenarios is critical to determining how to assess readiness in the economic component of total defence.

Readiness of What?

The economy comprises diverse sectors, each with its own unique characteristics. Consequently, determining the appropriate timeframe for preparing these sectors adequately is essential, accounting for anticipated challenges specific to each sector. Readiness "of what" is contingent upon "for what" and "for when." With consensus established on the type and timing of potential crises or conflicts a nation must prepare for, it can identify which capabilities and systems within the economic component of total defence should remain accessible in the short term, including necessary material and technical resources.

Key Elements of Economic Readiness

These can be summarized as follows:

Risk assessment: Identifying potential threats and vulnerabilities that could adversely affect the economy and analyzing their potential impact.
Contingency planning: Developing comprehensive plans and strategies to address various economic crises and emergencies effectively.
Financial stability: Ensuring the stability of financial institutions and markets to prevent systemic risks and promote confidence in the economy.
Supply chain resilience: Strengthening supply chains to maintain the availability of essential goods and services even in adverse circumstances.
Diversification: Reducing reliance on a narrow range of industries, trading partners, or revenue sources to enhance economic stability.
Infrastructure protection: Safeguarding critical infrastructure and services to ensure their continuous operation during disruptions.
Strategic reserves: Maintaining reserves of essential goods and resources to address shortages during emergencies.
Human capital development: Investing in education, training, and workforce development to build a skilled and adaptable labor force.
Public–private cooperation: Collaborating with the private sector to coordinate economic defence efforts and leverage resources effectively.
Innovation and technology: Encouraging research, development, and technological advancements to foster economic growth and competitiveness.

To conclude, concerning the economic aspect of total defence, accurate answers to the three questions *Readiness for When? Readiness for What? and Readiness of What?* enable to make assumptions regarding the nature of anticipated crises or conflicts, their impact on the country's economy, strategic warning signs, and the specific preparedness measures required across different sectors of the economic component of total defence. This ensures a timely and effective response to crises or conflicts while upholding the strength, efficiency, and sustainability of the economy.

Summary (Conceptual and Comparative Conclusion)

This part of the paper explores the concept of economic defence within the context of international security, focusing on the experiences of selected nations including Singapore, Israel, Sweden, and Switzerland. It discusses the evolving strategies and challenges faced by these countries in safeguarding their economic interests and ensuring national security.

The Total Defence model in Singapore emphasizes a comprehensive approach involving government, business, and the public, with a particular focus on economic resilience and technological innovation.

Israel prioritizes economic development and technological superiority as integral components of its defence posture, leveraging defence exports and research capabilities to strengthen global alliances.

Sweden's total defence concept integrates military preparedness with civil resilience and economic defence, highlighting the importance of industry–government collaboration and adaptability.

Switzerland's security policy, rooted in neutrality and independence, combines military readiness with economic preparedness to ensure comprehensive defence, serving as a model for other nations seeking to balance defence capabilities with economic resilience.

Overall, the comparative analysis underscores the importance of economic defence strategies in maintaining national security and navigating uncertain global landscapes, particularly for small states. By learning from these diverse experiences, small states can enhance their defence capabilities, strengthen resilience, and safeguard national interests in an increasingly complex and interconnected world.

References

Betts, R. K. (1995). *Military readiness: Concepts, choices, consequences*. Brookings Institution.

Defence Science and Technology Agency. (n.d.). *Defence Science and Technology Agency (DSTA)*. https://www.dsta.gov.sg/home

Eisenkot, G., & Siboni, G. (2019). *Israel's national security strategy*. The Washington Institute for Near East Policy.

Factsheet – About Total Defence. (n.d.). *Government of Singapore*. https://tinyurl.com/4thf4mhy

Federal Department of Foreign Affairs. (FDFA, n.d.). *The late Middle Ages and beyond*. https://www.aboutswitzerland.eda.admin.ch/en/the-history-of-switzerland

Government Offices of Sweden. (2024). *Total defence*. https://www.government.se/government-policy/total-defence/

Institut des Hautes Études de Défense Nationale (IHEDN). (2023). Economic defence: A new approach to dealing with new threats. https://ihedn.fr/en/lundis-de-lihedn/defense-economique-une-approche-nouvelle-pour-traiter-de-nouvelles-menaces/

Matthews, R., & Bintang Timur, F. (2023). Singapore's total defence strategy. *Defence and Peace Economics*, 1–21. https://doi.org/10.1080/10242694.2023.2187924

Royal Swedish Academy of War Sciences (KKRVA). (2023). *The role of industry in Sweden's total defence: Past, present, and future*. https://kkrva.se/the-role-of-industry-in-swedens-total-defence-past-present-and-future/

Segell, G. (2020). Israel's security facing a nuclear Iran. *London Institute of Security Policy / NATO Strategic Report*. https://tile.loc.gov/storage-services/master/gdc/gdcebookspublic/20/20/43/52/34/2020435234/2020435234.pdf

Singapore Economic Development Board. (2020). *About the economic development board*. https://www.edb.gov.sg/en/about-edb/who-we-are.html

Spillmann, K. R. (1987). *Beyond soldiers and arms: The Swiss model of comprehensive security policy*. https://tinyurl.com/4bkvc4jp

Swiss Federal Council. (1973). *Conception of general defence*. Fedlex. https://www.fedlex.admin.ch/eli/fga/1973/2__103_/fr

Chapter 7

Economic Defence in Wartime and Transatlantic Solidarity: The Case of Ukraine and NATO

Ivan Okromtchedlishvili

Sulkhan-Saba Orbeliani University, Tbilisi, Georgia

Abstract

This chapter analyses economic defence in wartime conditions through the case of Ukraine during the Russian–Ukrainian war. It places it within the broader framework of transatlantic economic and security cooperation. It examines how war has affected Ukraine's macroeconomic stability, industrial base, financial system, and fiscal sustainability. It highlights the critical role of international financial assistance from the European Union, the United States, and international financial institutions. The chapter further explores the role of NATO and the transatlantic alliance as pillars of collective economic and security stability, including the economic foundations of NATO power, the shift in EU–NATO relations toward strategic autonomy, and the economic benefits of alliance membership. The chapter concludes with policy-oriented lessons on economic resilience, international solidarity, and collective economic defence in high-intensity conflict environments.

Keywords: Economic defence; war economy; Ukraine; NATO; transatlantic solidarity; resilience; reconstruction

JEL Codes: H56; F52; D74; F34; O52

Enhancing Transatlantic Solidarity in Collective Defence: Navigating Increased Defence Expenditures, Cyber Security, and Emerging Risks, 131–144

doi:10.1108/978-1-80686-259-720261007

Introduction – Economic Defence and Resilience: Lessons from the Russian–Ukrainian War

A strong and stable economy and properly organized economic defence play a crucial role in a nation's resilience during crises and conflicts.

Ukraine, known for its vast natural resources and diverse industries, has long struggled with economic stability issues predating the Russian–Ukrainian war. Despite its wealth of resources, Ukraine has faced challenges in maintaining economic stability, exacerbated by the collapse of the Soviet Union. This led to deindustrialization and difficulties in transitioning to a market economy, despite sectors like metallurgy, energy, and agriculture forming the backbone of its economy.

Prior to the conflict, Ukraine was already grappling with significant economic challenges, characterized by a modest real GDP of merely $160 billion (Roberts, 2023). Ukraine's business landscape comprised approximately 500 major enterprises generating turnovers surpassing US $100 million, alongside around 400,000 small and medium-sized enterprises (SMEs) and nearly 1.6 million individual entrepreneurs. Larger enterprises typically faced hurdles related to entering new markets and securing foreign investment. SMEs, on the other hand, dealt with corrupt governmental bodies and burdensome taxation, particularly administrative tax obligations. Common challenges shared by both large corporations and SMEs included deficiencies in the judicial system, inadequate safeguards for property rights, and a shortage of skilled labor (CEPR, 2022).

In peacetime, economic defence encompasses a range of policies and measures aimed at enhancing the resilience and adaptability of the economy to withstand various challenges. Ukraine, like other nations, implemented strategies to bolster its economic defence, including efforts to diversify industries, attract foreign investment, and improve governance and regulatory frameworks. However, the onset of the Russian–Ukrainian war presented unprecedented challenges to these defence mechanisms.

The Russian invasion of Ukraine in 2022 inflicted severe damage on the country's economy, causing a sharp contraction of 29.2% in GDP and widespread destruction of infrastructure (The World Bank, 2023). The war disrupted supply chains, led to the displacement of millions of people, and resulted in significant economic losses across various sectors. Agribusiness, a key contributor to Ukraine's economy, faced challenges in exporting grain due to port blockades and increased costs, exacerbating the economic crisis (Roberts, 2023).

The war precipitated an acute shortage of hard currency like US dollars, prompting national currency depreciation and inflationary pressures. Efforts to stabilize the exchange rate proved challenging, as the government grappled with fiscal sustainability amidst increased defence spending. However, Ukraine's banking sector remained resilient, ensuring the continued functioning of the economy by facilitating financial transactions and supporting government operations (IMF, 2022).

Amidst the economic turmoil caused by the war, international financial support emerged as a crucial lifeline for Ukraine (Gramer & Mackinnon, 2022).

The European Union, United States, and international financial institutions like the International Monetary Fund (IMF) played a pivotal role in providing financial assistance to Ukraine, helping to stabilize its economy and mitigate the impact of the conflict. This support was essential for financing the war effort, supporting basic services, and fulfilling foreign obligations.

The European Union, as Ukraine's largest trading partner, has been instrumental in providing financial aid and implementing assistance programs aimed at supporting economic reforms and reconstruction efforts. The EU's financial assistance package has included grants, loans, and technical assistance, focusing on areas such as infrastructure development, energy security, governance reforms, and humanitarian aid.

Similarly, the United States has been a key ally of Ukraine, providing substantial financial assistance and military aid to bolster its defence capabilities and support its economic recovery. The United States has allocated billions of dollars in aid to Ukraine, including military equipment, humanitarian aid, and economic assistance, underscoring its commitment to Ukraine's sovereignty and territorial integrity.

International financial institutions, particularly the above-mentioned IMF, have also played a critical role in supporting Ukraine's economy during the conflict. The IMF has provided financial assistance packages to Ukraine, aimed at stabilizing its economy, restoring macroeconomic stability, and implementing structural reforms. These programs have helped Ukraine address fiscal imbalances, stabilize its currency, and restore investor confidence amidst the uncertainty of war.

Furthermore, other international organizations and donor countries have contributed to Ukraine's economic resilience through financial assistance, technical support, and humanitarian aid. Multilateral development banks, such as the World Bank and the European Bank for Reconstruction and Development (EBRD), have financed infrastructure projects and provided policy advice to support Ukraine's economic recovery.

The importance of international support to Ukraine cannot be overstated, as it has been instrumental in sustaining the country's economy and helping it navigate through the challenges of war. International assistance has provided crucial funding for defence expenditures, humanitarian aid, and reconstruction efforts, enabling Ukraine to continue military operations, maintain basic services, and fulfill its international obligations.

Moreover, international support has bolstered investor confidence, restored macroeconomic stability, and facilitated the implementation of structural reforms aimed at improving governance, transparency, and the business environment. By providing financial assistance and technical expertise, international partners have helped Ukraine strengthen its institutions, modernize its economy, and lay the foundation for sustainable growth and development in the post-conflict era.

International support has also served as a demonstration of solidarity and commitment to Ukraine's sovereignty and territorial integrity, sending a strong message to Russia and other aggressors that the international community stands united in support of Ukraine's independence and right to self-determination.

As the conflict persists, Ukraine faces formidable challenges in rebuilding its economy and restoring infrastructure. The costs of reconstruction are expected to be substantial, requiring significant investment and international assistance (The World Bank, 2023). Moreover, the country must address underlying structural issues, including corruption, weak governance, and the need for institutional reforms, to ensure sustainable economic growth in the long term.

It's important to highlight that Ukraine's economic forecast is highly uncertain, with the country facing particularly elevated levels of unpredictability, as classified by the IMF. In contrast to the IMF's typical approach of relying on a single central scenario, Ukraine's situation necessitates consideration of multiple potential outcomes, primarily due to uncertainty surrounding the duration of the conflict. The baseline scenario outlined in 2023 anticipated the conclusion of the war by the first half of 2024, leading to a phase of tangible investment and reconstruction. Conversely, the pessimistic scenario anticipates a prolonged and intensified conflict, resulting in more severe economic repercussions than projected in the baseline scenario. This scenario would impede the return of displaced individuals, exacerbate infrastructure damage, and further hinder economic activity (IMF, 2023).

Ukraine's economic policy during wartime, backed by the IMF, aims to achieve macroeconomic and financial stability, secure external financing, and establish a structural policy framework to pave the way for post-war recovery and eventual EU accession.

Key elements include:

Fiscal policy: The immediate focus is on ensuring adequate resources for priority spending, maintaining robust tax revenues, and upholding fiscal and debt sustainability. Medium-term objectives involve developing a national revenue strategy, reinstating the medium-term budget framework, and enhancing government investment management to support reconstruction and social spending.

Monetary and exchange rate policy: The primary goal is to sustain disinflation[1] and exchange rate stability by prudently managing foreign exchange reserves and excess liquidity during wartime.

Financial sector: Policies prioritize maintaining financial stability and preparing for post-war recovery through emergency planning, banking diagnostics, and addressing issues with troubled banks and non-performing assets.

Governance and growth: Strengthening independent anti-corruption institutions is crucial to improving governance, fostering public trust, and enhancing donor confidence in future reconstruction efforts. Deepening integration with the EU single market and aligning with EU membership requirements are essential for institutional and structural reforms.

---

[1]Disinflation is used to describe the slowing of price inflation. In other words, it is a decrease in the rate of inflation. The term should not be confused with deflation, which is used to describe a negative inflation rate. https://corporatefinanceinstitute.com/resources/economics/disinflation/

Financing strategy and debt sustainability: The government program aims to restore debt sustainability by restructuring both official and foreign commercial debts to meet funding needs during the program period (IMF, 2023).

Privatization: Despite the war, Ukraine continues its privatization process, which was briefly suspended at the onset of full-scale conflict but resumed on a smaller scale in September 2022. While small-scale privatization generated 1.7 billion hryvnia in 2022, larger-scale privatization remains challenging amid the conflict, with limited prospects for attracting strategic investors (GMK, n.d.).

Anti-corruption efforts: Corruption and weak oversight over public funds persist as significant challenges, particularly amidst the ongoing conflict. Addressing concerns about potential misappropriation of investment funds and ensuring transparency in the recovery process are priorities (Euronews, 2023). While the Zelensky government has taken steps to combat corruption and shown progress in law enforcement reforms and anti-corruption institution appointments, challenges persist, as evidenced by allegations of misallocation of funds for reconstruction efforts in the Kiev region (Bihus.info, 2023).

However, despite the challenges ahead, there are reasons for cautious optimism about Ukraine's prospects for post-conflict recovery. The resilience and adaptability of the Ukrainian people, coupled with continued international support, provide a strong foundation for rebuilding the economy and restoring stability. With sustained commitment from the international community and concerted efforts from Ukrainian authorities, the country can overcome the challenges of war and embark on a path of sustainable development and prosperity.

To summarize, the Russian–Ukrainian war has had far-reaching economic implications for Ukraine, testing the resilience of its economy and highlighting the importance of robust economic defence mechanisms. However, amidst the turmoil of conflict, *international support has emerged as a crucial lifeline for Ukraine*, providing essential funding, technical expertise, and solidarity in its time of need. As Ukraine continues to navigate through the challenges of war and rebuild its economy, the support of the international community remains indispensable in ensuring a brighter and more prosperous future for the country and its people.

Transatlantic Solidarity: Collective Economic Defence

Amidst shifting security landscapes, increasing economic interconnectivity, and rapid technological progress, the notion of collective economic defence has gained unprecedented importance, especially within the context of transatlantic solidarity. As nations struggle with the complexities of modern security challenges, such as escalating defence expenditures and the ever-present specter of cyber threats, the imperative for collaborative action among transatlantic partners becomes increasingly apparent.

At the heart of collective economic defence lies the principle of shared responsibility and mutual assistance among allied nations. The transatlantic alliance, comprising North American and European partners, represents a cornerstone of global security architecture, built upon shared values, interests, and commitments to collective defence. Against the backdrop of escalating defence expenditures, characterized by substantial investments in military capabilities and technological modernization, fostering transatlantic solidarity assumes heightened importance in leveraging resources efficiently, mitigating duplication of efforts, and enhancing overall defence capabilities.

Moreover, the proliferation of cyber threats poses a formidable challenge to national security and economic resilience, underscoring the need for a coordinated and cohesive response. As cyber attacks transcend borders and target critical infrastructure, cooperation in cybersecurity emerges as an imperative for safeguarding collective interests and ensuring the uninterrupted flow of economic activities. By sharing intelligence, best practices, and technological expertise, transatlantic partners can enhance their cyber defence capabilities, bolster resilience against emerging threats, and mitigate the disruptive impact of cyber incidents on economic stability.

Transatlantic Solidarity for the Defence: A Cornerstone of the Alliance

The principle of collective defence has been at the core of NATO's mission since its inception. Born out of the post-World War II era, when the specter of Soviet expansionism loomed over Europe, NATO's founding treaty cemented the commitment of its members to mutual protection. This solidarity, enshrined in Article 5 of the North Atlantic Treaty, has served as a cornerstone of the Alliance, forging an unbreakable bond among its members.

Article 5 of the North Atlantic Treaty embodies the essence of collective defence within NATO. It stipulates that an armed attack against one member shall be considered an attack against all members, compelling each member to come to the aid of the aggrieved party. This provision underscores the shared responsibility of NATO allies to uphold the security and integrity of the North Atlantic area.

NATO's commitment to collective defence extends beyond mere words. In response to various security challenges, the Alliance has undertaken collective defence measures, demonstrating its readiness to confront threats to its members' security.

Moreover, in the wake of Russia's illegal annexation of Crimea and the rise of terrorist threats, NATO has implemented significant enhancements to its collective defence posture.

As security threats evolve, NATO remains steadfast in its commitment to adapt and reinforce its defensive capabilities. Recognizing the changing geopolitical landscape, the Alliance has undertaken measures to bolster deterrence and defence across its eastern flank.

The deployment of multinational battlegroups in countries like Estonia, Latvia, Lithuania, and Poland, along with the strengthening of the NATO Response Force, reflects NATO's resolve to ensure the security of all its members. Moreover, the acknowledgment of cyberspace and space as new operational domains underscores NATO's readiness to confront emerging threats in the digital age (NATO, 2024).

Central to NATO's collective defence efforts is transatlantic solidarity – the enduring bond between North American and European allies. This partnership, rooted in shared values and mutual commitment, forms the bedrock of the Alliance's cohesion.

Events such as Lucio Gussetti's presentation[2] on transatlantic solidarity highlight the ongoing discourse on defence cooperation between the European Union and NATO. By fostering dialog and cooperation, both entities seek to enhance their respective defence capabilities and reinforce the broader framework of collective security (Yale MacMillan Center, 2023).

As NATO continues to confront complex security challenges, solidarity remains paramount. Whether in the face of terrorism, regional aggression, or emerging threats, the Alliance stands united in its commitment to collective defence.

By upholding the principles of Article 5 and strengthening transatlantic partnerships, NATO reaffirms its role as a bulwark of stability and security in an ever-changing world. As threats evolve and new challenges emerge, the Alliance remains steadfast in its mission to protect the European continent and uphold the values of freedom, democracy, and peace.

The Shift of the Transatlantic Link on Defence: From Dependency to Autonomy

As the landscape of global security evolves, so too do the strategies and alliances that underpin it. The relationship between the European Union (EU) and the North Atlantic Treaty Organization (NATO) has undergone significant evolution in recent years, reflecting a shift from dependency to autonomy in European defence strategies. This transformation is crucial in ensuring the security and stability of the European continent in an increasingly complex geopolitical environment.

The evolution of European defence strategies can be traced through key documents such as the European Security Strategy (European Union, 2009), the EU Global Strategy (EU Global Strategy, 2019), and the Strategic Compass (EEAS, 2022). These documents reflect a growing recognition within the EU of the need to assert greater autonomy in defence while maintaining strong cooperation with NATO.

The European Security Strategy of 2003 acknowledged the significant role played by the United States through NATO but did not prioritize the Alliance as central to European security. While NATO was recognized as an important actor, the strategy emphasized effective multilateralism, positioning NATO alongside other international actors. Moreover, the strategy highlighted the need for EU

---

[2]On April 19, 2023, Lucio Gussetti, EU Visiting Fellow, presented a second talk related to his research project entitled, "Every Inch of NATO Territory: Transatlantic Solidarity for the Defence of the European Continent and Some Lessons from the Creation of the US Federal Armed Forces."

operational capabilities to be reinforced, including through arrangements with NATO such as the Berlin Plus agreements. However, these arrangements also highlighted a dependency on the United States, limiting the EU's autonomy and flexibility in crisis management. Additionally, political disparities among EU member states hindered efforts to assume a leading role in defence, with some viewing enhanced security cooperation as a threat to NATO's influence (European Union, 2009).

The EU Global Strategy (2019), published amidst political instability due to Brexit, presented an opportunity for the EU to assert greater autonomy in defence. It emphasized the need for Europeans to have sufficient capabilities to defend themselves and contribute decisively to collective defence efforts. Importantly, the strategy advocated for the EU to act autonomously when necessary, signaling a departure from dependency on the United States.

Furthermore, the EU Global Strategy sought to deepen the partnership with NATO while also emphasizing the EU's ambition for strategic autonomy. This shift in approach was aimed at strengthening European defence capabilities and balancing transatlantic efforts, recognizing that a more credible European defence is essential for a healthy transatlantic partnership (EU Global Strategy, 2019).

The Strategic Compass 2022 builds upon the EU Global Strategy, emphasizing the need for the EU to take more responsibility for its own security. Against the backdrop of geopolitical shifts, such as the invasion of Ukraine, the Strategic Compass underscores the urgency for the EU to enhance its collective ability to address global threats. Additionally, the Compass reflects the EU's preference for multilateralism over bilateral alliances, highlighting the importance of European cooperation in facing shared security challenges. By investing in strategic thinking and decision-making, the EU aims to strengthen its role as a global security provider (EEAS, 2022).

The evolution of European defence strategies signals a clear intent to assert greater autonomy while maintaining strong ties with NATO. By enhancing its defence capabilities and assuming greater responsibility for its security, the EU seeks to strengthen the transatlantic partnership (González-Ripa, 2024).

Moreover, events such as Brexit and geopolitical crises have underscored the importance of transatlantic solidarity. Despite challenges, the United States and its allies in Europe are experiencing a strong moment of cooperation, recognizing the mutual benefits of a united approach to security (Cusick, 2023).

In conclusion, as the EU moves toward greater autonomy in defence, it simultaneously reinforces the transatlantic alliance by becoming a stronger and more capable partner. By embracing its role as a global security provider, the EU contributes to a more stable and secure world, grounded in the principles of cooperation and solidarity.

The Economic Basis of the Alliance: Understanding NATO's Power Dynamics (NATO GDP, Power Asymmetry)

The North Atlantic Treaty Organization (NATO) stands as a cornerstone of international security, built upon a foundation of collective defence, and shared values among member states. While NATO's significance in geopolitical affairs is widely acknowledged, its economic underpinnings often receive less attention. However, a closer examination reveals that the economic prowess of NATO member states plays a pivotal role in shaping the alliance's capabilities and influence on the global stage.

According to Hartwell (2024), the combined Gross Domestic Product (GDP) of NATO's 32 member states, based on nominal GDP in 2022, amounts to a staggering $45.93319 trillion. This figure, when juxtaposed with the global GDP of approximately $100.562 trillion, underscores NATO's economic dominance, constituting nearly 45.65 percent of the world's total economic output. Such economic heft provides NATO with substantial leverage in international affairs, allowing member states to wield significant influence in shaping global economic policies and security strategies.

To comprehend the scale of NATO's economic might, it is instructive to compare its GDP with that of other major global players. China, often regarded as an economic powerhouse, boasts a GDP of $17.963 trillion, while Russia's GDP stands at $2.240 trillion. In comparison, NATO's GDP surpasses China's by 2.554 times and Russia's by an astonishing 20.5 times. This stark contrast underscores NATO's economic superiority, reaffirming its status as a formidable force in the international arena.

The disparity between NATO's economic prowess and that of Russia is particularly noteworthy. Once touted for its economic potential as part of the BRIC acronym, Russia has since faltered, grappling with structural challenges and the so called oil curse phenomenon. The overreliance on mineral wealth has hindered diversification and modernization efforts, resulting in a stagnant economy that lags behind its peers. As NATO continues to assert its influence, Russia's economic vulnerabilities may further exacerbate its geopolitical isolation and diminish its ability to counter the alliance's strategic objectives (Hartwell, 2024).

Despite NATO's economic supremacy, *challenges persist in translating economic power into effective strategic action.* The decision-making process within the alliance is complex, requiring consensus among member states with diverse economic interests and policy objectives. Moreover, economic strength alone does not guarantee success in achieving strategic objectives. Effective utilization of resources, diplomatic finesse, and coherent policy formulation are imperative for realizing the alliance's full potential.

To conclude, the economic basis of the alliance serves as a crucial determinant of NATO's strength and influence in the contemporary global landscape. The combined GDP of member states underscores NATO's economic dominance, positioning the alliance as a key player in shaping international security and economic policies. *However, realizing the full potential of NATO's economic power necessitates strategic coordination, diplomatic acumen, and proactive engagement to address emerging challenges and seize opportunities for collective prosperity and security.* As the alliance navigates an increasingly complex and dynamic geopolitical environment, leveraging its economic might remain paramount in advancing its core objectives of peace, security, and stability.

The Economic Impact of NATO Membership: A Catalyst for Prosperity and Stability

NATO, the North Atlantic Treaty Organization, has long been recognized for its role in ensuring the security of its member states. However, beyond its primary function of collective defence, NATO membership brings about profound economic benefits. The economic effect of NATO membership extends far beyond mere security considerations, encompassing various facets of economic development and prosperity. This part of the paper explores the intricate relationship between NATO membership and economic growth, drawing upon empirical evidence and case studies to elucidate the tangible benefits experienced by member states.

At the heart of NATO's economic impact lies the stability it provides to member states. Since its inception after World War II, NATO has aimed to create a secure environment conducive to economic growth and prosperity. The stability afforded by NATO membership instills confidence among investors, both domestic and foreign, fostering a conducive climate for economic activity. Countries such as the United States, Germany, and France, among others, exemplify how NATO membership correlates with robust economic development, with these nations ranking among the world's most prosperous.

Conversely, countries outside the NATO fold, such as Bosnia and Herzegovina, Serbia, and Kosovo, often face economic challenges due to the absence of the security umbrella provided by the alliance. These nations struggle to attract significant foreign investment, hindering their economic progress. Despite widespread support for NATO membership among citizens and politicians in these countries, political obstacles and external influences impede their integration into the alliance, exacerbating their economic woes (IGES, 2021).

Empirical data provide compelling evidence of the economic benefits associated with NATO membership. Following accession to NATO, countries experience significant increases in GDP, foreign direct investment, and trade volumes. For instance, Estonia and Latvia witnessed substantial economic growth and a surge in foreign investment after joining NATO in 2004. Similarly, countries like Bulgaria, Lithuania, and Slovenia saw enhanced economic activity and heightened trade integration with Europe and Central Asia, bolstering their economic resilience.

Furthermore, NATO membership catalyzes regional economic and political integration, fostering diversification and resilience within member states' economies. Integration initiatives facilitate increased trade and cooperation, contributing to peace and security in the region. The synergy between NATO and EU integration tracks underscores the importance of a holistic strategy in promoting democratic governance and economic development.

In addition to fostering economic growth, NATO membership enables member states to invest in critical sectors such as education and healthcare. By ensuring political stability and security, NATO membership creates an environment conducive to increased expenditure on education and healthcare, leading to improved human capital development and enhanced quality of life for citizens (Guruli, 2016).

In conclusion, the economic effect of NATO membership is profound and far-reaching. Beyond its primary function of ensuring security, NATO membership serves as a catalyst for economic growth, stability, and prosperity. Empirical evidence demonstrates the tangible benefits experienced by member states, ranging from increased GDP and foreign investment to enhanced trade integration and investment in critical sectors such as education and healthcare. As the world continues to struggle with complex geopolitical challenges, NATO remains a cornerstone of economic stability and development for its member states.

Summary (Ukraine + NATO + Transatlantic Link)

This part of the paper discusses transatlantic solidarity and collective economic defence within NATO, stressing collaborative action amid evolving security landscapes and rising defence expenditures. It emphasizes shared responsibility among allied nations for efficient resource use and enhanced defence capabilities.

The evolution of European defence strategies toward autonomy has been explored, alongside the significance of transatlantic solidarity amidst geopolitical shifts like Brexit.

NATO's economic dominance and its role in shaping global policies have been highlighted, emphasizing benefits like increased GDP and investment associated with membership. The paper emphasizes the profound economic and strategic impact of transatlantic solidarity and NATO membership on stability, prosperity, and collective security.

Conclusions and Recommendations

In conclusion, the dynamics of modern security landscapes underscore the indispensable role of economic defence in safeguarding national security and resilience. As highlighted throughout this paper, economic defence encompasses a comprehensive array of policies, strategies, and measures aimed at bolstering the resilience, adaptability, and stability of national economies. Economic strength and stability are fundamental to a nation's ability to respond effectively to security challenges. Drawing upon international experiences from Singapore, Israel, Sweden, Switzerland, and the lessons learned from the Russian–Ukrainian conflict, it is evident that economic readiness is a crucial component of total defence, requiring proactive planning, coordination, and collaboration across multiple sectors.

Establishing an effective system of economic defence requires significant efforts from the government. It must ensure, both with its own internal resources and in cooperation with its allies, the development of potential capabilities in the field of economic defence in such a way that the country has sufficient potential and is able to maintain the efficiency and stability (resilience) of the economy in the event of a crisis or conflict.

The imperative for transatlantic solidarity in economic defence cannot be overstated, particularly amidst escalating security risks and cyber threats. As nations confront multifaceted challenges that transcend traditional boundaries, collaboration among transatlantic partners assumes unprecedented significance. By fostering collective action and mutual assistance, transatlantic allies can leverage their resources effectively, enhance defence capabilities, and mitigate the disruptive impact of emerging threats on shared interests and prosperity.

Recommendations

- *Strategic timing assessment*: Governments should conduct strategic timing assessments to accurately determine the timeframe available for the transformation of potential economic defence capabilities into actual ones. By addressing questions related to readiness for when, policymakers can ensure timely and adequate preparation for potential crises or conflicts. This involves understanding the lead time required to mobilize economic resources effectively and adjusting policies and strategies accordingly to minimize the peacetime disparity between current and potential economic capacities. Additionally, by discerning the specific timing requirements for different sectors of the economy, governments can prioritize preparedness efforts and allocate resources more efficiently to enhance overall economic readiness and resilience.
- *Enhancing economic resilience*: Governments should prioritize enhancing economic resilience through proactive risk assessment, contingency planning, and financial stability measures. By identifying potential threats and vulnerabilities and developing comprehensive strategies to address them, nations can mitigate the impact of crises and ensure the continuity of economic activities.
- *Strengthening supply chain resilience*: Governments should focus on strengthening supply chain resilience to maintain the availability of essential goods and services during disruptions. This can be achieved through diversification, redundancy, and strategic stockpiling of critical resources, as well as fostering collaboration between public and private sectors to address supply chain vulnerabilities.
- *Investing in human capital*: Investing in education, training, and workforce development is essential to building a skilled and adaptable labor force capable of navigating economic challenges. Governments should prioritize initiatives aimed at enhancing human capital development to ensure the long-term competitiveness and sustainability of the economy.
- *Promoting innovation and technology*: Governments should promote innovation and technological advancements to drive economic growth and competitiveness. By investing in research and development, fostering public–private partnerships, and leveraging emerging technologies, nations can enhance their economic resilience and adaptability in an increasingly complex and interconnected world.
- *Facilitating public–private cooperation*: Collaboration between the public and private sectors is crucial for effective economic defence. Governments should foster a conducive environment for public–private cooperation, encouraging information sharing, joint planning, and resource mobilization to address common challenges and enhance economic resilience.

- *Strengthening collaboration*: Transatlantic partners should enhance collaboration in economic defence through information sharing, joint exercises, and capacity-building initiatives. By leveraging collective expertise and resources, allied nations can enhance their resilience against evolving security threats and ensure the continuity of economic activities.
- *Enhancing strategic coordination*: Addressing the challenges of translating economic power into strategic action within NATO necessitates enhanced coordination among member states. This involves fostering greater consensus-building mechanisms and streamlining decision-making processes to accommodate diverse economic interests and policy objectives. Additionally, investing in diplomatic skills and coherent policy formulation is crucial to ensuring the effective utilization of resources and maximizing the alliance's strategic impact. By prioritizing strategic coordination, NATO can better leverage its economic supremacy to address evolving security challenges and uphold collective defence commitments effectively.
- *Investing in cybersecurity*: Given the proliferation of cyber threats, nations should prioritize investments in cybersecurity capabilities and resilience. By sharing intelligence, best practices, and technological expertise, allied nations can bolster their cyber defence capabilities and mitigate the impact of cyber incidents on economic stability.
- *Drawing lessons from conflict*: Nations should study the economic defence and resilience strategies employed by Ukraine during the Russian–Ukrainian war to draw valuable lessons for enhancing their own defence mechanisms. Analyzing the challenges faced by Ukraine, such as disruptions to supply chains, currency depreciation, and the need for international financial support, can inform the development of more robust economic defence strategies. By learning from Ukraine's experiences, nations can strengthen their economic resilience and preparedness to mitigate the impact of conflicts and crises on their economies.
- *Upholding international solidarity*: The Russian–Ukrainian War underscores the critical importance of international support in times of crisis, particularly for nations facing aggression or conflict. The solidarity demonstrated by the European Union, the United States, and international financial institutions toward Ukraine serves as a powerful example of collective action to uphold sovereignty and territorial integrity. In light of this, nations should prioritize fostering strong diplomatic ties and collaborative partnerships to ensure swift and effective responses to crises, bolstering global stability and security. Additionally, efforts to strengthen international institutions and frameworks for conflict resolution and peacebuilding can enhance the collective capacity to address emerging threats and promote peace and prosperity worldwide.
- *Supporting Ukraine and other vulnerable states*: The international community, including transatlantic partners, should continue to support Ukraine and other vulnerable states facing security challenges. By providing financial assistance, technical support, and solidarity, allied nations can help mitigate the impact of conflicts and crises on economic stability and promote sustainable recovery and development.

In summary, by embracing a collaborative approach and investing in economic defence capabilities, transatlantic partners can navigate the complexities of modern security challenges, strengthen resilience, and safeguard shared interests and prosperity in an ever-evolving global landscape.

References

Bihus.Info. (2023). *Reconstruction of Kyiv region: Misuse of funds report*. https://tinyurl.com/3pzrc77t

Centre for Economic Policy Research (CEPR). (2022). *Rebuilding Ukraine: Principles and policies* (Paris Report 1). https://cepr.org/system/files/publication-files/178114-paris_report_1_rebuilding_ukraine_principles_and_policies.pdf

Cusick, C. (2023). *Brexit, trade and a new era for transatlantic solidarity*. UNC Global Affairs. https://tinyurl.com/2rawup5p

EU Global Strategy. (2019). *The European Union's global strategy three years on*. https://tinyurl.com/yck6m27s

Euronews. (2023). *Ukrainians concerned about corruption as donors pledge billions*. https://tinyurl.com/ys4y2v45

European External Action Service. (2022). *A strategic compass for security and defence*. https://tinyurl.com/y9hsd8pp

European Union. (2009). *European security strategy: A secure Europe in a better world*. https://tinyurl.com/658pytax

GMK. (n.d.). *Large-scale privatization continues in Ukraine during the war*. https://tinyurl.com/yx4f4k5a

González-Ripa, I. (2024). *The shift of the transatlantic link on defence: From dependency to autonomy*. https://tinyurl.com/mr2t2k6v

Gramer, R., & Mackinnon, A. (2022). *The battle to save Ukraine's economy from the war*. Foreign Policy. https://tinyurl.com/3znnnez2

Guruli, I. (2016). *The economic effect of NATO*. Forbes Georgia. https://forbes.ge/the-economic-effect-of-nato/

Hartwell, D. L. (2024). *What is the combined GDP of all NATO members?* Medium. https://tinyurl.com/hwvwrbw2

Institute for Geopolitics, Economy and Security. (2021). *NATO membership brings stability and economic growth*. https://tinyurl.com/4ferb9f8

International Monetary Fund. (2022). *How Ukraine is managing a war economy*. https://tinyurl.com/53fhs3vf

International Monetary Fund. (2023). *Amid war, Ukraine is maintaining macroeconomic stability and embarking on reforms*. https://tinyurl.com/mvjekf4z

NATO. (2024). *Collective defence – Article 5*. https://www.nato.int/cps/en/natohq/topics_110496.htm

Roberts, M. (2023). *Russia–Ukraine: One year of war – The economics*. CADTM. https://www.cadtm.org/Russia-Ukraine-one-year-of-war-the-economics

World Bank. (2023). *Russia's invasion of Ukraine and cost-of-living crisis dim growth prospects in emerging Europe and Central Asia*. https://tinyurl.com/mr3d9pzu

Yale MacMillan Center. (2023). *Transatlantic solidarity for the defence of the European continent*. https://tinyurl.com/bdcrh4an

Chapter 8

Developing Human Resource Reserves During Security Crises: Theoretical and Practical Perspectives on Normality and Challenges

Dorel Badea, Diana Elena Ranf and Elisabeta-Emilia Halmaghi

"Nicolae Bălcescu" Land Forces Academy, Sibiu, Romania

Abstract

The war in Ukraine will undoubtedly remain a disruptive event, with paradigmatic value in the field of resource management for defense, in the contemporary history of humanity. The whole spectrum of security was put in a different light, with significance for civilians and the military alike, from the point of view of causality and effects, of the civil–military relationship, and of the domino effects produced in different fields, more or less close to the military one. Continuing the previously addressed lines of research, we intended to make a contribution that would highlight the role and importance of human resources in the military field, transcending an administrative-territorial management approach and converging on a flexible, scalable, adaptable, and responsive managerial approach to the current security context.

The need for study of proposed topic is justified by the resulting importance for resilience, and, within it, the role of capabilities and human resources in particular. As a finding, it is necessary to reject the idea that the quantitative approach in this framework is entirely insufficient. From a practical perspective, a proactive, multidimensional approach to national security management is useful, as it facilitates the transition from a state of peace to a state of crisis. The methodology used for the research is

Enhancing Transatlantic Solidarity in Collective Defence: Navigating Increased Defence Expenditures, Cyber Security, and Emerging Risks, 145–172

Published under exclusive licence by Emerald Publishing Limited
doi:10.1108/978-1-80686-259-720261008

primarily descriptive, with open sources used for the quantitative aspects that need to be exposed, corroborated by bibliometric research.

Keywords: War; human resources; military capacities; conscription; recruitment

JEL Codes: H12; O15; O38

1. Introduction

The high hybridization of the means of conducting the conflict as well as the challenges of international collaboration are sufficient reasons for considering the conflict as an event of major interest of the 21st century.

A war is a human tragedy for the inhabitants of any country in the world, and the current war in Ukraine is no exception. In the case of Ukraine, according to Bebler (2023), this armed conflict is the largest, bloodiest, and longest war in Europe since 1945 and, among all the wars fought in the world after 1945, it is strongly distinguished by the inverse ratio of military mortality and the civil one.

The Russian–Ukrainian war began on the morning of February 24, 2022, around 06:00 Moscow time, after the mobilization of the Russian army on the border of Ukraine with Belarus, a mobilization disguised as military exercises. To justify the invasion, Vladimir Putin, the president of the Russian Federation, said the same morning, according to the media, that he had decided to lead a special military operation to try to prevent a genocide against Russian speakers and promised a demilitarization and denazification of Ukraine. At the same time, the actions taken by Russia were aimed at protecting Ukraine "from those who have taken Ukraine hostage" (Sheftalovich, 2022) and there is no desire to occupy Ukrainian territory.

In addition to the effects of the COVID-19 pandemic, climate change or existing conflicts, there are also the challenges caused by the conflict in Ukraine. It is a conflict that has exacerbated existing challenges, locally, regionally, and globally. Migration of the civilian population, food insecurity, rising food and energy prices, inflation, lack of quality health and education services, massive pollution and deteriorating environmental factors are just some of the elements that have led to demographic, food, energy, financial, health and education, or environmental crises. The conflict in Ukraine has intensified the global cost of living crisis and led to a fall in living standards.

2. The Russian–Ukrainian War, Crises, and Risk Perception: Overview

Discussions about Ukraine's demographic situation are challenging because part of the population is located in the territories annexed by Russia in 2014 (the Autonomous Republic of Crimea and Sevastopol). Rogoża (2023) notes that it is not easy to make an analysis of the demographic situation in Ukraine due to both the lack of official data and the discrepancy in the information published by various Ukrainian and international institutions.

In general, information on the population of Ukraine is based on the last census conducted in 2001 (State Statistics Service of Ukraine, 2018). But since then and until now, the Russian Federation annexed the Autonomous Region of Crimea and Sevastopol (2014), the Donetsk and Lugansk regions separated from Ukraine (2014), and the Russian–Ukrainian conflict broke out. Libanova (2023) appreciates that it is difficult to obtain reliable data on the population – namely its size, composition, and movement – currently living in government-controlled territories. It is even harder to know what is happening to people in the occupied regions (parts of Kherson, Donetsk, Luhansk, and Zaporizhzhia regions). The next census should have been carried out in 2013, but it was postponed, initially until 2016, then 2020, and finally 2023, when, due to the war, it could no longer be organized (Rogoża, 2023).

If at the beginning of the 1990s there was an increase in the population of Ukraine, starting from 1995 it began to decrease, one of the causes being the emigration of Ukrainians to the West, to the Russian Federation or to other states. Malynovska (2006) estimates that more than 2,500,000 Ukrainians emigrated between 1991 and 2004, most of them young people, which, according to Raymond (2024), reduces Ukraine's ability to sustain its population in the long term. A significant decrease in the number of inhabitants also occurs as a result of the annexation of the Autonomous Republic of Crimea and Sevastopol. According to Eurostat (2024), in the period 2015–2021, Ukraine's population decreased by 3.1%.

Currently, Ukraine continues to face a severe demographic crisis. According to WorldData (2024), in 2022, the population of Ukraine experienced the highest negative growth rate, that is −13.29 percent and currently there are no signs that it will start to grow. At least as long as the war with the Russian Federation continues, Ukraine's population will continue to decline. Predictions about the population of Ukraine at the end of hostilities are different, but they have one thing in common: pessimism. Rogoża (2023) states that by 2030, Ukraine's population could be one of the oldest in Europe, with a high proportion of people suffering from depression, multiple illnesses, disabilities or post-traumatic stress disorder (PTSD).

It is appreciated that after the end of the war, due to the existing situation on the territory of the country, there is a possibility that part of the population will choose to emigrate to other parts of the world. According to Smart (2023), who takes the opinion of different experts, at the end of the war, there is a probability that up to 5 million inhabitants will leave Ukraine.

According to the website of the United Nations High Commissioner for Refugees (UNHCR, 2024), the conflict in Ukraine has triggered one of the fastest growing humanitarian and displacement emergencies in recent history. In a relatively short time of a few weeks, more than a quarter of the population sought refuge abroad or in other parts of Ukraine that were not involved in the conflict. The conflict has caused and continues to cause suffering to the Ukrainian people, displaced millions, and destroyed civilian infrastructure (UN Women, 2023).

Since the start of the so called special military operation launched by President Vladimir Putin, fearing bombing, many civilians in Ukraine live without access to food, water, or electricity (RESCUE, 2023). In the first month after hostilities began, more than 10 million people were displaced either as refugees abroad or within the country (Tymchyshyn, 2024). According to UNHCR (2024), most of the refugees arrived in the countries neighboring Ukraine, such as Poland, the Czech Republic, the Republic of Moldova, Slovakia, Romania, etc., or in Slavic-speaking states. Some of the Ukrainians chose to take refuge in Belarus (42,785 as of February 29, 2024) and the Russian Federation (1,212,585 as of June 30, 2023). The largest number of Ukrainian refugees is in Germany (1,139,000 as of March 02, 2024, of which 1,053,050 requested asylum) and the small number is in Bosnia and Herzegovina (225) and Lichtenstein (590).

The existing number of refugees does not mean a reduction in the population of Ukraine by this figure, but a particularly important problem arises when it comes to the repatriation of refugees. Once integrated into their countries of refuge, it is not certain that refugees will return to a largely war-torn country with a collapsed economy, no infrastructure, hospitals, and schools.

During conflicts, in the absence of protection of any kind, children are the most vulnerable. All the traumatic experiences they go through during the course of the conflict – separation from parents and caregivers, the loss of a parent, the obligation to relocate – leave their mark on a child's mental health. Kadir et al. (2018) show that the direct (death, physical and psychological trauma) and indirect (inadequate living conditions, separation from family, lack of education, etc.) effects of war on children are associated with immediate and long-term problems.

According to the Children of War platform, which receives information from the National Police of Ukraine, the Prosecutor General's Office and the National Intelligence Bureau, 'it is impossible to establish the exact number of injured children due to active hostilities and the temporary occupation of a part of Ukrainian territory' (https://childrenofwar.gov.ua). Table 8.1, based on information taken from the Children of War platform, shows the situation of children in Ukraine from the beginning of the war until now (the period February 24, 2022–April 8, 2024).

The conflict in Ukraine has a strong psychological impact on children in conflict zones. It is estimated that since the start of the war, due to air raids on Ukrainian cities located on the front line, children in these areas have spent between four and seven months in shelters organized in subway stations or in the basements of buildings. The most difficult period was represented by the winter months when, due to the intensification of air raids, many families were left without electricity, heating and access to water or were forced to take shelter in unsanitary basements.

All this has negatively affected children's future and has taken its toll on their mental health and their ability to learn. According to Pfeiffer et al. (2024), the invasion of Ukraine has led to an increase in the number of children and adolescents experiencing armed conflict and other traumatic experiences, which could lead to increased PTSD tubulations in an entire generation.

Table 8.1. The Situation of Children in Ukraine from the Beginning of the War to the Present (Period February 24, 2022–April 08, 2024).

Crt. No.	The Situation of Children	Number of Children	Remarks
1	Deceased	539	According to the Attorney General's Office
2	Wounded	1.284	According to the Attorney General's Office
3	Missing	2.073	According to the National Police of Ukraine
4	Found	25.236	According to the National Police of Ukraine
5	Deportees and/or forcibly displaced persons (children and adults)	19.546	According to the National Intelligence Bureau
6	Returned	388	According to the National Intelligence Bureau
7	Sexual abused	15	According to the Attorney General's Office

Source: The authors, based on the information on the website https://childrenofwar.gov.ua.

A special case is Ukrainian children from conflict zones brought to Russian territories. The exact number of children taken to Russian territories is not known as each party involved estimates different numbers. According to Reuters (2023), the head of the international committee in the Council of the Federation stated on July 03, 2023, that 700,000 children were taken from the conflict zones in Ukraine to the territory of Russia, while Ukraine's Ministry of Integration and Occupied Territories stated that they are currently considered 19,492 Ukrainian children illegally deported. Regardless of the number of children taken to Russia, it cannot be estimated whether at the end of the conflict they will return to Ukraine.

3. Characteristics of Generation Z

The attitude of Generation Z, which includes people born between 1997 and 2010, toward the conflict in Ukraine is also of interest. Generation Z, also known as Gen Z, iGen or postmillennials, is the generation that has used tablets and smartphones from an early age, its members being true "digital natives" (Bolboacă, 2020), communicating predominantly online and therefore, in the opinion of Kelly (2024) their interpersonal skills – or soft skills – suffer. Generation Z is a more realistic generation, more liberal but not necessarily more democratic, more tolerant, concerned with economic, environmental, and volunteering issues. It's a generation that faces loneliness, stress, anxiety, financial problems and feels that the future is uncertain. De Witte (2022) appreciates that

> is a self-driver who deeply cares about others, strives for a diverse community, is highly collaborative and social, values flexibility, relevance, authenticity and non-hierarchical leadership, and, while dismayed about inherited issues like climate change, has a pragmatic attitude about the work that has to be to address those issues.

In July–August 2017, the New Europe Center and Friedrich-Ebert-Stiftung in cooperation with the sociological company GfK Ukraine conducted a survey involving representatives of generations Y and Z. The sample consisted of 2,000 respondents from Ukraine, aged between 14 and 29. Residents of the Autonomous Republics of Crimea and Sevastopol and the territories of Donetsk and Lugansk regions were excluded. The survey aims to understand and assess the feelings of young Ukrainians throughout the period of Ukrainian independence (Gaidai et al., 2017). According to the results published in the work 'Ukrainian "Generation Z": Attitudes and Values', young Ukrainians are concerned about five major issues: the armed conflict in eastern Ukraine, the state of the economy, the general decline in living standards, finding a job, corruption and incompetence of the authorities (Gaidai et al., 2017).

Knowing the characteristics of Generation Z is particularly important for the education system, but also for employers or the military system. In the case of the armed forces, "Gen-Z comprises virtually all junior enlisted personnel and a significant share of junior officers, not to mention nearly the entire current recruiting pool. From a manning perspective alone, Gen-Z is critical to the military's mission" (Clark & Atkinson, 2023). Currently, recruitment is a weak point for the military organization, being influenced by several factors: the constant decrease in the confidence of citizens in the army, demographic changes, drug use, the existence of a criminal record, other physical or mental health problems (Berger, 2022). It is worth noting the loss of interest of young people in the military career, as a result of the evolution of society, the change of mentality and the emergence of new opportunities on the labor market.

Generation Z gets involved in fighting for important causes, but "the question that the armed forces must wrestle with is not whether Gen-Z possesses a fighting spirit but how to tap into it and apply it to the military mission. To do that, the armed forces must help Gen-Z to establish a clear link between their service and the betterment of the world" (Clark & Atkinson, 2023).

4. Bibliometric Analysis of Human Resource Recruitment Policies to Increase Global Mobilization

This subchapter aims to identify, by analyzing the scientific literature, to what extent researchers have emphasized in the published articles on this need to increase the reserve of human resources within the army. Thus, starting from a search for the terms "war," "people," and "recruitment," a database consisting of 151 scientific publications from the period 1992–2023 was obtained. The number of articles is relatively low for such an extensive period, but the distribution of scientific output by country is interesting. Fig. 8.1 highlights the main countries grouped by correspondence authors' affiliation. The United States of America leads the ranking, also demonstrating a high scientific concern for the military field, a performance that is added to other indicators of economic and military performance, such as the world leader in terms of technology and the largest defense budget (over 750 billion USD). Thus, 23 authors of correspondence come from the United States of America, and 4 represented the country working in collaboration with authors from other countries.

Not far behind are the United Kingdom and Russia, which, although they are in the top three countries in terms of the number of publications, demonstrate that the aggressive policy they lead is not necessarily reflected by adequate research.

The amount of scientific production over time is shown in Fig. 8.2. The figure highlights the total number of affiliated articles in five countries, of which the United States of America is also distinguished, with a number of 50 publications. Russia is also in third place on this criterion, with a low number of scientific publications. An explanation (Comisia Europeană, 2023) may also be Russia's censorship policy (censorship laws, entered into force in March 2022 and updated in 2023) regarding the spread of negative information regarding the Russian armed forces, thus restricting the realistic nature of scientific research and the number of publications.

To generate the network and the wordcloud, we started from the frequencies of the words used in the abstracts of the analyzed articles (Fig. 8.3). In addition to the keywords on the basis of which the database was created, namely,

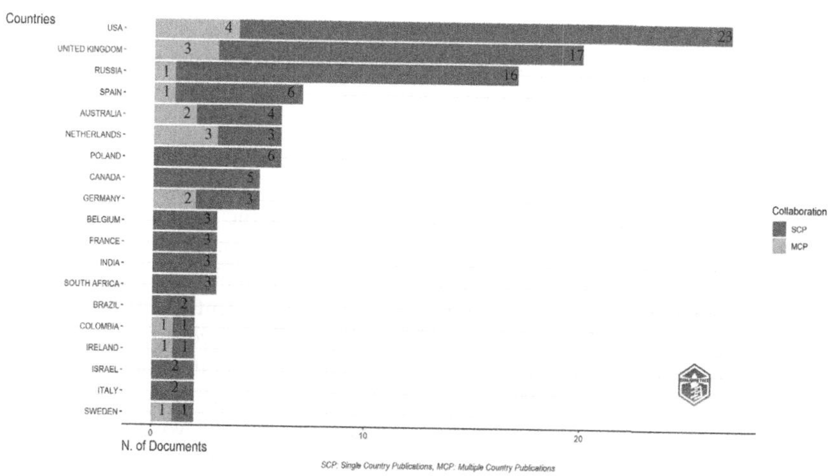

Fig. 8.1 List of the Most Relevant Countries by Correspondence Authors. *Source*: Authors' processing in *Bibliometrix*.

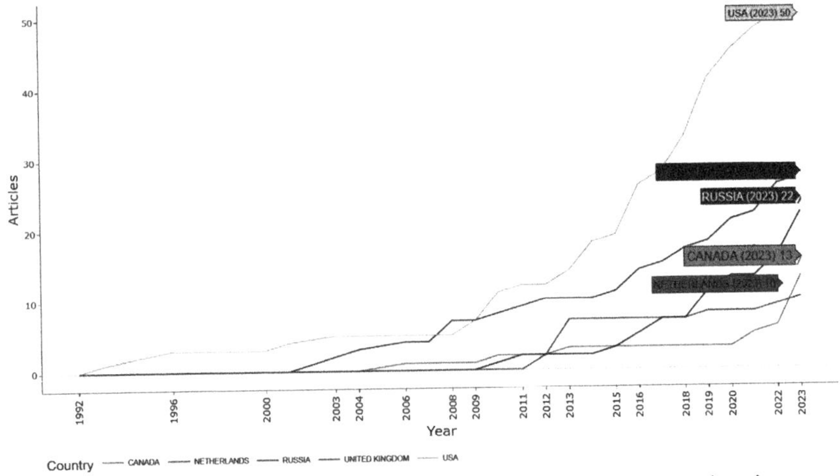

Fig. 8.2 Scientific Production of Countries over Time. *Source*: Authors' processing in *Bibliometrix*.

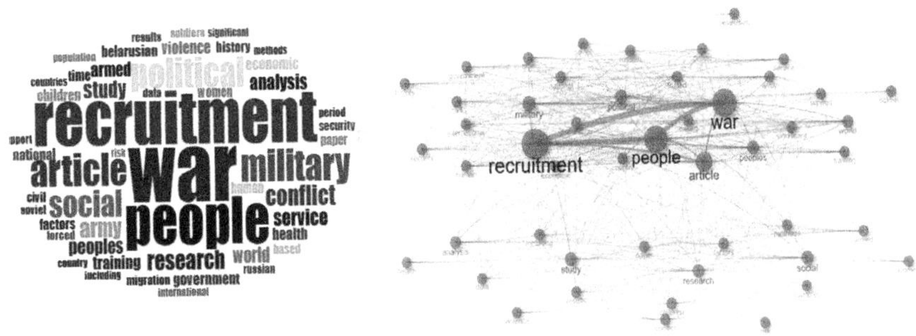

Fig. 8.3 The Most Used Words and the Co-occurrences Created Between Them. *Source*: Authors' processing in *Bibliometrix*.

war, *people*, and *recruitment*, there are also terms specific to scientific analysis (*research*, *article*, *study*), as well as terms specific to the security field (*army*, *conflict*, *armed*, *violence*, *soldiers*, *government*, *training*, *political*, etc.).

The keyword network made using the *bibliometrix* tool is duplicated by an analysis using the *VOSviewer* tool in Fig. 8.4. *VOSviewer* identified 782 keywords, and adding the restriction of at least 2 occurrences of the words in the text of the articles, a network with 11 clusters was generated that integrates 100 keywords.

The network in Fig. 8.4 differs from the one illustrated with the *Bibliometrix* tool because it analyzes more than the frequency and links of words in abstracts, it considers the full articles. Also, based on conceptual relations emphasized in Fig. 8.4, one can observe words that capture elements of sensitivity of the

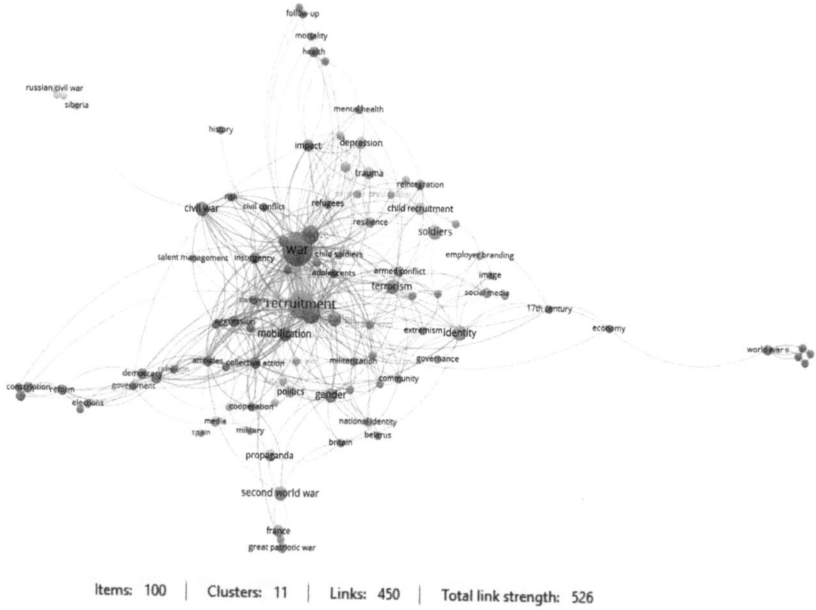

Fig. 8.4 Keyword Network. *Source*: Generated by authors processing in *VOSviewer.*

phenomenon: *child recruitment, child soldiers, terrorism, extremism, trauma, refugees, mortality, depression, propaganda*, etc. The term *conscription* should also be highlighted with three occurrences in the text and a strength of link 7, used in the context of bringing back into discussion at the European level the need to reintroduce mandatory military training.

Table 8.2 contains a classification of the 10 main terms analyzed in Fig. 8.4, ordered according to the number of occurrences in the text.

Table 8.2 contains a comparison of how keywords are grouped according to frequency of occurrence and the links they generated. As frequency of appearance, we distinguish violence, identity, soldiers. The logic of these appearances is justified through the prism of the conflict in Ukraine, where issues of national identity also appeared in the discussion. Analyzing the table from the point of view of the powers of the created links, the terms *war, recruitment, conflict* are distinguished. The common elements are *conflict, mobilization, civil war*, and *identity*.

The most cited article analyzed the political legacy of Uganda's violent conflict (the 1986–2010 civil war), trying to identify a link between rebel group violence and increased political engagement among ex-combatants. Among the worst atrocities committed is the recruitment of people by kidnapping (especially children) and turning them into criminals. The article tries to find justification for

Table 8.2. Keyword Ranking Based on Occurrences and Strength of Links Created in the Network.

Crt. No.	Keyword	Occurrences	Keyword	Total Link Strength
1	Violence	9	War	88
2	Identity	6	Recruitment	74
3	Soldiers	6	Conflict	49
4	Civil war	5	Violence	37
5	Mobilization	5	Insurgency	25
6	Gender	5	Civil war	23
7	Terrorism	5	Impact	19
8	Second world war	5	Mobilization	19
9	Migration	5	Attitudes	18
10	Impact	4	Identity	18

Source: Generated by authors processing in *VOSviewer*.

the apolitical behavior of the community, although a high level of violence was witnessed (Blattman, 2009).

Another example related to recruitment mentions how insurgencies stimulate recruitment by offering inclusive social services, believing that this legitimizes their claim to sovereignty in front of domestic and international audiences. This behavior is a strategic tool that, in ethnic conflicts in Africa, rebels have used to achieve their long-term goal of independence (Stewart, 2018). Recruitments in such conflicts were based on decisions that have political as well as economic and social real causes (Tezcür, 2016).

Classic fights are increasingly duplicated by cyberwars conducted in the online environment. Even terrorist groups like Isis invade the online space with professionally filmed and edited videos, online messages, or various applications with the aim of spreading propaganda and ideology to thousands of online sympathizers around the world (Awan, 2017).

Resistance to recruitment was brought up in the context of the movements against the wars in Vietnam and Iraq, when those who opposed conscription were considered accomplice citizens and thus generated a sense of personal responsibility for the war (Brissette, 2016).

Very interesting was Britain's approach to creating a sense of national belonging and national unity in the recruitment campaign led by the Chamberlain government in 1938–1939. Civil defense was promoted in newspapers, posters, leaflets, guidebooks, radio broadcasts, speeches, and rallies, with the intention of reinforcing in Britain the idea that any future conflict would be a "people's war, in which every citizen would contribute to equal way to victory" (Maartens, 2015).

5. Evidence and Perspectives of the Human Component in the Russian–Ukrainian War

To begin with, it is necessary to have an overall picture for the two states, regarding the military forces. An estimated centralizing situation at the level of 2024 regarding the possible military forces to be engaged in military operations is offered by one of the specialized sites frequently cited in specialized literature and in the media. It is relevant to be mentioned the fact that, for both active and reserve military personnel, the ratio is approximately 1.5–1.6 in favor of Russia. Also of interest regarding the preparation of the territory for defense (the demographic potential for defense) is the situation regarding available manpower, and here a ratio of 3.14 is recorded.

It is difficult to know exact figures on the human losses caused by the war at the level of combatants and the civilian population, for strategic reasons each side tries to minimize its own and increase those of its opponents. According to the data of the British Ministry of Defense (Askew, 2024), more than 355,000 Russian soldiers were killed and wounded in the war in Ukraine; on the other hand, the number of dead combatants was estimated, in February 2024, at approximately 31,000. We are talking about a war that started over two years ago (765 days at the time of writing the study), a war of attrition in every respect. The importance of the operational and general reserve and the generation of forces adequately to the needs of the war also appear in this context. It is implicit that human losses and the need to regenerate the forces, for both sides, will be correlated to the pace of military operations, according to the strategies adopted by the two warring camps. Also, considering the duration, the need to regenerate the forces is given and amplified (corroborated by the losses) also by the combat fatigue factor, present both at the level of the leadership and at the level of the troops. After the 2014 Crimean crisis, Ukraine reintroduced compulsory military service for men between the ages of 18 and 26. For the spring recruitment of Russian citizens to complete military service (for one year), from April 1 to July 15, 2024, the recruitment target is approximately 150,000 citizens aged 18–30 (AGERPRES, 2023). Russia is part of the states with mandatory conscription.

As was normal and expected, in relation to the human way of understanding and relating to the phenomenon of war, some of the citizens capable of mobilization proceeded to different solutions in order not to be recruited and not to participate. Although these data are difficult to prove, it is emphasized (Kazdobina & Hedenskog, 2024, p. 3) that:

> the international press has reported on the widespread practice of draft dodging, which is not unusual for a country at war. According to the BBC, nearly 20,000 Ukrainian men illegally fled Ukraine between February 2022 and 31 August 2023. Some had swum a dangerous river to get to neighboring Romania. A similar number of people had not managed to escape.

These data add to the reality of war migration, estimated (UNHCR, 2024), for Ukraine at 6,486,000 refugees. The fact that some of them represent the working population implicitly leads to the reduction of the internal possibility of supporting the war economy. The fact that no one comes behind, in the sense of replacement after long periods of mobilization for war, substantially affects another fundamental indicator of combat power, the will to fight. The effects of the long-term stay in the front line are also reflected in the increase in the number of desertions within the Russian units. In the case of the Russian military, clear refusal to fight is punishable by an average of two years and three months in a criminal court, but desertion receives a more severe punishment. On the border between propaganda and reality, the Russian side claimed in early April 2024 that the attack on the concert hall near Moscow led to an increase in the number of people who presented themselves for conscription into the armed forces.

6. National Particularities Regarding the Generation of Human Resources in Romania

According to the legislation (Legea nr. 446/2006) in force in Romania, the mobilization reserve consists of human resources that can be used for training, complementing the forces intended for defense and carrying out some missions during the state of emergency, the state of siege, the state of mobilization or state of war and consists of the operational reserve (volunteer reservists assigned to positions in the states of organization of the units; reservists included in the mobilization plans of the units) and the general reserve (citizens with military obligations who are not part of the operational reserve).

Voluntary reservists represent (Legea nr. 270/2015) personnel selected on a voluntary basis, who agree, on the basis of a fixed-term individual contract, to assign positions in the organizational states of military structures. They come from both reservists and citizens who have not completed active military service, but who opt for military reserve service as a voluntary reservist. When the state of siege is established, as well as when the state of mobilization or the state of war is declared, the contracts of the volunteer reservists are suspended, and they are appointed/mobilized, under the law, and are assigned to the same positions.

According to Law no. 80/1995 on the status of military personnel, reserve military personnel are persons who are not in a service relationship with the institutions of defense, public order, and national security and meet the conditions to perform military service, without exceeding the age of 65.

In the framework of the same legislative source cited previously (Legea nr. 446/2006), it is also clarified that the preparation of Romanian citizens for the defense of the country is carried out by performing military service and participating in other forms of training organized by the institutions of national defense and national security (the training of people with management duties in the public administration system at the central and local level; the pre-military training of young people; the training on the mode of action in civil emergency situations; the training in voluntary health formations). Active military service is carried out as a professional soldier, part-time soldier, and pupil or student at educational institutions in the national defense and security system, with the exception of high school and military college students.

An essential component is the preparation of the Romanian institutions with attributions in the preparation of the national economy and the territory for defense, this concept being described by

> the set of measures and actions that are established and carried out in peacetime, in order to use the economic and human potential of the country, to meet defense needs and ensure the continuity of economic and social activities in case of mobilization or war. (Legea nr. 477/2003)

Together with other military institutions, the National Administration of State Reserves and Special Problems, a governmental structure, has the role of "intervening operatively for the protection of the population, the economy and the defense of the country, in exceptional situations determined by natural calamities, epidemics, industrial accidents or nuclear, social or economic phenomena, external circumstances and in case of war" (A.N.R.S.P.S., 2024). In this framework, together with specialized structures, they participate in mobilization exercises, which also evaluate the human potential that can be employed by economic operators, organizations, and county institutions to support the defense effort. The military centers are responsible for updating the personal data of the reservists in the records.

The exceptional situations provided by Romanian legislation, when there are implications on the provision and regeneration of the human resource needed in special security contexts, are state of emergency, state of siege, state of mobilization, state of war.

Starting from January 1, 2007, performing the mandatory military service, as a full-time military and a short-term military (for graduates of higher education), was suspended, switching to voluntary military service.

The central concept brought into discussion particularly for the state of mobilization and war is that of generating human resources, explained by Vladu (2015, p. 62) through the following coordinates:

> the activity carried out by the military administrative structures for the purpose of selection, training and perfecting the training of the personnel with military obligations necessary to complete the military structures that have registered losses during the military actions.

Each state sizes and organizes this system starting, as fundamental elements, from the following conceptual lines: the mission of the defense system, the structure of this peace system, the characteristics of the geopolitical context of which it is a part and influences its functionality. Regarding this last aspect, it is worth detailing as possible geopolitical states of a state and implicitly of the military institution, the membership of organizations, initiatives, treaties, international conventions and the possibility of the manifestation or even the deployment of a military conflict in the vicinity of the borders. Also, regarding national obligations, it is useful to refer to Article 5 of the North Atlantic Treaty, which stipulates that

> The Parties agree that an armed attack against one or more of them, in Europe or North America, shall be considered an attack against all, and accordingly agree that, if such armed attack occurs, each of them, in the exercise of the right of individual or collective self-defense recognized by Article 51 of the Charter of the United Nations, shall support The Party or Parties attacked by taking immediately, individually or jointly with the other Parties, any action it considers necessary, including the use of armed force, to restore and maintain the security of the North Atlantic area. (MAE, 2024)

Military educational institutions play an important role in the generation of human resources in the context of the above. In Romania, each category of forces has a military academy for officer training and a school for military warrant officers and non-commissioned officers.

Obviously, concretely speaking, the human resource generation system is also related to the national demographic potential. The main demographic data specific to Romania (Worldometers, 2024a) indicate a decrease in the population: four places lower (66th place in the general ranking by country) in a four-year interval starting with the base date of 2020, combined with a decrease of the fertility rate indicator (live births per woman) (Worldometers, 2024b). It is thus clear that, regarding the demographic potential for defense, the situation is not an encouraging one. According to the same source of demographic data, the situation worsens in the perspective of 2050 (fertility rate 1.71), which additionally impacts on the need to rethink the resource assurance system for defense, public order, and security. Additionally, it should be mentioned (Stancu, 2023) and the fact that the demographic aging index registered an increase from 121.1 (on July 1, 2022) to 124.9 elderly people per 100 young people (on July 1, 2023).

7. Beyond Speeches. Contemporary European Realities Regarding the Generation of Human Resources

This subchapter starts from the quantitative analysis of the speeches of some notable personalities on the scene of the recent events that have happened since the beginning of 2023. The aim is thus to identify trends or messages beyond the first impression created by the events.

For this purpose, all the public statements of the NATO Secretary General, Jens Stoltenberg, starting from January 01, 2023, and until the end of March 2024, were taken into account. A database was created that includes 210 public interventions consisting of press statements, interviews, public speeches, etc., available online on the web page www.NATO.int. The contents of the press materials were analyzed using the *QDA Miner* software, a tool that can process data from different sources and with different properties, capable of merging and resampling these data and building models based on them (Kenda et al., 2015).

Fig. 8.5 includes a wordcloud highlighting the main words used by the NATO Secretary General in public interventions. The frequency of words can be analyzed in Table 8.3. To compile the table, those words that are relevant in the context of the analysis were selected.

The second most used word in Jens Stoltenberg's speeches is Ukraine, followed by allies, defense, support, and war. A string of simple words defines a far-reaching NATO-wide concern. The outbreak of the war in Ukraine in February 2022 led to changes in priorities and the need to reassess defense capabilities. From the order of the words, it follows that the main concern of the NATO bloc is a reassurance of the defense commitment in the context of the conflict between Russia and Ukraine. Ensuring support from the Allies in the conditions of a direct non-involvement of the North Atlantic Alliance in the conflict constituted the challenge of the moment.

The mention of the names of the states in the speeches of the Secretary General has several arguments: Ukraine, the most mentioned country in the context in which it was established in a military conflict zone, followed by Russia which is associated with terms such as invasion and aggression. As for Sweden, in 2019 favorable Swedish public opinion regarding popular support for NATO

Fig. 8.5 Wordcloud of Keywords Used in Jens Stoltenberg's Speeches. *Source*: Authors, own processing in *QDA Miner.*

Table 8.3. The Frequency of the Most Used Words in the NATO Secretary General's Speeches.

Crt. No.	Words	Frequency	Rate per 10,000 words
1	NATO	5,296	135
2	Ukraine	2,972	75.7
3	Allies	1,897	48.3
4	Defence	1,342	34.2
5	Support	1,304	33.2
6	War	1,091	27.8
7	Security	1,029	26.2
8	Russia	966	24.6
9	Sweden	920	23.4
10	Summit	541	13.8
11	Finland	522	13.3
12	Europe	492	12.5
13	Forces	489	12.5
14	China	478	12.2
15	Putin	394	10
16	Türkiye	338	8.6
17	Weapons	305	7.8
18	Nuclear	281	7.2
19	Peace	268	6.8
20	Capabilities	264	6.7
21	Commitment	211	5.4
22	Aggression	219	5.6
23	Invasion	202	5.1
24	America	126	3.2
25	Resilience	98	2.5

Source: Authors, generated by processing in *QDA Miner.*

increased, although there were still ambiguities and paradoxes complicating this process, and the public was overwhelmingly in favor of continuing to adopt a policy of military non-alignment (Ydén et al., 2019). The outbreak of the conflict in Ukraine subsequently produced changes regarding the security paradigm, and on March 07, 2024, Sweden becomes a member of the North Atlantic Alliance. In this context, Sweden was mentioned in speeches with a similar frequency to Russia.

Finland, which shares a 1,340 km border with Russia, hastened the accession process, becoming a NATO member on April 4, 2023. Analyses have been made on generational differences among parliamentarians whose parties have long opposed the prospect of Finland joining NATO (Fittante, 2023). It was found that the 25- to 34-year-old population showed an increase in the level of support for membership. Also, Finns with university education and higher income tended to approve of NATO membership in higher proportions than those with no university education and lower income. This can be justified by the fact that the political elite comes from the first category of the population and there is a tendency to align between the elected and the voters.

Nuclear weapons have also been mentioned in response to the Russian president's repeated threats, with Putin also mentioned 394 times since 2022. Nuclear weapons and talk of nuclear war are intended to intimidate, amplify states of confusion.

Another analysis took into account the statements of Ursula von der Leyen, President of the European Commission. The purpose of the investigation is to make a comparison between two representative figures involved in zonal politics with economic and security implications. Starting from the news published on the website of the European Commission, a database was created with 69 public interventions by President Ursula von der Leyen. Fig. 8.6 contains a word cloud graphic representation for a visualization of the most used words in the analyzed materials. Table 8.4 contains the words with the highest frequency of use.

Fig. 8.6 Wordcloud of Keywords Used in Ursula von der Leyen's Speeches. *Source*: Authors, own processing in *QDA Miner*.

Table 8.4. The Frequency of the Most Used Words in the Speeches of the President of the European Commission.

Crt. No.	Words	Frequency	Rate per 10,000 Words
1	Ukraine	429	63.4
2	European	420	62
3	Union	304	44.9
4	Europe	275	40.6
5	Support	181	26.7
6	People	178	26.3
7	War	143	21.1
8	Russia	140	20.7
9	EU	121	17.9
10	EUR	119	17.6
11	Energy	110	16.2
12	Market	106	15.7
13	Commission	84	12.4
14	Plan	76	11.2
15	Ukrainian	75	11.1
16	President	74	10.9
17	Reforms	74	10.9
18	Humanitarian	67	9.9
19	Peace	67	9.9
20	Defence	63	9.3
21	Economic	63	9.3
22	Gaza	63	9.3
23	Putin	61	9
24	Solidarity	39	5.8
25	Cooperation	38	5.6

Source: Authors, generated by processing in *QDA Miner*.

Analyzing Table 8.4 by comparison with Table 8.3, it can be seen that the object of the declarations is a common one, although NATO is a political and military organization, and the European Union (EU) is a political and economic organization. The idea of cooperation between NATO and the EU is not a recent one and is due to the increase in the complexity of the European security environment, especially in the context of the conflict in Ukraine since 2014, the more assertive behavior of Russia in terms of foreign policy, as well as considering the management operations of ongoing crises in Africa, the Mediterranean and the Middle East (Ewers-Peters, 2023).

Russia's invasion of Ukraine prompted EU member states and NATO allies to step up their activity and cooperation, demonstrating their full unity and shared determination to condemn Russia's war of aggression and support Ukraine to defend and protect itself and its population. The analysis of the frequency of words used by representatives of these two organizations in public statements once again demonstrates an alignment of long-term and short-term objectives. The EU contributes through direct financial support to Ukraine, while NATO can only reassess and strengthen its endowment capabilities while maintaining its neutrality toward the conflict. The Allies, on the other hand, granted aid to Ukraine in various forms, financial or humanitarian, in their own name.

The discussions and statements broadcast in the public space by the European Commission revealed aspects of the general spectrum of resources, once by the character given by the attacks of the Russian army directed toward the critical infrastructure of Ukraine, causing major damages and exacerbating some deficits, then by the devastating effect of the consuming battles of all categories of resources. An example of this is the June 2023 destruction of the Nova Kahovka dam in Ukraine. The EU's response was prompt, providing facilities related to access to drinking water, assistance on health issues, energy supply, and the creation of shelters for affected people (European Council, 2024). The EU and Ukraine connected their electricity grids in March 2022, shortly after the Russian invasion began, so Ukraine can receive emergency electricity from Europe, with Romania being one of the suppliers.

The word *euro* has a frequency of use similar to energy, and the association with the terms *support*, *war*, and *Ukraine* brings to mind the high number of interventions in support of the Ukrainian people. At the last update of March 25, 2024, the number of sums provided or committed by the EU and its member states for aid to Ukraine was published on the website of the Council of the European Union, namely 143 billion euros. The aid targeted several directions, such as financial support, budgetary, and humanitarian assistance; military support; support for refugees within the EU; grants, loans and guarantees provided by EU member states. The terms *president* and *Ukrainian* are also highly used, indicating constant meetings between Volodymyr Zelenskiy and representatives of the European Commission.

Another category of resources, very important in supporting and conducting an armed operation, is the human resource. Since Ukraine is not a NATO ally, there is no question of sending combatants to the Ukrainian front. Human aid arrived in the form of volunteering, through personal or group initiatives. The specialized literature has also analyzed the need to introduce critical military studies because military conscription is poorly understood in the social and political sciences, a view impacted by the efforts of activists and protest movements against military conscription in the United States of America and Great Britain (Rech, 2014).

Other words frequently used in public appearances, such as *peace, solidarity and cooperation* indicate the way in which this form of political organization, the

European Union, intervenes in solving problems and conflicts of any nature that it has faced since its foundation. An example of a crisis successfully managed by the EU was the COVID-19 crisis, in which case EU leaders managed not only to launch an ambitious response plan based on joint actions but also to restore unity between member states, the basis for ensuring both of social solidarity as well as political stability (Ferrera, 2023). The new challenge at the level of the EU leadership is to demonstrate the same solidarity in the context of a security crisis.

Beyond the discourses, the generation of human resources for the needs of waging war is a complex process, influenced by a multitude of specific factors and sub-factors. From the total population of the country, the male population is of particular interest (but many states also allow women to be part of the armed forces) and especially the medically and psychologically fit segment and over 18 years of age to satisfy the military service. The more the age percentage of this segment is in the range of 18–35 years, the better it is for the generation and regeneration of the human resource. As an example, a majority percentage located over 50 years loses its relevance in providing human potential for defense, this segment being more relevant for the appreciation of the reserve component of the forces. Another important characteristic is the level of education in the sense that a high percentage of graduates of higher education constitutes a solid basis for recruitment and selection for the officer corps of various arms and military specialties. The fact that a certain percentage of the population fit for military service has education in the technical field is auspicious given the increased level of technical knowledge specific to the use of new generations of military technologies. No less important, even if we are talking about defense in crisis conditions, is the issue of the costs involved. Of course, within defense budgets, the main category of costs relates to investments in technology and major new endowment programs. However, as important as the volume is the financial resource required for recruitment, selection, training, maintaining the performance potential specific to the human resource. Salary packages and benefits must be competitive compared to those in the labor market in order to succeed in attracting the necessary human resource, quantitatively and qualitatively. The aspect of compulsory military service puts additional pressure financially if we consider the costs of training large numbers of soldiers. In many states where the obligation to perform military service has been waived, the problem of the necessary infrastructure also arises, there are situations when the previously existing infrastructure, as a result of the termination of the obligation of conscription, is degraded or has in the meantime acquired other destinations regarding the use.

Most states in Europe face problems in securing human resources for defense. Some have an aging population and then recruitment (possible pool) is at risk from the start. Most have abolished conscription and are facing a dwindling operational reserve. If we also add the fact that the young person of the 21st century has a set of values and expectations that are hardly compatible with the purely vocational aspects of training (as an active military or voluntary reservist) for the profession of arms, we have a very bleak picture of the possibilities. In this context, many states are considering the possibility of reintroducing mandatory military service.

The problem of ensuring human resources for security crisis situations becomes, through the multidimensionality of the social aspects involved, a matter of national resilience (seen in a double key, as a characteristic of a nation but also as the sum of the component multi-domain resiliencies). If we accept that, in general, in management, human resources constitute the strategic resource of organizations, then it can be inferred that also at the level of national resilience, the human component constitutes a strategic dimension, with complementary political–military valences. In the Romanian strategic documents (Administrația prezidențială, 2000), resilience is approached as "the inherent capacity of entities – individuals, communities, regions, state – to resist and adapt in an articulated way to violent events, causing stress, shock, disasters, pandemics or conflicts, on the one hand, and the ability of these entities to quickly return to a functional, normal state, on the other hand." The research carried out between September 14 and October 5, 2022, by a team of the University of Bucharest regarding the conduct of a consistent survey on national resilience in Romania showed that:

> They tend to be more concerned about the expansion in Romania of the war that Russia is waging in Ukraine, especially the following population categories: women, people over 60 years old, retired citizens, unemployed people, residents of the urban environment (except Bucharest), respectively from the West and South-East regions. Young people, those with a higher income and the residents of Bucharest are less worried than the rest of the population about the expansion in Romania of the war that Russia is waging in Ukraine. (Universitatea din București, 2022)

It is obvious that the declaration of the state of war is a moment of unrest for a state's population, both as a threat to their own safety and also from the point of view of putting into practice plans to mobilize the population. The lessons identified as a result of the Russian–Ukrainian war also impact NATO's defense and security policies. In this regard, it is relevant to recall the exercise planned and carried out in 2024, Steadfast Defender, in which approximately 90,000 soldiers were mobilized, an otherwise impressive force.

Another important element that must be taken into account for the efficiency of human resource generation campaigns for security and defense, especially during a security crisis, is related to the media framework through which recruitment targets are reached, especially on the volunteering component freely committed. Like the content, the message must be well balanced by coagulation of some motivational items referring to necessity as well as utility and advantages. Apart from the situations of dictatorial regimes where we are talking about imposition and mandatory standardized necessity, in order to gain the adhesion of a young person for military service, the information-recruitment staff must reach the specific values of the respective generation considered of interest, on which to fold the military interests, in the sense of those stated before. The approach can only be interdisciplinary, with multidisciplinary teams (army, psychology, sociology, etc.). Campaigns carried out through mass media must be finished by face-to-face meetings, within specific activities of recruitment-information offices, at their headquarters or in places (parks, malls, etc.) or public institutions (schools, high schools, universities, etc.). The fact that the young people of the current generation mostly prefer communication through social media platforms is an impediment to knowing the personal profile of the possible candidate, but an advantage for information. Once more, a robust security culture in place at the societal level ultimately facilitates the effectiveness of force generation. An example of good practice in this sense is offered by the United States of America through the ROTC program – Reserve Officers' Training Corps.

8. Conclusions and Discussions

The chapter briefly reviews the main issues specific to the provision of human resources for defense and security. Both theoretical aspects of the specific scientific research produced over time and practical aspects of the proposed subject are addressed, with particularities at the level of NATO and Romania, and in the context of the recent war in Ukraine. Only found public sources are used, part of the limitations of the wider development of certain subsumed discussion topics coming from this stream. An original contribution of the collective of authors is also given by the bibliometric analysis undertaken. The graphic device used complements and further highlights the treated aspects by providing multidimensional perspectives to the basic topics in question presented.

The objective of the bibliometric research was to analyze the approach to recruitment, the war, in the context of security crises, from a scientific point of view, of the reflection in the specialized literature. A main conclusion that emerges is that there is a discrepancy demonstrated by some countries between involvement in conflict generation and published military studies. Thus, Russia, a militarily active state, is in third place after the United States of America and Great Britain in terms of the number of authors who have published studies on the possibilities of recruiting human resources for increasing the army.

From the bibliometric processing, it is also possible to observe the way of scientific collaboration between the authors; worth mentioning is the collaboration between Russia and Belarus which does not interact or create scientific links with other authors from other states. From the network of scientific collaborations, it can be seen that American and English researchers create the most links between themselves and with other countries, demonstrating an openness to interaction as a basis for the generation of new knowledge.

Most of the articles that looked at recruitment techniques made reference to ethnic conflicts and the techniques that certain rebel groups used to increase the number of soldiers. It should be emphasized that the use of the term conscription also emerged from the analysis of the literature, although with a reduced frequency. The currently existing deficit in the Romanian army and in most European armies has generated high-level discussions on the disadvantages and advantages of reintroducing mandatory military training.

The second quantitative analysis aimed to position the two major organizations EU and NATO in relation to the security crisis in Ukraine through the public statements of the representative figures. Thus, the speeches of Jens Stoltenberg and the president of the European Commission, Ursula von der Leyen, were analyzed starting from January 2023 and until March 2024. From the analysis of the public interventions of the two personalities, the common concern for providing support and assistance in resolving the conflict is concluded from Ukraine. The collaboration between the EU and NATO has been the subject of analysis for a long time. At one point, there were certain ambiguities regarding their role and identity, such as, for example, the decision to implement the Common Security and Defense Policy, the main policy framework through which member states can develop a European strategic security and defense culture. However, the joint management of the conflict in Ukraine, the common front it creates through all kinds of support, shows that the EU–NATO relationship has reached a high level of maturity. Community states understood that only through the relationship with NATO and not in contradiction with it, the EU could aspire both to autonomy and to the consolidation of the transatlantic alliance (Howorth, 2019), so necessary for the prevention and management of local, regional, or global conflicts.

The already difficult circumstances of Ukraine's demographic situation were aggravated by the invasion of the Russian Federation, leading to the prospect of a demographic catastrophe. If in the 1990s Ukraine was one of the most populated countries in Europe, it is currently facing a sharp decrease in population, which will have dramatic effects on development and reconstruction at the end of the Russian–Ukrainian conflict. As of February 2022, following the Russian invasion, the causes of the decrease are determined by the increased mortality among the civilian population and military participants in the conflict, and the increased number of refugees. It is impossible to estimate how many of the refugees will return to Ukraine at the end of the conflict.

When the war is over, the reconstruction of the economy and badly damaged infrastructure of the war will be done with an impoverished and war-weary, aging and in some cases sick population. The aging and sick population will present a challenge to public services in terms of assisting the provision of daily livelihoods.

At the same time, the conflict in Ukraine leaves deep traces in the physical and mental health of the Ukrainian population and has favored the emergence of a negative trend in the decision of the young generation regarding the increase in the birth rate. This negative trend also appears due to the uncertainty related to the evolution of the economic and social situation after the end of the conflict with the Russian Federation.

The negative effects of the displacement of the population or its evacuation from the conflict zone, the destruction of schools, hospitals, infrastructure, the damage caused to the environment, the economic sanctions are just as many causes that endanger children's access, throughout the duration of the conflict, to a peaceful life in family, food, proper education, medical care. All the trauma suffered by children during conflicts affects the physical and mental health of the child throughout their lives, even in adulthood. As with adults, it is impossible to estimate how many of the child refugees, who no longer have a family, will return to Ukraine at the end of the conflict to participate in the country's reconstruction.

Generation Z, with a specific characteristic of relating to purpose in life, is an informed generation that needs transparency, information, and data. When they understand why they need to complete a task, motivation and commitment to the cause emerge. However, due to pragmatism and way of thinking, patriotism and nationalism began to decline, anti-war and non-involvement beliefs emerged, evidence that in the case of the conflict in Ukraine more and more young people choose to flee the country instead of enlisting and fighting on the battle fields.

The transition from peace to mobilization and/or war is a complex process, legislated specific to each state, through which a state's level of defense readiness is tested and validated. Within this process, the generation and regeneration of the human resource necessary to carry out the actual military action (but also the associated support activities) contribute to determining operational success. Quantitatively well-proportioned but also qualitatively appropriate forces, in terms of the level of training, constituted in military capabilities, can create, under restrictive conditions of operationalization in a time-frame, the differences in capability that lead to the expected operational effect. Regarding the process of ensuring the specific resource itself, the essence remains that of the management of military human resources in the sense of an integration of the two essential aspects, spaces (given by the positions in organizational charts) and faces, with differences (larger or smaller at the level of different armies) for peace and war. It is essential that in approaching the processes of transformation of capabilities, these two states are correlated, in the sense that a capability achieved by a package of forces is as sustainable as possible during the transition to the state of war. The starting point for manpower requirements is the military strategy and the assumed mission, correlated to the security context. Then, going through the sequence of manpower programming, planning, and distribution, the projected readiness is reached. The military assistance received by Ukraine, appreciated (Marsh, 2023) as the most consistent delivered after the Second World War, is a component that remains important but insufficient if it is not also supported by the generation of human resources, from the point of view of the potential to increase the operational effect. Hypothetically, if for a period of time, security and defense recruitment issues arise for a military, a direction to develop the desired capability package that can be applied (which does not mean abandoning strategies to attract the right personnel) takes into account the insistence on the technical development component (to minimize some quantitative and qualitative personnel deficiencies), but this is not possible with the placement of a balance below a certain tolerated limit, set as a reference. Also, the transition of belligerent states to a war economy, beyond the necessary changes related to the functionality of industrial capacities, is also obstructed by deficiencies in the line of human resource generation, which will also be valid in the post-conflict reconstruction stage. The issue of continuity and the transfer of experience and expertise between the generations active in the field of defense also comes into play here. Until the specialized analysis undertaken to analyze the force ratio, active and reserve force numbers can be impactful to the adversary, accompanied by appropriate media campaigns.

The existence of a high level of security culture among the active population is a major advantage regarding the quality of regenerated resources for defense and security, but for a high level of security culture maturity, time is needed and a certain consistency of specific approaches. Associations of reservists can be involved in activities that consist of certain forms of counseling and mentoring for the training of new generations of active military personnel as well as reservists. Negative demographic indicators negatively affect the potential for force generation. Combined with the change in options regarding the preference of young people for military service, it results in the need to rethink the strategies for ensuring the human resource for defense.

References

Administrația Prezidențială. (2000). *Strategia națională de apărare a țării pentru perioada 2020-2024*. Retrieved March 20, 2024, from https://www.presidency.ro

AGERPRES. (2023, April 01). *În Rusia începe campania de recrutare de primăvară, în care sunt chemați sub arme 147.000 de tineri*. Retrieved March 20, 2024, from https://www.agerpres.ro/politica-externa/2023/04/01/in-rusia-incepe-campania-de-recrutare-de-primavara-in-care-sunt-chemati-sub-arme-147-000-de-tineri–1085841

A.N.R.S.P.S. (2024, March 25). http://www.anrsps.gov.ro/index.html

Askew, J. (2024, March 03). *Russia likely suffered at least 355,000 casualities in Ukraine war – UK MoD*. Retrieved March 25, 2024, from https://www.euronews.com/2024/03/03/russia-likely-suffered-at-least-355000-casualties-in-ukraine-war-uk-mod

Awan, I. (2017). Cyber-extremism: Isis and the power of social media. *Society*, *54*(2), 138–149. https://doi.org/10.1007/s12115-017-0114-0

Bebler, A. (2023). The war in Ukraine in a comparative perspective. *Teorija in Praksa*, *60*(4), 776. https://doi.org/10.51936/tip.60.4.775

Berger, D. H. (2022, November). *Recruiting requires bold changes*. Retrieved April 08, 2024, from https://www.usni.org/magazines/proceedings/2022/november/recruiting-requires-bold-changes

Blattman, C. (2009). From violence to voting: War and political participation in Uganda. *American Political Science Review*, *103*(2), 231–247. https://doi.org/10.1017/S0003055409090212

Bolboacă, A. O. C. (2020). *Generația Z: cine este și ce o caracterizează*. Retrieved April 06, 2024, from https://www.jurnaldedigitalmarketing.com/digital-marketing/generatia-z-ce-inseamna-si-ce-o-caracterizeaza/

Brissette, E. (2016). From complicit citizens to potential prey: State imaginaries and subjectivities in US war resistance. *Critical Sociology*, *42*(7–8), 1163–1177. https://doi.org/10.1177/0896920515582091

Children of War. (2024, March 28). https://childrenofwar.gov.ua/en/

Clark, I., & Atkinson, K. (2023, January 31). *Gen-Z will fight: But first, they need to know why. S*. Retrieved April 08, 2024, from https://www.usni.org/magazines/proceedings/2023/january/gen-z-will-fight-first-they-need-know-why

Comisia Europeană. (2023, March 10). *O nouă zi neagră pentru mass-media și libertatea de exprimare din Rusia*. Retrieved April 08, 2024, from https://romania.representation.ec.europa.eu/news/o-noua-zi-neagra-pentru-mass-media-si-libertatea-de-exprimare-din-rusia-euvsdisinfo-2023-03-10_ro

De Witte, M. (2022, January 3). *Gen Z are not "coddled". They are highly collaborative, self-reliant and pragmatic, according to new Stanford-affiliated research*. Retrieved April 10, 2024, from https://news.stanford.edu/2022/01/03/know-gen-z/

European Council. (2024, March 28). *EU response to the dam breach in Ukraine.* https://www.consilium.europa.eu/ro/policies/eu-response-ukraine-invasion/eu-response-ukraine-dam-breach/

Eurostat. (2024, March 28). *Ukrainian citizens in the EU.* https://ec.europa.eu/eurostat/statistics-explained/index.php?title=Ukrainian_citizens_in_the_EU#Population_of_Ukraine

Ewers-Peters, N. M. (2023). Positioning member states in EU-NATO security cooperation: Towards a typology. *European Security*, *32*(1), 22–41. https://doi.org/10.1080/09662839.2022.2076558

Ferrera, M. (2023). The European Union and cross-national solidarity: Safeguarding 'togetherness' in hard times. *Review of Social Economy*, *81*(1), 105–129. https://doi.org/10.1080/00346764.2021.2024872

Fittante, D. (2023). Generation-based position taking: Unpacking Finland's decision to join NATO. *Party Politics*. https://doi.org/10.1177/13540688231188479

Gaidai, D., Zarembo, K., Litra, L., Lymar, O., & Solodkyy, S. (2017, November 22). *Ukrainian "Generation Z": Attitudes and values*. Retrieved April 09, 2024, from http://neweurope.org.ua/en/analytics/ukrayinske-pokolinnya-z-tsinnosti-ta-oriyentyry/

Howorth, J. (2019). Strategic autonomy and EU-NATO cooperation: A win-win approach. *L'Europe en Formation*, *389*(2), 85–103. https://doi.org/10.3917/eufor.389.0085

Kadir, A., Shenoda, S., Goldhagen, J., & Pitterman, S. (2018). The effects of armed conflict on children. *Pediatrics*, *142*(6), e20182586. https://doi.org/10.1542/peds.2018-2586

Kazdobina, J., & Hedenskog, J. (2024, March 8). *Challenges of the Ukrainian mobilization.* SCEEUS ReportNo. 5. Retrieved March 29, 2024, from https://www.ui.se/globalassets/ui.se-eng/publications/sceeus/challenges-of-the-ukrainian-mobilization-2.pdf

Kelly, J. (2024, February 20). *Gen-Z faces financial challenges, stress, anxiety and an uncertain future*. Retrieved April 9, 2024, from https://www.forbes.com/sites/jackkelly/2023/09/29/gen-z-faces-financial-challenges-stress-anxiety-and-an-uncertain-future/?sh=648313db4f14

Kenda, K., Skrjanc, M., & Borstnik, A. (2015). *Modelling of the complex data space architecture and use cases from NRG4CAST project.* 6th International conference on information, intelligence, systems and applications (IISA). Corfu, Greece, 1–4. https://doi.org/10.1109/IISA.2015.7388056

Legea nr. 80 din 11 iulie 1995 privind Statutul cadrelor militare, in: Monitorul Oficial nr. 155 din 20 iulie 1995.

Legea nr. 270 din 10 noiembrie 2015 privind Statutul rezerviştilor voluntari, in: Monitorul Oficial nr. 846 din 13 noiembrie 2015.

Legea nr. 446 din 30 noiembrie 2006 privind pregătirea populaţiei pentru apărare, in: Monitorul Oficial nr. 990 din 12 decembrie 2006.

Legea nr. 477 din 12 noiembrie 2003 privind pregătirea economiei naţionale şi a teritoriului pentru apărare, in: Monitorul Oficial nr. 824 din 20 noiembrie 2003.

Libanova, E. (2023, June 27). *Ukraine's demography in the second year of the full-fledged war*. Retrieved March 31, 2024, from https://www.wilsoncenter.org/blog-post/ukraines-demography-second-year-full-fledged-war

Maartens, B. (2015). To encourage, inspire and guide National service, the people's war and the promotion of civil defence in interwar Britain, 1938-1939. *Media History*, *21*(3), 328–341. https://doi.org/10.1080/13688804.2015.1053386

MAE. (2024). *Tratatul Atlanticului de Nord.* Retrieved March 25, 2024, from https://www.mae.ro/sites/default/files/file/pdf/TRATATUL%2520NORD-ATLANTIC.pdf

Malynovska, O. (2006, January 1). *Caught between East and West, Ukraine struggles with its migration policy*. Retrieved April 01, 2024, from https://www.migrationpolicy.org/article/caught-between-east-and-west-ukraine-struggles-its-migration-policy

Marsh, N. (2023). Responding to needs: Military aid to Ukraine during the first year after the 2022 invasion. *Defense & Security Analysis, 39*(3), 329–352. https://doi.org/10.1080/14751798.2023.2235121

Pfeiffer, E., Garbade, M., & Sachser, C. (2024). Traumatic events and posttraumatic stress symptoms in a treatment-seeking sample of Ukrainian children during the war. *Child and Adolescent Psychiatry and Mental Health, 18*(25). https://doi.org/10.1186/s13034-024-00715-1

Raymond, E. (2024, January 3). *War on two fronts: Ukraine's demographic crisis.* Retrieved April 04, 2024, from https://theloop.ecpr.eu/war-on-two-fronts-ukraines-demographic-crisis/

Rech, M. F. (2014). Recruitment, counter-recruitment and critical military studies. *Global Discourse, 4*(2–3), 244–262. https://doi.org/10.1080/23269995.2014.909243

RESCUE. (2023, August 15). *Ukraine War: What are the impacts on the world today?* Retrieved April 05, 2024, from https://www.rescue.org/article/ukraine-war-what-are-impacts-world-today

Reuters. (2023, July 3). *Moscow says 700,000 children from Ukraine conflict zones now in Russia.* Retrieved April 07, 2024, from https://www.reuters.com/world/europe/moscow-says-700000-children-ukraine-conflict-zones-now-russia-2023-07-03/

Rogoża, J. (2023). *Ukraine in the face of a demographic catastrophe.* Retrieved April 08, 2024, from https://www.osw.waw.pl/en/publikacje/osw-commentary/2023-07-11/ukraine-face-a-demographic-catastrophe

Sheftalovich, Z. (2022, February 24). *Battles flare across Ukraine after Putin declares war.* Politico. Retrieved March 31, 2024, from https://www.politico.eu/article/putin-announces-special-military-operation-in-ukraine/

Smart, J. J. (2023, December 24). *Analysis: Ukraine's impending demographic crisis.* Retrieved April 01, 2024, from https://www.kyivpost.com/analysis/25730

Stancu, C. (2023, October 27). *Îmbătrânește România. Câți români locuiesc oficial în țară.* Date complete INS. Capital. Retrieved March 27, 2024, from https://www.capital.ro/populatia-romaniei-date-statistice-ins.html

State Statistics Service of Ukraine. (2018). *All-Ukrainian population census.* Retrieved April 06, 2024, from https://www.ukrcensus.gov.ua/eng/

Stewart, M. A. (2018). Civil war as state-making: Strategic governance in civil war. *International Organization, 72*(1), 205–226. https://doi.org/10.1017/S0020818317000418

Tezcür, G. M. (2016). Ordinary people, extraordinary risks: Participation in an ethnic rebellion. *American Political Science Review, 110*(2), 247–264. https://doi.org/10.1017/S0003055416000150

Tymchyshyn, I. (2024, February 23). *Twice displaced by war in Ukraine, but refusing to give up.* Retrieved April 01, 2024, from https://www.unhcr.org/ua/en/68153-twice-displaced-by-war-in-ukraine-but-refusing-to-give-up.html#

UNHCR. (2024). *Ukraine refugee situation.* Retrieved March 25, 2024, from https://data.unhcr.org/en/situations/ukraine

Universitatea din București. (2022, December 13). *Universitatea din București produce prima cercetare consistentă pe tema rezilienței sistemului de guvernanță a României.* Retrieved March 20, 2024, from https://unibuc.ro/universitatea-din-bucuresti-produce-prima-cercetare-consistenta-pe-tema-rezilientei-sistemului-de-guvernanta-a-romaniei/

UN Women. (2023, February 22). *In focus: War in Ukraine is a crisis for women and girls.* Retrieved April 01, 2024, from https://www.unwomen.org/en/news-stories/in-focus/2022/03/in-focus-war-in-ukraine-is-a-crisis-for-women-and-girls

Vladu, M. (2015). Considerații privind limitele conceptului românesc de generare și regenerare a forțelor în situații de criză. In B. Sfârlog (coord.). *Teoria și practica generării forței.* Studii. Editura Academiei Forțelor Terestre "Nicolae Bălcescu", Sibiu, p. 62.

WorldData. (2024). *Ukraine*. Retrieved March 31, 2024, from https://www.worlddata.info/europe/ukraine/populationgrowth.php

Worldometers. (2024a). *Romania demographics*. Retrieved March 27, 2024, from https://www.worldometers.info/demographics/romania-demographics/

Worldometers. (2024b). *Romania demographics*. Retrieved March 27, 2024, from https://www.worldometers.info/world-population/romania-population

www.NATO.int

Ydén, K., Berndtsson, J., & Petersson, M. (2019). Sweden and the issue of NATO membership: Exploring a public opinion paradox. *Defence Studies*, *19*(1), 1–18. https://doi.org/10.1080/14702436.2019.1568192

Chapter 9

Reassessing Collective Defence: NATO, Russia, and the Return of Territorial Threats

Roman Janjulia[a] *and Bachuki Gakharia*[b]

[a]*Defence Institution Building School, Defence and Security Training and Analytical Center Head of the National and Regional Security Directorate, Georgia*
[b]*School of Education, Humanities, and Social Sciences, American Studies Program, International Black Sea University, Georgia*

Abstract

With a particular focus on the Baltic States, this study examines NATO's evolving readiness and strategic orientation in response to Russia's increasingly assertive posture. It analyzes historical lessons, the evolution of NATO's deterrence posture, and the role of initiatives such as the NATO Response Force (NRF) and the Very High Readiness Joint Task Force (VJTF) in strengthening Alliance readiness and deterrence. The study also explores contemporary challenges related to interoperability, operational readiness, resilience, and territorial defence.

Keywords: Deterrence; interoperability; strategic planning; resource allocation; crisis response; operational readiness; burden-sharing

JEL Code: H560 National Security and War

Enhancing Transatlantic Solidarity in Collective Defence: Navigating Increased Defence Expenditures, Cyber Security, and Emerging Risks, 173–200

doi:10.1108/978-1-80686-259-720261009

Introduction

24 February 2014. Under the pretence of being local military forces, the Russian military quickly seized essential government facilities and infrastructure in the Crimean Peninsula of Ukraine. The international community was alarmed by this blatant act of aggression, which also marked a significant turning point in European security. The Ukraine crisis provided a sharp reminder of NATO's founding principle – collective defence against external threats – for an organization formed in the furnace of the Cold War. The alliance had to adjust to tackle this emerging threat as Russian military moved across the Ukrainian border, presenting NATO with the harsh reality that the post-Cold War era of relative stability and peace had abruptly ended.

Since its establishment in 1949, the North Atlantic Treaty Organisation (NATO, 1949) has experienced substantial strategic changes in response to evolving global geopolitics, advances in military technology, and new security challenges. This study analyses NATO's strategic evolution using a qualitative research methodology, concentrating on the organization's current posture in the Baltic region in reaction to Russia's resurgent aggression. This study attempts to thoroughly grasp NATO's preparedness and difficulties in guaranteeing collective defence and deterrence in the modern era by looking at historical parallels, current military drills, and strategic concepts.

The Formation of NATO: Collective Defence in the Post-World War II Era

NATO's Role in Shaping Post-World War II Defence

In this chapter, we examine how NATO shaped the post–World War II security perspective, focusing on the Alliance's role in collective defence and the containment of Soviet influence. This chapter examines the Alliance's establishment, the strategic objectives outlined in documents such as D.C. 6/1, and the broader geopolitical context of the Cold War, which shaped NATO's formation and strategic orientation.

The rapid expansion and modernization of the Soviet military, coupled with increasingly assertive political maneuvering across Eastern Europe, underscored the urgent need for a unified defence strategy among Western nations. The North Atlantic Treaty, signed on April 4, 1949, established the North Atlantic Treaty Organization (NATO, 1949) (Milestones: 1945–1952 – Office of the Historian, 1949a, 1949b). The Alliance's establishment was "part of an overall effort to achieve the following goals: deter Soviet expansionism, prevent the rise of nationalist militarism in Europe through a robust North American presence, and foster European democratic cohesion" (NATO, 1949). Therefore, the NATO founding states signed the agreement that enshrined the principle of collective defence, decreeing that "an armed attack against one or more member states shall be considered an attack against them all" (Milestones: 1945–1952 – Office of the Historian, 1949a, 1949b).

The document D.C. 6/1, a foundational Strategic Concept from 1949, addresses post-World War II security concerns and the establishment of NATO (North

Atlantic Council, 1949). It emphasizes the integration of political, economic, and military means for North Atlantic defence, as well as the principles of democracy, liberty, and collective defence (as discussed in Strategic Concept, 1949). The document further advocates coordinated planning among member nations, taking into account geography, industrial capacity, and military capabilities, while stressing standardised operational procedures and proportional contributions. Finally, the document outlines peacetime deterrence and wartime defence objectives, including strategic bombing and the protection of communication lines.

The Soviet Threat and Geopolitical Flashpoints

Post-World War II, the Soviet Union's military build-up was accompanied by efforts to seize political opportunities and achieve strategic goals through political, economic, informational, and intelligence means, expanding communism's reach. As they strengthened their armed forces, they used propaganda and intelligence to pressure Western states. The Soviets forcibly annexed the Baltic states, parts of Germany, Poland, Bulgaria, Romania, Hungary, and eastern Finland (The Soviet Union and the Eastern Front | Holocaust Encyclopaedia, 2022).

The rapid expansion of Soviet power was seen as a serious threat to Europe's free nations.

> By 1952, one NATO intelligence report estimated that the strength of Soviet bloc ground forces approached 6.5 million men, organized into 235 divisions. That number included sixty divisions from the satellite nations of Albania, Bulgaria, Czechoslovakia, Hungary, Poland, and Romania. Paramilitary forces in East Germany – trained, equipped, and supervised by the Soviets provided an additional one hundred thousand soldiers. (Millett, 2015, p. 35)

Facing this significant Soviet threat, European states recognized the need to seek security guarantees. Given the magnitude of the Soviet nuclear capability, these European nations inevitably turned to the United States as the only power capable of effectively countering the U.S.S.R. (NATO Information Service, 1959).

Soviet ambitions, however, extended beyond Europe. The Korean War (1950–1953) demonstrated that communist expansionism was perceived as a global phenomenon, reinforcing the rationale for NATO's collective defence framework. Soviet and Chinese support for North Korea against South Korea heightened international tensions and strengthened Western concerns regarding the spread of communism beyond the European theatre (The Korean War Article; 1950s America | Khan Academy, 1950).

Moreover, it was evident that the Soviet Union had commenced the illegal occupation and annexation of states it had conquered during the war, with no indication that it intended to cease its efforts to expand its sphere of influence beyond Eastern Europe. This Soviet aggression provoked the European states to seriously contemplate establishing a collective defence mechanism to prevent further communist expansion and deter potential aggression from the Soviet bloc.

Without the USA's timely implementation of the Truman Doctrine and George C. Marshall's Plan Turkey and Greece might have succumbed to communism, significantly altering the geopolitical landscape (The Marshall Plan and Postwar Economic Recovery, 2022). These initiatives were pivotal in shaping the Cold War era and curbing the spread of communism in Europe.

U.S. Support and European Recovery: The Truman Doctrine and Marshall Plan

The European Recovery Program, and Marshall Plan as it was formally called, was a 1948–1952 U.S.-sponsored program that attempted to revive the economies of 17 Western and Southern European nations. Secretary of State George C. Marshall proposed this plan in reaction to Europe's severe post-World War II conditions. Its goals were to preserve democratic institutions and reduce the economic conditions that made communist parties appealing to European populations. The proposal included $13 billion in financial aid from the United States, which went a long way toward helping Western European businesses and sectors recover (Marshall Plan | Summary & Significance | Britannica, 2024).

In addition, the Marshal plan was backed by the Truman Doctrine, which was based on George Kennan's report known as the Long Telegram' which highlights key points such as the Soviet belief in the impossibility of peaceful coexistence with capitalism (George Kennan's 'Long Telegram', n.d.). European governments realized how urgently they needed to protect their independence and security in light of the Soviet Union's growing danger and continuous aggression.

By the mid -1950s, NATO sought to improve force readiness and mobilisation capabilities in response to the growing Soviet military threat. However, achieving and sustaining such levels of readiness proved financially and politically difficult for Alliance member states (Kugler, 1990). Consequently, the United States recalibrated its defence strategy through the adoption of the "New Look" policy (1952–1953), which prioritized the utilization of nuclear capabilities (The New Look of 1952–53). This strategic shift was articulated in NSC 162/2, dated October 30, 1953, which emphasized the importance of maintaining credible conventional and nuclear capabilities as central components of the United States' deterrence strategy against the Soviet Union. The document reflected growing Western concerns regarding Soviet military and atomic capabilities and reinforced the role of retaliatory power in preserving the security of the Western alliance (NSC 162/2, 1953).

MC 48 concluded that "…NATO forces-in-being must be equipped with an integrated atomic capability" (North Atlantic Military Committee Decision on M.C. 48.Pdf, n.d., p. 10). This document pushes NATO military leaders to be authorized and free to use sufficient atomic, thermo-nuclear weapons. In this document, it is believed that if a major war could start, it would be by a surprise attack from the Soviet Union with massive use of nuclear weapons, and for this, it was necessary to have NATO leaders' feasibility of using nuclear weapons.

Moreover, MC 48 called for additional priority improvements, such as the provision of adequate early warning and modern alert systems, including "systems in operation designed to ensure early warning of attack" (North Atlantic Military Committee Decision on M.C. 48, 1954., p. 2). Through these systems, NATO would be able to fully exploit its land, sea, and air power and thus ensure the defeat of the Soviets.

When NATO first began to rely upon U.S. strategic nuclear weapons for the defence of Europe, the territory of the United States was not threatened by nuclear weapons because the Soviet Union did not possess delivery systems with sufficient range to reach the United States. However, the deployment of long-range jet bombers by the U.S.S.R., notably the Tu-16 and Tu-95, during the 1950s, eroded the sense of invulnerability within the United States, instigating a notable shift in perceptions (The Soviet Union and the Eastern Front | Holocaust Encyclopedia, n.d.). In 1957, the Soviets successfully tested the first intercontinental ballistic missile (ICBM), the R-7 Korolev (R-7 | Intercontinental, Soviet, ICBM | Britannica, n.d.). Later that year, in October 1957, they launched the first artificial satellite, 'Sputnik' (U.S.S.R. Launches Sputnik, n.d.). These technological advancements demonstrated the Soviet Union's military and technological capabilities, raising concerns about United States defence strategies. The events marked a turning point in the Cold War arms race and heightened tensions between the two superpowers.

Nuclear Deterrence and the European Quest for Autonomy

There emerged fears that the United States would not be willing to deploy its nuclear weapons to defend Europe under all conditions. Leaders across Europe increasingly shared a concern later articulated by French President Charles de Gaulle: "No U.S. President will exchange Chicago for Lyon'" (Legge, 1983, p. 9). (Theatre Nuclear Weapons and the NATO Strategy of Flexible Response.pdf, n.d., p. 9). As a result, proposals emerged for Europe to develop an autonomous nuclear deterrent. However, as Frank C. Zagare and D. Marc Kilgour argued, when two players can damage each other, the value of mutual punishment is not practical for deterrence; instead, it can trigger war (Zagare & Kilgour, 2000, p. 129). Due to this rising uncertainty, the necessity for a united military policy distinct from that of the United States became a topic of more discussion and debate among European states.

On April 20, 1961, the National Security Council issued a secret directive titled National Security Action Memorandum (N.S.A.M.) 40, delineating United States policy toward NATO. Within its military provisions, N.S.A.M. 40 advocated for prioritizing NATO programs in the European theater to address foreseeable contingencies "Priority be given, in NATO programs for the European areas to prepare for the more likely contingencies, i.e., those short of nuclear or massive non-nuclear attack" (National Security Action Memoranda [N.S.A.M.], n.d., p. 11). The memorandum emphasized the necessity for the United States to advocate for adopting this policy shift within NATO through a constructive interpretation of existing doctrine, reserving the formulation of a new doctrine only if indispensable to mobilize European resources and achieve consensus on revisions.

Secretary General Stikker presented a special report on NATO defence policy, focusing on the political control of nuclear weapons. The report recommended consultation on nuclear weapon use, with automatic use in Soviet attacks.

In September 1962, Stikker circulated a paper advocating for early NATO defence discussions on medium-range ballistic missiles and nuclear force development. This paper emphasized the importance of maintaining a strong deterrent against potential Soviet aggression (NATO Secretary General, 1962). Stikker's proactive approach aimed to ensure NATO's readiness in the face of evolving security threats.

However, the push for increased flexibility within NATO remained a contention among member nations in the following years. Ultimately, this disagreement highlighted the challenges of maintaining unity within the Alliance. During the same period, the Cuban missile crisis occurred (Milestones: 1961–1968 – Office of the Historian, 1949). This event further tested the strength of NATO's unity and collective defence capabilities. The crisis ultimately resulted in a renewed commitment to cooperation and solidarity among member nations. However, nuclear flexibility was paused.

Following the assassination of U.S. President Kennedy in November 1963 (22 November 1963, n.d.), the government of Lyndon B. Johnson quickly grew more and more focused on the U.S. military's expanding presence in Southeast Asia (Lyndon B. Johnson and the Vietnam War, n.d.). Improvements to NATO strategy would not be made again until March 1966, when the French government declared its intention to leave the NATO-integrated military system (France and NATO – Historical Events in the European Integration Process (1945–2009), n.d.).

But based, MC 14/3 considered that the Soviet Union would continue its military build-up on land, air, navy, and ultimately nuclear forces as well as anti-ballistic missile defence and air defence capabilities. The MC *14/3* delineated three distinct military responses to aggression against NATO: Direct Defence countered aggression at the adversary's chosen level. Deliberate Escalation expanded conflict cautiously, potentially leading to nuclear deterrence through intensified non-nuclear actions or selective atomic strikes. General Nuclear Response was the ultimate deterrent, reinforcing NATO's defence posture (NATO Military Committee, 1968).

In conclusion, NATO's formation in the aftermath of World War II was a direct response to the growing threat posed by the Soviet Union's military expansion and aggressive political maneuvering. From its inception in 1949, NATO's primary objective was to ensure collective defence, as enshrined in Article 5 of the North Atlantic Treaty. The Alliance's strategy evolved in response to the geopolitical realities of the Cold War, shifting from conventional deterrence to nuclear reliance and flexible response doctrines.

As the Soviet Union expanded its sphere of influence through military build-up, propaganda, and strategic annexations, NATO member states recognized the necessity of a unified military strategy to deter potential aggression. Early strategic concepts, such as D.C. 6/1 and MC 48, emphasized integrating political, economic, and military means to maintain security in the North Atlantic region. However, the Soviet Union's advancements in nuclear technology and intercontinental ballistic missile capabilities introduced new challenges, heightening fears of an existential threat to both Europe and the United States.

The Cold War's escalating tensions, exemplified by the Korean War, the Cuban Missile Crisis, and Soviet intervention in Eastern Europe, reinforced the need for NATO to adapt its military posture. The introduction of strategies like the "New Look" and MC 14/3 reflected a shift toward nuclear deterrence and flexible response, seeking to counter Soviet aggression at multiple levels. However, internal divisions within NATO, such as France's withdrawal from the integrated military command in 1966, demonstrated the difficulty of maintaining Alliance cohesion in the face of evolving security concerns.

Ultimately, NATO's establishment and strategic development in the early Cold War laid the foundation for its enduring role in European and transatlantic security. The Alliance's ability to adapt to Soviet threats while maintaining political unity was crucial in deterring aggression and preserving the balance of power. While the Cold War continued to evolve, the core principles of collective defence and deterrence remained central to NATO's mission, shaping its role in global security for decades to come.

NATO's Response to Emerging Threats: Failures in Threat Assessment and Anticipation

The 1991 NATO Strategic Concept and Addressing New Security Risks

The post-Cold War security landscape presented NATO with both opportunities and challenges as it sought to redefine its strategic priorities. The 1991 NATO Strategic Concept reflected a shift from traditional collective defence toward crisis management, peacekeeping, and cooperative security, particularly in response to instability in Eastern Europe. Initially, NATO pursued diplomatic engagement with Russia, fostering economic cooperation and arms control agreements in hopes of integrating Russia into a stable European security framework. However, as Russia regained strength, its geopolitical ambitions resurfaced, leading to increasing opposition to NATO's influence and interventions.

This chapter examines the evolution of NATO's strategic approach in response to Russia's shifting policies, from early cooperation to growing confrontation. It explores key milestones, including NATO's enlargement, peacekeeping operations, and diplomatic agreements, as well as Russia's violations of international norms, culminating in its aggressive actions in Georgia and Ukraine. By analyzing the limitations of non-military responses and the resurgence of conventional threats, this study highlights the challenges NATO faces in adapting to an increasingly assertive Russia and underscores the necessity of a credible deterrence strategy.

The 1991 NATO Strategic Concept articulates the Alliance's post-Cold War security and defence framework, focusing on collective defence, deterrence, and resilience against aggression toward member states (NATO, 2022). It underscores NATO's role as a pivotal platform for allied consultation and consensus-building on security and defence policies, guided by the principles enshrined in the Washington Treaty. Numerous security risks were addressed by the 1991 NATO strategic concept, like

> Risks to Allied security are less likely to result from calculated aggression against the territory of the Allies, but rather from the

> adverse consequences of instabilities that may arise from the serious economic, social and political difficulties, including ethnic rivalries and territorial disputes, which are faced by many countries in central and eastern Europe (NATO, n.d.-e, p. p.3/13).

It turned out that events unfolded in line with it.

As the Soviet Union broke up quickly, tensions erupted between the newly formed governments and different ethnic groups. NATO's reaction to these issues encompassed humanitarian assistance, peacekeeping operations, military interventions, and backing for the democratic transitions occurring in Eastern Europe. Adding former Warsaw Pact nations to its membership further cemented the alliance's position as a leader in regional peace and security.

For example, after the collapse of the Soviet Union, Yugoslavia was broken apart into several countries: Slovenia, Croatia, Bosnia-Herzegovina, Macedonia, and Montenegro as successor states to old Yugoslavia, and later Kosovo also declared independence. This led to ethnic conflicts and violence in the region, prompting NATO and the USA to intervene through military campaigns, peacekeeping missions, and diplomatic negotiations. The USA and NATO's involvement helped stabilize the situation and prevent further escalation of violence, showcasing the organization's commitment to promoting peace and security in Europe (Milestones: 1989–1992 – Office of the Historian, 1949).

Russia's Seductive Policy Changed NATO's Strategy and Its Impact on the Geopolitical Landscape

Gorbachev's withdrawal of military forces from West Germany and his support for German reunification were pivotal in reshaping the geopolitical landscape of Europe. These actions contributed to the end of the Cold War. They paved the way for incorporating former Warsaw Pact countries into NATO (The Reshaping of Europe – Geopolitical Upheavals in Europe after 1989, n.d.).

Gorbachev's cooperation with the US during the Gulf War, where he supported the US-led coalition against Saddam Hussein's invasion of Kuwait, further demonstrated a shift toward a more cooperative relationship between the superpowers (Gorbachev's "Diplomatic Marathon" to Prevent the 1991 Persian Gulf War | National Security Archive, n.d.). Nevertheless, not everybody supported this peaceful initiative in the Kremlin. For example, the Soviet military's opposition to the European peace deal stemmed from concerns about losing influence and infrastructure (Rumer, 1995, p. 9).

The signing of the START treaty at the Moscow Summit in July 1991 was a landmark event in arms control efforts between the United States and the Soviet Union. This treaty aimed to reduce the number of strategic nuclear weapons held by both countries, marking a significant step toward nuclear disarmament and easing tensions between the two nations (Listen to Bush and Gorbachev Sign the START I Treaty | HISTORY Channel, n.d.). Overall, Gorbachev's decisions and collaborations with the United States, including the START treaty, played a crucial role in shaping NATO's strategy and fostering a more cooperative relationship between the superpowers during a critical period in international relations.

Gaining the Western state's positive attitude, Russia's political steps moved toward democracy and signed the PFP in 1994, which had to influence EU security positively. Russia asked for credit from the International Monetary Fund (IMF), which the IMF approved.

> The International Monetary Fund (IMF) approved a request by the Russian Federation for a 12-month stand-by credit, authorizing drawings up to the equivalent of SDR 4,313.1 million (about US$6.8 billion) to support the Government's 1995 economic stabilization and reform program. (Press Release, n.d., p. 1/4)

Moreover, in 1996, another 10.1 billion was given to Russia by the IMF and 2.4 billion by Germany and France (Deni, 2017, p. 47). Russia–NATO relations were further developed not only in the Economic domain but also in security.

On May 27, 1997, The NATO–Russia Founding Act was signed, which emphasized cooperation and rejected the notion of adversarial relations between the two parties. "NATO and Russia do not consider each other as adversaries" (NATO, n.d.-c, p. 1/9). The document highlights NATO and Russia's shared interest in promoting democracy and establishing a stable security framework. The Act acknowledges Russia's efforts to reduce its military presence in Europe, taking ballistic missiles to Russian territory and withdrawing land, naval, and air forces from Europe and the Baltic States. These actions are seen as positive steps toward enhancing security and peace in Europe, reflecting Russia's commitment to democratic principles and regional stability (NATO, n.d.-c).

The disappearance of conventional threats after the Cold War, the emerging ethnic grievances and terrorism, and Russia's positive signs of changing regimes and diplomatic relations with the United States and NATO changed NATO's approach to force development, employment, and composition dispositions, dramatically reducing NATO's force posture. NATO, transforming it from a defensive alliance into an organization, engaged in peacekeeping and crisis management (NATO – Topic: NATO's Role in Kosovo, n.d.).

The NATO Strategic Concept of 1999, approved at the Washington Summit, was a response to the profound political and security developments that had taken place since the end of the Cold War. This new Strategic Concept aimed to guide the Alliance in the coming years, providing a strategic framework for Alliance military planners and setting forth NATO's role in Euro-Atlantic security. The 1999 Strategic Concept was the sixth document to be approved by NATO, and this last document did not mention Russia as a threat to NATO (4/24/99: Fact Sheet – NATO Strategic Concept, n.d.).

NATO1999 strategy was responsive to changes in the Euro-Atlantic security environment and focused on key elements such as collective defence, military capabilities, new missions, new members, strengthened partnerships, and European capabilities. The Concept reaffirmed the Allies' determination to enhance Alliance defence capabilities by ensuring forces that are more mobile, sustainable, survivable, and able to engage effectively on the full spectrum of NATO missions. It also called for improvements in NATO's capability to undertake new missions to respond to a broad spectrum of possible threats to the Alliance's common interests, including regional conflicts, the proliferation of weapons of mass destruction and their means of delivery, and transnational threats like terrorism (NATO, n.d.-f).

At the same time, NATO continued enlargement, and in 1999, former Warsaw Pact member states joined NATO. Hungary, the Czech Republic, and Poland post-Cold War was the first NATO enlargement. This expansion was seen as a way to promote regional stability and security but also heightened tensions with Russia. The decision to include former Warsaw Pact countries in NATO was met with criticism from Moscow, leading to strained relations between Russia and the West.

Despite some disagreements, Russia–NATO relations were developing further to stabilization of security. On May 28, 2002, the NATO–Russia Council (NRC) was established.

> The NATO-Russia Council (NRC) was established as a mechanism for consultation, consensus-building, cooperation, joint decision-making, and joint action. Within the NRC, the individual NATO member states and Russia have worked as equal partners on a wide spectrum of security issues of common interest (NATO, n.d.).

This collaboration aimed to enhance mutual understanding and trust between Russia and NATO, ultimately contributing to regional stability and security. The NRC has since facilitated dialogue on various issues such as counter-terrorism, non-proliferation, and crisis management. But it lost its aim in 2014 when Russia illegally annexed Crimea (Iulian, 2022, p. 60).

Exposing Russia's Real Interests and Zero-sum Approach

Russia was winning the hearts and minds of NATO and the USA, but as soon as it became stronger economically and politically, it condemned NATO operations. Sergei Karaganov sharply criticizes NATO's military operations in Kosovo (1999), Iraq (2003), and Serbia (1995), characterizing them as "barbaric bombing" (Deni, 2017, p. 53). Russia exposed its Zero-sum approach, and the success of the West was a loss for them.

Additionally, he underscores the intertwining of social and security dimensions, citing the imposition of visa requirements for Russian travelers to Europe. At the same time, citizens of the European Union and NATO member states enjoy unrestricted travel privileges. This critique highlights the multifaceted nature of contemporary security challenges and accentuates the destabilizing impact of Western policies on regional security arrangements. Karaganov's thesis offers a critical perspective on Western actions, framing them as significant contributors to the destabilization of security frameworks in Europe, thus emphasizing the imperative for a nuanced understanding of the implications of military interventions on broader security architectures (Deni, 2017).

Russia's Violations of International Norms and Agreements and the Limitations of Non-military Responses to Russian Aggression

NATO underscored the importance of trust, transparency, and dialog with Russia, and Russia violated international agreements and norms spanning multiple key documents in 2008, invading Georgia, and later, in 2014, invading Ukraine. Firstly, Russia's actions have been scrutinized in light of its violations of the 1975 Helsinki Declaration, particularly Articles III and IV, which emphasize the principles of sovereignty, territorial integrity, and non-interference in the internal affairs of other states. Russia's annexation of Crimea in 2014 and its ongoing war were condemned as direct contraventions of these foundational principles (CSCE, 1975).

Secondly, the 1994 Budapest Memorandum, signed by Russia, Ukraine, the United Kingdom, and the United States, provided assurances of Ukraine's territorial integrity and sovereignty in exchange for relinquishing nuclear weapons. Russia's subsequent actions in Crimea and eastern Ukraine have been viewed as flagrant breaches of this agreement, undermining the trust and security assurances it had pledged (UNTC, n.d.). Moreover, Russia's actions have raised significant questions regarding its adherence to established international legal frameworks, including the United Nations Charter and International Humanitarian Law.

However, despite Western hopes of curbing Russia's aggression through diplomatic and economic sanctions, these measures proved insufficient to deter Moscow's actions. Ultimately, the escalation culminated in a war of aggression in 2022 in Ukraine, demonstrating the limitations of non-military responses in deterring aggressive behavior. Despite concerted efforts, the West could not prevent the outbreak of hostilities, underscoring the challenges of effectively countering military aggression through diplomatic means alone.

In summary, NATO's post-Cold War strategic adaptations were shaped by evolving security dynamics, initially fostering cooperation with Russia through diplomatic agreements and economic engagements. However, as Russia regained political and economic strength, it increasingly opposed NATO's actions, revealing a zero-sum worldview that positioned Western influence as a direct threat. While NATO's strategic concepts evolved to address emerging threats like terrorism and regional instability, the alliance's gradual military downsizing reflected an optimism that ultimately proved misplaced. Russia's growing assertiveness, culminating in its actions in Georgia and Ukraine, exposed the fragility of diplomatic frameworks and highlighted the limitations of non-military deterrence.

The violations of international agreements, including the Helsinki Final Act and the Budapest Memorandum, demonstrated Russia's disregard for established norms, challenging NATO and the broader global security order. Diplomatic efforts and economic sanctions failed to prevent the escalation of conflict, underscoring the necessity of a robust deterrence strategy. The 2022 invasion of Ukraine reaffirmed that strategic ambiguity and reliance on political and economic pressures alone are inadequate against revisionist powers with expansionist ambitions. NATO's response must now incorporate a balance of military readiness, strengthened alliances, and credible deterrence to counter future threats and preserve stability in the Euro-Atlantic region.

NATO in the Post-Cold War Era: Transformation, Strategic Adaptation, and Emerging Challenges

The U.S. Role in Preserving NATO

Military alliances often dissolve without a common enemy, yet the U.S. played a key role in NATO's preservation. The United States believed that NATO's existence in Europe was essential for military cooperation, but they also claimed that NATO is such an ally that "partner of first refusal" (Garey, 2020, p. 206). In 1989, President Bush proposed a major reduction of conventional forces in Europe to counter Soviet presence and pressure Gorbachev into scaling back troops (Zoellick, 2000). Following the Cold War, NATO troop levels declined, with U.S. forces in Europe reduced to 100,000 (SUBSTANTIAL CUT URGED IN U.S. NATO TROOPS, 2024). The 1999 Treaty on Conventional Armed Forces in Europe (CFE) Adaptation Agreement enhanced stability and transparency, leading Russia to withdraw from Moldova and reduce forces in Georgia (STRENGTHENING NATO AND EUROPEAN SECURITY, 1999).

NATO's Transformation: Operational Challenges and Alliance Cohesion

The 9/11 terrorist attacks dramatically altered NATO's security strategy. Article 5 was invoked for the first time, marking a shift in NATO's collective defence doctrine and highlighting the United States's dominant role (NATO, n.d.-b). However, Afghanistan mission exposed NATO's challenges, including unclear strategic goals, weak command structures, and unrealistic timelines. Coordination with international actors and local stakeholders was insufficient, delaying reconstruction efforts and limiting operational effectiveness. Future NATO engagements must prioritize strategic planning, resource optimization, and risk management to ensure sustainable security outcomes (SIGAR 21-46-LL What We Need to Learn: Lessons from Twenty Years of Afghanistan Reconstruction, n.d.).

Furthermore, Libya operation revealed NATO's weaknesses, particularly in funding and resource allocation. Robert Gates criticized NATO's insufficient funding, which constrained operations despite political consensus (Council, 2011). Initial plans called for 300 air sorties, but only 150 were executed due to logistical shortfalls and ammunition shortages (Council, 2011). These deficiencies highlight NATO's struggle to translate political will into effective military action. Addressing funding gaps and logistical challenges remains essential for ensuring NATO's operational effectiveness in future conflicts.

Burden-sharing has long been a contentious issue within NATO. Traditionally cantered on financial contributions, the debate now encompasses broader security responsibilities (McInnis & Fata, 2023). The collapse of the Soviet Union led to decreased defence spending, but investments should align with NATO priorities. The 2022 Russian invasion of Ukraine reinforced the need for burden-sharing, driving renewed NATO–EU cooperation (A New Burden-Sharing Formula in the Making? | DGAP, n.d.). NATO members are now meeting the 2% GDP defence spending target, a significant shift from 2014's 1.47% (NATO, 2024b). Some analyses suggest a range of 2%–4% GDP should be allocated to defence, resilience, and crisis response (McInnis et al., 2024).

Threat Perception Within NATO

NATO's 2022 research across 30 allies, including Finland and Sweden, revealed significant differences in threat perception (NATO, 2023). While 69% of NATO citizens support defending allies, perspectives vary. For example, 74% of Montenegrins feel safe, compared to only 42% of Poles, who share a border with Russia (NATO, 2023, p. 11). Likewise, 12% of Montenegrins support increased defence spending, compared to 38% in Poland (NATO, 2023, p. 4). NATO's cohesion depends on reconciling these perspectives to ensure effective collective defence.

Differences are also evident in the Baltic Sea region. Poland and the Baltic states view Russia as an existential threat, while Germany sees it as a broader concern (The Baltic Sea Region, 2023).

Europe's 31% decline in defence investment from 1995 to 2015 weakened collective defence capabilities (NATO's 2022 Strategic Concept: One Year On, 2023, p. 7). Perceptions of U.S. security guarantees further influence European investment in NATO defence.

Recent decisions to supply Ukraine with ammunition and tanks (Fact Sheet on Efforts of Ukraine Defence Contact Group National Armaments Directors, n.d.) underscore NATO's shifting role in addressing security threats. NATO must enhance deterrence, interoperability, and defence capabilities while fostering closer coordination with partners. Lessons from past conflicts should guide NATO's strategic evolution to maintain resilience and adaptability in an increasingly complex security landscape.

The Need for a New Strategic Approach to Russia

Weighing Escalation Risks and Narratives: The Seeds of Conflict, Georgia, and Crimea

Some scholars (Friedman, 1998) adopt the Kremlin's narrative, portraying Russia's actions in Georgia, Ukraine, and beyond as defensive (Carpenter, 2022). Putin says that the West and NATO, in particular, are not fulfilling their promises and, despite the agreement, are expanding eastward to Russia's borders (Russia, 2014). To dispel any doubts that Russia's actions are purely defensive in response to NATO expansion, extensive evidence points to Russia's proactive and aggressive military posturing, including its invasions of Georgia in 2008 and Ukraine in 2014 and 2022, as well as its continued deployment of advanced offensive capabilities in regions like Kaliningrad, which significantly exceed defensive needs. Mark Kramer thoroughly analyses of the available data (Record of Conversation between Mikhail Gorbachev and James Baker in Moscow. | National Security Archive, n.d.) of the 1990 conference between Germany, the United States, the Soviet Union, Britain, and France in his article, confirming that the Soviets never mentioned the subject of NATO expansion (Kramer, 2009). This expression by the Russian leader is essentially Russia's attempt to defend the illegitimate takeover of Crimea. Russia has its agenda connecting to the Russian Eurasian worldview (Zakheim, 2024) Which includes bringing back the former soviet republics in their share of influence (The Return of History, n.d.) and rebuilding Great Russia (великая держава) (Иванова, 2023).

Russia's unprovoked invasion of Ukraine in 2022 underscored the threat of state actors "acting irrationally" and reignited concerns over Moscow's apparent determination to reassert control over its former sphere of influence (Mackintosh, 2022). Such territorial ambitions directly contradict the core principles of sovereignty and territorial integrity that NATO was founded to uphold. Aggressive actions like the 2022 invasion of Ukraine demonstrate Russia's willingness to use military force to violate these norms with regard to former Soviet republics.

Looking back, the failure to impose truly crippling costs on Russia for its 2008 and 2014 acts of aggression emboldened the Kremlin to undertake the full-scale invasion of Ukraine in 2022. The origins of the current tensions between NATO and Russia can be traced back to the 2008 Russian invasion of Georgia. Expert on NATO and Eastern Europe F. Stephen Larrabee predicted a chain of events following Russia's invasion of Georgia, demanding that the West respond quickly to punish Russia (Russia's Offensive in Georgia a Signal to NATO to Stay Away from Its 'Space', n.d.). Despite widespread international condemnation, Russia's military intervention to support the separatist regions of South Ossetia (Samachablo) and Abkhazia went largely unchecked by the West (Dickinson, 2021). This weak response from NATO and European powers emboldened Moscow, signaling that it could act aggressively against its neighbors with limited consequences. This pattern repeated itself in 2014, when Russia annexed Crimean peninsula in Ukraine. Exploiting political instability in Kyiv following the Euromaidan protests, Russian forces seized control of the strategic location without firing a shot (Press, 2014).

The West's sanctions undeniably pressure the Russian economy, impacting technology, energy, and finance industries (Impact of Sanctions on the Russian Economy, 2023). However, despite these economic consequences, the Kremlin has not been deterred from using force against independent nations when it believes it will further its geopolitical objectives (NATO Review – Sanctions after Crimea, 2015). The assumption that the West lacked a sense of urgency for a protracted conflict was reinforced by this setback, which gave the Kremlin the impression that the West was unprepared to invoke Article 5 and launch a retaliatory offensive (Does the West's Ukraine Policy Need a Reality Check?, 2024). Russia has managed its internal economy, leveraged energy exports, diversified trade partnerships, and stabilized its currency in order minimize the anticipated effects of the sanctions (Rutland, 2023). This has undermined the West's plan to use economic pressure to force Russia to pull out from the conflict or alter its behavior by enabling Vladimir Putin to carry out the ongoing conflict in Ukraine. It will be important to keep Russia's political and economic pressure by imposing more sanctions as response strategy (Pfaff, 2022, p. 10).

This acknowledgment indicated a lack of determination to oppose Russia's activities, which strengthened the Kremlin's perception that the West is hesitant to participate in a risky conflict (Bugayova et al., 2024). The lack of any significant limitations on Russian revisionism in Georgia and Crimea gave the Kremlin confidence that it could regain its dominance across post-Soviet space. This action by Kremlin can be viewed as Vladimir Putin's ambitions to assert political control over the former imperial sphere regions (Dickinson, 2023). The 2022 attempt to invade Ukraine, then, represents the culmination of this long-standing imperial ambition. Arming and supporting Ukraine more robustly prior to 2022 may have improved Kyiv's defensive capabilities and deterred further Russian aggression. Correspondingly, by supporting Ukraine, Russia's rhetoric about NATO intrusion, would have given Russia's claim more legitimacy than it actually has (Pfaff, 2022, p. 10). NATO's apparent unwillingness to escalate in defence of Ukraine in these earlier crises likely reinforced Moscow's calculus that the West lacked the political will for a prolonged, high-stakes confrontation.

With a focus on managing escalation, NATO leaders established boundaries for Russian aggression. President Biden announced goals to strengthen NATO, assist Ukraine, and avoid confrontation with Russia. These conditions included refraining from pursuing war with Russia, thwarting attacks on NATO allies, and abstaining from efforts to remove Putin from office. In an effort to avoid unintentional escalation and preserve international support against Russian aggression, the United States also issued a warning against the use of nuclear weapons (Escalation Management in Ukraine, 2023).

Lessons Unlearned and Escalating Aggression

In the lead-up to the 2022 attempt of invasion Ukraine, "NATO had to carefully weigh the escalation risks of taking actions that Russian leadership could portray as overtly provocative or corroborating long-standing grievances against the Alliance's eastward expansion" (Escalation Management in Ukraine, 2023). This hesitancy appears to be motivated by concerns about intensifying the confrontation with Russia, indicating some self-deterrence on the part of the West in its dealings with Moscow (Bugayova et al., 2024). Despondently, the amount of additional aid promises to Ukraine fell by almost 90% between August and October 2023 compared to 2022, indicating a major slowdown in support for the country (Ukraine Support Tracker, n.d.). Some residents of NATO members oppose their nation's continued support for Ukraine, citing worries about the conflict's possible escalation and the money being diverted from domestic needs (NATO, 2023, p. 18).

Anticipating Future Threats and Emerging Operational Domains

To safeguard the security of its member states and uphold a robust defence posture, NATO must constantly detect new threats, closely examine existing dangers, and assess viable offensive and defensive solutions. Systems thinking is essential to NATO's operational adaptation as it allows for early reactions to changing combat situations (Bartholomees & Army War College (U.S.), 2010, p. 253). By understanding complex interactions between various components, NATO troops improve their agility and effectiveness.

Acknowledging the revolutionary potential of emerging and disruptive technologies (EDTs) such as artificial intelligence (AI) and quantum technologies, NATO works in partnership with both public and private sectors to sustain its technological supremacy. In order to ensure the security and efficacy of the Alliance, NATO's innovation strategies seek to utilize EDTs while protecting against any adversary usage (NATO, 2024a). In addition, NATO's transformation initiatives are vital for sustaining military superiority and fulfilling its defence, security, and crisis management responsibilities in the future. Allied Command Transformation (ACT) of NATO is spearheading a Long-Term Military Transformation (LTMT) program to equip the Coalition to handle all potential "instability situations" by 2035 and beyond (Framework for Future Alliance Operations, 2020). The LTMT program uses two key publications to anticipate future challenges:

a. *Strategic Foresight Analysis (SFA)*, which identifies potential global patterns and their military implications for NATO (NATO, Allied Transformation, 2023).
b. *Framework for Future Alliance Operations (FFAO)*, which outlines necessary operational modifications for future readiness (NATO, Allied Transformation, 2023).

Incorporating systems principles allows NATO to make proactive modifications, ensuring readiness for changing threats and the complexities of contemporary conflict scenarios. While military deterrence remains a cornerstone of NATO's mission, the alliance increasingly recognizes that 21st-century collective defence requires addressing a broader range of existential threats to societal resilience. The imperative for civil preparedness stems from the need to fortify member states against destabilizing forces such as climate change-induced disasters, uncontrolled mass migration, and global pandemics. Converging phenomena like rising sea levels, drought, and extreme weather events could overwhelm national emergency response capabilities if not coordinated through NATO frameworks. Similarly, irregular migration surges driven by conflict, natural disasters, or economic privations pose the potential to spark humanitarian crises and social unrest exploitable by adversaries.

Developing and operationalizing resilience at political, military, operational, and tactical levels is crucial for NATO. The alliance is advancing the Layered Resilience Concept, which aims to strengthen both civil and military resilience layers, thereby sustaining the overall military instrument of power (Van Mill, 2023, p. 85). Lessons learned from the Russian–Ukrainian war underscore the need for better preparation, response, and adaptation to increase societal resilience. This includes forming partnerships and collaborating with civilian sectors to minimize vulnerabilities and promote collective defence (NATO, 2023b).

NATO partners, including the EU, prioritize societal resilience, exemplified by the joint EU-NATO declaration from 2016 (IDEAS, 2022). Allies seek to enhance societal resilience by meeting seven fundamental readiness needs in response to the shifting strategic environment (NATO Review – Resilience, 2019).

1. Assured continuity of government and critical government services;
2. Resilient energy supplies;
3. Ability to deal effectively with uncontrolled movement of people;
4. Resilient food and water resources;
5. Ability to deal with mass casualties;
6. Resilient civil communications systems;
7. Resilient civil transportation systems.

NATO also incorporates exercises to bolster resilience as part of its Total Defence Concept, such as the Trident Juncture exercises (Deterrence and defence in NATO's north, n.d.). In 2018, NATO evaluated each ally's resilience capacity using seven baseline standards, identifying areas needing improvement (The Secretary General's Annual Report 2018, 2018, p. 22). Institutional adaptations like the Defence Innovation Accelerator for the North Atlantic (DIANA) and multinational cooperation frameworks offer avenues for NATO to harness innovation and share the burden of capability development more effectively (NATO, 2023a). Canada's designation of The Launch as a NATO DIANA test site marks a significant milestone in defence innovation. The Launch works with DIANA to test, improve, and implement innovations to meet NATO challenges (Baird, 2024). For example, out of almost 1,300 applications, 44 businesses were selected in 2023 to develop dual-use solutions for secure information exchange, underwater sensing and surveillance, and energy resilience (DIANA | Challenges, n.d.). Currently, DIANA scientists and researchers are developing innovative solutions for modular microgrids that can function independently (NATO-DIANA, 2023).

Implications for NATO's New Strategic Approach

Developing a comprehensive, long-term strategy that credibly threatens severe consequences – whether through economic/diplomatic pressure, military assistance to partners, or the potential for direct confrontation – will be essential to check Moscow's revisionist ambitions going forward. Failure to adopt such a resolute posture risks further emboldening Russia to pursue additional territorial gains, confident that the West will once again stop short of a forceful response. NATO must demonstrate that the costs of continued aggression will be prohibitively high, no matter the Kremlin's efforts to justify its actions through nationalist narratives. Only by appreciating the historical roots of the current crisis, and the strategic missteps that enabled it to metastasize, can the Alliance craft an approach capable of deterring and, if necessary, decisively defeating Russian revanchism for the long term. Effectively countering this threat will be crucial not only for Ukraine's future, but for safeguarding the broader rules-based international order that NATO was created to uphold. Developing a range of credible deterrent options – from economic/diplomatic, military, and pressure to asymmetric support for irregular resistance – may be crucial for NATO to regain strategic leverage against Russia's revanchist ambitions.

Confronting the Readiness–Resource Mismatch

Due to Russian strategic doctrine and the belief that the Kremlin has the right to reclaim its lost strategic depth following the dissolution of the Soviet Union (Murphy, 2016) – the risk of a Russian attack on the Baltic States remains a constant concern. Moscow has bolstered its military posture in Central Europe, most notably in Kaliningrad, by deploying a wide spectrum of anti-aircraft and missile systems designed to neutralize both short- and long-range threats (Read "Regional Ballistic Missile Defence in the Context of Strategic Stability" at NAP. Edu, n.d.). This concentrated buildup has made the Baltic States, already constrained by outdated Soviet-era equipment, increasingly vulnerable.

Importance of Jointness and Operational Art

Russia's military modernization is exemplified by large-scale exercises such as the 2018 "Vostok exercise," which reportedly involved 300,000 personnel and joint operations with China and Mongolia (Russia's Vostok-2018, n.d.). These exercises not only demonstrate Moscow's ability to mobilize vast numbers of troops rapidly but also underscore its commitment to strengthening military alliances and enhancing its operational art. In addition to its conventional forces, Russia employs asymmetric tactics – including information warfare, psychological operations, and coercion – to complicate NATO's decision-making and delay an effective response (House of Commons – Towards the next Defence and Security Review: Part Two-NATO – Defence Committee, 2014). Despite extensive monitoring of these exercises and of Russia's incursions (for example, during and after the annexation of Crimea), NATO's own efforts at capacity-building have been uneven (Power Projection, n.d.).

Improving NATO's response time is critical. Enhanced joint exercises and training that emphasize multi-domain operations and the integration of operational art are essential. Outgoing Estonian air chief Riivo Valge (Herem, 2019) and Millet (Millet, 2020, p. 47). Stress that training programs must "shift from being linear to embracing ambiguity" to develop deep operational competencies while capitalizing on the benefits of jointness. Yet within NATO, significant disparities persist. While some member nations invest heavily in modernizing their forces, others have scaled back defence spending. This uneven distribution of capabilities raises serious concerns about NATO's ability to rapidly mobilize, deploy, and sustain forces across the European theatre. The Baltic republics, in particular, face acute shortages of critical conventional assets modern artillery, armored vehicles, and effective air defence systems exacerbated by their reliance on obsolete Soviet-era technology. RAND Corporation wargames conducted between 2014 and 2015 indicate that Russian forces could reach Tallinn or Riga in under 60 hours, highlighting the grave risk posed to NATO's weakest members (Shlapak & Johnson, 2016, p. 4).

NATO's Evolving Posture and Persistent Gaps

In response to these challenges, NATO has sought to reconfigure its military posture by establishing formations such as the NRF, the VJTF, and an enhanced Forward Presence (eFP) that deploys multinational battle groups to the Baltics and Poland (McKinney, 2022, p. 7). These initiatives signal a renewed commitment to collective defence. However, persistent gaps remain that could severely limit NATO's effectiveness in a crisis:

- *Reinforcement delays*: There is concern that, due to inadequate readiness or unclear categorization of national forces, reinforcements under the NRF might be delayed by up to 30 days. During such a window, adversary forces could exploit their initial advantages.
- Capability shortfalls: Critical assets such as long-range fires, modern air defence systems, and robust early warning networks remain in short supply (Vershbow & Breedlove, 2019, p. 31). These shortfalls significantly impair NATO's deterrence and operational response.
- *Command and control challenges*: Fragmented command and control structures across the Baltic region and limited military mobility infrastructure throughout Europe further hinder rapid reinforcement and coordinated operations. Establishing a coherent, cross-border headquarters for joint planning among the Baltic States is essential to streamline these efforts.

Enhancing Situational Awareness

A key element of NATO's defence capability is its ability to maintain continuous situational awareness. Currently, this is achieved largely through Intelligence, Surveillance, and Reconnaissance (ISR) platforms. AWACS (Airborne Warning & Control System) aircraft, for instance, provide critical real-time intelligence to the Joint Air Operations Centre (NATO Airborne Early Warning and Control, n.d.). However, the survivability of AWACS assets is increasingly in doubt given the threat posed by advanced Russian long- and very long-range air-to-air missiles (Outsmarting Agile Adversaries in the Electromagnetic Spectrum, 2023, p. 114). To counter this vulnerability, NATO is exploring emerging ISR solutions. Technologies such as microsatellites and the "Alliance Persistent Surveillance from Space" (APSS) initiative – developing a virtual network known as "Aquila" that integrates both commercial and national satellites – are being developed to ensure a continuous, resilient flow of intelligence (Vershinin, 2020, p. 14). These enhancements are expected to improve NATO's ability to detect and respond to adversary movements across a contested battlespace (Faleti, 2024).

Defensive Barriers and the Challenge of Rapid Reinforcement

Despite NATO's efforts to reinforce the Baltic States, some scholars argue that Russia might still attack, reasoning that aggressors may take the risk if they believe defenders will accept minor territorial losses rather than escalate to full-scale war (Reiter & Poast, 2021, p. 39). If Russia were to launch an invasion, its capability to quickly construct multi-layered defensive lines would pose a formidable barrier to NATO's reinforcement efforts. Lieutenant General Yuri Stavitsky (Генерал Ставицкий, 2024) has noted that Russian forces in Ukraine managed to establish defensive positions up to 120 km deep in a remarkably short time, within eight months. Should similar fortifications be built in the Baltics, NATO would face significant delays in breaching these lines, thereby allowing Russian forces to consolidate their advantage. In such a scenario, counter-mobility measures become critically important. For example, Lithuania has initiated efforts to harden its borders with Belarus and Russia by reforesting border areas, upgrading bridges and roads, and deploying mines. These measures aim to delay enemy advances and buy valuable time for NATO reinforcements. Coordinated counter-mobility efforts among Lithuania, Estonia, and Latvia could further impede an adversary's rapid progress (How Lithuania Is Preparing to Fortify Its Border with Russia, Belarus, 2024).

Urban Warfare and the Protection of Critical Infrastructure

Beyond the conventional battlefield, urban warfare and the protection of critical infrastructure present additional layers of complexity. The UK Future Operating Environment 2035 report (FOE.Pdf, n.d., p. 25) highlights that urban areas are among the most challenging operational domains, with nearly half of intense fighting occurring in cities (Fridbertsson, 2022, p. 2). In the Baltic context, where densely populated urban centers often coexist with military bases and essential infrastructure, the stakes are particularly high. Robust, multi-layer air and missile defence systems are essential not only for protecting population centers but also for safeguarding key assets such as power plants, transportation hubs, and communication networks. Recent studies (Joint Communication to the European Parliament, The European Council, The Council, The European Economic and Social Committee and The Committee of The Regions on the Defence Investment Gaps Analysis and Way Forward, 2022, p. 7) emphasize that without adequate protection, critical infrastructure remains highly vulnerable to precision strikes that could disrupt national functions and undermine public confidence. Russia's use of FAB-1500 bombs, transformed into guided glide bombs, devastates Ukrainian defences and critical infrastructure, underscoring the urgent need for Baltic countries to deploy longer-range air defence systems and harden vital resources (Pleitgen, 2024). Although the Baltic republics have invested in medium-range air defence, their limited budgets and small forces leave significant coverage gaps. This shortfall argues for larger NATO members to contribute additional, possibly pooled, air defence systems (VAN TOL et al., 2022, p. 37). Moreover, by adopting a "mini-A2/AD" strategy using a mix of short- and long-range precision-guided weapons the Baltics could further hinder Russian advances and delay enemy operations, making it harder for Russia to quickly achieve its objectives (VAN TOL et al., 2022, p. 24).

Interoperability and the "4 30s" Concept

A major obstacle to effective defence in the Baltics is the interoperability gap among NATO members. Outdated Soviet-era hardware and insufficient communication systems hinder the seamless integration of forces across different domains (Curtis, 2023, p. 182). NATO's ambitious "4 30s" force concept which envisions 30 fighter squadrons, 30 land battalions, and 30 ships ready to deploy within 30 days (NATO, 2019) remains largely aspirational in the face of these challenges. Without modern, interoperable systems and standardized training, rapid reinforcement and coordinated operations will continue to be compromised. Former Estonian Defence Forces General Martin Herem (Herem, 2019) has argued for treating the Baltic region as a single operational zone. Such an approach would allow for pooling of resources, improved interoperability, and a unified deterrent posture against potential aggression.

Enhancing EU–NATO Synergy

Due to Russia's conventional military shortcomings compared to NATO, the Kremlin is increasingly turning to asymmetric tactics that exploit its strengths (House of Commons – Towards the next Defence and Security Review: Part Two-NATO – Defence Committee, 2014). Strengthening NATO–EU collaboration is essential to counter these hybrid threats, as the EU offers resources such as justice, security, and development tools – that NATO lacks. Better cooperation would help identify and address vulnerabilities across Europe. For example, if a Russian business tries to acquire a strategic Baltic port, uncoordinated investment screening might leave critical infrastructure exposed. Regional cohesion would enable a unified assessment of risks and coordinated protection of shared interests (The Baltic Sea Region, 2023).

Conclusion and Recommendations

NATO's evolution from a Cold War bulwark to a modern security alliance highlights the enduring relevance of nuclear deterrence while underscoring the necessity for a diversified defence strategy. Historical lessons affirm the efficacy of nuclear deterrence, yet contemporary threats demand robust land, air, and naval capabilities. The deployment of the VJTF and NRF reflects NATO's commitment to high readiness and rapid response.

For NATO to address the readiness-resource mismatch, it must prioritize agility, resilience, and capability within its force structure. These activities involve enhancing coordination and interoperability with allied nations, ensuring consistent training and operational standards, and maintaining readiness for conventional warfare scenarios. Increasing the resistance and resilience of partner nations, particularly in the Baltic region, is critical for robust territorial defence.

The Russian threat to the Baltic States, amplified by strategic doctrines and military modernization, underscores the urgent need for NATO to adapt and reinforce its deterrent posture. The effectiveness of deterrence relies not solely on nuclear capabilities but on a comprehensive approach that includes land, air, and naval forces. Agile and resilient forces, capable of rapid deployment and sustained operations, are essential to countering threats and ensuring regional stability.

Furthermore, improving coordination and interoperability with partner nations enhances NATO's collective defence capabilities. Consistency in training, standards, and operational readiness ensures a unified and effective response in any conflict scenario. By addressing these areas, NATO can sustain its relevance and effectiveness in an increasingly complex and impulsive geopolitical landscape.

Ultimately, the burden-sharing and responsibility-sharing debate within NATO requires a holistic assessment of how allies contribute to the alliance's overall security. The 2022 Russian invasion of Ukraine highlights the importance of burden sharing and territorial defence in European and Euro-Atlantic security debates. A new burden-sharing formula between NATO and the EU, focusing on a comprehensive assessment of risk-sharing and security contributions, is essential for strengthening the alliance.

Recommendations

1. *Enhance permanent presence*: Increase the permanent deployment of allied forces in the Baltic region to strengthen deterrence and rapid response capabilities.
2. *Intensify joint training and exercises*: Conduct more frequent and comprehensive joint training exercises with member and partner nations, focusing on multi-domain operations to improve readiness and interoperability.
3. *Develop non-kinetic capabilities*: Invest in non-kinetic tools such as cyber capabilities and electronic warfare to effectively counter Russian Anti-Access/Area-Denial (A2/AD) systems.
4. *Secure critical infrastructure*: Enhance the resilience of critical infrastructure in the Baltic States through improved civil-military cooperation, ensuring sustained defence and deterrence.
5. *Modernize defence systems*: Support the Baltic States in upgrading their defence systems to modern, interoperable technologies, overcoming current limitations, and enhancing overall defence capabilities.
6. *Strengthen territorial defence*: Increase the resilience and resistance of partner nations through improved defence infrastructure, strategic planning, and resource allocation, bolstering NATO's collective security framework.

References

4/24/99: Fact Sheet – NATO Strategic Concept. (n.d.). Retrieved April 20, 2024, from https://1997-2001.state.gov/regions/eur/nato/fs_990424_nato_strategy.html

A New Burden-Sharing Formula in the Making? | DGAP. (n.d.). Retrieved April 22, 2024, from https://dgap.org/en/research/publications/new-burden-sharing-formula-making

Baird, M. (2024, March 28). *Technology test bed.* Gazette - Memorial University of Newfoundland. https://gazette.mun.ca/research/technology-test-bed/

Bartholomees, J. B., &Army War College (U.S.). (Eds.). (2010). *The U.S. Army War College guide to national security issues* (4th ed.). Strategic Studies Institute, U.S. Army War College.

Bugayova, N., Kagan, F. W., & Stepanenko, K. (2024, March 27). *Denying Russia's only strategy for success.* Institute for the Study of War. http://dev-isw.bivings.com/

Carpenter, T. G. (2022, February 28). Many predicted Nato expansion would lead to war. Those warnings were ignored. *The Guardian.* https://www.theguardian.com/commentisfree/2022/feb/28/nato-expansion-war-russia-ukraine

Cold War Europe Military Alliances Map | World History Commons. (n.d.). Retrieved April 17, 2024, from https://worldhistorycommons.org/cold-war-europe-military-alliances-map

Conference on Security and Co-operation in Europe. (1975, August 1). *Final act. Organization for Security and Co-operation in Europe.* https://www.osce.org/files/f/documents/5/c/39501.pdf.

Council, A. (2011, June 10). *Text of speech by Robert Gates on the future of NATO.* Atlantic Council. https://www.atlanticcouncil.org/blogs/natosource/text-of-speech-by-robert-gates-on-the-future-of-nato/

Curtis, A. (2023). Interoperability challenges in an era of systemic competition. In M. Weissmann & N. Nilsson (Eds.), *Advanced land warfare* (1st ed., pp. 173–192). Oxford University PressOxford. https://doi.org/10.1093/oso/9780192857422.003.0009

Defence Expenditures of NATO Countries as a Percentage of GDP 2023. (n.d.). *Statista.* Retrieved May 16, 2024, from https://www.statista.com/statistics/584088/defence-expenditures-of-nato-countries/

Deni, J. R. (2017). NATO and Article 5: *The transatlantic alliance and the twenty-first-century challenges of collective defense.* Rowman & Littlefield.

Deterrence and Defence in NATO's North. (n.d.). Retrieved April 29, 2024, from https://www.rand.org/randeurope/research/projects/deterrence-defence-nato-northern-flank.html

Development, Concepts and Doctrine Centre. (2014, November 30). Future operating environment 2035 (1st ed.). Ministry of Defence. https://assets.publishing.service.gov.uk/media/68cd3ba8c908572e81248a68/ARCHIVE-FOE_35.pdf

DIANA | Challenges. (n.d.). Retrieved May 20, 2024, from https://diana.nato.int/challenges.html

Dickinson, P. (2021, August 7). *The 2008 Russo-Georgian War: Putin's green light.* Atlantic Council. https://www.atlanticcouncil.org/blogs/ukrainealert/the-2008-russo-georgian-war-putins-green-light/

Dickinson, P. (2023, April 25). *Putin's dreams of a new Russian Empire are unraveling in Ukraine.* Atlantic Council. https://www.atlanticcouncil.org/blogs/ukrainealert/putins-dreams-of-a-new-russian-empire-are-unraveling-in-ukraine/

Does the West's Ukraine Policy Need a Reality Check? A Brookings Debate. (2024, February 15). *Brookings.* https://www.brookings.edu/articles/does-the-wests-ukraine-policy-need-a-reality-check-a-brookings-debate/

Escalation Management in Ukraine: Assessing the U.S. Response to Russia's Manipulation of Risk. (2023, August 9). *Johns Hopkins SAIS.* https://sais.jhu.edu/kissinger/programs-and-projects/kissinger-center-papers/escalation-management-ukraine-response-russias-manipulation-risk

Fact Sheet on Efforts of Ukraine Defence Contact Group National Armaments Directors. (n.d.). *U.S. Department of Defence.* Retrieved February 3, 2025, from https://www.defence.gov/News/Releases/Release/Article/4026238/fact-sheet-on-efforts-of-ukraine-defence-contact-group-national-armaments-direc/https%3A%2F%2Fwww.defence.gov%2FNews%2FReleases%2FRelease%2FA

rticle%2F4026238%2Ffact-sheet-on-efforts-of-ukraine-defence-contact-group-national-armaments-direc%2F
Faleti, J. (2024, February 21). *NATO to Strengthen partnership with space industry, launches APSS*. SpaceWatch.Global. https://spacewatch.global/2024/02/nato-to-strengthen-partnership-with-space-industry-launches-apss/
Forging the Shield The U.S. Army in Europe, 1951–1962.pdf. (2015).
Framework for Future Alliance Operations: Adapting NATO to New Security Contexts – Finabel. (2020, July 14). https://finabel.org/framework-for-future-alliance-operations/
France and NATO – Historical Events in the European Integration Process (1945–2009). (n.d.). *CVCE.EU by UNI.LU*. Retrieved April 9, 2024, from https://www.cvce.eu/en/recherche/unit-content/-/unit/02bb76df-d066-4c08-a58a-d4686a3e68ff/c4bbe3c4-b6d7-406d-bb2b-607dbdf37207
Fridbertsson, N. T. (2022). *The future of warfare*.
Friedman, T. L. (1998, May 2). Opinion | Foreign affairs; now a word from X. *The New York Times*. https://www.nytimes.com/1998/05/02/opinion/foreign-affairs-now-a-word-from-x.html
Garey, J. (2020). *The US role in NATO's survival after the cold war*. Springer International Publishing. https://doi.org/10.1007/978-3-030-13675-8
George Kennan's "Long Telegram." (n.d.). Retrieved May 2, 2024, from https://nsarchive2.gwu.edu/coldwar/documents/episode-1/kennan.htm
Gorbachev's "Diplomatic Marathon" to Prevent the 1991 Persian Gulf War | National Security Archive. (n.d.). Retrieved April 16, 2024, from https://nsarchive.gwu.edu/briefing-book/russia-programs/2021-02-26/gorbachevs-diplomatic-marathon-prevent-1991-persian-gulf-war
Herem, M. G. M. (2019, December 2). Estonian chief of Defence Forces: Regional cooperation as the main enabler. *Defence News*. https://www.defencenews.com/outlook/2019/12/02/estonian-chief-of-defence-forces-regional-cooperation-as-the-main-enabler/
House of Commons – Towards the Next Defence and Security Review: Part Two-NATO – Defence Committee. (2014, July 31). https://publications.parliament.uk/pa/cm201415/cmselect/cmdfence/358/35805.htm#a4
How Lithuania Is Preparing to Fortify Its Border with Russia, Belarus. (2024, February 20). Lrt.Lt. https://www.lrt.lt/en/news-in-english/19/2199884/how-lithuania-is-preparing-to-fortify-its-border-with-russia-belarus
Ideas, L. (2022, May 10). NATO's resilience: The first and last line of defence. *Medium*. https://lseideas.medium.com/natos-resilience-the-first-and-last-line-of-defence-89c42ac47eb0
Impact of Sanctions on the Russian Economy. (2023, October 12). https://www.consilium.europa.eu/en/infographics/impact-sanctions-russian-economy/
Iulian, R. I. (2022). Why Nato-Russia council has failed after 20 years of existence. *Proceedings of CBU in Social Sciences*, *3*, 57–63. https://doi.org/10.12955/pss.v3.305
Johnson, L. B. and the Vietnam War. (n.d.). Retrieved April 9, 2024, from https://prde.upress.virginia.edu/content/Vietnam
Joint Communication to the European Parliament, The European Council, The Council, The European Economic and Social Committee and the Committee of the Regions on the Defence Investment Gaps Analysis and Way Forward. (2022). European Commission.
Kramer, M. (2009). *TWQ: The myth of a No-NATO-Enlargement pledge to Russia – Spring 2009*. https://www.csis.org/analysis/twq-myth-no-nato-enlargement-pledge-russia-spring-2009
Kugler, R. L. (1990). Laying the Foundations: *The Evolution of NATO in the 1950s* (RAND Note N-3105-FF/RC). RAND Corporation.

Listen to Bush and Gorbachev Sign the START I Treaty | HISTORY Channel. (n.d.). *The HISTORY channel*. Retrieved April 16, 2024, from https://www.history.com/speeches/bush-and-gorbachev-sign-the-start-i-treaty
Mackintosh, E. (2022, February 24). *What does Putin want in Ukraine? The conflict explained*. CNN. https://www.cnn.com/2022/02/24/europe/ukraine-russia-conflict-explainer-2-cmd-intl/index.html
Marshall Plan | Summary & Significance | Britannica. (2024, March 28). https://www.britannica.com/event/Marshall-Plan
McInnis, K., & Fata, D. (2023). *From burden sharing to responsibility sharing*. https://www.csis.org/analysis/burden-sharing-responsibility-sharing
McInnis, K., Fata, D., Jensen, B., & Iii, J. M. M. (2024). *Pulling their weight: The data on NATO responsibility sharing*. https://www.csis.org/analysis/pulling-their-weight-data-nato-responsibility-sharing
McKinney, M. M. (2022). *Deterrence by denial to prevent a Russian Invasion of The Baltic States* (0704–0188; p. 19). Naval War College.
Milestones: 1945–1952 – Office of the Historian. (1949a). Retrieved April 23, 2024, from https://history.state.gov/milestones/1945-1952/nato
Milestones: 1945–1952 – Office of the Historian. (1949b). Retrieved April 15, 2024, from https://history.state.gov/milestones/1945-1952/nato
Milestones: 1961–1968 – Office of the Historian. (1949). Retrieved April 9, 2024, from https://history.state.gov/milestones/1961-1968/cuban-missile-crisis
Milestones: 1989–1992 – Office of the Historian. (1949). Retrieved April 17, 2024, from https://history.state.gov/milestones/1989-1992/breakup-yugoslavia
Milestones in the History of U.S. Foreign Relations – Office of the Historian. (1949). Retrieved May 2, 2024, from https://history.state.gov/milestones/1945-1952/truman-doctrine
Millet, J.-M. (2020). Why there is more to OPERATIONAL ART than what meets the "Joint" eye. *The Three Swords Magazine*.
Murphy, M. (2016, September 12). *Understanding Russia's concept for total war in Europe*. The Heritage Foundation. https://www.heritage.org/defence/report/understanding-russias-concept-total-war-europe
National Security Action Memoranda [NSAM]: NSAM 40, Policy Directive Regarding NATO and the Atlantic Nations | JFK Library. (n.d.). Retrieved April 9, 2024, from https://www.jfklibrary.org/asset-viewer/archives/jfknsf-329-015
National Security Council. (1953). Report to the National Security Council on NSC 162/2.
NATO Allied Command Transformation. (2023, February). Strategic foresight analysis 2023. https://www.act.nato.int/wp-content/uploads/2024/01/SFA2023_Final.pdf
NATO Allied Command Transformation. (2018, May 14). *Future forces analysis 2018*. https://www.act.nato.int/images/stories/media/doclibrary/180514_ffao18-txt.pdf
NATO. (2023, March 20). *Annual tracker report*. https://www.nato.int/content/dam/nato/webready/documents/public-opinion/230320-annual_tracker_report.pdf
NATO. (n.d.-a). *A short history of NATO*. NATO. Retrieved April 15, 2024, from https://www.nato.int/cps/en/natohq/declassified_139339.htm
NATO. (n.d.-b). *Collective defence and Article 5*. NATO. Retrieved April 20, 2024, from https://www.nato.int/cps/en/natohq/topics_110496.htm
NATO. (n.d.-c). *Founding act on mutual relations, cooperation and security between NATO and the Russian Federation signed in Paris, France*. NATO. Retrieved April 18, 2024, from https://www.nato.int/cps/en/natohq/official_texts_25468.htm
NATO. (n.d.-d). *NATO-Russia Council (NRC)*. NATO. Retrieved April 20, 2024, from https://www.nato.int/cps/en/natohq/topics_50091.htm
NATO. (n.d.-e). *The Alliance's 1991 strategic concept*. NATO. Retrieved April 16, 2024, from https://www.nato.int/cps/en/natohq/official_texts_23847.htm

NATO. (n.d.-f). *The Alliance's 1999 strategic concept*. NATO. Retrieved April 20, 2024, from https://www.nato.int/cps/en/natohq/official_texts_27433.htm
NATO. (1959). *Facts about NATO*. https://archives.nato.int/uploads/r/null/1/4/145639/0012_Facts_about_NATO_1959_ENG.pdf
NATO. (2019, October 24). *Press conference by NATO Secretary General Jens Stoltenberg following the meeting of NATO Defence Ministers*. NATO. http://www.nato.int/cps/en/natohq/opinions_169936.htm
NATO. (2022, July 1). *The Alliance's 1991 strategic concept*. NATO. https://www.nato.int/cps/en/natohq/official_texts_23847.htm
NATO. (2023a). *Defence innovation accelerator for the North Atlantic (DIANA)*. NATO. https://www.nato.int/cps/en/natohq/topics_216199.htm
NATO. (2023b, October 10). *Deterrence and defence*. NATO. https://www.nato.int/cps/en/natohq/topics_133127.htm
NATO. (2024a). *Emerging and disruptive technologies*. NATO. https://www.nato.int/cps/en/natohq/topics_184303.htm
NATO. (2024b, February 14). *Secretary General welcomes unprecedented rise in NATO defence spending*. NATO. https://www.nato.int/cps/en/natohq/news_222664.htm
NATO – Topic: NATO's Role in Kosovo. (n.d.). Retrieved April 20, 2024, from https://www.nato.int/cps/en/natolive/topics_48818.htm
NATO Airborne Early Warning and Control. (n.d.). *Ac.Nato.Int*. Retrieved May 13, 2024, from https://ac.nato.int/missions/indications-and-warnings/AWACS.aspx
NATO-DIANA (Director). (2023, July 31). *DIANA challenges: Energy resilience – Harnessing Microgrid Tech for disaster & conflict recovery* [Video recording]. https://www.youtube.com/watch?v=TK1II_gu3Pw
NATO Review – Resilience: The First Line of Defence. (2019, February 27). *NATO review*. https://www.nato.int/docu/review/articles/2019/02/27/resilience-the-first-line-of-defence/index.html
NATO Review – Sanctions After Crimea: Have They Worked? (2015, July 13). *NATO review*. https://www.nato.int/docu/review/articles/2015/07/13/sanctions-after-crimea-have-they-worked/index.html
NATO's 2022 Strategic Concept: One Year On. (2023). *LSE IDEAS strategic update*. ideas@lse.ac.uk
NATO Military Committee. (1968, January 16). Overall strategic concept for the defense of the North Atlantic Treaty Organization area (MC 14/3 Final). NATO Archives. nato.int
NATO Secretary General. (1962, April 17). Annual political appraisal: Special report by the Secretary General on NATO defence policy (C-M(62)48). NATO Archives. nato.int
North Atlantic Defense Committee. (1949). D.C. 6/1: Strategic concept for the defence of the North Atlantic area (1 December 1949). NATO. PDF.
North Atlantic Treaty Organization (NATO). (1959). *Facts about NATO. NATO Information Service*. https://archives.nato.int/uploads/r/null/1/4/145639/0012_Facts_about_NATO_1959_ENG.pdf
North Atlantic Military Committee. 1954. Decision on M.C. 48.
November 22, 1963: Death of the President | JFK Library. (n.d.). Retrieved April 9, 2024, from https://www.jfklibrary.org/learn/about-jfk/jfk-in-history/november-22-1963-death-of-the-president
Outsmarting Agile Adversaries in the Electromagnetic Spectrum. (2023). RAND corporation. https://doi.org/10.7249/RRA981-1
Pfaff, C. A. (2022). *Coercing fluently: The grammar of coercion in the twenty-first century*.
Pleitgen, F. (2024, March 10). *Russia's new guided bomb inflicts devastation and heavy casualties on the Ukrainian frontlines*. CNN. https://www.cnn.com/2024/03/10/europe/russian-guided-bomb-ukraine-frontline-intl/index.html

Power Projection: Comparing NATO and Russian Military Exercises. (n.d.). *RadioFreeEurope/RadioLiberty*. Retrieved May 3, 2024, from https://www.rferl.org/a/data-visualization-nato-russia-exercises/27212161.html
Press, A. (2014, March 1). *Russian troops seize Crimea*. POLITICO. https://www.politico.com/story/2014/03/russian-troops-crimea-ukraine-104130
Press Release: IMF Approves Stand-by Credit for Russia. (n.d.). *IMF*. Retrieved April 20, 2024, from https://www.imf.org/en/News/Articles/2015/09/14/01/49/pr9521
R-7 | Intercontinental, Soviet, ICBM | Britannica. (n.d.). Retrieved April 9, 2024, from https://www.britannica.com/technology/R-7
Read "Regional Ballistic Missile Defence in the Context of Strategic Stability" at NAP.edu. (n.d.). https://doi.org/10.17226/24964
Record of conversation between Mikhail Gorbachev and James Baker in Moscow. | National Security Archive. (n.d.). Retrieved March 25, 2024, from https://nsarchive.gwu.edu/document/16132-document-18-record-conversation-between
Reiter, D., & Poast, P. (2021). *The truth about tripwires: Why small force deployments do not deter aggression*. 4.
Rumer, E. B. (with United States & Project Air Force (U.S.)). (1995). *Russian national security and foreign policy in transition*. Rand.
Russia (2014, March 20). *Address by President of the Russian Federation*. President of Russia. http://en.kremlin.ru/events/president/news/20603
Russia's Offensive in Georgia a Signal to NATO to Stay Away from Its 'Space'. (n.d.). *Council on foreign relations*. Retrieved April 4, 2024, from https://www.cfr.org/interview/russias-offensive-georgia-signal-nato-stay-away-its-space
Russia's Vostok-2018: A Rehearsal for Global War? | Lowy Institute. (n.d.). Retrieved March 28, 2024, from https://www.lowyinstitute.org/the-interpreter/russia-s-vostok-2018-rehearsal-global-war
Rutland, P. (2023, February 21). How Putin has shrugged off unprecedented economic sanctions over Russia's war in Ukraine – For now. *The Conversation*. http://theconversation.com/how-putin-has-shrugged-off-unprecedented-economic-sanctions-over-russias-war-in-ukraine-for-now-199718
Shlapak, D., & Johnson, M. (2016). *Reinforcing deterrence on NATO's Eastern flank: Wargaming the defence of the Baltics*. RAND Corporation. https://doi.org/10.7249/RR1253
SIGAR 21-46-LL What We Need to Learn: Lessons from Twenty Years of Afghanistan Reconstruction. (n.d.).
The Baltic Sea Region: A Laboratory for Overcoming European Security Challenges. (2023, December). https://carnegieendowment.org/research/2023/12/the-baltic-sea-region-a-laboratory-for-overcoming-european-security-challenges?lang=en
The Korean War (article) | 1950s America | Khan Academy. (1950). https://www.khanacademy.org/humanities/us-history/postwarera/x71a94f19:the-korean-war/a/the-korean-war
The Marshall Plan and Postwar Economic Recovery. (2022, March 30). *The National WWII Museum | New Orleans*. https://www.nationalww2museum.org/war/articles/marshall-plan-and-postwar-economic-recovery
The Reshaping of Europe – Geopolitical Upheavals in Europe After 1989. (n.d.). *CVCE.EU by UNI.LU*. Retrieved April 16, 2024, from https://www.cvce.eu/en/education/unit-content/-/unit/1f5d29d1-bc79-44af-ae41-6fdb3f41608e/7239caaa-e861-47fc-a4bb-7dbe4276f17a
The Return of History: The Post-Soviet Space Thirty Years after the Fall of the USSR. (n.d.). Retrieved March 25, 2024, from https://huri.harvard.edu/news/return-history-post-soviet-space-thirty-years-after-fall-ussr
The Secretary General's Annual Report 2018 (p. 136). (2018). https://www.nato.int/nato_static_fl2014/assets/pdf/pdf_publications/20190315_sgar2018-en.pdf

The Soviet Union and the Eastern Front | Holocaust Encyclopedia. (2022). Retrieved March 31, 2024, from https://encyclopedia.ushmm.org/content/en/article/the-soviet-union-and-the-eastern-front

Threater Nuclear Weapons and the NATO Strategy of Flexible Response.pdf. (n.d.).

Ukraine Support Tracker: New Aid Drops to Lowest Level Since January 2022. (n.d.). Kiel Institute. Retrieved April 5, 2024, from https://www.ifw-kiel.de/publications/news/ukraine-support-tracker-new-aid-drops-to-lowest-level-since-january-2022/

UNTC. (n.d.). Retrieved April 21, 2024, from https://treaties.un.org/Pages/showDetails.aspx?objid=0800000280401fbb

U.S. Department of State. (n.d.). The new look of 1952–53.

Van Mill, J. (2023). The future of NATO's resilience. *Royal Netherlands army concepts, capability integration and experimentation branch*. NATO Joint Warfare Centre.

Van Tol, J., Bassler, C., Kjellström Elgin, K., & Hacker, T. (2022). *Deterrence and defence in The Baltic Region new realities* (p. 86) [Policy]. Center for Strategic and Budgetary Assessments (CSBA).

Vershbow, A. R., & Breedlove, P. M. (2019). *PERMANENT DETERRENCE enhancements to the US Military presence in North Central Europe*. Atlantic Council.

Vershinin, A. (2020). *The challenge of dis-integrating A2/AD zone*. National Defence University Press.

Zagare, F. C., & Kilgour, D. M. (2000). *Perfect deterrence*. Cambridge University Press. http://www.cambridge.org

Zakheim, D. S. opinion contributor. (2024, March 22). Putin, in the footsteps of Potemkin, is trying to recreate the Russian Empire [Text]. *The Hill*. https://thehill.com/opinion/international/4548668-putin-in-the-footsteps-of-potemkin-is-trying-to-recreate-the-russian-empire/

Zoellick, R. B. (2000, September 1). *Two Plus Four [Text]*. The National Interest; The Center for the National Interest. https://nationalinterest.org/article/two-plus-four-1205

Генерал Ставицкий: Система рубежей обороны повысила живучесть ВС РФ в 5-6 раз. (2024, January 19). *Российская газета*. https://rg.ru/2024/01/19/general-stavickij-sistema-rubezhej-oborony-povysila-zhivuchest-vc-rf-v-5-6-raz.html

Иванова, М. О. (2023). СССР как «великая держава»: Имперские нарративы и статус государства, 1920–1935. *Quaestio Rossica*, *11*(3), 1041–1056. https://doi.org/10.15826/qr.2023.3.833

Chapter 10

Defence Resources Implications of the Conflict in Ukraine on European Countries

Maria Constantinescu[a] *and Paul Tudorache*[b]

[a]*Regional Department of Defence Resources Management Studies, "Carol I" National Defense University, Romania*
[b]*"Nicolae Bălcescu" Land Forces Academy of Sibiu, Romania*

Abstract

This chapter aims to examine the various areas in which the Ukrainian conflict influenced the EU approach to the common defence policy, with focus on defence expenditures, as overall trend and in terms of destination of expenditures and changes in procurement policies. The research questions envisaged are related to the potential influence of the war in Ukraine on the European Countries defence expenditures and to the specific steps they took in order to enhance their defence from the perspective of defence resources management. Qualitative research methods were used, based on a combination of examination of the literature, comparative analysis, and indirect observation.

The main findings of the chapter are that the invasion of Ukraine has significantly influenced European countries' defence expenditures, prompting many EU members to increase their defence budgets and armament purchases. The war exposed the need for stronger, interoperable defence systems and highlighted weaknesses in the EU's defence cooperation, military industries, and supply of ammunition. The upside of the events is that they have led to unprecedented unity among EU member states, with new initiatives focusing on self-reliance in military matters and a larger role for the European Commission. Despite the progress, uncertainties persist whether these trends will persist post-conflict, as future elections and

Enhancing Transatlantic Solidarity in Collective Defence: Navigating Increased Defence Expenditures, Cyber Security, and Emerging Risks, 201–224

Published under exclusive licence by Emerald Publishing Limited
doi:10.1108/978-1-80686-259-720261010

shifting political priorities could affect defence policies and spending. The practical implications are related to the need for an increased cooperation, more streamlined decision making processes and the need for the EU to diversify its strategic partnerships while maintaining strong ties with NATO.

Keywords: EU; defence; industry; Ukraine; war; implications

JEL Code: H56

1. Introduction

1.1. Need for the Study

The attack on Ukraine by Russia in February 2022 can be considered a seminal moment which abruptly brought into the attention of the EU member states, politicians and civil society a harsh reality: a large regional conflict on the European territory is no longer unimaginable. The Ukrainian war emphasized the need for a critical change in the security domain and defence policy of the EU and in its priorities in terms of allocating defence resources, encouraging defence investments and increasing total defence spending of EU member-states. After a long period characterized by prioritizing economic issues and denial of the potential security risks, the serious challenges for the European defence generated by the regional security environment were finally brought to the decision makers and public's attention. Such challenges are related to the need to increase the investments in defence capabilities, the worrying reductions in armaments and ammunition stockpiles among European countries due to providing military support to Ukraine, or the disintegration of the EU national defence industries interests.

Related to defence spending, the EU member states started to realize that the increase in their defence expenditures following the events in Crimea in 2014 was not enough to counter the current problems and a change in paradigm related to the EU's role as a security provider began to emerge, marking the beginning of a change in defence policies of its members.

In terms of defence planning, the Ukrainian conflict has brought to the attention the fact that at the level of the EU, there still is no coordinated mechanism of defence planning to support ambitious ideas such as the strategic autonomy or the European army (La Baume & Herszenhorn, 2018), promoted by the French president Macron. Defence planning is not yet a unitary process at EU level, as it consists of a patchwork of national planning processes, the NATO defence planning process for the EU members who are also members of the Alliance and the EU defence planning process, under the umbrella of the Common Security and Defence policy, comprised of several components: the Capability Development Mechanism – introduced in 2003, the Capability Development Plans coordinated by the European Defence Agency (EDA) – introduced in 2008, the Permanent Structured Cooperation (PESCO), and the Coordinated Annual Review on Defence – introduced in 2017. Progress has been made in the last years in terms of enhancing the coordination of defence planning, but not sufficient defence project investments were developed in cooperation among EU countries. Defence is still viewed as the main task of the EU and NATO member states cooperate when they have the incentives of their national interests in terms of national defence plans, national defence industries or in terms of political relations. Defence projects are costly and take a long time to develop, so many EU countries prefer off-the-shelf weapon systems, from strategic partners such as the United States.

The Ukrainian conflict generated a change in the mind-set of the European Union, which was quite unthinkable a decade ago, from an economic and political union toward a regional security and defence actor. This change is illustrated by a recent speech of Ursula von der Leyen in the European Parliament Plenary, on consolidating European defence in a dynamic geopolitical landscape (European Commission, 2024a, 2024b, 2024c), referring to the

> urgent need to rebuild, replenish and modernize Member States' armed forces. In doing so, Europe should strive to develop and manufacture the next generation of battle-winning operational capabilities and to ensure it has the sufficient quantity of material and the technological superiority that we may need in the future. That means turbocharging our defence industrial capacity in the next five years…At the heart of this must be a simple principle: Europe must spend more, spend better, spend European…this will help us reduce fragmentation and increase interoperability.

The president of the European Commission highlighted the importance of increasing support for the defence industry, through the identification of European Defence Projects of Common Interest and innovation to promote EU's technological progress in terms of defence products. The changes went beyond words, as EU member states have mostly showed cohesion and unity in providing financial and military assistance to Ukraine and renewed their common security commitments through the creation of new mechanisms such as solidarity corridor or a munitions plan.

1.2. Purpose

This chapter aims to examine the various areas in which the Ukrainian conflict changed the EU approach to the common defence policy, with focus on defence expenditures, as trend and in terms of destination of expenditures and the changes in procurement policies.

In support of the research goal and objectives, the following research questions have been considered:

(1) Did the invasion if Ukraine have an influence on the European Countries defence expenditures? (main research question);
(2) What are the specific steps the EU countries took in order to enhance their defence from the perspective of defence resources management (policies, procurement programs, cooperation agreements, infrastructure investments, and recruitment and retention policies)?

1.3. Methodology

In order to provide an answer the main purpose and subordinate research questions, qualitative research methods were used, based on a combination of examination of the literature, comparative analysis, and indirect observation.

2. The Impact of the Ukrainian Conflict on the EU Strategic Stance and the Evolution of the EU Countries Defence Expenditures

For the last two decades following the end of the Cold War, the EU countries did not feel the need to increase (or at least maintain constant) their defence expenditures, as the security and defence environment did not appear to justify such expenses. After the separation of the Soviet Union, the tensions in Europe were greatly reduced, as the former enemies were viewed as partners (some of them becoming members of the EU themselves, others included in various formats of cooperation). Consequently, many European countries reduced their defence budgets significantly. The focus in the defence area shifted toward demilitarization, arms controls, and peacekeeping and humanitarian operations, as in the first decade after 1990 there was an increased emphasis on peacekeeping and humanitarian operations, particularly in the Balkans and later in the Middle East and Africa. The level of military spending required by these operations was limited, and the emphasis was placed on smaller, professional armed forces and the reallocation of resources to other sectors, such as social welfare and infrastructure.

Following the emergence of new asymmetric threats and the involvement of many of the EU members that were also NATO members in various operations under the concept of War on Terror, some of the EU countries did start to increase their defence spending, but in a limited manner. The increases were aimed at specific areas such as intelligence, Special Forces, and homeland security, which were directly linked to countering the emerging threats, but the overall level of defence expenditures remained stagnant.

The financial crisis in 2008 was another factor that negatively influenced the evolution of defence spending in the EU countries, as the ensuing economic recession meant a contraction of the EU economy for five consecutive quarters, with a return to economic growth only in the second part of 2009. In addition, the EU government debt, which had remained relatively stable to approximately 60% of gross domestic product (GDP) from 2000 to 2008, increased sharply to 73% GDP in 2009, as a result of the measures taken to mitigate the effects of the financial crisis (Szczepanski, 2019). Government expenditures at the level of the EU were mainly directed toward navigating the financial crisis aftermath and the cuts in defence spending were easy to justify in a security environment in which there were no perceived state foes for the EU.

Starting with 2010, concerns about Russia's assertiveness in Eastern Europe and the shift of the United States center of interest away from Europe toward Asia Pacific, generated the first stages of realization from some of the EU countries that there was a need for greater strategic autonomy from the United States. This led to a renewed focus on European defence integration, driven in part by efforts of the EDA and initiatives like PESCO, aimed to promote cooperation and coordination among EU member states in defence matters. Still, these developments were not translated into significant increases in the military budgets of the EU members and the defence expenditures continued their downward trend.

The invasion of Crimea in 2014 can be considered a turning point, as many EU countries slowly began to realize that Russia's aggressive stance was not limited to indirect interventions in places outside Europe (like Syria). The defence expenditures of the EU members started to increase, at a slower pace at first, and then in a more accelerated manner following the election of Donald Trump as the US president in 2016. The Trump administration meant unprecedented challenges in the transatlantic relations, as uncomfortable questions arose about the credibility of the USA as a security guarantor and even related to the existence of NATO itself (Nielsen & Dimitrova, 2022). The pressures exerted by the Trump administration for EU countries to increase defence spending to meet NATO's level of ambition of spending 2% of GDP on defence capabilities and the less than amicable messages send through press statements and economic measures slowly began to convince at least some of the EU countries to reassess their confidence on NATO and consider the need for stronger EU defence capabilities (Kirshner, 2021).

Despite the geopolitical shifts, including Russia's annexation of Crimea, disputes in the Middle East, and increasing tensions with China which prompted some EU countries to re-evaluate their defence postures and increase military spending to address perceived threats and safeguard their national interests, the overall EU defence expenditures remained below the 2% reference point throughout the entire period, at an average of 1.5% of GDP, which means that the EU members need to collectively further increase their defence spending with 76 billion euro to reach 2% of the EU's GDP (European Defence Agency).

The European security architecture was dramatically changed by Russia's attack on Ukraine, as even the most optimistic and cooperation-inclined members of the EU came to the realization that armed conflict in Europe was no longer a thing of the past. The year 2022 market the approval of the more ambitious EU Strategic Compass for Security and Defence and an unprecedented increase in most of the EU members defence spending.

A 2024 speech (Von der Leyen, 2024) that would have been hard to imagine a decade ago held by Ursula von der Leyen stressed how serious the implications of the war in Ukraine have been regarding changing the EU's security paradigm. Von der Leyen admitted that the very foundation on which the EU was build, namely that of prosperity could prevent war, was no longer valid and that EU is doing enough in terms of its security is an illusion. The main areas of security mentioned are economic, military, and cyber security, hinting at some of the most important lessons identified from Russia's attack on Ukraine.

The speech is remarkable in the sense that it highlights what von der Leyen calls "EU's strategic responsibility" in the face of a changed reality, characterized by a degradation of the security landscape in Europe and worldwide. The support of Ukraine's fight against Russia is mentioned, as part of this strategic responsibility, but the speech also mentions EU's enlarged responsibilities through its naval operation Aspides, in the Indian Ocean and Red Sea, "aimed at protecting vital global trade routes and our supply chains against Houthi terrorists supported by the Iran" through the means of will European warships and early warning systems sent to the Red Sea, Gulf of Aden and nearby waters. Although this operation is not a very large one, it highlights EU's increased role as a security actor. Von der Leyen acknowledges the need for the member states to increase their coordination in security matters and to increase their contribution within and to NATO. While the Trump administration failed to achieve this through its heavy handed approach of pressuring the EU allies to increase their defence spending, the war in Ukraine managed to change the perception of at least a significant number of members related to the need to step up their security, at a national and collective level (Badawi & Zrcik, 2025).

The speech also mentions that as a result of the war in Ukraine, several taboos have fallen, such as Europe providing military assistance to a country under attack and training troops involved in a European interstate war. In 2017, the French president Emanuel Macron generated quite a controversy by highlighting the need for EU's greater "strategic autonomy," including the creation of a joint doctrine, a joint defence budget and a joint force (Macron, 2017). While Angela Merkel and the former Italian Prime Minister Paolo Gentiloni supported this idea, the reactions (Vohra, 2023) from the United States, United Kingdom, and Poland were quite strong against it, arguing that it would undermine NATO and create divisions within the Western alliance. Now, following the events in Ukraine in the last two years, most of the EU member states most opposed to the idea (like Poland) have had quite a change of heart regarding the need for Europe to defend itself, manifested also in the level of their defence allocations.

Going even further, Ursula von den Leyen's speech reminded that the EU integration project was built on economic AND security considerations, in the aftermath of a devastating conflict. The mention of economic security hints at the fact that economic policy decisions (such as Germany's development model based on cheap energy from Russia) should not ignore the long term security implications and reminds the member states that

> most of our Union's policies have direct security implications: from trade to research, from energy to communications…and we must once again think of our Union as, intrinsically, a security project…. this is the real paradigm shift that Europe still needs, towards a true European Defence Union. (Von der Leyen, 2024)

From a highly contested strategic autonomy in 2017 to strategic responsibility and a European Defence Union in 2024, the change in discourse is quite impressive.

The military and economic considerations are brought together in relation to Europe's defence industries, as the speech acknowledges the need to

> mobilize Europe's defence industry to support a country's war effort. For example, with our new law to support ammunition production, we have helped to quadruple European ammunition production capacity. And we are now expanding a similar approach to other critical industrial supply lines. We are asking our defence industry to go into war mode, so that the rest of Europe does not have to. (Von der Leyen, 2024)

Von den Leyen's message is very pragmatic and realistic, as it draws the attention on the fact that simply increasing the defence spending is a good step ahead, but it is not enough, as in 2023 "almost 80% of it went outside the EU," emphasizing the need for an increased competitiveness of the European industry for defence and to increase Europe's self-reliance through the establishment of robust and reliable supply chains in times of crisis.

Finally, the mention of cyber security as an important component of security is also noteworthy, as the use of cyber-attacks and information warfare in parallel with military actions has been a defining feature of the war in Ukraine and is a threat that is only going to increase in the future.

The issues highlighted by the president of the European Commission are supported by the evolution of the EU members defence expenditures.

European Union defence expenditure increased by 24.6 per cent from $207.3 billion in 2014 up to $258.3 billion in 2022 (European Defence Agency data) and almost 300 billion in 2024 (Von der Leyen, 2024). Despite the renewed commitments to a stronger EU defence, the defence expenditures of the EU members did not evolve in a coordinated manner, as in the absence of a commonly agreed benchmark, their level is primarily dependent of the national interests, values, threat perceptions, and economic considerations, as main drivers of the member states defence policies. The EU member states in closer geographical proximity to Ukraine and Russia (Romania, Hungary, Slovakia, the Baltic States, Sweden, Poland, Finland) had the highest increases in their defence spending in 2023. The leader in Poland, with 3.9% of GDP for defence, followed by Estonia with 2.74%, Lithuania with 2.54%, Finland with 2.45%, and Romania with 2.44% (SIPRI Military expenditures database). Poland, Sweden, and Finland have started to significantly increase their defence budgets even before the February 2022 attack. In 2022 compared to 2021, Poland increased its defence budget with 11%, Sweden with 12%, while Finland with an impressive 36% (Institute Delors, 2023).

Greece already had a high degree of military spending due to the enduring tensions in their bilateral relations with Turkey, so in this case, the Ukrainian conflict did not have a significant direct influence on the defence spending. The countries of Western Europe and others of Central Europe are more restrained in increasing their defence spending, with the countries furthest from the conflict (such as Portugal and Spain) and smaller countries such as Luxembourg and Belgium, registering smaller increases.

Most of the EU countries are still below the NATO guideline of 2% of GDP for defence. Although the 2% figure should not be equated with the military power of a country (as it is mostly a political signal, showcasing the dedication of a country to contributing to burden-sharing at the level of NATO), the numbers still illustrate the gap the EU member states need to fill before being able to reduce their reliance on the United States from a military perspective.

In terms of individual countries, France has planned to achieve the 2% of GDP guideline until 2025, having a budget planned for that year around €50 billion (€45.4 billion in 2023), and around €69 billion in 2030. In the same vein, Germany intends to increase its defence spending to 60 billion in 2024 and to create a special €100 billion fund used to modernizing the Bundeswehr, while Poland, who already exceeds the 2% guideline, intends to accompany the increase in military spending with a policy of massive arms purchases, notably from the United States and South Korea and significantly increase the size of its Land Forces, from 115.000 to 300.000 manpower, making it the most representative Land Force in Europe (Institut Delors, 2023).

3. Material Resources and Defence Procurements

Although the overall EU level of defence expenditures definitely needs to be increased, with some countries lagging behind while others are more aware of this requirement, the level of defence investments apparently offers a more optimistic picture. If we are to consider NATO's guideline of 20% of defence spending for investments, the EU member states have exceeded the guideline from the year 2019, reaching an average of 24.2% in 2022 (European Defence Agency, Defence Data 2021–2022). Only 5 EU members are below the 20% of the defence spending allocated for defence guideline (Austria 9.4%, Germany 18.35%, Ireland 10.75%, Malta 13.21%, and Portugal 18.37%). Surprisingly given the size of the country and its military, but not surprising from the point of view of its economically driven policy, Germany is among the countries that falls below the 20% guideline.

Unfortunately, if we are to take a closer look at the way the EU members have invested in their defence capabilities, the picture becomes less optimistic. Since 2007, the European Defence Agency attempted to set some collective benchmarks for investment so as to improve the level of modernization of the EU members armed forces and enhance cooperation (20% of total defence spending for equipment procurement, 2% of total defence spending for R&T, 35% of total equipment spending from European collaborative procurements, and 20% of total R%T spending from European collaborative defence R&T) (European Defence Agency, 2007). In reality, the starting point of any functioning defence policy should be the political will, the agreement and commitment of the political decision makers to embark on a specific course of action. Simply establishing benchmarks at the level of a specialized agency, without any instruments to enforce the achievement of those benchmarks, is not the most effective method of stimulating the development and modernization of the armed forces, at national or EU member states level. The lack of interest of the EU members in military matters, the fact that these were collective benchmarks, applied to the total amounts of money spent by all EDA member states together, the fact that they were purely voluntary and the countries were not bound to turn them into national targets, the lack of timelines for their implementation meant that in reality they were more an exercise in wishful thinking than a proper tool for defence planning.

The lack of a deadline, the dissolution of individual state responsibility encouraging free riding, and the lack of consequences for those member states falling below the benchmarks would be considered bad management at the level of a company, but they were still considered for many years sufficient in terms of EU military ambitions, mainly due to the lack of a specific threat. The war in Ukraine has fundamentally altered the perception, but the EU has still a long way to go before becoming a credible military force. Increasing the defence spending is an encouraging development, but the EU members need to take a hard look at their significant capabilities gaps, especially in terms of strategic airlift and mobility, major equipment and supplies of ammunition, ISR capabilities.

The apparently sufficient defence investment expenditures (amounting to 55 billion EUR invested in equipment acquisition in 2023 [Institute Delors, 2023]) are not enough to provide the require defence capabilities, with one of the primary causes being the disintegration of the EU defence market. Considering the diverging national interests of the member states and the lack of interest of the EU in regard to developing a European military, the defence industries and the support of the defence companies were considered mainly a matter of national interests and policy.

The lack of a common policy for the EU defence manifests itself in the area of defence acquisitions and defence industrial base, in a duplication of effort which generates high costs. The concept of capabilities based planning had its origins in the US precisely to avoid such issues (Walker, 2005), as before its implementation the capabilities were developed and acquired individually by the services of the US Department of Defence, resulting into duplication, inefficient use of resources, and only partially interoperable capabilities. As the EU does not have a common military doctrine or a clear joint process of acquisition of weapons systems, the result is the inefficient use of the defence spending, increase costs and reduced economies of scale, related to military capabilities. Regarding investment and innovation of the EU defence industry, it is faced with limitations, as the defence companies are highly dependent on national orders for keeping functioning and are faced with steep competition from companies outside the EU (especially the United States, where large defence companies are also supported by large orders from the DOD and have enough financing to be able to invest into production lines). To illustrate this point, the EU operates 17 different main battle tanks, as opposed to 1 by the United States (the M1 Abrams), 29 types of destroyers/frigates versus only 4 types operated in the United States, and 20 fighter aircraft models as opposed to 6 by the United States (European Defence Agency, Coordinated Annual Review On Defence Report, 2022).

The EU has two competing programs for the development of 6th generation fighter jets – the Future Combat Aircraft System developed by Spain, France, Germany, and the TEMPEST project, developed under umbrella of United

Kingdom, Italy, and Japan. The FCAS project can be viewed as an example of the problems faced by the entire European defence industry in terms of cooperation, as it has been plagued by a series of difficulties, such as sharing the workload between France and Germany. Each of the two participant countries wants to defend its own industries, there are marked differences in levels of ambitions and political interests in terms of European autonomy versus close relations with NATO, and the project is fraught with difficulties in collaboration, technological difficulties, and issues related to intellectual property rights (Finabel, 2020).

Another example of the benefits offered by increased cooperation in the development of weapon systems within the EU, but also of the numerous challenges to be overcome is the "Main Ground Combat System" (MGCS), whose development was agreed in 2018 between Germany and France in order to commonly develop a replacement of their respective main battle tanks, the Leopard 2 and the Leclerc. The program was aimed at developing a next-generation technology, and the tank was the response to the operational requirements derived from the current and future operational environment, in order to provide a state of the art system in terms of its offensive and defensive capabilities. One such characteristic is the fact that the future tank capability was required to be fully networked, as the development of a joint multi-national capability from the start made perfect sense from the perspective of the effectiveness of military operations. The bilateral program was also driven by economic considerations, such as economies of scale and the need to share the burden of the significant financial investments and know-how and infrastructure requirements, which would be difficult to bear for a single nation.

One of the main challenges in setting the terms of the program derived from the need to balance the domestic interests of both nations, both in political terms and in terms of defence industry contractors. A major hurdle appeared over the disagreement between the contractors regarding which company (the German Rheinmetell or the French KMW) should be the consortium leader (Cafarella, 2023). Other challenges resulted from the various rules for exporting arms of the two countries, scarcity of funds available for financing following the Covid 19 pandemic (the invasion of Ukraine in 2022 contributing to a positive change for the program in this respect), and the definition of contractor structures for further research and technology activities (Dean, 2023).

Another challenge faced by the EU defence industry is its fragmentation, as it is comprised of a large number of multinational companies and more than 2.000 medium-sized and small enterprises (Clapp, 2023). This means that many of the latter companies, and some of the large ones, are dependent on the national defence policies and the orders placed by the national governments, with strong intra-European competition, leading to smaller market shares, fewer funds available for investment and lower output, making a sudden surge in demand like the one generated by the war in Ukraine difficult to satisfy.

This generates difficulties in collaboration but also has negative financial implications. According to a 2023 study by the European Parliamentary Research Service (EPRS, 2023), a greater coordination of the EU defence policy, procurement and spending could lead to savings between 24.5 billion EUR per year if a "moderate approach" is adopted, up to 75.5 billion EUR per year if a more ambitious approach would be implemented.

The most important potential gains, according to the EPRS (EPRS, 2023), even in the case a moderate approach is adopted, derive from efficiency gains in industrial production (14.2 billion) and savings on offsets (7.8 billion), in other words from a coordinated defence industrial policy.

The Commission and the EDA have identified a series of capability issues, to be solved in short, medium, and long term. According to their findings (European Commission, 2024b), the most urgent capability issue that should be solved by the EU defence industry are:

1. *Replenish stockpiles*, "in order to ensure the combat readiness of armed forces and coordinate competing national demands, avoiding price spiraling and ensuring that most exposed countries have access to required capabilities" (European Commission, 2024b). The war in Ukraine has been the primary catalyst for the realization that the EU member states need to urgently increase the ammunition and equipment stocks, as the countries which sent military aid to Ukraine found their reserves seriously diminished and incapable of producing enough ammunition to sustain a war of attrition: "European nations have been found lacking not only adequate munitions stockpiles, but also the industrial base required to refill inventories to keep up with Ukraine's continued pleas for weapons" (Elgin & Hacker, 2024). The situation is very serious, as according to other sources, "taking into account that Ukraine's artillery uses around 45,000 shells per week, within two months the entire annual production of the European Union could be consumed" (Psara, 2023).
2. *Replace*: "Phase out existing Soviet era legacy systems still in use within EU Armed Forces with European solutions (such as: Main Battle Tanks, Armoured Fighting Vehicles, Infantry Fighting Vehicles, Armoured Personnel Carriers, heavy artillery, etc.), as part of a wider effort to augment existing capabilities and supporting interoperability and enhancing security of supply" (European Commission, 2024b). This issue does not concern only the EU members that were part of the former Warsaw pact, which indeed still have a lot of work ahead in replacing the old soviet times equipment still in use. The decision of the EU members to help Ukraine by providing military equipment and initiatives such as the EU's European Peace Facility (EPF), which provided incentives for EU member states to give military equipment to Ukraine by reimbursing them for some of the costs led to a situation in which now the European states have realized they cannot continue with the same rate of support as it would mean providing Ukraine with newer, more expensive equipment (as most of the old equipment has been divested) and diminishing their own capabilities. Most EU members need to increase the modernization level and the number of operational systems and military equipment, as decades of defence budget cuts have led to "the armed forces in European NATO and European Union member states are hollowed-out, plagued by unserviceable equipment and severely depleted ammunition stocks" (IISS, 2023).

3. *Reinforce*: The Ukrainian war has showcased the urgent need for the EU members to increase their capabilities in terms of Main Battle Tanks, which have made a resurgence as the backbone of land operations and air defence Anti Area Access Denial A2/AD, as the intensive use of capacities like cruise missiles, ballistic missiles or UAV's in the operations in Ukraine have proven air defence to be a critical capability, of utmost importance for the protection of the population, critical infrastructure, and own forces. Enhanced Military Mobility, through enhanced C2, Air and Sea Lift capabilities, and sustainment possibilities are also a priority direction for reinforcing the capabilities, and projects already underway within PESCO (such as Strategic Air Transport for Outsized Cargo or Future Medium-size Tactical Cargo) would need to be accelerated (European Commission, 2024a). Defence in space and European Patrol Class Surface Ships are also mentioned in the designated documents (Annex to the Defence Investment Gaps Analysis and Way Forward).

The war in Ukraine has brought to the attention a long-ignored situation, namely the fact that overall defence expenditures are not a substitute for a strong defence production capacity. Restarting production lines or increasing production for defence products takes time, at least two or three years, due to financial requirements, workforce requirements, supply chain issues and bottlenecks caused by the limited number of suppliers in the EU. BAE Systems stated that recently it would require between 30 and 36 months to restart M777 production, a Rheinmetall CEO declared that specialized steel for tank armor would take from 8 to 12 months to be provided and that lead times for certain electronic components for tank production can be no more than 24 months (IISS, 2023).

Still, the EU officials are reluctant to address the root cause of the issue (the fact that the EU was built for an economic purpose, in a different security context) and persist on insisting that the solution is not a common defence policy, but more investing. According to a recent statement by Joseph Borell

> defence is and will remain for the foreseeable future an exclusive competence of our Member States...We have no choice if we consider the scale of the needs both to support Ukraine and to enable our Member States to replenish their stocks and acquire essential new equipment. But, above all, it's about spending together to fill gaps, avoid duplication and increase the interoperability of our equipment. (Borell, 2024)

The statement highlights the real need to increase the defence spending and cooperation, but it offers no concrete planning framework to achieve these goals, beyond the familiar pattern of creating initiatives for financial support. More money allocated for defence and armaments production is of course useful, cooperation is to be encouraged, but the fact remains that defence planning starts with a common perception of threats, goals, objectives, missions and plans, which are still lacking. Although acknowledging the fact that the EU has "delegated our external security to the United States for too long... and that the American involvement in the defence of Europe is becoming less certain in the long term," Joseph Borell reiterates the same narrative of the EU assuming its "strategic responsibility by becoming capable of defending Europe by ourselves, and to do so build a strong European pillar within NATO" (Borell, 2024), without addressing the elephant in the room – will NATO still exist (together with NDPP – the NATO defence planning process) if the United States decide to withdraw from the Alliance?

The loss of U.S. leadership could lead to mistrust and resentment among European allies, who may feel abandoned or betrayed by their closest strategic partner, hindering cooperation on critical security issues and weakening NATO's ability to react effectively to emerging threats. At the same time, it may increase the level of threat in Europe, as it might embolden Russia who may see an opportunity to expand its influence or challenge international norms without fear of U.S. intervention, as the EU has yet to prove it can successfully counterbalance the military power of Russia without U.S. help.

With the absence of U.S. military support, European nations would need to develop robust crisis management capabilities to respond effectively to security crises within the region. This includes strengthening rapid response forces, improving interoperability among national militaries, and enhancing intelligence-sharing mechanisms to address security threats in a timely and coordinated manner.

European militaries are heavily reliant on U.S. defence technologies, equipment, and systems. A U.S. withdrawal could disrupt supply chains and create technological dependencies, making it challenging for European nations to maintain their defence capabilities. European defence industries would need to accelerate efforts to develop indigenous technologies and reduce reliance on U.S. imports.

The European Commission (EC) has taken some steps toward solving these numerous challenges, as the Russia–Ukraine war provided the incentive for the EU members to strengthen the European Defence Technology and Industrial Base (EDTIB) and consolidate the Common Security Defence Policy. Consequently, the Ukrainian war ensured the background for the adoption of a series of initiatives such as the first European Defence Industry Strategy (EDIS, 2023), its associated European Defence Industry Program (EDIP, 2023), or the Act in Support of Ammunition Production (ASAP) and the European Defence Industry Reinforcement Procurement Act (EDIRPA).

The first ever EDIS provides an ambitious background for developing a more competitive and effective EU defence industry, by addressing the issues mentioned by Ursula von den Leyen (the reliance of the EU member states on arms imports from outside the EU and the lack of coordination in procurement). Consequently, the strategy sets medium term objectives such as increasing the internal EU defence trade more than 35% by 2030, for the members should procure more than 40% of their defence equipment in a collaborative manner until 2030, more than 50% of EU members defence procurement budget directed to procurement from the EDTIB by 2030 and 60% by 2035, with the aim of reducing the dependence of the EU member stated armed forces on military systems produced in the United States.

The EDIS is accompanied by the EDIP, aimed at providing a more specific framework for the implementation of the Strategy. The Program proposes objectives such as the provision of financial support for Ukraine of €1.5 billion from the EU budget between 2025 and 2027, consolidating the competitiveness and responsiveness of the EDTIB, ensuring the opportunity and supply of defence products and promoting the cooperation with Ukraine on the recovery, reconstruction, and modernization of its defence industry (EDIP, 2023). A positive aspect of EDIP is that it acknowledges that short-term measures such as ASAP and EDIRPA, which are the result of EU's emergency response to the events on Ukraine, are not enough and that medium- and long-term actions are required to ensure the European defence industry preparedness, on a more permanent basis.

The EDIP is an important step forward, as it goes beyond the broad declarations of intentions and strategies, offering a more specific framework of action. For example, in order to overcome the challenge of supply chain issues and bottlenecks, the document proposes the

> set up a modular and gradual EU Security of Supply regime to enhance solidarity and effectiveness in response to tensions along the supply chains or to security crises and allow for the timely identification of potential bottlenecks...a regulatory support to remove existing bottlenecks such as access to skilled personnel, raw materials...and to draw up a list, identifying the crisis-relevant defence products, raw materials or components thereof, that are affected by disruptions or potential disruptions of the functioning of the Single Market and its supply chains leading to significant shortages. (EDIP, 2023, p. 23)

Acknowledging that defence companies often lack the funds to allocate the required investments for de-risking measures, the document proposes that the EU should support them through various grants and by stimulating the collaboration for joint procurement.

In terms of short-term measures, the war in Ukraine has prompted the EU to take reactive measures, such as the adoption of the European defence industry reinforcement through common procurement act (EDIRPA, 2024), through which incentives of 310 million EUR are provided to compensate the drawbacks of joint procurement. The stated aim of EDIRPA is "incentivizing cooperation in defence procurement between Member States to jointly coordinate and acquire the most urgent and critical defence product needs, especially those amplified from Russia's aggression against Ukraine" (European Commission, EU Defence Industry, 2024). The lessons identified from the war in Ukraine are evident in the three main areas supported for common procurement by the EDIRPA Work Program, namely ammunition (e.g., mortars, rockets, artillery ammunition, small arms), air defence, missile defence, platforms, and replacement of legacy systems. Such short-term initiatives (EDIRPA is aimed for 2024 and 2025), are definitely useful, but in order to have military relevance, a permanent framework for coordinated procurement (perhaps similar to the NATO Support and Procurement Agency) would be desirable.

Another short-term initiative related to Ukrainian war is the Act in Support of Ammunition Production (ASAP), aimed at "ramping-up of ammunition production capacity across Europe and with this, helping Member States refill their stocks and deliver ammunition to Ukraine by anticipating bottlenecks and shortages in the defence supply chains (ASAP, 2024)." The ASAP requires calls for the production of ammunition elements as explosives, shells, powder and propellant, missiles, with total allocated budget of approximately €500 million, supplemented by estimated co-funding by industry up to €1.5 billion. The calls of proposals presented below are to be signed in May 2024 (ASAP Facts Sheet, 2024). Defence companies from 13 EU countries (Belgium, Czech Republic, Germany, Finland, Sweden, Italy, France, Greece, Slovakia, Hungary, Latvia, Poland, and Romania) have placed calls for proposals for the production of the required defence products. Some of these proposals will have effects even at the end of 2024 and despite the benefits of ASAP, the temporary character of the initiative has to be acknowledges. The companies activating in the defence industry need a steady and dependable level of orders from governments in order to economically justify the investments required to develop/upgrade their production lines and increase production, as there is no guarantee that the surge of demand caused by the war in Ukraine will not disappear after peace will be re-established. The companies providing dual use products may potentially be able to adapt, but producers of military specific items, such as weapons or ammunition, are completely dependent on the size of orders placed by the armed forces, and it would not be the first time when defence budgets were cut in situations when the military threats were not considered serious enough.

Initiatives such as ASAP are beneficial, but a more reliable mechanism needs to be established at EU level in order to incentivize the defence industries companies to allocate funds for developing production facilities, with a timeframe between 5 and 10 years. This is another argument in the favor of a joint EU defence policy that would make the evolution of the European members more predictable. Lacking such predictability, closing the ammunition gaps solely through the efforts of the governments of the producer countries is not going to be a viable solution, as at EU level these private companies will remain in competition on the open market. Many EU member states have a short term approach to defence procurement, driven by national interests and national political considerations. EU countries (in cooperation with NATO) need to take into consideration, within the defence planning framework, the potential of a major regional conflict and ensure a better correlation between the defence planning processes at national level, European level and NATO level and the development of the defence industry capacities, in conjunction with their economic policies and to ensure the planning framework and the required funding necessary to permit a sudden increase in production capacities in case of contingency.

The Russian economy and defence industry have been proven by the war in Ukraine to be more resilient than anticipated, due to a combination of factors, but one of them is the most relevant for the purpose of the aspects analyzed in this chapter: the Russian economy and its defence industry switched to a war economy quite early on in the timeframe of the conflict, which meant that most of the country's resources were redirected toward the war effort. The country increased its defence spending at levels that no Western country, in peacetime, would be willing to commit (according to some reports 40% of Russia's GDP is allocated for the military spending) (Oliphant et al., 2024). It ramped up the manufacturing of military products and even converted shopping malls, civilian factories, and infrastructure for arms production, and recruited parts of the population to support the war effort, by working six days/week and volunteering for work in arms factories (Oliphant et al., 2024). According to Russian sources (which should of course be considered with caution in terms of reliability), in the last 2 years 520.000 new jobs were created in the military industry, meaning around of 3.5 million employees, or 2.5% of the population (Savitsky, 2024). The result is that the Russian managed to produce between 2.5 million and 5 million artillery shells per year (Roth, 2024), with the potential to increase in the following years.

The unexpected resilience of Russia's armaments industry stems from a series of specificities, some of which make it less competitive compared to the EU defence industry, but at the same time more suited for coping with a sudden surge in demand, in quantitative terms. The thousands of factories composing the Russian arms industry were kept afloat by state subsidies, seldom generating profit, but at the same time keeping a larger production capacity. As legacy of the former USSR arms industry, it is not particularly focused on economic efficiency or being competitive in international markets, but rather a result of a military doctrine of attrition, aimed at being able to produce large quantities of unsophisticated ammunition in order to sustain a military conflict and the government's military policy. In Russia's case, government control over the sector and military planning considerations came first, even if very costly from an economic perspective. The result has been that Russia's intensive use of artillery and the huge quantity of ammunition it managed to produce and use outpaced Ukraine's and its European and U.S. allies capacity to produce, to a degree amounting to 6 shells fired by Russia for every shell fired by Ukraine (By Deutsch & Lopatka, 2024).

The nomination of an economist, Andrei Belusov, in May 2024 as a replacement for general Shoigu as Minister of Defence is another indication that Russia is aiming to support the continuation of its war economy for a longer term, to achieve a balance between using its resources (especially the human resource) on the frontline and supporting the war economy, to manage the long-term rearmament plans and the high levels of spending in the military industry (Berg, 2024).

The developments on the frontline in Ukraine and Russia's capacity to mobilize its arms industry should serve as a serious warning about the need for the EU and NATO members and allies to change their mind-set in regard to the place of the defence industry in the national and European approach to defence policy and to acknowledge and mitigate the drawbacks caused by systemic challenges.

Most European defence companies are private companies, functioning in an open market economy, with a development model based on exports first and demand from national governments second, motivated by the maximization of profit and value for the shareholders. There is no central authority in the EU with the power grant subsidies to inefficient companies in order to keep them as backup for a sudden need of increased ammunition, and the national governments are limited in their support of national defence industries by EU legislation designed to prevent unfair competition. Although it is possible for a member state to subsidize a domestic manufacturer, under the Treaty for the EU Functioning, allowing exemptions for national defence and security in the production and trade of arms, war equipment and ammunitions, these subsidies need to be notified to and approved by the European Commission, in order to ensure they do not distort competition more than necessary and they comply with internal market rules. The European Commission will then assess if such subsidies are suitable to the EU's internal market regulations, in terms of necessity, proportionality and potential impact on competition. The bureaucratic process is lengthy, complicated and geared toward the economic aspects, as it is not aligned with a common defence policy or doctrines.

The initiatives at EU level based on the lessons learned from the Ukrainian war are encouraging, but the implementation of the goals outlined in the aforementioned documents is fraught with difficulties. The EU is not a federal country, it is a union composed of various nations, with sometimes diverging security and economic interests and priorities. The implementation of these initiatives would require the harmonization of political actions, overcoming the national interests of the member states that may still favor a close relation with the US or even Russia (as is the case of Hungary). They would also require the coordination with NATO in terms of capability requirements and overcoming the lack of a common defence planning process, as the EU Headline Goal and capability planning for defence should be substantially reviewed in the light of the current developments in the European defence environment and be better correlated with the NDPP. The increase of the production capacities of the EU defence industry will also require overcoming the tendency to protect the national producers in large countries, the reluctance of some smaller member states to spend EU funds on defence products and sizeable investments, far exceeding the current allocation of funds. For instance, according to a statement from retired general Marc Thys, the former commander of the Belgian army land command, that has caused a lot of controversy, "it would require investment in the order of €5 billion to €7 billion in Belgium alone to make enough shells to fight a two-month conflict" (Posaner, 2023). Regulatory challenges are also ahead, as the EU's massive legal framework is poorly equipped for handling the coordination of security, defence planning and defence industry areas in a functional and rapid manner. Production, technological, and manpower challenges at the level of the defence manufacturers are other areas where significant challenges are likely to manifest on short and medium term.

4. Changes in the Defence Policies of Member States

From a military perspective, an effective European defence would require a common defence policy as an expression of a response to commonly perceived security threats and interests, but from a political point of view, this remains in the theoretical realm. While the Ukrainian war has proven that the threat of a military conflict in Europe is not over, we will see if it will be sufficient to galvanize the EU member states into a coordinated response, as the differences between interests, economic, defence, and foreign policies still persist. The countries nearer the source of conflict (such as Poland and the Baltic states) have taken important steps in building stronger military forces, in investing in armament procurement and in forging new relationships with arms producers outside the EU. At the level of declarations, the most influential EU members (France and Germany) have acknowledged the need to improve the European defence, but their cooperation still faces many unresolved challenges. It remains to be seen how committed is Germany to changing its economic development model, based on exports and cheap energy from Russia and if Germany will not wish to renew the project of Nord Stream 2 once the war is over. Other EU members already do not share the view that Russia is the major threat to their security, with Hungary openly presenting a pro-Russian foreign policy.

In the case of France, the invasion of Russian Federation into Ukrainian territory has generated an important change in France's defence policy. In the early stages of the war, despite its advocacy on strategic autonomy, France appeared to underestimate and underplay the Russian threat, as president Macron attempted to integrate Russia into the European security framework. France positioned itself, through the actions of president Macron, as an intermediary and negotiator between Russia and Ukraine, and promoted a policy of appeasement even after the beginning of the war (Cragg, 2022) by calling the Western countries "not to humiliate Russia." The evolution of the Ukrainian war has led France to the realization that Russian Federation is a serious threat, and these changes have been reflected in a change in its defence policy, through calls for a stronger European deterrence beyond the EU and a more robust European defence response to Russian aggression (Macron, 2024). In terms of concrete actions, France established substantial funds for Ukraine to procure French weapons and the signing a significant bilateral security agreement with Kyiv (Elysee, 2024) and strengthened the bilateral relations with some Central European countries such as Poland. Initiatives such as the EU Political Community, designed as a framework for countries "that subscribe to our shared core values to find a new space for cooperation" on politics, security, infrastructure, investment, energy, and migration (Greene et al., 2023) are also a signal that France's defence policy is changing focus from the North African regions toward Europe, but France is still far from assuming a leading role in developing a more defence-oriented EU.

Germany's defence policy has also changed following the war in Russia, from a "pragmatic" approach driven by its energy dependence on Russian energy supplies, a heavy reliance on the United States and NATO for its defence and a reluctance to strengthen the defence of NATO's eastern borders, toward an increased awareness of Russia as a security threat. That is quite an impressive change, from the notorious moment when Germany offered 5,000 protective helmets to Ukraine in response to a request for military support in 2022 (Boffey & Oltermann, 2022) to the Chancellor Olaf Scholz's significant speech in the

Parliament notifying "a turning of the times," or "Zeitenwende" (Scholz, 2022) underscoring unprecedented changes to Germany's defence policy and emphasis on the country's military capabilities. Pragmatic and economically rational Germany even set up a significant fund of €100 billion that will be invested in improving the German army, accompanied by the promise to raise the defence expenditures to 2% of GDP.

This is a dramatic change from Germany's defence policy pre-Ukraine war, but time will show if this change will be enough to determine a sufficient reaction in terms of concrete actions to develop the German armed forces and defence industry, increase cooperation at EU level in the area of defence and a more active role as a leader of a EU as a defence actor. According to a recent study (Graf et al., 2023), the German society's macro culture has not significantly changed, as the main approach on these matters of the German citizens proved stable in favor of multilateral approaches in international affairs, a transatlantic orientation in terms of defence and a preference of civilian over military means. The reaction of the German society and government to the war in Ukraine may be proven to be just temporary, once peace will return.

Poland showcased the most dramatic change in defence policy following the war in Ukraine. The country was already reacting through a change in defence policy and increase in armaments purchased (following the increase in tensions with Belarus and the use of hybrid war tactics by Russia even before February 2022), and the country had already embarked on a road to transform and modernize its armed forces in order to increase its deterrence capabilities (Frick, 2020).

The attack on Ukraine has marked a decisive movement toward becoming one of the most military powerful countries in the EU. Poland was already spending more than the NATO 2% guideline before the 2022 attack, but the war in Ukraine has provided the incentive to raise the spending in defence to 4% of GDP and the proportion of budget spend to equipment acquisitions to over 50% (Reuters, 2023). This defence policy orientation is enduring, despite the political changes in the government, in a rare display of political consensus and vision in respect to strengthening the national defence compared to other EU member countries. Through the voice of its foreign minister, Radoslaw Sikorski, Poland also advocated a closer collaboration between the UK and the EU in defence matters, supporting "the deepest possible inclusion of the United Kingdom in the EU security and defence structures, if you so wish" (Wintour, 2024).

5. Conclusions and Practical Implications

The main conclusions of this chapter are that the invasion of Ukraine had indeed an influence on the European Countries defence expenditures, as most of the EU members took steps toward increasing their defence spending and armaments purchases and changed the European countries' defence outlook, prompting the need to reassess the national and common approaches to defence, in terms of military and defence industry strategies, defence spending, and collaborative efforts. The re-emergence of traditional warfare in Europe has led EU member states recognize the need for strong, interoperable defence systems capable of responding quickly to emerging threats. The Ukrainian war has exposed weaknesses in the processes and frameworks that underline the defence cooperation within the EU, in the EU members defence industries and underscored the importance to invest not only in technological advancements and cyber defence, but also in producing large quantities of weapons and ammunition.

The EU has responded with unexpected unity and implemented initiatives that were hard to imagine ten years ago (such as calls for an increased self-reliance in military matters and an increased role for the European Commission in this respect), but we will see if these momentum will continue and the current trends of increased defence spending and improvement in the defence posture will continue after the war is ended.

Many of the EU member states foreign policy depend on the results of upcoming elections, and the perception on the threat and priorities for courses of action and allocation of funds may change following the EU Parliament elections. The current EU Commission has taken bold steps toward ensuring a more active and coordinated role for the EU in the area of defence, but the nature of the EU is still that of an organization built for peace-time, with a functioning framework centered toward lengthy and complex negotiations, supported by a large bureaucratic apparatus. It is an organization better equipped to deal with a more stable environment, focused on markets and economic considerations and capable of dealing with crises through financial allocations and the set-up of cooperation frameworks (such as in case of Covid 19 crisis), than to make fast coordinated decisions in military matters. Most of the EU members still consider that the common defence should take place within the umbrella of NATO and are still reluctant to take the necessary measures to reduce their military dependence on the United States. It remains to be seen if the possibility of the United States withdrawing from NATO as a result of the re-election of Donald Trump would be a sufficient shock to change the current status quo, but at the present moment, the war in Ukraine has not yet provided a sufficient incentive for a change toward a common defence policy.

A NATO without the United States would face significant challenges, including reduced military capability, financial burdens, and the need for new strategic and operational frameworks. However, it would also present opportunities for European strategic autonomy, enhanced cooperation, and a more focused regional security approach. The success of such a transition would depend on the willingness and ability of European NATO members to invest in their defence, adapt to new leadership dynamics, and maintain political cohesion. Ultimately, while a NATO without the United States would be fundamentally different, it could still play a vital role in ensuring European and transatlantic security through innovation, adaptation, and strengthened European cooperation.

Looking ahead, continued collaboration, innovation, and adaptation will be crucial for the EU to effectively navigate the complex security landscape and uphold its commitment to peace, stability, and sovereignty in Europe and beyond. The EU should focus on accelerating its military integration by enhancing the operational effectiveness of existing initiatives like PESCO and the European Defense Fund. This would require streamlining decision-making processes to allow faster deployment of joint military forces, increasing defence spending among member states, and fostering the development of advanced military technologies within Europe. The EU could also establish a rapid-response command structure that bypasses lengthy negotiations in times of crises, ensuring a more agile and coordinated defence mechanism.

Simultaneously, the EU should work to diversify its strategic partnerships while maintaining strong ties with NATO. This could include strengthening defence collaborations with non-NATO countries, deepening cooperation on cybersecurity, intelligence sharing, and military exercises. Additionally, Europe should reduce its over-reliance on the United States by boosting its own military capabilities, particularly in areas like logistics, air defence, and nuclear deterrence. Doing so would give the EU more leverage and ensure it is better prepared to defend itself autonomously, even if U.S. involvement in NATO diminishes.

References

ASAP. (2024). *Act in support of ammunition production – Boosting defence production.* https://defence-industry-space.ec.europa.eu/eu-defence-industry/asap-boosting-defence-production_en

ASAP Facts Sheet. (2024). https://defence-industry-space.ec.europa.eu/regulation-support-ammunition-production-asap-aims-reinforcing-and-ramping-ammunition-production_en

ASAP Results. (2024). https://defence-industry-space.ec.europa.eu/document/download/b694b109-fa2c-493e-bf1e-87768ae6469e_en?filename=ASAP%20factsheet.pdf

Badawi, H., & Zreik, M. (2025). Counting allies' coins: Trump's NATO strategy and its implications for transatlantic relations.*Journal of Transatlantic Studies*. https://link.springer.com/article/10.1057/s42738-025-00135-9

Berg, M. (2024). *Russia's war economy takes the front seat*. Politico. https://www.politico.com/newsletters/national-security-daily/2024/05/13/russias-war-economy-takes-the-front-seat-00157636

Boffey, D., & Oltermann, P. (2022). Germany's offer to Ukraine of 5,000 helmets is 'joke', says Vitali Klitschko. *The Guradian*. https://www.theguardian.com/world/2022/jan/26/russia-ukraine-germany-under-pressure-to-back-eu-military-training-mission-in-ukraine

Borell, J. (2024). *Europe Day 2024: The need of a paradigm shift for the EU*. https://www.eeas.europa.eu/eeas/europe-day-2024-need-paradigm-shift-eu_en

Cafarella, F. (2023). *Overcoming challenges: Advancing the MGCS future Main Battle Tank*. https://defence-industry.eu/overcoming-challenges-advancing-the-mgcs-future-main-battle-tank/

Clapp, S. (2023). *European Parliament Briefing PE 749.805*. https://www.europarl.europa.eu/RegData/etudes/BRIE/2023/749805/EPRS_BRI(2023)749805_EN.pdf

Cragg, G. (2022). *Macron draws new wave of criticism over call not to 'humiliate' Russia*. https://www.france24.com/en/europe/20220606-macron-draws-new-wave-of-criticism-over-call-not-to-humiliate-russia

Dean, S. (2023). *Main Ground Combat System (MGCS): A status report*. European security and defense. https://euro-sd.com/2023/01/articles/29122/main-ground-combat-system-mgcs-a-status-report/

Deutsch, A., & Lopatka, J. (2024). Inside Europe's drive to get ammunition to Ukraine as Russia advances. *Reuters*. https://www.reuters.com/world/europe/inside-europes-drive-get-ammunition-ukraine-russia-advances-2024-03-06/

EDIP. (2023). *European defence industry programme*. https://defence-industry-space.ec.europa.eu/eu-defence-industry/edip-future-defence_en

EDIRPA. (2024). *European defence industry reinforcement through common procurement act*. https://ec.europa.eu/commission/presscorner/detail/en/ip_24_1495

EDIS. (2023). *European defence industry strategy*. https://defence-industry-space.ec.europa.eu/eu-defence-industry/edis-our-common-defence-industrial-strategy_en

Elgin, K. K., & Hacker, T. (2024). NATO has a munitions problem, and Europe needs to step up. *Defence News*. https://www.defensenews.com/opinion/2024/02/01/nato-has-a-munitions-problem-and-europe-needs-to-step-up/#:~:text=In%20March%2C%20European%20Union%20countries,to%20deliver%20on%20its%20promise

Elysee. (2024). *Agreement on security cooperation between France and Ukraine*. https://www.elysee.fr/en/emmanuel-macron/2024/02/16/agreement-on-security-cooperation-between-france-and-ukraine

European Commission. (2024a). *Annex to the joint communication to the European parliament, the European council, the council, the European economic and social committee and the committee of the regions on the Defense investment gaps analysis and way forward*. https://commission.europa.eu/document/download/45d28cb2-e9de-4b92-972c-16903a007198_en?filename=join_2022_24_1_en_annexe_autre_acte_con-joint_cp_part1_v1.pdf

European Commission. (2024b). *Joint communication to the European parliament, the European council, the council, the European economic and social committee and the committee of the regions on the Defense investment gaps analysis and way forward*. https://commission.europa.eu/document/download/4bcf9a69-ed82-4a74-836f-b85bb16725f6_en?filename=join_2022_24_2_en_act_part1_v3.pdf

European Commission. (2024c). *Speech by President von der Leyen at the European Parliament Plenary on strengthening European defense in a volatile geopolitical landscape*. https://neighbourhood-enlargement.ec.europa.eu/news/speech-president-von-der-leyen-european-parliament-plenary-strengthening-european-defence-volatile-2024-02-28_en

European Commission, EU Defence Industry. (2024). *EDIRPA | Procuring together defence capabilities*. https://defence-industry-space.ec.europa.eu/eu-defence-industry/edirpa-procuring-together-defence-capabilities_en

European Defence Agency Data. https://eda.europa.eu/publications-and-data/defence-data#

European Defence Agency Data. (2007). https://eda.europa.eu/docs/default-source/documents/defence-data/defence-data-2007.pdf

European Defence Agency. *Coordinated annual review on defence report 2022*. https://eda.europa.eu/docs/default-source/eda-publications/2022-card-report.pdf

European Defence Agency. *Defence data 2021-2022/key findings and analysis*. https://eda.europa.eu/docs/default-source/brochures/2022-eda_defencedata_web.pdf

European Parliamentary Research Service. (2023). *European added value unit study PE 734.690*. https://www.europarl.europa.eu/RegData/etudes/STUD/2023/734690/EPRS_STU(2023)734690_EN.pdf

Eurostat Data. https://www.ceicdata.com/en/european-union/eurostat-foreign-direct-investment-outward-by-country-bpm6/fdi-flow-outward-eu-27e-russia

Finabel. (2020). *Seven issues with the ambitious future combat air system for participating nations*. https://finabel.org/seven-issues-with-the-ambitious-future-combat-air-system-for-participating-nations/

Frick, M. (2020). *Strengthening the flank – Poland updates its defense strategy and reconfirms its role in NATO. Concordiam* (pp. 38–45). https://www.marshallcenter.org/sites/default/files/files/2020-10/pC_V6N3_en_Fryc.pdf

Graf, T., Steinbrecher, M., & Biehl, H. (2023). From reluctance to reassurance: Explaining the shift in the Germans' NATO alliance solidarity following Russia's invasion of Ukraine. *Contemporary Security Policy*, *45*(2), 298–330. https://doi.org/10.1080/13523260.2023.2286771

Greene, S., Lucas, E., & Tenzer, N. (2023). *The road to Chişinău: The European political community*. Center for European Political Analysis. https://cepa.org/comprehensive-reports/the-road-to-chisinau-the-european-political-community/

IISS. (2023). *The guns of Europe: Defence-industrial challenges in a time of war*. Institute for International Security Studies. https://www.iiss.org/online-analysis/survival-online/2023/06/the-guns-of-europe-defence-industrial-challenges-in-a-time-of-war/

Institute Delors. (2023). https://institutdelors.eu/en/publications/european-defence-part-1-budgets/

Kirshner, J. (2021). Gone but not forgotten: Trump's long shadow and the end of American credibility.*Foreign Affairs*, *100*. https://heinonline.org/hol-cgi-bin/get_pdf.cgi?handle=hein.journals/fora100&section=35

La Baume, M., & Herszenhorn, D. M. (2018). *Merkel joins Macron in calling for EU army to complement NATO*. Politico. https://www.politico.eu/article/angela-merkel-emmanuel-macron-eu-army-to-complement-nato/

Macron, E. (2017). *President Macron gives speech on new initiative for Europe*. https://www.elysee.fr/en/emmanuel-macron/2017/09/26/president-macron-gives-speech-on-new-initiative-for-europe

Macron, E. (2024). *Europe – It can die. A new paradigm at the Sorbonne*. Geopolitique. https://geopolitique.eu/en/2024/04/26/macron-europe-it-can-die-a-new-paradigm-at-the-sorbonne/

Nielsen, K. L., & Dimitrova, A. (2022). Trump, trust and the transatlantic relationship. In *The Trump administration*. Taylor & Francis. https://www.taylorfrancis.com/chapters/edit/10.4324/9781003259923-23/trump-trust-transatlantic-relationship-kristian-nielsen-anna-dimitrova

Oliphant, R., Barnes, J., Rothwell, J., & Kilner, J. (2024). *From scones to drones: Inside Putin's arms race that is leaving the West behind. The Telegraph*. https://www.telegraph.co.uk/world-news/2024/01/26/russia-arming-itself-faster-than-nato/

Posaner, J. (2023). Belgian army will be throwing 'stones' within hours of a war starting, laments ex-general. *Politico*. https://www.politico.eu/article/belgian-army-throwing-stones-within-hours-war-ex-general-marc-thys/

Psara, M. (2023). EU countries failing to meet ammunition production demands for Ukraine. *Euronews*. https://www.euronews.com/my-europe/2023/11/14/eu-countries-failing-to-meet-ammunition-production-demands-for-ukraine

Reuters. (2023). *Poland's 2024 budget to see big spending on defense, social benefits*. https://www.reuters.com/world/europe/polands-2024-budget-see-big-spending-defence-social-benefits-2023-08-24/

Roth, A. (2024). A lot higher than we expected: Russian arms production worries Europe's war planners. *The Guardian*. https://www.theguardian.com/world/2024/feb/15/rate-of-russian-military-production-worries-european-war-planners

Saballa, J. (2024, April 8). Italy military 'Absolutely Undersized,' below 'Limit of Survival': Officials. *The Defence Post*. https://www.thedefensepost.com/2024/04/08/italy-military-undersized/

Savitsky, V. (2024). Defense industry workers are being offered higher salaries than "office plankton" and even IT specialists. *Moscow Times*. https://www.moscowtimes.ru/2023/11/15/rabochim-oboronki-nachali-predlagat-zarplati-vishe-chem-ofis-nomu-planktonu-i-dazhe-aitishnikam-a113294

Scholz, O. (2022, February 27). *Government statement by federal chancellor Olaf Scholz*. https://www.bundesregierung.de/breg-de/suche/regierungserklaerung-von-bundeskanzler-olaf-scholz-am-27-februar-2022-2008356

Stockholm International Peace Research Institute Military Expenditure Database. https://www.sipri.org/databases/milex

Szczepanski, M. (2019). *A decade on from the crisis Main responses and remaining challenges*. https://www.europarl.europa.eu/RegData/etudes/BRIE/2019/642253/EPRS_BRI%282019%29642253_EN.pdf

The European Union. *What it is and what it does*. https://op.europa.eu/webpub/com/eu-what-it-is/en/

Total bilateral aid commitments to Ukraine between January 24, 2022 and January 15, 2024, by donor and type, Feb 24, 2024, Statista. https://www.statista.com/statistics/1303432/total-bilateral-aid-to-ukraine/

Unterrichtung durch die Wehrbeauftragte, Jahresbericht. (2023). https://dserver.bundestag.de/btd/20/105/2010500.pdf

Vohra, A. (2023). *Foreign policy*. https://foreignpolicy.com/2023/07/03/strategic-autonomy-is-a-french-pipe-dream/

Von der Leyen, U. (2024). *Our strategic responsibility*. https://www.bruxelles2.eu/en/2024/05/avant-propos-notre-responsabilite-strategique-our-strategic-responsibility-ursula-von-der-leyen/?utm_source=mailpoet&utm_medium=email&utm_source_platform=mailpoet&utm_campaign=les-newsletter-total-derniers-articles-de-notre-blog_2

Walker, S. (2005). *Capabilities-based planning – How it is intended to work and challenges to its successful implementation*. USAWC Strategy Research Project. https://apps.dtic.mil/sti/pdfs/ADA434864.pdf

Wintour, P. (2024). Polish foreign minister calls for long-term rearmament of Europe. *The Guardian*. https://amp-theguardian-com.cdn.ampproject.org/c/s/amp.theguardian.com/world/article/2024/may/25/poland-foreign-minister-radoslaw-sikorski-long-term-rearmament-europe

Chapter 11

How Labor Management in Defence Is Affected by Biases on NATO's Eastern Flank: The Romanian Example

Vlad Dumitrache and Brîndușa Maria Popa

Regional Department of Defence Resources Management Studies, Brasov, Romania

Abstract

The increase of personnel numbers in defence has become a top priority for defence structures on the Eastern Flank following the war in Ukraine that has developed following the February 2022 invasion from the Russian Federation. Most countries that form NATO's Eastern Border have found out, however, that the modern process of recruitment in the military is a complicated and difficult one. Biases related to the military, a competitive private sector that is increasing in the emergent economies that have developed in countries like Poland, Estonia, Latvia, Lithuania, Romania, or Bulgaria, have created an environment where the military finds itself in a dilemma on how to pursue workforce that might be incentivized to join the armed forces.

The aim of this chapter is to understand where the above-mentioned nations find themselves in managing this overall process. While a descriptive analysis will be used to narrowly present the situation in each country, an emphasis will be made on the Romanian example, with a more in-depth analysis having the purpose to further break down the strategy concerning the personnel selection and recruitment process in this case.

Keywords: Recruitment; cognitive bias; economic behavior; defence management; defence personnel

JEL Code: H56

Enhancing Transatlantic Solidarity in Collective Defence: Navigating Increased Defence Expenditures, Cyber Security, and Emerging Risks, 225–238

doi:10.1108/978-1-80686-259-720261011

Introduction

When making decisions in management, the classical economic man model is preferred. This model refers to a decision-making process which is constructed on the idea that a rational process when taking actions or choosing an alternative will choose to do so in the most profitable manner possible. However, studies (insert-reference) have demonstrated that this is not always the case and a lot of heuristics influence decision makers into making choices of an irrational matter. For this reason, the study of behavior economics has developed and its influence in governmental economics and budgeting has a pivotal role in shaping overall long-term projects and decisions. This pattern is extrapolated to decision making in defence as well.

As defence resources are more than ever under reform following the Russian Invasion into Ukraine in 2022, it is the aim of this chapter to analyze if behavior economics and different biases can influence one particular resources, respectively, the human one, as it translates into the military personnel that builds national armies and helps develop and maintain military capabilities. For this chapter, the sample chosen to analyze is that of the group of countries that make the Eastern Flank of NATO as countries like Poland, Romania, The Baltic States or Bulgaria have been subject to increase defence spending, but the acquisition of defence weapons and armament has to be doubled by a conceivable effort of modernizing, upgrading and increasing in strength the existing human resources in each of these countries defence structures. A particular accent will be placed on the case study, which is the Romanian Defence Management System, in terms of personnel.

From the start it has to be mentioned that one particular bias from a behavior economic point of view has been that of the lack of need of an increased number of personnel in modern armies (a cognitive bias), as traditional threats were considered anachronic, while hybrid and cyber threats seemed to emerge. For this reason, many of the countries that build the Eastern Flank have seen a sunk and a major reduction of their armed forces following their entrance into NATO.

Over the years, behavior economics has been used when managing human resources especially in the recruitment process of western militaries like United States, United Kingdom, or Canada. Efforts related to better marketing due to understanding behavior and, therefore, arising interest for joining military forces has been considered a success in the last 20 years.

Personnel in the Military in the Eastern Flank

To better understand the dynamic of military expenditures on the Eastern Flank, we must first look at the strategy since these countries have joined NATO. Most of the former communist countries were able to join the alliance in the late 1990s and early 2000s. In that particular moment in time, the strategic tendency in NATO was to reduce military personnel numbers especially on the European continent.

Poland's Military Personnel Management

From all the Eastern Flank countries, Poland has become an example for success regarding recruitment in the military, as the Polish armed forces have constantly developed their numbers in the past 10 years, starting with 2014 following the Crimean invasion by the Russian Federation. A study from Poland (Kopka, 2019) demonstrates, however, that the country is facing the same bias as other eastern European countries. Even with increased salaries and other important incentives, the polish military recruitment comes mostly from lower middle-class categories except for the area of intelligence where recruitment is mostly from the higher educated class and the selection process is a complicated one. The reasons are related to migration from Poland to other western European countries and a decrease in demographics. While Poland has no silver bullet answer in terms of its strategy to increase military personnel, the polish governments of the past years have managed to reduce most biases toward the military and have promoted a system of compensation that tries to be as close as possible to normal NATO standards. This refers to higher salaries, incentives that create condition of labor inside the ministry of defence in Poland similar to that of well-developed countries like France, Germany, or the United Kingdom. By applying these types of policies, the military becomes a contender on the competitive labor market and jobs inside the system are no longer perceived as full of disadvantages and whatever biases might exist disappear.

The Baltic States

The Baltic countries find themselves in a particular situation. They are the only three states on the Eastern Flank that have maintained or reinstated conscription in the arm forces. Even so, with this theoretical regulated boost, the armies of three countries have difficulties in increasing the number of their personnel (Chmielewski & Tarociński, 2024). Demographic concerns make it difficult for Latvia to operationalize its national division while both Lithuania and Estonia have challenges in further developing their brigades. All three countries might under the influence of confirmation bias or that specific tendency to believe in the data that reinforces or supports their beliefs. For these countries, the belief is that because of their size, the only way to increase in numbers and to realize deterrence is to ultimately relay on collaboration with different partners, in most cases that being the possibility of creating joint international structures under NATO command.

Bulgaria

As we move further down from the north of the Eastern Flank to the south, we can analyze the cases of countries that border the Black Sea like Bulgaria and Romania.

Bulgaria's defence management approach in terms of developing their armed forces in the area of increased personnel has been a bumpy one to say the least

(2023 Defence Status report). For the Bulgarian military, recent years have brought a decrease in personnel numbers that passes 20% in 2023 compared to the desired numbers. Compared to other countries, the biases in regards to joining the military in Bulgaria deal with Russian propaganda against Ukraine that has increased ever since the Russian invasion in 2022. This recency bias example, a bias in which the perception of reality is altered because of events that have just happened or are very close to the present is shortfall that the Bulgarian decision makers in defence continue to struggle with and will still do so for the foreseeable future.

Romania's Management of Personnel Recruitment in the Context of Cognitive Bias

In the case of Romania, cognitive bias has represented an issue for a long period of time in accordance to joining the military. A subjective reality, in which the army is perceived as a rough environment compared to the private civilian sector, has impacted the selection process. Similarly, those that are part of the military forces have a subjective view on how the private sector operates and what types of opportunities exist there. For this reason, while in theory the Romanian armed forces have strategized about the need of increase in their armed forces in reality for the last decade the numbers have constantly decreased and the trend is very hard to stop. One major factor is that of the Romanian pension system regarding military forces, one very advantageous for exiting the system early, a challenge that the Romanian Ministry of National Defence has not been able to respond to so far.

The Romanian Armed Forces currently consist of approximately 74,695 active personnel[1] and 55,000 reserves. The breakdown of active personnel includes 35,500 in the Land Forces, 11,700 in the Air Force, and 6,800 in the Naval Forces. Additionally, there are 17,500 personnel in joint forces and about 15,000 in paramilitary units.[2]

Romania maintains a voluntary military service in peacetime, with conscription applicable only during times of war or national emergency, the country's defence spending is around 2.44% of its GDP, and its military strength is ranked 47 out of 147 according to Global Firepower.[3]

In terms of overall manpower, Romania has a total population of approximately 18.3 million, with about 9.5 million available for military service. Of those, around 7.8 million are considered fit for service, and about 201,590 individuals reach military age annually.[4] The Romanian military is structured to provide

[1]https://mfinante.gov.ro/domenii/bugetul-de-stat/numar-salariati-bugetari

[2]https://www.digi24.ro/stiri/actualitate/topul-celor-mai-puternice-armate-ale-lumii-in-2023-ce-efective-si-dotari-are-romania-si-ce-loc-ocupa-2364795

[3]https://www.globalfirepower.com/country-military-strength-detail.php?country_id=romania

[4]https://www.globalfirepower.com/country-military-strength-detail.php?country_id=romania

territorial defence, support NATO and EU missions, and contribute to regional and global stability.

Since the military service is no longer compulsory in Romania, as it was until 2007, but it is a service that lasts four months and it is done on a voluntary basis, the numbers of the enlisted have decreased. Young men who wish to enter the service will be paid for the four months when they train,[5,6,7] according to chapter V, article 53 of the Law for Volunteer Reserve Soldiers number 384 from 2006, and afterward they will be part of the operational reserve. The Ministry of National Defence has tried to raise young people's interest in the domain through different awareness and recruitment campaigns however, despite its efforts, the recruitment goals have not been met yet. In 2023, only around 72,000 positions were filled, and this number is believed to have decreased since there were resignations due to unattractive conditions for military personnel.[8] The government has considered reintroducing conscription to address the shortfall, aiming to increase the armed forces' strength from 80,000 to 100,000 troops, according to the Brussels Signal,[9] but no official actions have been taken yet.

The challenges in recruitment are attributed to low pay and poor working conditions, with salaries for non-commissioned officers ranging between €459 and €994 per month. This situation has prompted discussions on reintroducing compulsory military service to ensure sufficient personnel for national defence needs.[10]

Unfortunately, recruitment has been a significant issue for the Romanian defence forces primarily since 2007 when Romania transitioned to the Professional Armed Forces. Our country ended conscription and moved to an all-volunteer military force, and this transition marked the beginning of recruitment challenges as the military had to rely on volunteers instead of conscripted soldiers.

Among the possible challenges we shall mention:

- Competition with the Private Sector where jobs became more attractive, offering better pay and conditions than military service.
- *Emigration*: A substantial number of young Romanians emigrated for better opportunities in Western Europe, shrinking the pool of potential recruits.
- *Public perception*: The image of the military and its appeal to younger generations impacted recruitment. Many young people did not see the military as a desirable career path.

---

[5]https://lege5.ro/gratuit/geydamjqga/soldatii-si-gradatii-rezervisti-voluntari-lege-384-2006?dp=gmydcnbygu3do

[6]https://legislatie.just.ro/Public/DetaliiDocument/275330

[7]https://legislatie.just.ro/Public/DetaliiDocument/275081

[8]https://www.national.ro/social/disperare-la-mapn-val-de-demisii-si-retrageri-din-armata-romana-815009.html/

[9]https://brusselssignal.eu/2024/01/romania-set-to-join-europes-military-conscription-trend/

[10]https://brusselssignal.eu/2024/01/romania-set-to-join-europes-military-conscription-trend/

- Ministry of National Defence Budget constraints often meant limited resources for improving salaries, benefits, and working conditions in the military.
- *NATO commitments*: Romania's obligations as a NATO member required maintaining a certain level of military readiness and personnel, adding pressure to recruit sufficient numbers.

Starting with 2017, the focus on recruitment has increased. The Romanian government has recognized the ongoing recruitment issues and has implemented various measures to address them, such as increasing salaries, improving living conditions for soldiers, and running recruitment campaigns. The rising regional tensions and the need for a robust defence force have underscored the importance of addressing recruitment challenges more urgently. Overall, while recruitment has been a persistent issue for Romania's defence forces since the end of conscription in 2007, recent efforts aim to mitigate these challenges and bolster military personnel numbers.

According to Monitorul Oficial part III, no.220/20.V.2023,[11] the official gazette of Romania, where the official announcements and reports are published

> the activities for the promotion of the military profession have been developed according the Strategy for the promotion of the military profession between 2021–2025 and the Campaign Plan for the promotion of the military profession, on three priority axes of effort: the use of digital marketing technologies, the creation and the dissemination of promotional materials as well as the development of the infrastructure of the promotion activities with actions aimed at a better information regarding the Romanian Armed Forces[12]

Romania's recent recruitment campaigns have faced significant challenges. The Romanian Ministry of National Defence has organized several recruitment campaigns starting with 2017, but we shall focus our analysis on the situation starting with 2022 when the efforts to digitize the recruitment process materialized with the new recruitment site *recrutaremapn.ro* which has improved the registration process, facilitating the identification of the options and the documents submission of the candidates' documents. The year 2022 counted 20,000 for the recruitment procedures in the different regional recruitment offices. There were 10,000 less candidates than in 2021 however, the ratio between the seats available for competition and the candidate was good: 3:4 candidates per seat for the military colleges, 2:7 candidates/seat for the military higher education, and 1:2 candidates/seat for the professional soldiers. The only situation when there were less candidates that the existing seats was that of the post-secondary education. It seems that the causes for the decrease in the candidates' numbers are: low

---

[11]https://www.mapn.ro/rapoarte/documente/raport_20230719144129.pdf, page 8
[12]https://www.mapn.ro/rapoarte/documente/raport_20230719144129.pdf, page 9.

payments, the competition with other defence, security and public order institutions, and the security situation in the area. Other indirect causes which led to a reduced fill up of the seats advertised for competition, not related to the military system characteristics, are that part of the competitors did not meet some of the requirements like: having a driving license for the lack of or some medical requirements.

According to the same analysis, in 2022, the number of people who left the system surpassed the estimations thus, maintaining the gap between the necessary amount of people and the existing personnel. Therefore, in order to reduce the deficit, the government and Ministry of National Defence have taken some measures focused on the short and medium term by organizing another training session for professional soldiers and redistributing the unoccupied post-secondary education seats for warrant officers and non-commissioned officers positions. Also, on the medium term, they tried to change the personnel training paradigm[13] and the way the military college graduates are allocated to the military higher education institutions, focusing on using the educational capacity to the utmost in order to fulfill the necessities of the system.

The recruitment campaign from 2023 for reserve forces, which unfolded between May 22 and June 30, 2023, and was resumed between 7 August and August 25, 2023,[14] detailed in Monitorul Oficial, has achieved significant results. The campaign aimed to reinforce the numbers of the Romanian Armed Forces by attracting a diverse group of new recruits. This initiative was part of a broader strategy to enhance national defence capabilities and ensure readiness to address various security challenges.

The key outcomes of the campaign include:

- The Ministry of National Defence faced significant challenges with its recruitment campaign, reflecting ongoing difficulties in attracting enough candidates for military positions. Despite extensive recruitment efforts and multiple campaigns targeting both professional soldiers and reservists, the response has been mixed.
- The campaign aimed to recruit nearly 4,159 volunteer reservists between May and June 2023.[15] This initiative also aimed to reinforce the ranks by offering positions to citizens willing to serve in the reserves, but achieving these targets has remained challenging due to various factors, including demographic trends and societal attitudes toward military service.
- *Retention strategies*: Efforts were made not only to recruit new members, but also to retain current personnel through improved benefits, career development opportunities, and supportive measures.[16]

---

[13]https://legislatie.just.ro/Public/DetaliiDocument/275081
[14]https://www.recrutaremapn.ro/anunt.php?id=24
[15]https://www.recrutaremapn.ro/anunt.php?id=20
[16]https://www.mapn.ro/rapoarte/documente/raport_20230719144129.pdf

These results highlight the Romanian government's commitment to strengthening its defence forces through effective recruitment and retention strategies, ensuring the military is well-prepared for future challenges.

In 2024, the recruitment campaign took place from May 20 to June 27, aiming to fill nearly 5,000 volunteer reservist positions, including officers, non-commissioned officers, and other ranks also, 3,856 professional soldiers.[17] This campaign is part of a broader effort to bolster military numbers amid ongoing regional tensions, particularly with the proximity to the conflict in Ukraine.

According to DIGI24, which was citing an analysis of the Romanian General Staff, the recruitment and selection campaign took place in 41 counties and in the city of Bucharest, the interest index (ratio between the number of candidates and the number of places put up for competition): 1.3; number of admitted candidates: 2,626; admission rate (proportion of selected candidates from the total number of registered candidates): 40%.[18]

On the whole, the campaign had a national coverage and was based on message convergence on every channel used and for all the target audiences. It tried to be proactive and anticipate the needs and unclarities of the target public, to be transparent and non-discriminatory. The communicators tried to make use of all the channels, using not only the traditional media (TV and Radio) also, Facebook, Instagram, YouTube, and Twitter. However, direct contact with the target audience has been maintained through meetings organized by the regional recruitment offices in schools, high schools, and through events organized on different occasions like The Open Doors Days, The Romanian National Day, the days of the services, etc. They also maintained an active presence in the society using posters, fliers, videos, and publicity caravans thus aiming at enlarging the selection pool.

Therefore, even if there was a notable increase in applications and many targeted outreach efforts, the campaign aiming to strengthen the nation's defence capabilities, encountered several significant drawbacks that hindered its success. We shall try to discuss them below:

1. Salary system

The salary level for the professional soldiers and NCO positions is not very appealing. Salaries between €459 and €994 per month are considered relatively low taking into account the demands of military service and the present day security situation in the region. Additionally, the overall working conditions were seen as unattractive, contributing to a lack of interest among potential recruits.

Also, to attract and retain personnel, the Romanian military should consider increasing salaries and improving benefits for all ranks. Competitive

---

[17]https://www.mapn.ro/cpresa/18433_Noi-oportunit%C4%83%C8%9Bi-pentru-alegerea-unei-cariere-militare

[18]https://www.digi24.ro/stiri/actualitate/prima-serie-de-recrutare-pentru-armata-din-acest-an-cei-mai-multi-dintre-candidati-nu-au-trecut-proba-fizica-si-examenul-medical-2768191

compensation packages could make military careers more attractive. Enhanced benefits could include better healthcare, housing allowances, and retirement plans.

2. High resignation rates

The Romanian military faced ongoing challenges with retention, as many current personnel chose to leave the service. This high turnover further complicated the recruitment efforts, as new recruits were needed not only to expand the forces but also to replace those who had resigned.[19]

3. Unmet recruitment targets

Despite a focused campaign, the recruitment drive failed to meet its ambitious targets. Previous efforts had already shown a trend of falling short, and the recent campaign did not significantly reverse this trend. This shortfall indicates persistent issues in attracting sufficient numbers of volunteers to the military.

4. Need for conscription considerations

Due to the challenges in voluntary recruitment, there were serious discussions about reintroducing conscription. This move highlights the difficulty in relying solely on voluntary enlistment to meet the military's manpower needs. The consideration of conscription reflects the severity of the recruitment efforts.

A more targeted and appealing recruitment strategy could help attract a diverse range of candidates. The secondary and high education levels should be the focus of attention for professional militaries and specialist. Frequent activities, not only during the recruitment periods, with schools, universities, and community organizations should be carried out to promote military careers. Offering signing bonuses, educational scholarships, and career development opportunities to new recruits could be an approach.

5. Retention programs

Developing programs focused on retaining current personnel is essential. This can include:

- *Career advancement opportunities*: Providing clear paths for promotion and professional development.
- *Recognition and awards*: Implementing programs that recognize and reward outstanding service and achievements.
- *Mentorship programs*: Establishing mentorship and support networks within the military to help new recruits adjust and advance in their careers.

[19]https://lumeapolitica.ro/actualitate/armata-fara-ostasi-militarii-pleaca-din-armata-in-pas-vioi-iar-57-din-iesirile-din-sistem-au-fost-pensionari-anticipate/

6. Conscription with modern approaches

While conscription could help meet manpower needs, it should be implemented in a way that is acceptable to the public:

- *Short-term service options*: Offering shorter mandatory service periods with options to transition into voluntary service.
- *Civic service alternatives*: Allowing conscripts to choose between military service and other forms of national service, such as disaster relief or infrastructure projects.
- *Comprehensive training*: Ensuring that conscripts receive high-quality training and experience that can be valuable in civilian careers.

7. Engage with larger public and stakeholders

Open communication and engagement with the public and key stakeholders can build support for recruitment initiatives: Clearly communicating the goals, benefits, and challenges of military service can promote a good image based on transparency. The military community should be involved as much as possible, involving veterans, military families, and community influencing personalities in the recruitment efforts.

8. Invest in technology and innovation

Adopting new technologies can make military service more appealing and effective:

- *Cyber and IT training*: Offering training and career paths in high-demand fields such as cybersecurity and information technology.
- *Modern training methods*: Using simulators, virtual reality, and other advanced training tools to provide engaging and realistic training experiences.

9. Public perception and appeal

The campaign struggled to make the military service appealing to younger demographics and a broader population segment. The perception of the military as an unattractive career option due to low pay and challenging conditions likely deterred many potential recruits. These factors have impeded the achievement of recruitment targets, leading to discussions about reintroducing conscription as a means to bolster the armed forces' strength from 80,000 to 100,000 troops.[20] By addressing these areas, Romania can create a more attractive and sustainable environment for military service, ultimately enhancing its national defence capabilities.

[20] https://brusselssignal.eu/2024/01/romania-set-to-join-europes-military-conscription-trend/

Future Opportunities for the Romanian Defence Personal Management System

Summing up we can assess that the current situation regarding the Romanian military's recruits is characterized by several notable factors:

1. Increased demand for recruits

The Romanian Armed Forces have significantly ramped up their recruitment efforts due to geopolitical tensions, particularly the proximity to the ongoing conflict in Ukraine. This urgency has driven a focused campaign to attract more volunteers to the ranks.

2. Recruitment challenges

Despite the intensified efforts, the campaigns have faced significant obstacles:

- *Unattractive payment situation*: The salaries for military personnel, especially non-commissioned officers, are relatively low.
- *Retention issues*: The military has struggled with high resignation rates, which further complicates recruitment efforts.[21,22]
- *Unmet recruitment targets*: Previous campaigns fell short of their targets, highlighting persistent issues in attracting and retaining personnel.[23]

3. Government initiatives

The Romanian government has been proactive in addressing these challenges by:

- *Enhanced benefits*: Introducing better benefits and career development opportunities to make military service more attractive.
- *Targeted communication*: Utilizing targeted communication strategies to appeal to younger demographics and diverse groups.
- *National security emphasis*: Emphasizing the importance of national security and the role of the military in maintaining stability, especially in light of regional threats.

4. Public and official responses

The Romanian Official Gazette, Monitorul Oficial, details the structured approach and outcomes of the recruitment campaign. These official reports

[21]https://alephnews.ro/guvern/armata-exclude-serviciul-militar-obligatoriu-anul-trecut-6-000-de-militari-si-au-dat-demisia/

[22]https://brusselssignal.eu/2024/01/romania-set-to-join-europes-military-conscription-trend/

[23]https://brusselssignal.eu/2024/01/romania-set-to-join-europes-military-conscription-trend/

provide transparency and accountability regarding the efforts made and the results achieved.[24]

Conclusions

The potential war on the Eastern borders of Europe has determined most of the countries in the region to completely change their management objectives in defence as well as their strategy for personnel increase. While all countries have an objective to attract more personnel, some are more successful than others. For countries like Bulgaria and Romania, different biases toward joining the military as a public service sector instead of the alternative that exists in the public sector weighs in terms of really realizing the desired number of forces inside the army. The Baltic states and Poland are much more efficient in this regard. Their proximity to the Russian federation and several biases toward past events have enabled these countries to more successful in filling in the gaps that they might have in numbers.

Poland has the clear advantage with a policy that allows them for the next 10 years to double their effective numbers in personnel. Even for the polish state, however, the path to this objective is not a straight one several biases related to joining the military affecting the overall speed of the process.

One particular case that we were able to study was that of the Romanian strategy in this regard.

The Romanian military recruitment campaign reflects a critical effort to strengthen national defence amid challenging conditions. While there are significant hurdles, the government's commitment to improving conditions and exploring conscription indicates a strategic approach to bolstering military capabilities.

The Romanian Armed Forces are at a pivotal juncture, with the nation's defence apparatus actively seeking to bolster its ranks amid increasing geopolitical tensions. In light of the ongoing conflict in Ukraine and broader regional instability, Romania has launched an extensive recruitment campaign aimed at reinforcing its military capabilities. This initiative, spanning from May 20 to June 27, 2024, targeted nearly 5,000 volunteer reservist positions, reflecting a strategic effort to enhance national security. However, the campaign has faced significant obstacles. Despite the urgency and structured outreach efforts, recruitment targets have not been fully met, exacerbated by persistent issues such as low pay and challenging working conditions within the military. These challenges have prompted discussions around the potential reintroduction of conscription, a move aimed at addressing the manpower shortfall and ensuring a robust defence force capable of responding to current and future threats. However, such a possibility has not been confirmed by any of the government officials.

The Romanian government has shown a commitment to overcoming these challenges by improving benefits, enhancing career development opportunities, and emphasizing the importance of national security. These measures are aimed

[24]https://www.mapn.ro/rapoarte/documente/raport_20230719144129.pdf

at making military service more attractive and ensuring a more diverse and capable force.

To conclude, we can say that while the recruitment campaign has highlighted some relevant issues within the Romanian Armed Forces manning process, it has also demonstrated a proactive approach to addressing these challenges. The discussion about a potential reintroduction of conscription and the different governmental initiatives reflect a strategic effort to ensure that Romania's military is well-prepared to meet current and future security threats. The outcomes of this campaign will likely shape the future of Romania's defence strategy and its ability to maintain stability in an increasingly volatile region.

Even if the recruitment campaign faced several critical drawbacks and all these factors combined create a challenging environment for expanding the Romanian Armed Forces through voluntary enlistment. Addressing these issues will be essential for future recruitment efforts and ensuring a robust and capable military force.

Marketing strategies should include willingness to use economic behavior methods. It is for this reason that we have chosen to compare western selection methods and those more traditional that are found on the eastern flank.

References

2023 Defense Status Report: Bulgarian army faces staffing shortages. https://bnr.bg/en/post/101966352/2023-defense-status-report-bulgarian-army-faces-staffing-shortages

2024 Romania Military Strength. https://www.globalfirepower.com/country-military-strength-detail.php?country_id=romania

Chmielewski, B. I., & Tarociński, J. (2024). *On the warpath: The development and modernisation of the Baltic states' armed forces*. Centre for Eastern Studies. https://www.osw.waw.pl/en/publikacje/osw-commentary/2024-05-10/warpath-development-and-modernisation-baltic-states-armed

Fox, L. C. (2024). *Who in NATO is ready for war?* Military Review. Who in NATO Is Ready for War? (army.mil)

https://actmedia.eu/daily/defence-ministry-runs-new-volunteer-reservists-recruitment-campaign/108597

https://alephnews.ro/guvern/armata-exclude-serviciul-militar-obligatoriu-anul-trecut-6-000-de-militari-si-au-dat-demisia/

https://hotnews.ro/armata-voluntara-a-romniei-detalii-despre-proiectul-serviciului-militar-voluntar-pentru-tineri-cum-se-va-aplica-si-ce-presupune-18494

https://jurnaluldigital.ro/cati-angajati-are-armata-romaniei/

https://lege5.ro/gratuit/geydamjqga/soldatii-si-gradatii-rezervisti-voluntari-lege-384-2006?dp=gmydcnbygu3do

https://legislatie.just.ro/Public/DetaliiDocument/275081

https://legislatie.just.ro/Public/DetaliiDocument/275330

https://lumeapolitica.ro/actualitate/armata-fara-ostasi-militarii-pleaca-din-armata-in-pasvioi-iar-57-din-iesirile-din-sistem-au-fost-pensionari-anticipate/

https://mfinante.gov.ro/domenii/bugetul-de-stat/numar-salariati-bugetari

https://www.digi24.ro/stiri/actualitate/prima-serie-de-recrutare-pentru-armata-din-acestan-cei-mai-multi-dintre-candidati-nu-au-trecut-proba-fizica-si-examenul-medical-2768191

https://www.digi24.ro/stiri/actualitate/topul-celor-mai-puternice-armate-ale-lumii-in-2023-ce-efective-si-dotari-are-romania-si-ce-loc-ocupa-2364795

https://www.mapn.ro/cpresa/18433_Noi-oportunit%C4%83%C8%9Bi-pentru-alegerea-unei-cariere-militare

https://www.mapn.ro/rapoarte/documente/raport_20230719144129.pdf

https://www.national.ro/social/disperare-la-mapn-val-de-demisii-si-retrageri-din-armata-romana-815009.html/

https://www.recrutaremapn.ro/anunt.php?id=20

https://www.recrutaremapn.ro/anunt.php?id=24

Kopka, R. (2019). Social structure determinants of Polish military manpower. *Security and Defence Quarterly*, *26*(4), 67–97. https://securityanddefence.pl/Social-structure-determinants-of-Polish-military-manpower,109649,0,2.html

Notes from Poland. (2024). *Poland has NATO's third largest military, new figures show.* https://notesfrompoland.com/2024/07/16/poland-has-natos-third-largest-military-new-figures-show/

Pidgeon, T. (2024). *Romania set to join Europe's military conscription trend.* https://brusselssignal.eu/2024/01/romania-set-to-join-europes-military-conscription-

Sylvester, B., O'Keefe, D., Gooch, S., & Kalantzis, E. (2022). Behavioral economics in military personnel research and policy.*Handbook of Military Sciences*. https://link.springer.com/referenceworkentry/10.1007/978-3-030-02866-4_83-1

Chapter 12

The Geoeconomics of the Geopolitics of Maritime Security: The Crisis in the Middle East and Red Sea

Nikolaos Deniozos and Theodoros V. Stamatopoulos

Department of Accounting and Finance, School of Administrative, Economics and Social Sciences, University of West Attica, Greece

Abstract

The escalation of geopolitical tensions in the Middle East and the intensification of Houthi attacks in the Red Sea have disrupted global maritime trade, underscoring the critical geoeconomic role of maritime security in sustaining international supply chains. This paper examines the interactions among geopolitics, geoeconomics, and maritime security, focusing on freight transport corridors linking Asia with Europe via the Suez Canal and the Bab al-Mandab Strait. Using recent empirical data on vessel transits, freight rates, routing decisions, and energy flows, the study analyses the economic and operational consequences of heightened security risks, including large-scale vessel rerouting around the Cape of Good Hope, extended sailing distances, reduced transit volumes through strategic chokepoints, and increased greenhouse gas emissions. The findings indicate a decline of up to 66% in Suez Canal transits by early 2024, accompanied by container freight rate increases exceeding 300% on key Asia–Europe routes, while cost-push inflationary pressures are projected to persist in European markets if the crisis remains unresolved. The paper contributes to the limited literature on maritime geoeconomics by developing an analytical framework linking security risks with freight transport outcomes and proposing a diamond model for maritime security policy. Policy implications highlight the need for adaptive, technology-enhanced, and

Enhancing Transatlantic Solidarity in Collective Defence: Navigating Increased Defence Expenditures, Cyber Security, and Emerging Risks, 239–280

Published under exclusive licence by Emerald Publishing Limited
doi:10.1108/978-1-80686-259-720261012

institutionally coordinated maritime security strategies to enhance the resilience of global trade and energy supply networks.

Keywords: Maritime security; Red Sea crisis; Suez Canal disruption; Bab al-Mandab Strait; geoeconomics; geopolitical risk; container shipping; freight rates; vessel rerouting; supply chain disruption; CO_2 emissions; global trade resilience

JEL Codes: F13; F14; F51; L91; R41

Introduction

The geopolitical upheavals in the Middle East took the form of attacks on ships by the Houthis. This event highlights, in the most emphatic way, on the one hand, the geoeconomic consequences of sea corridors in the Red Sea region and, on the other hand, the geopolitical dimension of maritime security. The geopolitical dimension of maritime security lies in how geography directly or indirectly limits or informs maritime security policies, regulations, measures, and functions as well as how government actors, actors in the maritime industry, and/or international organizations take geography into account when developing their maritime security strategies. Therefore, geoeconomics as a component of geopolitics and Maritime Security are undoubtedly two sides of the same coin, which is nothing but a free from all kinds of threats and dangers navigation that ensures the uninterrupted conduct of maritime trade and the non-interruption of the supply chain – logistics as well.

In this light, the work attempts to highlight the geoeconomic aspect of Maritime Security and how it affects maritime freight transport from Asia to the West and Europe in particular. The approach to the matter in question takes place through presenting the geopolitical developments and actors in the area, as well as underlining the economic effects of the maritime security issues. These economic impacts substantially affect the number of vessels passing through the Suez Canal. Furthermore, vessels retouring affects the average cruising speed and are raising environmental impacts due to the CO_2 emissions because of the diversion from the Suez Canal's crossing and circumnavigation of Africa.

The contributions of the work are threefold. First it an analytical framework is initially developed that correlates geopolitics, geoeconomics, and maritime security, highlighting aspects justifying this relationship. Second, a holistic approach concerning the geopolitical and geoeconomical effects on chain supply because of Red Sea Crisis is being presented. Third, is being proposed a diamond – model for maritime security policy is being proposed related to the geoeconomic determinants influencing maritime freight transport from Asia to the West.

The chapter is structured as follows. In the next second section, we present the Literature review-conceptual approaches. The third section describes the geoeconomy of the region and geopolitical development in the region of Red Sea, while current impacts on various components of Maritime Transport are allocated to the fourth section. Fifth and sixth sections refer to vessels rerouting and CO_2 emissions impacts, respectively. The containers' freight rates impacts are presented in seventh section, while eighth and ninth refer to Alternative route and A Diamond-Model for Maritime Security Policy, related to the geoeconomics of the area in question, respectively. The paper's concluding remarks are presented in the 10th last section.

Literature Review: Conceptual Approaches

The Geopolitical Dimension

The concept of geopolitics was introduced by the Swedish political scientist Rudolf Kjellen, in his work *The State as a Form of Life* in 1916. Geopolitics includes two sub-strands, geostrategy and geoeconomics. These concepts of strategy and economics are correlated, that is, with the geographical factors that influence their formation.

Geopolitics is defined by the location of the deposits of natural resources and raw materials, on the one hand, and the lines of communication that connect them on the other, adding strategic value to specific areas and enabling the movement of goods and all kinds of goods, as well as the persons who manage it. Science is **geography** and the analytical method is **geopolitics**. The methodological background of geopolitical analysis is **economic geography**. According to Mazis (2002, 2012), geopolitics is:

> The geographical analytical method that studies predict and describes the redistribution of power and, more generally, the systems of unbalanced distribution of power in the international arena between independent and distinct international, national or ethnic actors,

and belongs epistemologically to economic geography. This is because, as he writes later in the book

> Geopolitics: Theory and Practice, the entire economic infrastructure that feeds and creates the superstructural ideological-political mechanisms is based on a single concept: **traffic** (Verkehr v. Ratzel). Without the circulation of information, goods, people and commodities there is no economic infrastructure, no political and ideological superstructure.

According to Germond (2015), the term "geopolitics" has been employed indiscriminately by both practitioners and scholars in reference to states' zones of interest or influence and how they clash with each other's. This meaning is both vague and limited; it does not account for the full significance of the term and even bears a negative connotation due to the emphasis on power politics. It aims at explaining how geography somewhat constrains politics, how states try to bypass those constraints, and (in the case of critical geopolitics) how they try to use geography to their advantage, including in discourses through series of geo-informed representations. In practice states and other international actors take into account the constraining impacts of geographical factors.

The Geoeconomic Dimension

Regarding the geoeconomic factor, it is noted that geoeconomics, according to Luttwak (1993), reflects the continued existence of the conflictual international scene and the manifestation of competitive relations under the guise of economic and commercial competition. In other words, in geoeconomic terms, the conflictual nature of the international system is now reduced to the level of use of economic means to achieve strategic ends, and the national interest is realized under the concrete reality. The roots of geoeconomic concept could be based on Thucydides (2008) who, during the Peloponnesian War, pointed out that *The war will not be decided in Attica, as some people think, but at the locations where Attica pulls out its resources.*

Luttwak (1993) further defines geoeconomics as a new form of primordial struggle between states, except that economic means are used here. In the era of geoeconomics, invested industrial capital provided or led by the state constitutes firepower, product development with the help of state subsidies is equivalent to the innovation of weapons systems, and the penetration of domestic enterprises into the international market with state support is the equivalent to the establishment of military bases on foreign soil, as well as diplomatic influence. Paraphrasing further the classic saying of Carl Von Clausewitz, it can be said that *geoeconomics is, in large part, the continuation of the primordial competition between nations by new industrial means*, or we would add post-industrial of the 4th revolution, such as artificial intelligence, machine learning, technological development, human capital (United Nations, 2018, SDG).

Also, geopolitical scholar Søilen (2012) believes that geoeconomics is the study of spatial, cultural, and strategic aspects of resources, to obtain a sustainable competitive advantage. It is the continuation of the logic of geopolitics, applied to the era of globalization. He also offers a new term that replaces the Heartland and the Rimland – the Nareland (reduction from English "Natural Resource Lands"). This new logic of dividing geographic places determines the shift from geopolitics to geoeconomics. The author validates this thesis with the example of the United States' presence in the Middle East, where there are hydrocarbon reserves, as well as China's interests in the agricultural and the oil sectors of the African countries.

Also, according to Sanjaya Baru (2012), geoeconomics can be defined in two different ways: as a relationship between economic policy and changes in national power and geopolitics (in other words, the geopolitical consequences of economic phenomena) and how economic consequences affect geopolitics and national power. Both the refrain that "international trade follows the flag" (that the projection of national power has economic consequences) and that "the flag follows international trade" (that there are essentially geopolitical consequences of economic phenomena), both highlight the importance of geoeconomics. After all, Scekic et al. (2016) on the issue of geoeconomics point out:

> [...] The end of the last and the beginning of the current millennium were marked by the escalation of mutual relations between the great powers. The race for resources globally has increased. Economic rivalries have become the dominant phenomenon. In this context, neoliberal ideology gave way to geoeconomics. The latter explains the geographical, economic, historical, political and institutional characteristics of a particular region...

In their book, Blackwill and Harris (2016) define geoeconomics as *The use of economic means to advance and defend national interests and produce beneficial geopolitical outcomes*. Also, geoeconomics includes

> the effects of the economic actions of other nations on the geopolitical goals of a country or defines the correlation between power and geographical space, analyzes and interprets the correlations of the web of economic interconnections at the international level with the strategic goal of economic control of areas that are also the goal of geopolitics. The ultimate goal of geoeconomics is not the occupation of geographical areas, but their broader economic control that will give advantages of superiority in the commercial and technological fields. (Kantas, 2005)

Maritime Security

Maritime Security is one of the latest "buzzwords" of international relations. Major actors in maritime policy, ocean governance, and international security have in the past decade started to include maritime security in their mandate or reframed their work in such terms. In 2014, the United Kingdom, the European Union, as well as the African Union (AU) have launched ambitious maritime security strategies. The North Atlantic Treaty Organization (NATO) included maritime security as one of its objectives in its 2011 Alliance Maritime Strategy (Bueger, 2015). The existing literature has focused more on semantics and the actual meaning of security. In the maritime context Klein (2010) has defined maritime security to mean *the protection of a state's land and maritime territory, infrastructure, economy, environment and society from certain harmful acts occurring at sea*.

Discussions of maritime security frequently do so by pointing to "threats" that prevail in the maritime domain. They refer to threats such as maritime interstate disputes, maritime terrorism, piracy, trafficking of narcotics, people and illicit goods, arms proliferation, illegal fishing, environmental crimes, or maritime accidents and disasters. The argument is then that maritime security should be defined as the absence of these threats (Klein, 2011; Kraska & Pedrozo, 2013; Roach, 2004).

Issues concerning maritime security topics are also used in geopolitical discourses as an argument justifying the projections of security beyond one's external boundary. In other words, geographical representations framed within the "safe/inside" versus "unsafe/outside" dichotomy encompass maritime elements (Germond, 2015). Consequently, the geopolitical dimension of maritime security also reflects the ongoing current – existing or future strategies on maritime security.

Maritime security is essentially a management of a mix of threats and activities by state and non-state actors. Under UNCLOS' 82 (United Nations Convention on the Law of the Sea, 1983), states distribute powers in maritime zones by ensuring their peaceful use and freedom of navigation. However, while security in the territorial sea is ensured and guaranteed, on the high seas, it is at stake. Thus, according to Professor Liakouras (2006), this Convention does not explicitly deal with security on the high seas beyond a general provision that stipulates the safety of freedom of navigation vis-à-vis the rights and obligations of states, which, however, is neither complete nor appropriate to address all threats. The status of the high seas has gaps. The exclusive jurisdiction of the flag State poses further obstacles to States' efforts to combat maritime terrorism, proliferation of weapons of mass destruction, illicit trafficking of drugs by sea, which are not addressed in UNCLOS. Usually, states that issue flags of convenience have no interest or incentive to comply with international rules.

As far as European Union (EU) initiative for Maritime Security is concerned, the adoption of the EU Maritime Security Strategy and its Action Plan have been in force since 2014. The most recent update of the Action Plan took place in 2018. The proposed update follows the Council conclusions on maritime security of June 2021, which invited the Commission and the High Representative to assess the need for this update.

Since 2014, the EU Maritime Security Strategy (EUMSS) and its Action Plan have provided a comprehensive framework to prevent and address maritime security challenges.

They have encouraged closer cooperation between civilian and military authorities, through the exchange of information.

Maritime security is also linked to economic development. Throughout history, the oceans were always of vital economic importance. The concepts of "blue economy" and "blue growth" – proposed at the 2012 Rio+20 world summit 2 and widely endorsed, for instance, in the European Union's Blue Growth Strategy – aim at linking and integrating the different dimensions of the economic development of the oceans and constructing sustainable management strategies for these. The blue economy is linked to maritime security since sustainable management strategies not only require the enforcement and monitoring of laws and regulations, but a secure maritime environment provides the precondition for managing marine resources. Therefore, ensuring freedom of navigation by ensuring maritime security is a key component of the geoeconomy of maritime transport, which in turn is an essential pillar of geopolitical power.

The issue of maritime security is a typical example of a pure public good and, as is well known, such goods are indivisible, non-competitive in consumption and no one can be excluded from their consumption. However, the production of maritime security services requires factors of production, labor and capital that are transformed into maritime security output. Of course, the production (service supply) of maritime security is subject to financial constraints that certainly refer to the resources of the budgets of both states and maritime industry and supply chain actors who have vital interests in the unhindered conduct of freedom of navigation by minimizing or eliminating threats and risks. In the bibliography, Kevork and Kollias (2018), using the theory of isoquants and isocost curves, present the production of security, with isoquant curves illustrating the different combinations of capital (K) and labor (L) and isocost curve illustrating economic constraints. The goal is to maximize the security production function so that the well-known condition:

$$TSB = P_K K + P_L L \text{ (TSB = Security Budget) is met.}$$

Concluding this section, it is necessary to briefly present the Port Security Risk Assessment Tool developed by the U.S. Coast Guard (2001) and is considered that can be extended to a wider range of maritime security field. In particular, the key players of this tool are:

1. The identification of hazardous areas and modus operandi of subjects that threaten and endanger the safety of navigation.
2. Identification of risk management strategies.
3. Calculation of coping mechanism effectiveness.
4. Identification of competent personnel and equipment.

The Maritime Security Risk Assessment Tool (Table 12.1 and Fig. 12.1) quantifies and classifies various risks that threaten the security of the maritime industry. The value of risk is derived from the basic equation:

$$\text{Risk} = (\text{Threat}) \times (\text{Consequence}) \times (\text{Vulnerability})$$

In particular, the above equation results as follows:

$$R = P \times C \qquad \text{(Equation 1)}$$

where R = relative risk score, P = probability, C = consequence.

Consequence is the sum of possible effects of the attack given the scenario (using the values shown in Appendix 1) which in this risk tool can be shown as:

$$\Sigma C = C_{\text{death/injury}} + C_{\text{economic}} + E_{\text{nvironment}} + C_{\text{defense}} + C_{\text{symbolic effect}} + C_{\text{Recoverability}} + C_{\text{Redundancy}} \qquad \text{(Equation 2)}$$

Table 12.1. Consequences and Vulnerabilities in Maritime Security.

Consequence	
Term	**Definition/Meaning**
Death and injury	The prospective number of lives lost and injuries occurring as a result of an attack scenario
Environmental impact	The potential environmental impact resulting from different attack scenarios
Economic impact	The potential economic impact resulting from different attack scenarios
National defense	The potential effect on national defense resulting from different attack scenarios on different assets/ infrastructures, including Department of Defense (DOD) assets/infrastructures
Symbolic effect	The potential that the asset/infrastructure is closely linked as a symbol with the American economy, political system, military, or public welfare against different attack scenarios
Recoverability	Resources required to recover or rebuild the asset/ infrastructure, estimated based upon the expected damage resulting from the scenario
Redundancy	The degree to which replacements or alternatives exist for the affected asset/infrastructure, and the extent to which the replacement will fulfill the asset/ infrastructure's function
Vulnerability	
Availability	The asset/infrastructure's presence and predictability as it relates to the ability to plan an attack
Accessibility	Access against different attack scenarios. It relates to physical and geographic barriers that deter the threat without organic security
Organic security	The ability of non-USCG security to deter the attack. It includes security plans, communication capabilities, guard force, intrusion detection systems, and timeliness of outside law enforcement to prevent the attack
Target hardness	The ability of an asset/infrastructure to withstand attack based on complexity of asset/infrastructure design and material construction characteristics

Source: Editing by authors on an idea of USCG port security risk assessment tool.

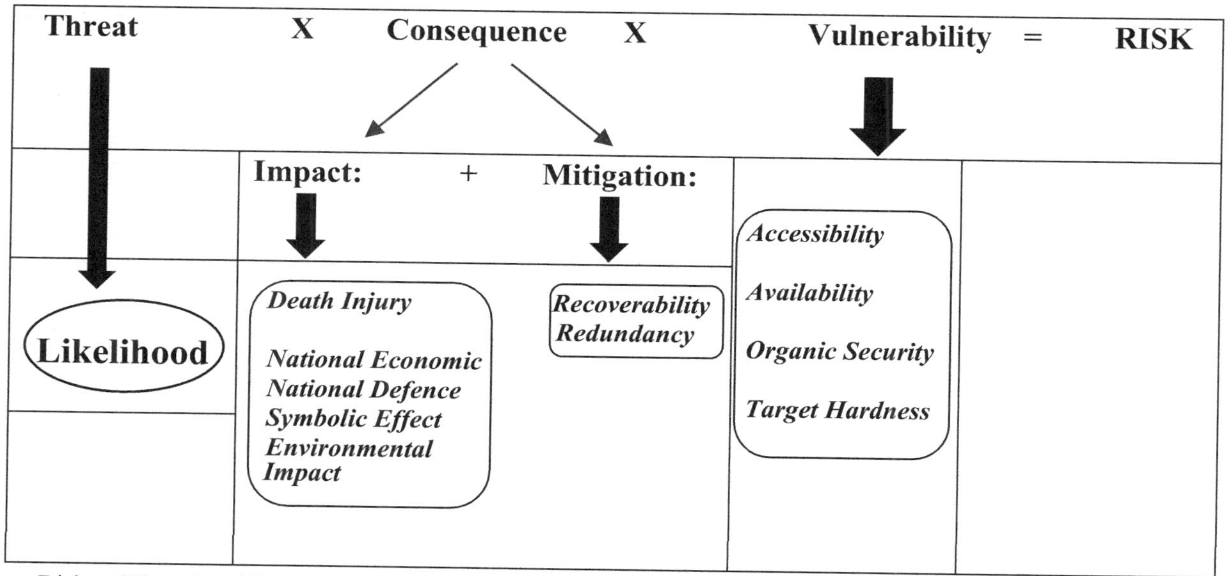

Fig. 12.1. Risk = (Threat) × (Consequence) × (Vulnerability). *Source*: Editing by authors on an idea of maritime security risk & threat.

Consequence tie breaker formula: The tie breaker formula adds in marginal values based on the consequence criteria values to allow for better ranking of assets by consequence score.

$$\Sigma C = C + C_{\text{death/injury}}(0.0000004) + C_{\text{economic}}(0.0000002) + C_{\text{environment}}(0.0000001) + C_{\text{defense}}(0.0000003) + C_{\text{symbolic effect}}(0.00000005) + C_{\text{Recoverability}}(0.0000005) + C_{\text{Redundancy}}(0.0000005) \quad \text{(Equation 3)}$$

The probability in Equation 1 is calculated in this risk tool by multiplying vulnerability by threat. This can be shown as:

$$P = V \times T \quad \text{(Equation 4)}$$

where V = vulnerability, T = threat

Vulnerability is the probability of success of an attack and is obtained by multiplying the probabilities (using the values shown in Appendix 2) associated with each of the four vulnerability categories:

$$\Pi V = V_{\text{availability}} \times V_{\text{accessibility}} \times V_{\text{organic security}} \times V_{\text{target hardness}} \quad \text{(Equation 5)}$$

Threat represents the probability of an attack (using the values shown in Appendix 1) based on the existence of intelligence and maritime domain awareness:

Thus, the resultant Risk Score for a scenario is:

$$\text{Risk} = \Sigma C \times \Pi V \times T \quad \text{(Equation 6)}$$

Note that the values used by the model to calculate the risk score are not the actual scores entered into the Worksheet. Rather, probabilities are assigned for the Vulnerability and Threat scores and equivalent values are assigned for each Consequence score. The three risk variables for each scenario result from databases and expert judgments

Ultimately, maritime security is a tool of geostrategy to enhance the geopolitical potential of the region under consideration, where power redistribution factors are evident. These power redistribution factors result, among others, from the operation of international maritime freight transport networks-corridors, which are geoeconomic variables. In turn, these geoeconomic variables are influenced and exploited by a power multiplier that is maritime security and that has to do mainly, on one hand, with strategic planning to achieve the objective of navigation free from threats and risks and, on the other hand, with tactics which is the way to achieve the goals. Strategy and tactics are two different things. This can be captured in his description by General and strategist Carl Von Clausewitz, who defined the relationship between tactics and strategy and said: *Tactics is the art of using forces on the battlefield, while strategy is the art of using battles in the final war.*

The Geoeconomy of the Region and Geopolitical Developments in the Region of Red Sea

The Geoeconomics of the Region in Question

The Red Sea is an important artery in global maritime transport, connecting the Mediterranean with the Arabian Sea and the Indian Ocean through two entrances: The Suez Canal in the North and the Bam Al Mandeb Strait in the south (Map 12.1). Blocking could cause a "heart attack" in supply chains and lead to a new spike in prices and inflation, as demonstrated both by the closure of the Suez Canal in 2021 due to the grounding of the cargo ship "Ever Given" and by the current crisis. According to UNCTAD data (UNCTAD, 2024), Suez Canal handled approximately 12% to 15% of global trade in 2023, while more than

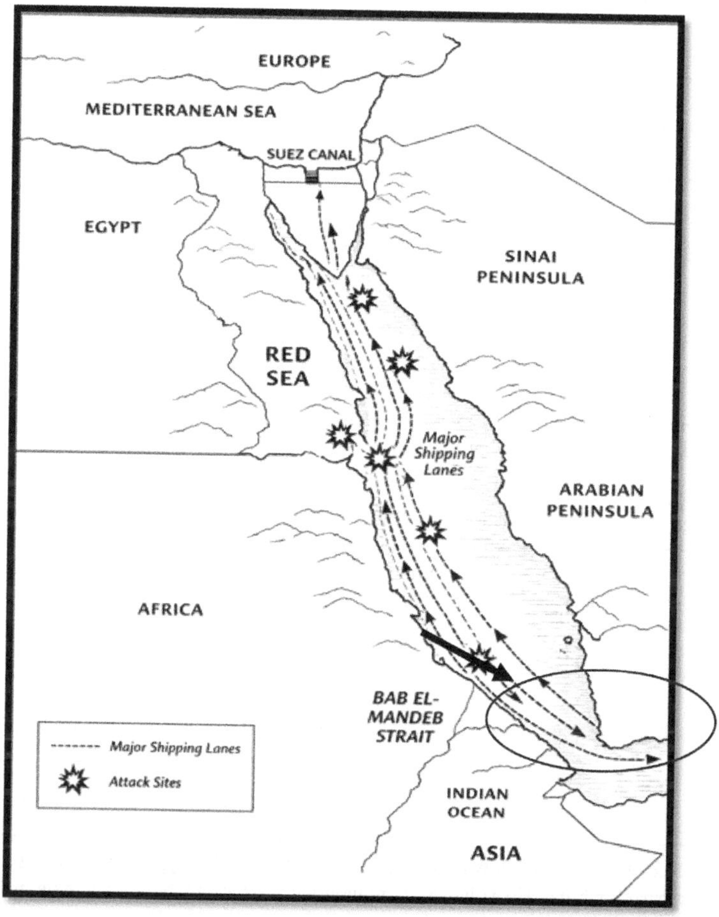

Map 12.1. Red Sea & Bab-al-Mandeb Strait. *Source*: Editing by authors.

13% of the world's crude oil transported, 8% of LNG transport and 21.5% of refined fuels were transported through this sea corridor. Additionally, the below-mentioned Tables 12.2 and 12.3 show the Oil Transit Volumes via Suez Canal & SUMED pipeline as well as Oil Transit Volumes via Bab el-Mandeb Strait for the years 2018-1H2023, highlighting the considerable geoeconomic and geopolitical importance of the region in question.

It should be noted that 40% of trade between the countries of Asia and Europe was conducted through this sea route, which means that for European economies the geopolitical situation in the region is of particular importance. In addition, 17,000 ships, merchant, and cruise ships crossed the Red Sea. Shipping Companies like Maersk, Hapag Lloyd, MSC, Evergreen, CMA, and Yang Ming Marine Transport, which immediately decided to divert their ferry routes, account for a total of 60% of world trade.

Oil and gas prices are particularly volatile to potential risks that could severely disrupt flows of these fuels from the main navigating straits in the Middle East. The

Table 12.2. Oil Transit Volumes – Suez Canal & SUMED Pipeline (2018–1H2023).

Year	Total Oil	Crude Oil & Condensate	Petroleum Products
2018	6.4	3.4	3.0
2019	6.2	3.1	3.1
2020	5.3	2.6	2.7
2021	5.1	2.2	2.9
2022	7.3	3.6	3.7
2023	8.6	4.4	4.3

Source: Editing by authors based on U.S. Energy information administration data.

Table 12.3. Oil Transit Volumes – Bab el-Mandeb Strait (2018–1H2023).

Year	Total Oil	Crude Oil & Condensate	Petroleum Products
2018	6.4	3.2	3.1
2019	6.0	2.8	3.2
2020	5.2	2.4	2.8
2021	5.4	2.2	3.2
2022	7.5	3.7	3.8
2023	8.6	4.3	4.4

Note: (a) SUMED pipeline transports crude oil north through Egypt and has a capacity of 2.5 million barrels per day. (b) Volumes are million barrels per day (b/d), a common metric for oil trade flow statistics.

Source: Editing by authors based on U.S. Energy information administration data.

reason is evident as more than 60% of the world's trade in oil, natural gas, LNG, and other energy products moves through sea transit by tankers, mainly from the – rich in deposits – Middle East to -bare- of deposits and thirsty for oil and energy Asia (China, Japan, and South Korea) and second to Europe. Tankers from Qatar, a top exporter of liquefied natural gas, are forced through all three Middle Eastern straits on their way to Europe. This fact escalates the energy risk for Europe, especially at this time when it is trying to wean itself off gas flows from Russia.

The Geopolitics of the Region in Question

The Strait of Aden and the southeastern part of the Red Sea are in a state of structural turmoil due to the most recent version of the Yemeni civil war, which in its initial phase began in 1962. In contrast to earlier phases of Yemen's division, the ongoing crisis triggered by the Houthi capture of the capital Sanaa in September 2014 differs in the following respects: (a) The internal conflict has not led to the division of the country between northern and southern Yemen, as happened many times between 1962 and 1990, but to the fragmentation of Yemen, as **a separatist movement has developed with the support of the UAE within southern Yemen that seized Aden in 2019**. (b) The risk of a complete Houthi victory caused Saudi Arabia's first-ever direct military involvement in a neighboring country between 2015 and 2020. (c) The Saudi intervention was imposed by the additional reason that the internal causes of division were for the first time, not of an ethnic-racial or ideological nature, but primarily of a national-religious nature, falling within the broader context of the sectarian **Shiite-Sunni conflict**. (d) The Yemeni civil war has become a subchapter of the broader multipolar cold war plaguing the wider Middle East between Riyadh and Tehran, which has taken advantage of Yemen's post-2020 ceasefire to expand the Houthi's ballistic capabilities and UAV arsenal. The expansion of Iranian influence in Yemen has created the impression that the Houthis have evolved into the southernmost analogue of **Hezbollah**, thus attributing the escalation of recent attacks on international shipping to Tehran instead of Sanaa. Although Tehran's degree of influence over the Houthis is undeniable, it would be a mistake to assume that the Houthis have the potential. Hezbollah's disciplined constitution and dependency vis-à-vis Tehran (Tsakiris, 2023).

Since the outbreak of the Israel-Gaza conflict following the October 7, 2023 attacks, the Houthis have shifted their military focus to the Red Sea, aiming to enforce an embargo on Israel and halt Tel Aviv's offensive on Gaza. In a continuous escalation, the Houthis initially targeted Israeli territory before subsequently expanding their objectives to vessels linked to or en route to Israel, as well as to US and UK warships and interests, continuously extending their pool of targets and effectively disrupting global trade transiting through the Red Sea.

Houthi operations targeting international shipping in the Red Sea and surrounding waterways have significantly relied on drones, with more than 40% of the events between October 2023 and June 2024 involving drones. However, the effectiveness of drone attacks to target international shipping has been considerably limited if compared to missile attacks. In fact, 75% of Houthi drone attacks on international shipping have been intercepted by international coalition forces deployed to the Red Sea and the Gulf of Aden region to counter the Houthi threat, compared to approximately 16% of missile attacks of the 85% of Houthi missile attacks that were not intercepted by international forces, 26% struck their target, while the rest impacted the water without causing any damage. Furthermore, among attacks that successfully hit the target, drones were used in only one out of five cases (Nevola & D'Hauthuille, 2006).

According to the researcher of ELIAMEP (Hellenic Foundation for European and Foreign Policy) (Papastavrides, 2024), Houthis have been engaged in different forms of attacks against shipping in the Red Sea. These attacks are not subject to the same classification under international law and cannot be addressed in the same manner by the target or third States. The potential in question classifications is the following: (a) Piracy; (b) Acts Related to Non-International Armed Conflict at Sea; (c) Acts of Maritime Terrorism or SUA Offences (Convention for the Suppression of Unlawful Acts against the Safety of Maritime Navigation –SUA Convention); (d) Claim of Sellf Defense (Papastavridis 2024).

As a response to the Israel-Gaza conflict, the group has sought to impose a blockade of Israel by targeting commercial shipping in the Red Sea and surrounding waterways, as well as carrying out attacks directly targeting Israeli territory. Since November 2023, more than 50% of all Houthi drone attacks have been launched toward targets outside of Yemen.

Of geopolitical significance, it is also pointed out that the Indian Ocean, – Arabian Sea – Red Sea navigation corridor is located in Rimland Spykman's (1944) theory as correction/integration of Mackinder's geopolitical theory of heartland (Map 12.2). In this way, Anglo-Saxon thinking organically integrates

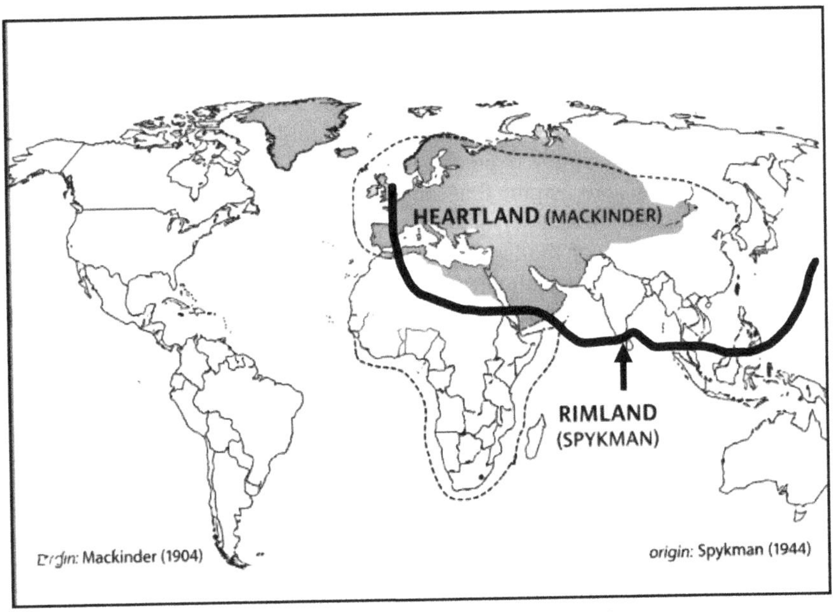

Map 12.2. Heartland & Rimland. *Source*: Editing by authors.

the geoeconomic factor into the geostrategic element, making the entire rimland a zone of military, political, and economic influence of the West, while highlighting the issue of maritime security as of paramount importance in the unhindered operation of maritime freight networks.

Furthermore, Alfred Mahan (1840–1914), a USA Navy Captain and President at Naval War College and father of Geostrategy, had characterized Great Britain as a pattern, and had referred in 1890 in the book "The Influence of Sea Power upon History 1600–1783," his admiration for its worldwide dominance as a sea power, with the control it was exercising through its powerful navy and its stations around the world (colonies, naval bases, maritime control of hub points of international trade and navigation, etc.). Mahan had pointed out: *For a country to become a great maritime power, it must have a long coastline, good-effective ports, and be located and control primarily the area north of the Suez Canal and the Panama Canal.*

Empirical Impacts, Evidence, and Policy Implications

Current Impacts on Various Components of Maritime Transport

Oil & Tanker Market

In the past, geopolitical crises in the Middle East had a significant impact on oil and tanker markets, which immediately translated into a rise in oil prices followed by higher tanker freight rates. One of these crises, the closure of Suez from 1967 to 1975, had a significant impact on the tanker market. It forced tankers to use longer routes around the Cape of Good Hope and resulted in a large increase in tanker sizes. Before 1967 there were no tankers larger than 200,000 dwt. The first of these Very Large Crude Carriers (VLCCW) was delivered in 1967. However, in the current situation and timing (August 2024), the reaction of the oil and tanker markets has been quite muted.

Crude Oil and Brent oil prices, shortly after the outbreak of the crisis in the Middle East and Red Sea, had presented the following features (Table 12.4):

It is noted that after the outbreak of the crisis the highest prices of Crude Oil occurred on 20/10/23: 86.612 USD/Bbl, on 05/04/24: 86.990 USD/Bbl. and 04/07/24: 83.967 USD/Bbl, while the price on 09/08/24 decreased to 76.080 USD/Bbl. In other words, from October 2023 till August 2024, a decline of 12.16% occurred.

Table 12.4. Crude Oil Prices & Brent Crude Oil Prices (in USD).

	30/12/2023	**03/01/2024**	**09/01/24**
Crude Oil	71.324	72.675	72.075
Brent	76.930	78.235	77.277

Source: Editing by authors, based on Trading Economics data.

Brent crude oil prices fluctuated around $79.2 per barrel on 09/08/24. Furthermore, prediction of a retributive strike by Iran against Israel, in response to assassination of a Hamas leader in Tehran, could escalate the Middle East conflict and raise concerns about regional oil supply. Meanwhile, Qatar, Egypt, and the United States have urged Israel and Hamas to resume ceasefire negotiations. After the outbreak of the crisis the highest prices of Brent Crude Oil occurred on 19/10/23: 90.554 USD/Bbl, on 05/04/24: 91.234 USD/Bbl. and 04/07/24: 87.380 USD/Bbl., while the price on 09/08/24 decreased to 79.144 USD/Bbl. In other words, from October 2023 till August 2024 a decline of 12.6% occurred. The rising tensions in the Middle East and Houthi attacks that significantly disrupted oil trade routes and pushed significantly upward freight rates. According to the Baltic Exchange Data, VLCC time charter equivalent rates peaked at a staggering USD 65,537 per day on February 2024, a 117% increase compared to the beginning of the year. However, according to the Fearnlays Data, VLCC time charter (T/C) equivalent rates was at 38,500 USD per day on February 2024 which remains stable until August 2024.

Concerning the SUEZMAX T/C equivalent rates was at 44,000 USD per day on March 2024 but in August 2024 there is a decline to 40,000 USD/per day, as shown in the Fig. 12.7. In other words, a decline of 9% occurred due to the rerouting of such a type of vessel.

Regarding the AFRAMAX T/C equivalent rate was at 42,000 USD per day at the end of February 2024, while in July 2024 and August 2024 the rate was at 43,500 USD/per day, recording an increase of 3.6%, due to the demand for this type of ship for a detour around Africa.

Vessels Rerouting

Shipping companies with vessels idling in or near the Suez Canal are considering taking a detour around Africa. The Cape of Good Hope route is considerably longer and burns more fuel, making it less popular than the Suez Canal option. A merchant ship's journey from Taiwan to the Netherlands via the Suez Canal takes 25.5 days, while circumnavigating Africa requires 34 days at an average speed of 16.48 knots (Map 12.3).

Furthermore, according to Sea Intelligence (2024a, 2024b)'s measurements, at Eastern Mediterranean were recorded the longest delays regarding ships calls from Asia. Thus, from the two sub-regions of Asia (North and Southeast Asia) and the three sub-regions of the Mediterranean (Eastern, Western, and Central Mediterranean), the average minimum transit time in the three months since the outbreak of the crisis (January–March 2024) increased on average by 39%, compared to the average time of the previous six months. On the Asia-Northern Europe routes, the increase in sailing days was 15%. In contrast, for the Eastern Mediterranean, the average minimum sailing time increased by 61%–63%, while for the Central Mediterranean by 39%–40%.

The existing data (Table 12.5) show that between the week 1/11/23–7/11/23 and the last week 22/07/24–29/07/24 there is a decrease in crossings through the

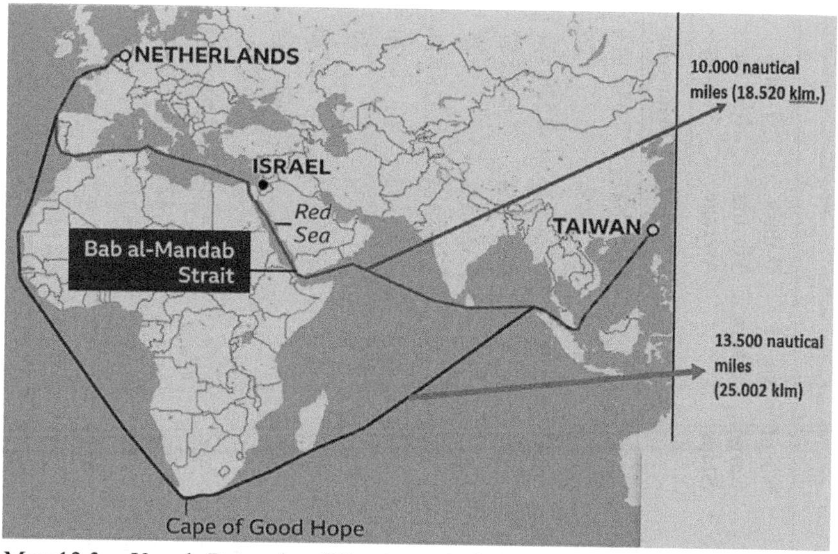

Map 12.3. Vessels Retouring (Distances via Suez Canel & Cape of Good Hope). *Source*: Editing by authors.

Suez Canal of the Cargo Ships by 54.75%. This fact is also reflected in Fig. 12.2. Concerning the Transit of Tankers via Suez Canal, between the same period a decrease in transit of 45.7% occurred. Fig. 12.3 reflects these developments.

Table 12.6 and Fig. 12.4 show that between 06/11/23 and 01/04/24 there was a decrease of 65.73% in total crossings via Suez Canal, reflecting emphatically this decline in comparison to a perspective increase of passage via Good Hope of 64.8% as has been pointed out considering the data of Table 12.5. This gap is obviously presented in mentioned Fig. 12.7, while the average weekly percentage decrease in crossings via Suez Canal, was 5%.

Table 12.7 and Fig. 12.5 show that between 06/11/23 and 01/04/24 there was a decrease of 60.72% in total crossings via Bab al Mandab. Furthermore, the average weekly percentage decreased 4.35%.

Table 12.8 and Fig. 12.6 illustrate that between 30/10/23 and 25/03/24 there was an increase of 64.8% in total crossings via Good Hope Cape.

Concluding, African ports face a multidute of hurdles and are unable to provide the same level of services as ports in the Red Sea or the Mediterranean. Therefore, shipping companiesand charterers have another factor to consider, as African ports are not the optimal choice when it comes to bunkering stops. Congestion and substandard services are not the only reason why reason why African ports are not an attractive option. The trip around the southern part of Africa is accompanied several times with particularly severe weather conditions. Therefore, ships consume more fuel faster.

Table 12.5. Suez Canal Daily Transit (30/10/23–29/7/24).

Dates	No. of Cargo Ships	No. of Tankers	7-days Moving Average	7-days Moving Average	Dates	No. of Cargo Ships	No. of Tankers	7-days Moving Average	7-days Moving Average
				Prior year					Prior year
30/10/2023 00:00	54	22	7,685,714	6,971,429	15/03/2024 00:00	19	11	3,642,857	7,657,143
31/10/2023 00:00	43	26	7,528,571	7,128,571	16/03/2024 00:00	24	10	3,471,429	75
01/11/2023 00:00	41	32	7,414,286	73	17/03/2024 00:00	23	9	3,371,429	7,528,571
02/11/2023 00:00	52	27	7,457,143	7,242,857	18/03/2024 00:00	19	14	34	7,442,857
03/11/2023 00:00	50	25	7,471,429	7,471,429	19/03/2024 00:00	21	11	3,328,571	75
04/11/2023 00:00	50	33	74	75	20/03/2024 00:00	19	13	3,185,714	7,328,571
05/11/2023 00:00	62	19	7,657,143	7,585,714	21/03/2024 00:00	21	10	32	76
06/11/2023 00:00	55	23	7,685,714	7,757,143	22/03/2024 00:00	21	9	32	74
07/11/2023 00:00	48	14	7,585,714	7,557,143	23/03/2024 00:00	30	10	3,285,714	75
08/11/2023 00:00	59	26	7,757,143	7,585,714	24/03/2024 00:00	28	5	33	7,485,714
09/11/2023 00:00	46	29	77	7,785,714	25/03/2024 00:00	24	16	34	7,128,571
10/11/2023 00:00	47	27	7,685,714	7,614,286	26/03/2024 00:00	22	14	3,457,143	7,242,857
11/11/2023 00:00	50	21	7,514,286	7,514,286	27/03/2024 00:00	27	13	3,571,429	7,357,143
12/11/2023 00:00	47	24	7,371,429	7,714,286	28/03/2024 00:00	17	8	3,485,714	69
13/11/2023 00:00	57	25	7,428,571	7,457,143	29/03/2024 00:00	22	7	3,471,429	6,928,571
14/11/2023 00:00	53	26	7,671,429	7,428,571	30/03/2024 00:00	22	14	3,414,286	6,742,857

15/11/2023 00:00	62	24	7,685,714	7,271,429	31/03/2024 00:00	21	10	3,385,714	7,071,429
16/11/2023 00:00	53	19	7,642,857	7,214,286	01/04/2024 00:00	25	15	3,385,714	7,157,143
17/11/2023 00:00	59	35	7,928,571	7,214,286	02/04/2024 00:00	27	18	3,514,286	7,242,857
18/11/2023 00:00	49	20	79	7,285,714	03/04/2024 00:00	22	8	3,371,429	69
19/11/2023 00:00	45	21	7,828,571	7,157,143	04/04/2024 00:00	26	9	3,514,286	7,371,429
20/11/2023 00:00	46	22	7,628,571	7,114,286	05/04/2024 00:00	23	14	3,628,571	7,428,571
21/11/2023 00:00	48	21	7,485,714	7,271,429	06/04/2024 00:00	22	10	3,571,429	7,642,857
22/11/2023 00:00	58	27	7,471,429	7,285,714	07/04/2024 00:00	27	11	3,671,429	7,528,571
23/11/2023 00:00	39	25	7,357,143	7,114,286	08/04/2024 00:00	29	13	37	7,657,143
24/11/2023 00:00	51	31	7,185,714	71	09/04/2024 00:00	19	10	3,471,429	76
25/11/2023 00:00	52	25	7,314,286	6,857,143	10/04/2024 00:00	17	13	3,471,429	77
26/11/2023 00:00	50	23	7,485,714	68	11/04/2024 00:00	30	13	3,585,714	7,614,286
27/11/2023 00:00	48	23	7,528,571	6,885,714	12/04/2024 00:00	20	14	3,542,857	77
28/11/2023 00:00	54	22	7,628,571	6,742,857	13/04/2024 00:00	26	8	3,571,429	7,785,714
29/11/2023 00:00	47	25	7,442,857	6,842,857	14/04/2024 00:00	19	9	3,428,571	7,642,857
30/11/2023 00:00	55	20	76	6,771,429	15/04/2024 00:00	23	18	3,414,286	7,685,714
01/12/2023 00:00	42	30	7,457,143	6,971,429	16/04/2024 00:00	33	13	3,657,143	76
02/12/2023 00:00	45	24	7,328,571	7,357,143	17/04/2024 00:00	24	12	3,742,857	7,771,429
03/12/2023 00:00	55	29	7,414,286	7,357,143	18/04/2024 00:00	19	11	3,557,143	7,671,429
04/12/2023 00:00	45	24	7,385,714	7,342,857	19/04/2024 00:00	31	7	3,614,286	80
05/12/2023 00:00	53	21	7,357,143	74	20/04/2024 00:00	24	4	3,528,571	7,828,571

(Continued)

Table 12.5. (*Continued*)

Dates	No. of Cargo Ships	No. of Tankers	7-days Moving Average	7-days Moving Average	Dates	No. of Cargo Ships	No. of Tankers	7-days Moving Average	7-days Moving Average
				Prior year					Prior year
06/12/2023 00:00	44	21	7,257,143	7,628,571	21/04/2024 00:00	31	18	3,828,571	7,842,857
07/12/2023 00:00	45	21	7,128,571	7,785,714	22/04/2024 00:00	27	16	3,857,143	7,985,714
08/12/2023 00:00	52	29	7,257,143	7,542,857	23/04/2024 00:00	23	6	3,614,286	7,914,286
09/12/2023 00:00	45	32	7,371,429	7,471,429	24/04/2024 00:00	21	9	3,528,571	80
10/12/2023 00:00	47	20	7,128,571	74	25/04/2024 00:00	16	10	3,471,429	7,914,286
11/12/2023 00:00	41	31	7,171,429	74	26/04/2024 00:00	32	7	3,485,714	78
12/12/2023 00:00	52	30	7,285,714	7,228,571	27/04/2024 00:00	15	13	3,485,714	7,857,143
13/12/2023 00:00	59	23	7,528,571	6,928,571	28/04/2024 00:00	23	10	3,257,143	7,871,429
14/12/2023 00:00	44	26	7,585,714	7,114,286	29/04/2024 00:00	24	8	31	7,885,714
15/12/2023 00:00	47	22	7,414,286	73	30/04/2024 00:00	21	15	32	7,885,714
16/12/2023 00:00	44	21	7,242,857	6,928,571	01/05/2024 00:00	15	9	3,114,286	8,157,143
17/12/2023 00:00	53	33	7,514,286	7,071,429	02/05/2024 00:00	20	9	3,157,143	8,071,429
18/12/2023 00:00	43	26	7,471,429	6,942,857	03/05/2024 00:00	23	7	3,028,571	8,085,714
19/12/2023 00:00	57	18	7,371,429	7,114,286	04/05/2024 00:00	27	10	3,157,143	8,157,143
20/12/2023 00:00	47	26	7,242,857	72	05/05/2024 00:00	20	5	3,042,857	8,185,714
21/12/2023 00:00	51	26	7,342,857	6,942,857	06/05/2024 00:00	21	11	3,042,857	8,114,286

22/12/2023 00:00	46	22	7,328,571	6,885,714	07/05/2024 00:00	18	17	3,028,571	8,157,143
23/12/2023 00:00	37	19	72	7,114,286	08/05/2024 00:00	25	14	3,242,857	78
24/12/2023 00:00	39	18	6,785,714	7,228,571	09/05/2024 00:00	27	15	3,428,571	7,842,857
25/12/2023 00:00	35	22	6,614,286	7,342,857	10/05/2024 00:00	18	14	3,457,143	78
26/12/2023 00:00	37	20	6,357,143	7,342,857	11/05/2024 00:00	25	9	3,414,286	7,657,143
27/12/2023 00:00	37	15	6,057,143	7,328,571	12/05/2024 00:00	21	11	3,514,286	76
28/12/2023 00:00	45	23	5,928,571	7,171,429	13/05/2024 00:00	42	16	3,885,714	75
29/12/2023 00:00	34	21	5,742,857	71	14/05/2024 00:00	18	10	3,785,714	7,628,571
30/12/2023 00:00	47	18	5,871,429	7,142,857	15/05/2024 00:00	23	12	3,728,571	7,657,143
31/12/2023 00:00	27	26	5,814,286	7,057,143	16/05/2024 00:00	22	12	3,614,286	7,757,143
01/01/2024 00:00	27	17	5,628,571	70	17/05/2024 00:00	18	11	3,571,429	7,914,286
02/01/2024 00:00	38	21	5,657,143	6,842,857	18/05/2024 00:00	15	10	3,442,857	7,957,143
03/01/2024 00:00	35	15	5,628,571	70	19/05/2024 00:00	20	13	3,457,143	8,128,571
04/01/2024 00:00	40	19	55	7,014,286	20/05/2024 00:00	23	13	3,142,857	8,085,714
05/01/2024 00:00	25	20	5,357,143	7,271,429	21/05/2024 00:00	23	14	3,271,429	7,771,429
06/01/2024 00:00	29	22	5,157,143	7,257,143	22/05/2024 00:00	21	14	3,271,429	8,042,857
07/01/2024 00:00	39	16	5,185,714	7,214,286	23/05/2024 00:00	27	11	3,328,571	7,942,857
08/01/2024 00:00	44	11	5,342,857	72	24/05/2024 00:00	26	13	3,471,429	7,314,286
09/01/2024 00:00	36	16	5,242,857	6,885,714	25/05/2024 00:00	17	13	3,542,857	75
10/01/2024 00:00	28	15	5,142,857	7,042,857	26/05/2024 00:00	26	13	3,628,571	7,314,286

(Continued)

Table 12.5. (*Continued*)

Dates	No. of Cargo Ships	No. of Tankers	7-days Moving Average	7-days Moving Average	Dates	No. of Cargo Ships	No. of Tankers	7-days Moving Average	7-days Moving Average
				Prior year					Prior year
11/01/2024 00:00	30	19	50	7,242,857	27/05/2024 00:00	24	8	3,571,429	7,585,714
12/01/2024 00:00	25	10	4,857,143	6,971,429	28/05/2024 00:00	26	7	3,514,286	7,671,429
13/01/2024 00:00	35	14	4,828,571	7,114,286	29/05/2024 00:00	18	14	3,471,429	7,571,429
14/01/2024 00:00	36	14	4,757,143	6,971,429	30/05/2024 00:00	25	14	3,485,714	7,557,143
15/01/2024 00:00	33	16	4,671,429	70	31/05/2024 00:00	17	12	3,342,857	7,742,857
16/01/2024 00:00	24	16	45	7,485,714	01/06/2024 00:00	24	14	3,457,143	7,742,857
17/01/2024 00:00	37	15	4,628,571	7,014,286	02/06/2024 00:00	30	11	3,485,714	7,657,143
18/01/2024 00:00	36	20	4,728,571	7,057,143	03/06/2024 00:00	26	8	3,514,286	7,257,143
19/01/2024 00:00	25	17	4,828,571	7,242,857	04/06/2024 00:00	24	13	3,571,429	73
20/01/2024 00:00	26	8	4,614,286	6,985,714	05/06/2024 00:00	21	14	3,614,286	7,057,143
21/01/2024 00:00	35	14	46	7,285,714	06/06/2024 00:00	25	13	36	73
22/01/2024 00:00	31	13	4,528,571	7,285,714	07/06/2024 00:00	18	14	3,642,857	7,585,714
23/01/2024 00:00	21	12	4,428,571	7,171,429	08/06/2024 00:00	23	7	3,528,571	7,371,429
24/01/2024 00:00	22	16	4,228,571	71	09/06/2024 00:00	22	13	3,442,857	76
25/01/2024 00:00	28	17	4,071,429	7,157,143	10/06/2024 00:00	20	12	3,414,286	7,757,143
26/01/2024 00:00	29	10	4,028,571	72	11/06/2024 00:00	23	12	3,385,714	7,828,571

27/01/2024 00:00	25	9	4,028,571	7,357,143	12/06/2024 00:00	23	14	3,414,286	7,814,286
28/01/2024 00:00	37	15	4,071,429	7,157,143	13/06/2024 00:00	22	13	3,371,429	7,657,143
29/01/2024 00:00	27	8	3,942,857	7,142,857	14/06/2024 00:00	28	9	3,442,857	7,442,857
30/01/2024 00:00	20	12	3,928,571	7,142,857	15/06/2024 00:00	19	13	3,471,429	75
31/01/2024 00:00	23	13	39	7,328,571	16/06/2024 00:00	13	11	3,314,286	7,314,286
01/02/2024 00:00	24	9	3,728,571	6,914,286	17/06/2024 00:00	13	13	3,228,571	7,514,286
02/02/2024 00:00	28	11	3,728,571	6,842,857	18/06/2024 00:00	21	10	3,171,429	7,357,143
03/02/2024 00:00	25	16	3,828,571	6,857,143	19/06/2024 00:00	25	11	3,157,143	7,157,143
04/02/2024 00:00	30	11	3,671,429	6,957,143	20/06/2024 00:00	21	15	3,171,429	7,071,429
05/02/2024 00:00	29	12	3,757,143	6,971,429	21/06/2024 00:00	19	8	3,028,571	75
06/02/2024 00:00	29	6	38	6,814,286	22/06/2024 00:00	19	12	3,014,286	7,442,857
07/02/2024 00:00	29	12	3,871,429	6,828,571	23/06/2024 00:00	16	13	3,085,714	7,857,143
08/02/2024 00:00	30	10	3,971,429	6,957,143	24/06/2024 00:00	27	11	3,257,143	7,871,429
09/02/2024 00:00	32	9	40	6,928,571	25/06/2024 00:00	25	8	3,285,714	7,814,286
10/02/2024 00:00	27	14	40	71	26/06/2024 00:00	13	15	3,171,429	81
11/02/2024 00:00	19	13	3,871,429	6,985,714	27/06/2024 00:00	18	6	30	83
12/02/2024 00:00	28	15	39	7,157,143	28/06/2024 00:00	20	8	3,014,286	7,614,286
13/02/2024 00:00	34	13	4,071,429	7,185,714	29/06/2024 00:00	22	15	31	78
14/02/2024 00:00	29	9	4,028,571	7,485,714	30/06/2024 00:00	20	7	3,071,429	7,471,429
15/02/2024 00:00	16	8	38	7,685,714	01/07/2024 00:00	31	9	31	7,357,143

(Continued)

Table 12.5. (*Continued*)

Dates	No. of Cargo Ships	No. of Tankers	7-days Moving Average	7-days Moving Average	Dates	No. of Cargo Ships	No. of Tankers	7-days Moving Average	7-days Moving Average
				Prior year					Prior year
16/02/2024 00:00	22	19	38	7,628,571	02/07/2024 00:00	31	7	3,171,429	7,414,286
17/02/2024 00:00	18	12	3,642,857	7,128,571	03/07/2024 00:00	15	13	3,171,429	7,185,714
18/02/2024 00:00	25	6	3,628,571	7,142,857	04/07/2024 00:00	26	9	3,328,571	7,185,714
19/02/2024 00:00	21	18	3,571,429	69	05/07/2024 00:00	21	11	3,385,714	7,342,857
20/02/2024 00:00	25	9	3,385,714	7,185,714	06/07/2024 00:00	22	11	3,328,571	7,071,429
21/02/2024 00:00	28	6	3,328,571	6,971,429	07/07/2024 00:00	17	10	3,328,571	7,185,714
22/02/2024 00:00	31	13	3,614,286	6,871,429	08/07/2024 00:00	19	7	3,128,571	7,057,143
23/02/2024 00:00	25	15	36	6,942,857	09/07/2024 00:00	20	11	3,028,571	7,371,429
24/02/2024 00:00	32	12	38	7,185,714	10/07/2024 00:00	17	5	2,942,857	7,314,286
25/02/2024 00:00	27	12	3,914,286	7,014,286	11/07/2024 00:00	17	19	2,957,143	6,842,857
26/02/2024 00:00	31	12	3,971,429	7,342,857	12/07/2024 00:00	26	10	3,014,286	7,014,286
27/02/2024 00:00	28	14	4,085,714	6,985,714	13/07/2024 00:00	19	11	2,971,429	7,271,429
28/02/2024 00:00	25	10	41	6,985,714	14/07/2024 00:00	16	9	2,942,857	7,271,429
29/02/2024 00:00	32	13	4,114,286	7,071,429	15/07/2024 00:00	20	7	2,957,143	73
01/03/2024 00:00	21	10	3,985,714	6,714,286	16/07/2024 00:00	24	9	2,985,714	6,828,571

02/03/2024 00:00	28	9	3,885,714	6,757,143	17/07/2024 00:00	15	12	3,057,143	72
03/03/2024 00:00	18	12	3,757,143	6,828,571	18/07/2024 00:00	20	10	2,971,429	7,528,571
04/03/2024 00:00	17	6	3,471,429	6,471,429	19/07/2024 00:00	28	12	3,028,571	7,585,714
05/03/2024 00:00	17	14	3,314,286	69	20/07/2024 00:00	22	12	3,085,714	7,414,286
06/03/2024 00:00	22	6	3,214,286	7,128,571	21/07/2024 00:00	18	11	3,142,857	7,328,571
07/03/2024 00:00	28	14	3,171,429	6,942,857	22/07/2024 00:00	22	9	32	7,314,286
08/03/2024 00:00	32	14	3,385,714	72	23/07/2024 00:00	25	7	3,185,714	7,485,714
09/03/2024 00:00	31	15	3,514,286	7,314,286	24/07/2024 00:00	13	17	3,228,571	7,257,143
10/03/2024 00:00	27	12	3,642,857	7,328,571	26/07/2024 00:00	15	19	3,185,714	71
11/03/2024 00:00	20	11	3,757,143	7,728,571	27/07/2024 00:00	19	13	3,157,143	7,028,571
12/03/2024 00:00	24	13	3,842,857	7,514,286	28/07/2024 00:00	24	6	3,171,429	69
13/03/2024 00:00	28	14	4,042,857	7,414,286	29/07/2024 00:00	25	9	3,214,286	6,857,143
14/03/2024 00:00	20	10	3,871,429	7,628,571					

Source: Editing by authors based on UK Statistical Office's data.

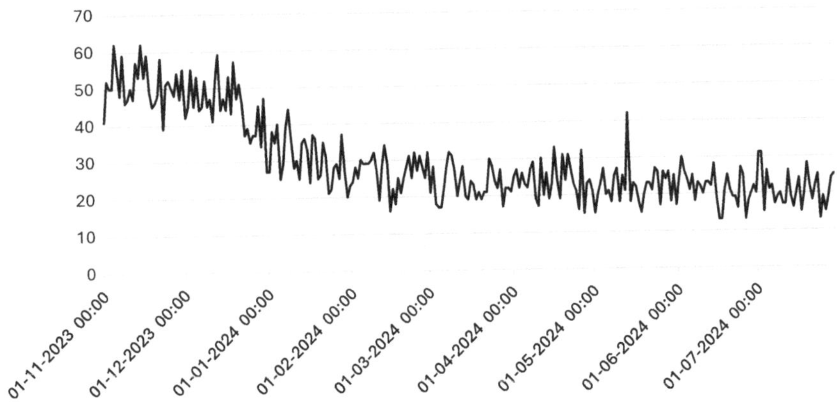

Fig. 12.2. Suez Canal Daily Transit of Cargo Ships (01/11/23–29/07/23).
Source: The Authors. Figure is created from Table 12.3.

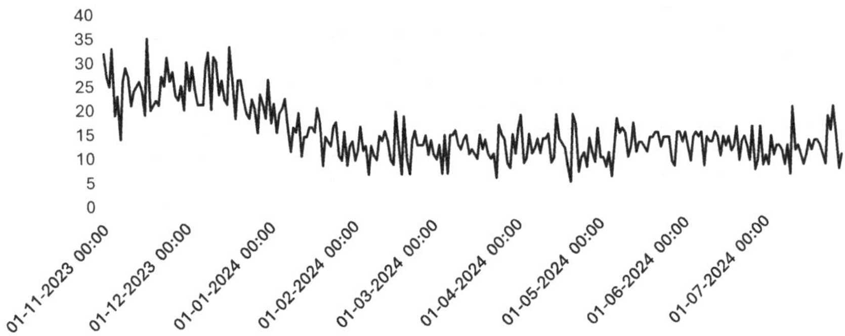

Fig. 12.3 Suez Canal Daily Transit of Tankers (01/11/23–29/07/23).
Source: The Authors. Figure is created from Table 12.3.

Table 12.6. Suez Canal Total Weekly Crossings (06/11/24–01/04/24).

Weeks	No. of Crossings
06/11/2023	467
13/11/2023	469
20/11/2023	453
27/11/2023	451
04/12/2023	427
11/12/2023	452
18/12/2023	407
25/12/2023	341
01/01/2024	316
08/01/2024	280
15/01/2024	271

Table 12.6. (*Continued*)

Weeks	No. of Crossings
22/01/2024	242
29/01/2024	221
05/02/2024	238
12/02/2024	210
19/02/2024	233
26/02/2024	212
04/03/2012	203
11/03/2024	169
18/03/2024	176
25/03/2024	157
01/04/2024	160

Source: Editing by authors based on UK Statistical Office's data.

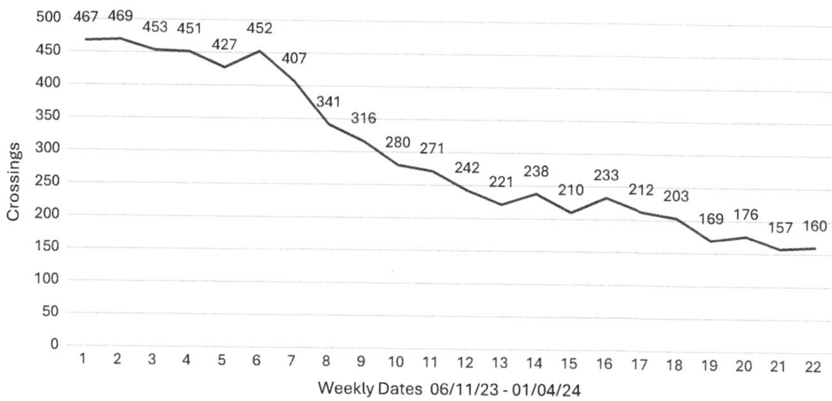

Fig. 12.4. Suez Canal Total Weekly Crossings (06/11/24–01/4/24).
Source: The Authors. Figure is created from Table 12.6.

Table 12.7. Bab Al Mandab Strait Total Weekly Crossings (06/11/23–01/4/23).

Week	Vessels Crossings
06/11/2023	499
13/11/2023	510
20/11/2023	545
27/11/2023	503
04/12/2023	508

(*Continued*)

Table 12.7. (*Continued*)

Week	Vessels Crossings
11/12/2023	498
18/12/2023	377
25/12/2023	358
01/01/2024	303
08/01/2024	288
15/01/2024	250
22/01/2024	226
29/01/2024	232
05/02/2024	228
12/02/2024	230
19/02/2024	241
26/02/2024	229
04/03/2012	212
11/03/2024	221
18/03/2024	207
25/03/2024	214
01/04/2024	196

Source: Editing by authors based on UK Statistical Office's data.

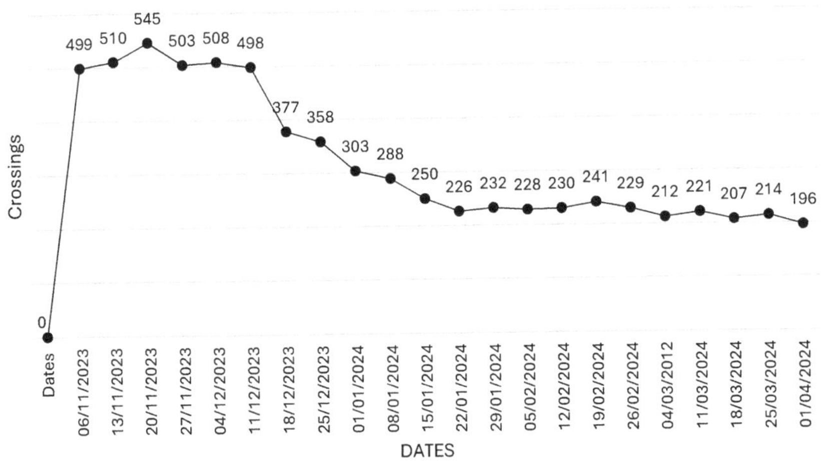

Fig. 12.5. Bab Al Mandab Strait Total Weekly Crossings (06/11/23–01/04/24).
Source: The Authors. Figure is created from Table 12.5.

Table 12.8. Cape Good Hope Passage.

Weeks	Vessels Crossings
30/10/2023	392
06/11/2023	374
13/11/2023	417
20/11/2023	393
27/11/2023	371
04/12/2023	387
11/12/2023	429
18/12/2023	393
25/12/2023	505
01/01/2024	592
08/01/2024	578
15/01/2024	559
22/01/2024	601
29/01/2024	648
05/02/2024	628
12/02/2024	686
19/02/2024	674
04/03/2012	679
11/03/2024	655
18/03/2024	606
25/03/2024	646

Source: Editing by authors based on UK Statistical Office's data.

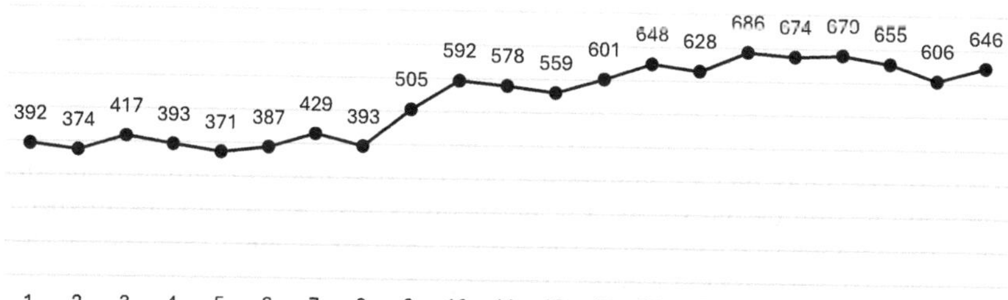

Fig. 12.6. Good Hope Care Weekly Passage (30/10/23–25/03/24), (21 Weeks).
Source: The Authors. Figure is created from Table 12.5.

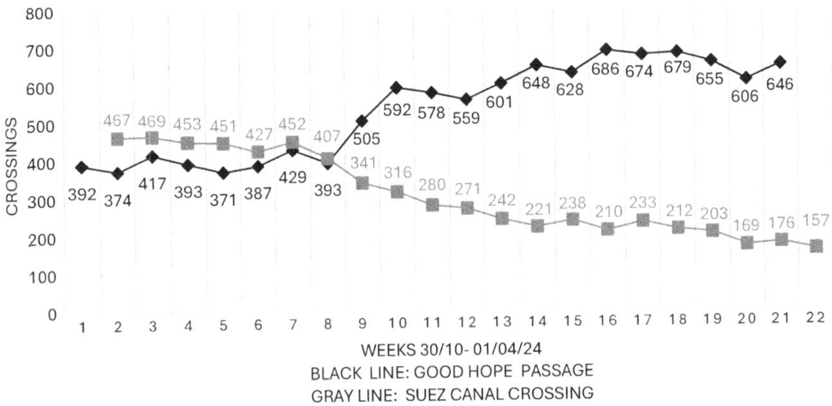

Fig. 12.7. Suez Canal & Good Hope Crossing Gap (Weeks 30/10/23–01/04/24). *Source*: The Authors. Figure is created from Tables 12.6 and 12.8.

CO_2 Emissions Impacts

According to the World Bank (2024), the crisis in question has far-reaching impacts, not only for the shipping industry but also for the environment. The longer routes required by the current situation have increased travel distances for cargo and tankers by up to 53%, causing a rise in CO_2 emissions due to the additional fuel burned.

A round trip from Singapore to Rotterdam via the Africa Retour leads to an increase in the ship's greenhouse gas emissions by up to 70%. For more than a decade, the shipping industry had reduced ship speeds to reduce fuel costs and greenhouse gas emissions. However, the crisis in the Red Sea and the avoidance of the Suez Canal are leading to new increased ship speeds to maintain routes, which leads to higher fuel consumption and more CO_2 emissions. For a large container ship, a speed increase of 1% usually leads to an increase in fuel consumption of 2.2%. An increase from 14 to 16 knots, for example, would increase the ship's consumption per mile by 31% (Sea intelligence, 2024). So, there is a clear correlation between these factors. Empirical data and academic theory suggest this correlation with the following equation:

$$B(S) = B_d\,(S)^k/\mathrm{Sd},$$

where $B(S)$ = daily fuel consumption at a given ship speed; B_d = daily fuel consumption at ship design speed; S = given ship speed; Sd = ship design speed, while the parameter; k depends on the type of ship, for example, for a typical ship whose speed is 18 to 20 knots, it has the value of 3.0 units.

Interesting and highly indicative is the analysis of Sea Intelligence according to which …*if the shipping lines use the exact same vessels, at the exact same speed, then emissions increase on a 1:1 ratio with increased sailing distances. As sailing distance around Africa are on average 31% and 66% longer for Asia to North Europe and Mediterranean, respectively, CO2 emissions will increase by these factors, at minimum.*

If the vessels also sail faster, then emissions will increase even further, as fuel consumption is not a linear function of sailing speed. As an example, based on our fuel consumption model, a 1 knot increase in speed from 16 to 17 knots, will increase emissions by 14%. On a TEU-basis, some of these smaller vessels see an increase in CO2 emissions of 141%, compared to conventional ULCVs. Putting all three components together, could lead to CO2 emissions increases of 260% and 354%, to North Europe and Mediterranean, respectively.

Containers Freight Rates Impacts

Indicatively, transport costs for a 12-meter container from Asia to Northern Europe increased by 16% in the week 07/12/23–21/12/23 at the beginning of crisis according to the Drewry World Container Index. Similarly, transport costs from Asia to South Europe (Genoa) in the same week increased by 15% (Table 12.9).

From the derived data of the above-mentioned Table 12.10, we see that for the period 14/12/23–04/01/24 there is a sharp increase in weekly container transport costs by 115% for the route Shanghai–Rotterdam and 114% for the route Shanghai–Genoa compared to the previously mentioned period 07/12/23–22/12/23.

From the above-mentioned Table 12.11, we can see that on 08/08/24 the cost of transporting the container was 7,929 USD for the route Shanghai–Rotterdam showing an increase compared to 4/01/24, which was 3,577 USD (Table 12.8), by 121.66%, while the annual change was 374%. Of course, between 25/07/24 and 08/08/24, there was a decrease in transport costs of 4%, while the weekly change between 25/07/24 and 08/08/24 was −3%.

Similarly, the increase in transportation costs between 04/01/24 (7,309 USD) and 08/08/24 (4,178 USD) for the route Shanghai–Genoa was of the order of 74.94%, while annually the increase was of the order of 253%. Of course, we are

Table 12.9. Drewry World Container Index (WCI) 07/12/23–21/12/24.

Route	07/12/23	14/12/23	21/12/23	Weekly Change (%)
Composite Index	$1,461	$1,521	$1,661	9%
Shanghai–Rotterdam	1,343	1,442	1,667	16%
Rotterdam–Sanghai	$443	$452	$466	3%
Sanghai–Genoa	1,608	1,697	1,956	15%

Source: Editing by authors based on Drewry WCI data (12/2023).

Table 12.10. Drewry WCI 14/12/23–04/01/24.

Route	**14/12/23**	**21/12/23**	**04/01/24**	**Weekly Change (%)**
Composite Index	$1,521	$1,661	$2,670	61%
Shanghai–Rotterdam	$1,442	$1,667	$3,557	115%
Rotterdam–Sanghai	$452	$466	$546	17%
Sanghai–Genoa	$1,697	$1,956	$4,178	114%

Source: Editing by authors based on Drewry WCI data.

Table 12.11. Drewry WCI 25/07/24–08/08/24.

Route	**25/07/24**	**01/08/24**	**08/08/24**	**Weekly Change (%)**	**Annual Change (%)**
Composite Index	$5,806	$5,736	$5,551	−3%	210%
Shanghai–Rotterdam	$8,260	$8,200	$7,929	−3%	374%
Rotterdam–Sanghai	$627	$626	$630	1%	20%
Sanghai–Genoa	$7,647	$7,610	$7,309	−4%%	253%

Source: Editing by authors based on Drewry WCI data.

talking about these two sea corridors because ships were crossing the Red Sea and the Suez Canal as well, while with the outbreak of the crisis most of them are forced to circumnavigate Africa.

Alternative Route

The India-Middle East-Europe Corridor (IMEC), which could bypass the Suez Canal and as a competitor to China's Belt and Road Initiative (BRI), is a project that USA promoted in September 2023, on the sidelines of the G20 summit. The USD 20 billion project would shorten distances by 40% to Suez by connecting India to Europe via a complex sea-rail multimodal transport network.

This corridor, according to the plan, starting in Mumbai, India, will connect by sea to Dubai. From there, the containers will be transferred to trains crossing Saudi Arabia to reach the Israeli port of Haifa, where from there the containers will be transported by sea to Piraeus and other Mediterranean ports, such as Marseille and Genoa, and from there by road or rail to the rest of Europe. According to Professor Haralambides (2024), his preliminary study concerning costings and timings shows that the number of necessary transshipments and the limited capacity of the railway leg do not pose a serious threat to either Suez or the Belt and Road Initiative (BRI).

A Diamond – Model for Maritime Security Policy Making, Related to the Geoeconomics of the Area in Question

Porter (1990) developed the "Diamond Model' in an attempt to explain why some economies are more developed than others. Although the author did not develop this theory for the analysis of a geoeconomic activity in a time of crisis, Diamond can be used and applied in order to trace and highlight the reasons that lead to effective treatment or minimization of damage from it.

The Diamond Model (Fig. 12.8) suggests that competitiveness is determined by four specific factors: (a) Factor Conditions; (b) Demand Conditions; (c) Strategy & Supporting Industries; (d) Strategy, Structure, & Rivalry. The diamond model can be translated to the maritime security sector related to the geoeconomics of the area in question, where the geopolitical crisis exists.

So, to the diamond can be added the factors: (d) Governmental Policies and International Initiatives adopted by International Organizations, for example, IMO, EU, NATO and (e) Random events. Consequently, the reshaping of the Diamond could be illustrated as below (Fig. 12.9).

Factor Conditions

These factors can be considered the resources used for the provision of maritime security services. Can either be location bound, indicating, for example, the geographical location of a vessel and maritime corridor, or non-location bound such as (a) technology and know-how on security issues (advanced non location bound). In this category belongs the Intelligence factor, especially those which,

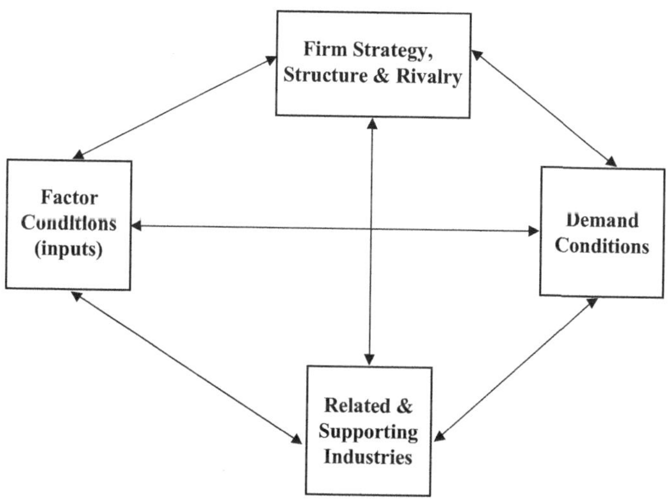

Fig. 12.8. The Diamond Model. *Source*: Editing by authors based on Porter's Diamond Model.

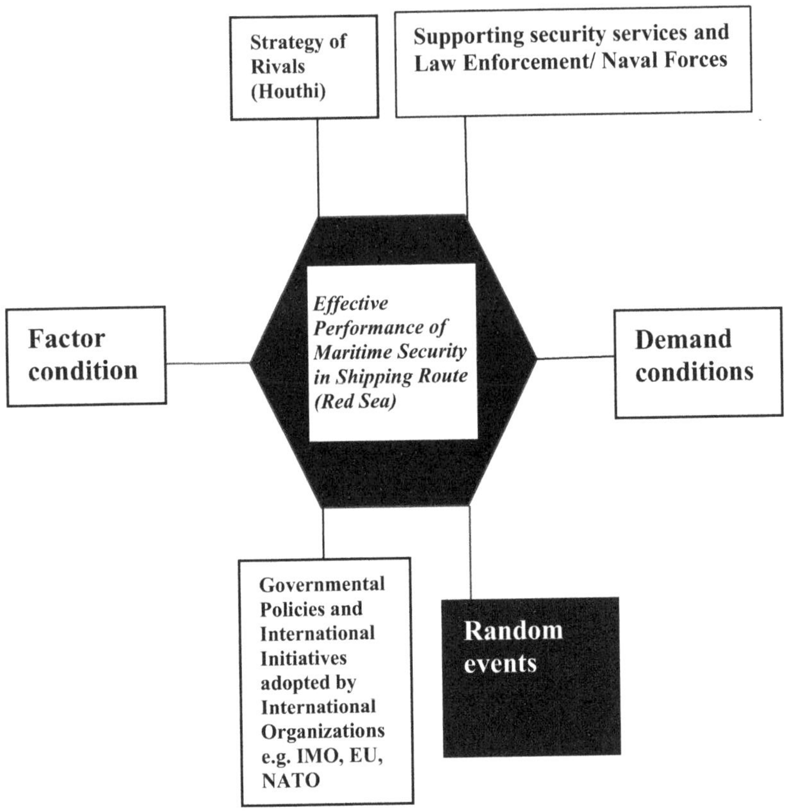

Fig. 12.9. The Diamond Model and Maritime Security. *Source*: Editing by authors based on the idea of Porter's Diamond Model implemented in Maritime Security.

if revealed, will operationally facilitate armed actions and of course actions that constitute asymmetric situations; (b) labor, capital infrastructural resources (basic non location bound). The quantity and quality of these factors dramatically increase the level of maritime security. Thus, effectiveness, prevention, and elimination of threats and risks to shipping depend on them.

Demand Conditions

These conditions are related to the requirements imposed by international trade and by the users of shipping services in the Indian Sea and Red Sea corridor. Demand conditions can, therefore, be considered determinants of the security power that the shipping industry should meet. Indeed, demand conditions push security services to constantly revise, upgrade, and innovate their output offered to the shipping industry.

Strategies and Structure of Rivals

The structure and organization of rivals, Houthi in this case, may have considerable impact upon the Effective Performance of Maritime Security in Shipping Route.

Supporting Security Services and Law Enforcement/Naval Forces

The efficient and effective maritime security procedure depends substantially upon the performance and efficiency of related and supporting security services within the shipping activity and the logistical support to them is of vital importance. The logistical support of the mandated services for maritime security is the process of linking it to the geoeconomic side. This logistical support, a component of the geoeconomic function, has two dimensions: The first refers to the material and appropriate equipment of the security forces, while the second refers to the human factor and logistics in general.

Random Events

The production-supply of maritime security output is clearly influenced sometimes by external factors which cannot be assessed accurately in advance. Such factors include, for example, sudden outbreak of armed conflicts, terrorist actions, political volatilities influencing the international trade, cyber-attacks, etc.

Governmental Policies and International Initiatives Adopted by International Organizations, for Example, IMO (International Ship Port Facility Security Code-ISPS Code), EU, NATO

Specifically, EUNAVFOR ASPIDES is an EU military operation contributing to the protection of freedom of navigation, to safeguarding maritime security, especially for merchant and commercial vessels in the Red Sea, the Indian Ocean and the Gulf under the EU Common Security and Defense Policy (CSDP). The EUNAVFOR ASPIDES within its defensive mandate is to provide maritime situational awareness, accompany vessels, and protect them against possible multi-domain attacks at sea. On the other hand, another operation takes place in the region in question named Operation Prosperity Guardian. This operation is a United States-led military operation consisting of a multinational coalition formed in December 2023 to respond to attacks by Houthi rebels on shipping in the Red Sea.

Furthermore, concerning Governmental Policies and International Initiatives the following issues are highlighted:

- Escalation of activities at sea. Actions include:

  - The organization of naval exercises at EU level;
  - The development of further coastguard operations in European sea basins;

- The designation of new maritime areas of interest for the implementation of the concept of coordinated maritime presence (a tool to enhance the coordination of Member States' naval and air assets located in specific sea areas)
- And strengthening security inspections in EU ports.

- Cooperation with partners
  - Deepen EU–NATO cooperation and intensify cooperation with all relevant international partners to uphold the rules-based order at sea, particularly the UN Convention on the Law of the Sea.
- Risk and threat management
  - Actions include conducting actual maritime exercises at regular intervals involving civilian and military actors, monitoring and protecting critical maritime infrastructure and ships (including passenger ships) from physical and cyber threats, and countering unexploded devices and mines at sea.
- Capacity building
  - Actions include developing common requirements for maritime defense technologies, stepping up work on projects such as the European patrol corvette (a new class of warship) and improving anti-submarine defense.
- Education and training
  - By strengthening hybrid and cybersecurity skills, for maritime security personnel, and by conducting training programs open to partners outside the EU.

Concluding Remarks

Maritime security as a major geopolitical factor influences and is affected by the geoeconomy of maritime freight transport. This is most emphatically demonstrated during the crisis in the Middle East and the Red Sea, causing repercussions on components of the maritime supply chain. Especially, changing the course of a ship to avoid the danger of the Red Sea and go around Africa is a complex issue. The possibility of re-routing depends on the exact terms agreed between charterer and shipowner as well as on the time of conclusion of the charterparty. So, when the passage through the Red Sea has been explicitly agreed, or the charterparty has been concluded after the escalation of tensions in the region, it may prove to be a challenge for shipowners to claim the right to be indemnified.

At the same time, the risks created by the attacks of the Houthi rebels have increased transport costs, among other things increasing war risk premiums, while persistent missile attacks by Houthi rebels on ships plying the Red Sea route have led to soaring emissions liabilities for shipping companies under the recently introduced Emissions Trading Scheme for shipping created by the European Union (EU ETS) as lengthy voyage diversions for Europe-bound vessels have multiplied fuel consumption.

Also, since the outbreak of the crisis, container freight rates on the Far East-Mediterranean route have "skyrocketed" by 253%, while on the Far East-Northern Europe route the increase has been 374%. Between 06/11/23 and 01/04/24, there was a decrease of 65.73% in total crossings via Suez Canal, reflecting emphatically this decline in comparison to a perspective increase of passaging via Good Hope of 64.8%. After a negative fourth quarter of 2023, major liner shipping companies posted profits again, as ship shortages caused by route diversions from the Red Sea pushed container shipping prices higher. Container freight rates increased by an average of 27% compared to the fourth quarter of 2023.

Finally, the adoption of Porter's Diamond model in the light of a holistic view of maritime security as a major geopolitical power factor, combined with the geoeconomic aspect in the specific geographical area where the crisis has occurred, could be a field of further consideration and research.

References

Baru, S. (2012). Geo-economics and Strategy. *Survival*, *54* (3), 47–58.

Blackwill, R. D., & Harris, J. M. (2016). *War by other means: geoeconomics and statecraft*. The Belknap Press of Harvard University Press.

Bueger, C. (2015). What is maritime security? *Marine Policy*, *53*, 159–164.

European Commission. (2023). ANNEX to the joint communication to the european parliament and the council on the update of the EU Maritime Security Strategy and its Action Plan "*An enhanced EU Maritime Security Strategy for evolving maritime threats*". Publications Office of the European Union.

European Union. (2014). *European Union maritime security strategy.*Council of the European Union, Doc. 11205/14.

Fearnlays. (2024). *Weekly report*. Retrieved August 08, 2024, from https://fearnpulse.com/#1

Germond, B. (2011). The EU's security and the sea: Defining a maritime security strategy. *European Security*, *20*(4), 563–584.

Haralambides, H. (2024). Maritime logistics, disruptions in global seaborn trade and alternative ways to deal with them. In *Shipbuilding the future* (pp. 217–227). Shipping 2024, *NAFTEMPORIKI*.

IMO (2003). *ISPS code*. https://portalcip.org/wp-content/uploads/2017/05/ISPS-Code-2003-English.pdf

Kantas, A. N. (2005). *Economics of defense and security* (in Greek). Papazisis, Athens.

Kevork, E., & Kollias, Ch. (2018). Defense and security economics (in Greek). In *Texts in defense and security economics* (pp. 9–25), University of Thessaly.

Kjellen, R. (1916). *Staten som lifsform*. Stockholm.

Klein, N. (2010). *Maritime security and the law of the sea*. Oxford University Press.

Klein, N. (2011). *Maritime security and the law of the sea*. Oxford University Press.

Kraska, J., & Pedrozo, R. (2013). *International maritime security law*. Martinus Nijhoff.

Liakouras, P. (2006). Intelligence gathering on the high seas. In *Unresolved issues and new challenges to the law of the sea*, Chapter 6: pp. 121–148, Brill | Nijhoff. Retrieved January, 2024, from https://doi.org/10.1163/ej.9789004151918.i-356.52

Luttwak, E. (1993). *The endangered American dream: How to stop the United States from becoming a third world economy and how to win the Geo-economic struggle for industrial supremacy*. Touchstone.

Mahan, A. T. (1898). *The influence of sea power upon history 1660-1783*. Little Brown and Company.

Mazis, I. Th. (2002). *Geopolitics, theory and practice* (in Greek). Papazisis, Athens.

Mazis, I. Th. (2012). *Metatheoretical critique of international relations and geopolitics, the neopositivist framework* (in Greek). Papazisis, Athens.

Nevola, L., & D'Hauthuille, V. (2006). *Six Houthi drone warfare strategies: How innovation is shifting the regional balance of power*. Retrieved August 07, 2024, from https://acleddata.com/2024/08/06/six-houthi-drone-warfare-strategies-how-innovation-is-shifting-the-regional-balance-of-power/

Papastavridis, E. (2024). Red Sea attacks and the international response: An international law insight. *ELIAMEP | Insights #2*.

Pauli, G. (2010). *The blue economy. 10 Years, 100 innovations, 100 million jobs*. Report to the club of Rome. Paradigm Publishers.

Porter, M. (1990). *The competitive advantage of nations*, Mc Millan.

Roach, J. A. (2004). *Initiatives to enhance maritime security at sea. Marine Policy*, *28*(1), 41–66.

S&P. (2024). *Global market intelligence, global-trade-disruptions*. Retrieved May 07, 2024, from https://www.spglobal.com/market-intelligence/en

Scekic, R., Draskovic, M., Delibasic, M. (2016). Neoliberalism in geoeconomics: The case of Southeast Europe. *Journal of International Studies*, *9*(1), 66–75. https://doi.org/10.14254/2071-8330.2016/9-1/5

Sea Intelligence. (2024a). Retrieved February 2024, from https://www.sea-intelligence.com/press-room/247-redsea-crisis-increase-in-co2-emissions

Sea Intelligence (2024b). Retrieved May 22, 2024, from https://www.sea-intelligence.com/press-room/266-avg-minimum-transit-time-up-39-on-asia-med

Søilen, K. S. (2012). *Geoeconomics*. Klaus Solberg Søilen & Ventus Publishing ApS. https://www.researchgate.net/publication/268188322_Geoeconomics

Spykman, N. J. (1944). *Geography of the peace*. Harcourt, Brace and Company.

Thucydides. (2008). *Peloponnesian War. Book Γ' (13)*. Translation in Modern Greek, Angelos Vlachos, Athens: Estia Bookstore.

Trading Economics. (2024). Retrieved August 09, 2024, from https://tradingeconomics.com/commodity/brent-crude-oil

Tsakiris, Th. (2023). *Structural destabilization of Red Sea* (in Greek). https://www.kathimerini.gr/economy/562799326/arthro-th-tsakiri-stin-k-i-domiki-apostatheropoiisi-tis-erythras-thalassas/

UNCTAD. (2024). *Red Sea, Black Sea and Panama Canal: UNCTAD raises alarm on global trade disruptions*. https://unctad.org/news/red-sea-blackseaand-panama-canal-unctad-raisesalarm-global-trade-disruptions

United Nations. (1983). *The law of the sea*. (Official Text of the United Nations Convention on the Law of the Sea), New York, UN.

United Nations. (2018). *Sustainable development goal report*. https://unstats.un.org/sdgs/files/report/2018/thesustainabledevelopmentgoalsreport2018-en.pdf

U.S. Coast Guard. (2001). *Port security risk assessment tool*. USCG Users' Manual.

U.S. Energy Information Administration. (2023). *Red Sea chokepoints are critical for international oil and natural gas flows*. https://www.eia.gov/todayinenergy/detail.php?id=61025

World Bank. (2024). *Navigating troubled waters: The Red Sea shipping crisis and its global repercussions*. Retrieved May 16, 2024, from https://blogs.worldbank.org/en/developmenttalk/navigating-troubled-waters-the-red-sea-shipping-crisis-and-its-

Appendix 1. Threat Category and Criteria

Category	Intelligence and Maritime Domain Awareness	Representative Likelihood of Attack (Probability)
5	Credible intelligence or operational information indicates that a specific type of attack will occur against a specific asset/ infrastructure at a specific time	0.60
4	Credible intelligence indicates that a specific type of attack is imminent against a class of assets/infrastructures	0.15
3	A terrorist attack on the same class of asset/ infrastructure has recently occurred AND/OR possible precursor/sentinel events that may indicate specific types of attacks on specific assets/infrastructures have been observed	0.05
2	Credible intelligence indicates that terrorist cells are operating with unknown assets/ infrastructures and methods of attack (default for baseline analysis)	0.01
1	No credible intelligence indicating the presence/activity of terrorist cells	0.001

Source: Editing by authors based on United States Coast Guard.

Example: Since the September 11th, 2001, attack, most scenarios should be scored "2." If specific intelligence indicates, for example, that an attack is likely in the immediate future on one of several bridges over a particular waterway, a score of "4" is appropriate. Additionally, information from outside the intelligence community may be sufficient to score a scenario "3" if the information may be evidence of a possible attack (a precursor/sentinel event) [United States Coast Guard]

Appendix 2. Vulnerability Categories and Criteria

Category	Availability Presence and Predictability of Asset/Infrastructure	Accessibility Restrictions that Deter the Threat Without Organic Security
5	Always available (e.g., continually present or present daily on a set schedule) Representative likelihood of failure (probability of 1.0)	No deterrence (e.g., unrestricted access to target and unrestricted internal movement) Representative likelihood of failure (probability of 1.0)
4	Usually available (e.g., present several times a week or on a relatively set schedule) Representative likelihood of failure (probability of 0.5)	Limited deterrence (easily defeated access barrier; unrestricted access up to perimeter of the asset/ infrastructure itself) Representative likelihood of failure (probability of 0.75)
3	Often available (e.g., present several times a month; arrival times predictable 1week to 2 months in advance; predictable departure times) Representative likelihood of failure (probability of 0.1)	Good deterrence (e.g., single substantial barrier; unrestricted access to within 100 yds of asset/ infrastructure) Representative likelihood of failure (probability of 0.3)
2	Limited availability (e.g., present several times a year or unpredictable arrival times/ departure times with < 1-week advanced notice of schedule) Representative likelihood of failure (probability of 0.01)	Substantial deterrence (e.g., multiple barriers that are difficult to defeat; unrestricted access to within 200 yds of asset/ infrastructure) Representative likelihood of failure (probability of 0.1)
1	Rarely available (e.g., no set schedule and on any given day presence highly unlikely and unpredictable; arrives once a year or less for a few hours and arrival is not publicly known) Representative likelihood of failure (probability of 0.001)	Excellent deterrence (expected to deter attack; access restricted to within 500 yds of asset/ infrastructure; multiple physical/ geographical barriers) Representative likelihood of failure (probability of 0.01)

Appendix 2. (*Continued*)

Category	*Organic Security* *Ability of non-USCG security to deter attack*	*Target Hardness* *Ability of asset/infrastructure to withstand attack*
5	No deterrence capability (e.g., no plan, no guard force, no emergency communication, outside L. E. [law enforcement] not timely for prevention, no detection capability) Representative likelihood of failure (probability of 1.0)	Intent of attack easily accomplished (e.g., readily damaged or destroyed) Representative likelihood of failure (probability of 1.0)
4	Limited deterrence capability (e.g., no plan, limited communications, outside L. E. not timely for prevention, unarmed minimal guard force) Representative likelihood of failure (probability of 0.9)	Limited capability to withstand attack (e.g., simple design and construction) Representative likelihood of failure (probability of 0.8)
3	Good deterrence capability (e.g., minimal security plan, some communications, armed guard force of limited size relative to the asset/ infrastructure; outside L. E. not timely for prevention, limited detection systems) Representative likelihood of failure (probability of 0.5)	Good ability to withstand attack (e.g., simple design and relatively strong construction) Representative likelihood of failure (probability of 0.3)
2	Substantial deterrence capability (e.g., detailed security plan, effective emergency communications, well trained and equipped guard force; multiple detection systems [camera, x-ray, etc.], timely outside L.E. for prevention) Representative likelihood of failure (probability of 0.05)	Substantial ability to withstand attack (e.g., good design and construction of asset/ infrastructure) Representative likelihood of failure (probability of 0.1)

(*Continued*)

Appendix 2. (*Continued*)

Category	*Organic Security* *Ability of non-USCG security to deter attack*	*Target Hardness* *Ability of asset/infrastructure to withstand attack*
1	Excellent deterrence capability expected to deter attack (e.g., all of #2 and covert security elements that represent additional elements not visible or apparent) Representative likelihood of failure (probability of 0.01)	Representative likelihood of failure (probability of 0.01)

Source: Editing by authors based on United States Coast Guard.

Example: An asset/infrastructure like the Statue of Liberty is always present and should be scored "5" for Availability. This equates to a probability of 1.0 for Availability, while a commuter ferry that operates several times per day on a fixed schedule should be scored "4" for Availability which equates to a probability of 0.5.

Index

Printed and bound by CPI Group (UK) Ltd, Croydon, CR0 4YY
21/09/2026
14966034-0004